Twenty Years of the Papua New Guinea Constitution

Twenty Years of the Papua New Guinea Constitution

edited by

ANTHONY J REGAN
Fellow Research School of Pacific and Asian Studies
Australian National University

OWEN JESSEP
Associate Professor of Law
University of New South Wales

and

ERIC L KWA
Lecturer and Dean of the Faculty of Law
University of Papua New Guinea

UPNG PRESS AND BOOKSHOP, 2010

Originally published in Sydney by Lawbook Co.

100 Harris St, Pyrmont NSW 2009

It is produced from final proofs provided by Professor Kwa and these have been checked against a copy of the Lawbook text.

ISBN 9980-939-53-2

Copies available from:

UPNG Press and Bookshop
Box 413
University Post Office
NCD 134
PAPUA NEW GUINEA

Table of Contents

[References are to page numbers]

Foreword

In 1996, the Law Faculty of the University of Papua New Guinea and the National Institute of Continuing Legal Education co-hosted a conference in Port Moresby, on the topic of 'the Papua New Guinea *Constitution*, 20 years on'. I am pleased to note that support for the conference was provided by the Judiciary and also by the Friedrich Ebert Foundation.

The three day conference was very well-attended, with both speakers and audience coming from many fields of experience and expertise. A highlight was the active participation of almost 20 people who had been active in the making and the events leading up to the coming into force of the *Constitution* in September 1975. They included not only members of the Constitutional Planning Committee (the body responsible for preparing the proposals for the *Constitution*) but also members and advisers of the government of the day. I am pleased to note that this book includes chapters by three of the constitution-makers (Sir Michael Somare, Mr John Momis and Mr Bernard Narokobi), as well as an edited transcript of a panel discussion involving those three plus another 12 constitution-makers.

The conference presented a fascinating opportunity to compare and contrast the views of the people who had been intimately involved in preparing the *Constitution*, and those of judges, lawyers, members of Parliament, public servants, academics and others who had been involved in implementation of the *Constitution* or who had observed its operation in the twenty years following independence. Listening to the presentations and discussions, I was struck by the thought that there can be few, if any, other post-colonial states where it was possible to sit back more than twenty years after independence, and consider the thoughts of the constitution-makers about their goals together with the views of those who had struggled to make the *Constitution* work. It seemed to me a striking testimony to the great contribution of the constitution-makers that, whatever the problems experienced in its first twenty years, the *Constitution* clearly not only had survived but undoubtedly was still making a great contribution to contemporary Papua New Guinea. Our constitution-makers certainly did Papua New Guinea a great service.

About 40 papers were presented to the conference, including several from representatives of 'civil society' organisations. Of course, it was not possible to include all those papers in this volume, but many of the key papers have been included. The editors are to be congratulated for their selection and revision of relevant papers, which have been organised according to a number of main themes. As a whole, the selection is designed to provide both historical insights and discussion and analysis of current constitutional issues in Papua New Guinea. This collection of papers will be of interest to members of the judiciary at all levels, and practising lawyers, as well as to students of law, history, political science and other disciplines, and to the general reader interested in our remarkable *Constitution*.

Of course, judges need no reminding of the continuing importance of the *Constitution*, since it underlies so much of the work of the courts – indeed, its provisions often give rise to the central issues in cases before the Supreme Court. I hope that this volume will help to bring home to many others the fact that the *Constitution* has much to say about many of the pressing public issues currently being confronted in this country – it is indeed a living document.

This book is one of a series prepared under the auspices of the Access to Laws in Papua New Guinea Project funded by the Australian Government through the Australian Agency for International Development (AusAID). The Access to Laws Project comprised three components aimed at improving access to the laws of this country. The Project involved updating and authenticating all the current legislation of this country and the extensive case law developed by the courts. The legislation and judicial decisions have been produced in the modern electronic CD-ROM format. Equally importantly, the Project included the production of a number of legal textbooks to record the distinctive developments in the laws of this country.

The book publishing component of the Access to Laws Project was under the direction of the Publications Committee that I had the pleasure of chairing. The other members of the Publications Committee were, the Commissioning Editor, Professor Don Chalmers, the Chief Magistrate, Mr George Manuhu, the Deputy Chief Magistrate, John Numapo, the Hon. the Attorney-General, Mr Francis Damen (previously Mr Sao Gabi, Mr Michael Gene), the Access to Laws Project Manager, Mr Bruce Fulton, the Project Team Leader, Mr Eric Kwa (previously Dr. Val Haynes), representatives of AusAID (Mr Stuart Schaefer, Ms Pauline Doonar, Ms Debbie Bowman, Mr John Prescott, Ms Katherine Ruiz-Avila) a representative of the PNG Law Society, Ms Catherine Davani and the Dean of the Law School, Mr Eric Kwa (previously Mr Gerry Linge). The Publications Committee was responsible for choosing authors, settling the contents, assessing the quality and appointing referees for each of the texts. At an early meeting of the Publications Committee it was decided that it was appropriate that Papua New Guinean authors or authors with considerable experience in Papua New Guinea should be chosen.

I am delighted that Anthony Regan, Owen Jessep and Eric Kwa agreed to accept the invitation of the Commissioning Editor on behalf of the Publications Committee to agree to prepare this text. On behalf of the Publications Committee I commend the learned authors for their work and scholarship. I am confident that this text with the others in this series will be of great value to judges, magistrates, legal practitioners, academics, students and the citizens of this country. If the underlying law is to be developed according to the precepts and principles embodied in our Constitution and *The Underlying Law Act* 2000, it is essential that the Papua New Guinea community has access to texts which state the Papua New Guinea law concisely, authoritatively and accurately. On behalf of the Publications Committee I commend the editors for their contribution to this important endeavour.

The Hon Sir Arnold Amet, Kt, CBE, LLD Chief Justice of Papua New Guinea,
Chair of the Publications Committee,
Access to Law in Papua New Guinea
Port Moresby April 2001

ACKNOWLEDGMENTS

The conference on Twenty Years of the Papua New Guinea Constitution held in Port Moresby from 28 to 30 March 1996 was organised by the Faculty of Law, University of Papua New Guinea, and the Papua New Guinea National Institute for Continuing Legal Education. Our thanks are due to both bodies for the provision of support and resources needed to organise the conference. The Friedrich Ebert Foundation and the National Judicial System both provided financial support critical to the success of the conference, thereby also contributing greatly to this book. The National Judicial System also made available a transcription service which enabled us to include in this volume the edited transcript of the panel discussion by constitution-makers which appears as the Appendix.

The success of the conference was also dependent on a large number of organisers and participants, too many for them all to be mentioned here. However, in relation to organisation, particular thanks are due to James Baker and other members of the board of the National Institute of Continuing Legal Education; to the Chief Justice (Sir Arnold Amet); to the Registrar of the Supreme Court, Mr Lawrence Newell; and to our colleagues at the Faculty of Law, University of Papua New Guinea. In relation to participants, thanks are due to all who chaired sessions, presented papers, participated in panels, and attended sessions of the conference.

Finally, thanks are due to various sources of support for the production of this book. The AusAID *Access to the Laws Project* has provided financial support. Professor Don Chalmers has headed the Committee co-ordinating that project and has given invaluable assistance. The State, Society and Governance in Melanesia Project and the Department of Political and Social Change, both in the Research School of Pacific and Asian Studies at The Australian National University, have provided funding and administrative support critical for turning the papers into a book. Thanks are also due to Karen Haines for her keyboard work and to Jill Wolf for preparation of tables of statutes and cases, the list of references and the index.

Anthony Regan	Owen Jessep	Eric Kwa
Canberra	Sydney	Port Moresby

March 2001

Table of Abbreviations

ASEAN	Association of South-East Asian Nations
CDC	Constitutional Development Committee (of the House of Assembly)
CEDAW	Committee on the Elimination of Discrimination Against Women
CILM	Commission of Inquiry into Land Matters
CRC	Constitution Review Commission
CPC	Constitutional Planning Commission
CRA	Conzinc Riotinto Australia
CSD	Commission for Sustainable Development
DFA	Department of Foreign Affairs
GCC	General Constitutional Commission
ILO	International Labour Organisation
IMF	International Monetary Fund
MUG	Minimum Unconditional Grant
NCDIC	National Capital District Interim Commission
NEC	National Executive Council
NFC	National Fiscal Commission
NGDP	National Goals and Directive Principles
NPEP	National Public Expenditure Plan
OLPG	Organic Law on Provincial Government
PNGDF	Papua New Guinea Defence Force
PSC	Public Services Commission
RPNGC	Royal Papua New Guinea Constabulary
UCC	Uganda Constitutional Commission
UNCED	United Nations Conference on Environment and Development

UNHCR	United Nations High Commissioner for Refugees
UNICEF	United Nations Children's Fund
WHO	World Health Organisation

CONTRIBUTORS

This list notes the position held by the contributors at the time of the Conference on Twenty Years of the Constitution in March 1996, save in respect of the Papua New Guinean constitution-makers and the editors of this book, in respect of whom some additional details are provided.

Sir Arnold Amet was the Chief Justice of Papua New Guinea.

James Baker was a private legal practitioner in Port Moresby and a member of the board of the National Institute of Continuing Legal Education.

Brian Brunton was a lawyer working for the Individual and Community Rights Advocacy Forum.

David Cannings was Deputy Legal Counsel, Ombudsman Commission of Papua New Guinea.

Jill Cottrell was Senior Lecturer, Faculty of Law, University of Hong Kong.

Yash Ghai was Sir YK Pao Professor of Public Law, University of Hong Kong in 1996. He served as a Visiting Specialist Consultant to the Constitutional Planning Committee for periods in 1973 and 1974.

Graham Hassall was Research Fellow at the Centre for Comparative Constitutional Studies, University of Melbourne.

Rudi James was Professor, Faculty of Law, University of Papua New Guinea.

Owen Jessep was Associate Professor, Faculty of Law, University of New South Wales, and in 1996 was a Visiting Fellow in the Faculty of Law, University of Papua New Guinea.

Eric Kwa was Lecturer in Law, Faculty of Law, University of Papua New Guinea in 1996, and at the time of publication is Dean, School of Law and Business, University of Papua New Guinea.

John Momis was Member of Parliament for Bougainville Regional Electorate in 1996, a seat he has held from 1972. He was a member of the House of Assembly and the National Constituent Assembly before independence and was the Deputy Chairman of the Constitutional Planning Committee from 1972 to 1974.

Bernard Narokobi was Member of Parliament for Wewak Open Electorate in 1996. He was a Permanent Consultant to the Constitutional Planning Committee from 1972 to 1974.

Michael Ntumy was Associate Professor, Faculty of Law, University of Papua New Guinea.

Anthony Regan was Senior Lecturer, Faculty of Law, University of Papua New Guinea in 1996, and at the time of publication is Fellow, Research School of Pacific and Asian Studies, The Australian National University, Canberra.

Sir Michael Somare was Member of Parliament for East Sepik Regional Electorate. Before independence he was a member of the House of Assembly and the Chief Minister, and a member of the National Constituent Assembly. He was also Chairman of the Constitutional Planning Committee from 1972 to 1974.

Meg Taylor was a private legal practitioner and consultant in 1996. Prior to independence she served on the staff of the then Chief Minister, Sir Michael Somare.

Greg Toop was Legal Counsel, Ombudsman Commission of Papua New Guinea.

Tiffany Twivey was lecturer, Faculty of Law, University of Papua New Guinea.

Edward Wolfers was Professor of Politics, Department of History and Politics, University of Wollongong in 1996. He was a Permanent Consultant to the Constitutional Planning Committee from 1972 to 1974.

Table of Cases

[References are to page numbers]

Table of Papua New Guinea Organic Laws and Statutes

[References are to page numbers]

Table of References to the Constitution

[References are to page numbers]

Amendments to the Constitution

INTRODUCTION

INTRODUCTION

ANTHONY J REGAN

In the first 20 years of its operation since independence in 1975, the Papua New Guinea *Constitution* has proved a remarkably resilient document. Long, complex and in many respects unusual for a national constitution, it has provided the framework for the establishment and operation of the Independent State of Papua New Guinea and, more generally, for what Ghai (Chapter 4) calls a "liberal democratic polity". Yet this has been achieved in a new country where the circumstances seem designed to test the viability of not only introduced state structures, but also "Western" notions of constitutionalism.

Perhaps the most basic challenge for the *Constitution* and the ambitious enterprise involved in it arises from the unparalleled cultural and linguistic diversity in Papua New Guinea. It is a country created by the vagaries of 19th century map drawing exercises by European powers in the last throes of colonial expansion. In a little over 100 years a modern state has emerged from perhaps several thousand small, stateless societies. Since independence rapid economic and social change has produced new political and economic forces, making control of the state central to the access of the small but growing elite to economic and political power. These developments have contributed to political instability (although mainly within the parliamentary framework), corruption and mismanagement. At the same time, however, the vast majority of people is still heavily reliant on village-based subsistence agriculture and has continuing strong loyalties to traditional societies. Not only do these conditions limit the scope for development of national identity but they also make for multiple cleavages and tensions that are far from simple to manage within the framework of a national constitution.

Under these circumstances, the fact that the independence *Constitution* and the state it provides for have survived is a major achievement. But, undoubtedly, the *Constitution* has done more than survive. While it has not achieved anywhere near the lofty aspirations held for it by the main constitution-makers – the pre-independence Constitutional Planning Committee (CPC) – the *Constitution*'s unique combination of characteristics has made important contributions to shaping and developing the complex, flexible and resilient "liberal democratic polity" of Papua New Guinea 20 years on.

Despite both its unusual characteristics and its important contribution to Papua New Guinea, there has been limited analysis of the operation of the *Constitution* in its first 20 years, and especially during the second 10 years. This book seeks to contribute to improving understanding of the operation of the *Constitution* and the extent to which it has achieved its complex and idealistic goals.

ASPECTS OF THE CONSTITUTION

Much that is unusual about the *Constitution* flows from the fact that it is largely based on the recommendations of one of the most extensive popular consultation exercises about national constitution-making that had occurred anywhere (to that time). That exercise was carried out from 1972 to 1974 by the CPC, which was concerned to ensure that the independence *Constitution* represented the views and aspirations of the people. This was not just a matter of seeking legitimacy for the proposed *Constitution*, for the key members of the CPC also embarked on the consultative exercise with a deeply idealistic view of what a national constitution could do. This was nothing less than self-determination and the shaping of a new society.

> "We see the planning of our own constitution as a vital aspect of the process of self-determination. It is not just a matter of our people determining that they should govern themselves. We have the opportunity of determining *how* we shall govern ourselves. To answer this question we must know what philosophy of life we wish to live by, what social and economic goals we wish to achieve, what kind of society we wish Papua New Guinea to be."[1]

In the process of consultation with the people, the CPC communicated its vision and undoubtedly raised high expectations. By the end of the consultative process, the CPC was convinced that it knew what the people wanted of an independent Papua New Guinea, and how the *Constitution* should contribute to the enterprise.

The CPC vision involved shaping a new, humane, egalitarian, and Christian Papua New Guinea that at the same time would be built firmly on the foundations of a resurgent traditional culture. Hence the CPC envisaged a constitution committed to setting the development of society in new directions based on "integral human development" for all. To do this it was necessary to overturn what the CPC saw as the evils of the colonial system of government and to create a new system of government and a new legal system directed towards developing the new society.

The pre-independence government was far from comfortable with such broad aims. Its views were much closer to the assumptions of many other post-World War II constitutions: that a national constitution for a new state should be relatively short and at the same time flexible, providing little more than the main structures of government, and leaving the new government relatively free to adapt to new and changing circumstances. The CPC's consultative efforts and the resulting high public standing of its leaders made it difficult for the government of the day to ignore its proposals. Eventually, although some of the CPC recommendations were not accepted, the majority survived. As a result the Papua New Guinea *Constitution* is based on the assumption that it reflects the real concerns and goals of the people as discerned by the CPC.

This assumption is a major factor underlying three important characteristics of the *Constitution.* First, it contains much programmatic and directive (as opposed to enforceable) material. Secondly, it covers an extremely wide range of subjects in considerable detail. Thirdly, it is far from easy to change. As background that may help the reader of the essays in this book, each of these characteristics deserves brief comment, as do two additional matters; namely, the question of whether or not the *Constitution* is "home-grown", and the ready availability of the constitution-makers' views on the *Constitution* and the uses that can be made of those views.

Programmatic and directive material

Such material is found in many parts of the *Constitution*, and not solely in the unusually long and detailed statement of political and policy goals and aspirations contained in the National Goals and Directive Principles. It is also found in the Basic Social Obligations, the Leadership Code, in directives to the judiciary to develop "indigenous jurisprudence" and to apply the National Goals

[1] CPC, *Final Report of the Constitutional Planning Committee: Part I* (Port Moresby: Government Printer, 1974), p 1/3/12. See also pp 2/1-2/2.

and the Basic Social Obligations, and in "in principle" statements found in various parts of the *Constitution*.

The National Goals and Directive Principles are a statement of the directions intended for the society as a whole and for all government bodies as well as other bodies of all kinds. There are five broad goals; namely: "Integral Human Development"; "Equality and Participation"; "National Sovereignty and Self-reliance"; "Natural Resources and Environment"; and "Papua New Guinean Ways". For the CPC, these goals and associated principles were to "provide for the full development of our people" and "guide the government and our people", and were seen to "express the needs and aspirations of our people".[2] The CPC thus saw them as reflecting the true needs of Papua New Guinea, and as a result sought to use them as the basis of its recommendations for the rest of the *Constitution*.[3]

The Basic Social Obligations were to be applied to all persons in Papua New Guinea as the quid pro quo in relation to the constitutional guarantee of human rights. Like the National Goals, they are set out in the Preamble to the *Constitution*. They involve requirements: to "respect and act in the spirit of the *Constitution*"; for "active participation in the development of the national community as a whole"; protecting Papua New Guinea and safeguarding "the national wealth, resources and environment"; working "in socially useful employment"; respecting the rights and freedoms of others; contributing to state revenues "required for the advancement of the Nation"; and for parents to assist children and for children to respect their parents.

While they are "non-justiciable" (not judicially enforceable), the National Goals and Directive Principles and the Basic Social Obligations are intended to be applied and given effect to by all governmental bodies and, in particular, to be given effect to by the courts as far as possible (ss 25 and 63). Further, they are intended to be justiciable in so far as they apply to the Leadership Code (ss 25(4) and 63(4)), and the Ombudsman Commission can inquire into the justifiability of government policies if they are contrary to the National Goals (s 219(3)).

Little needs to be said here about the enforceable code of conduct for both political leaders and senior bureaucrats found in the Leadership Code, as it is the subject of Chapter 14, "The Leadership Code: The Ombudsman Commission and Official Corruption" by Gregory Toop. It is, however, most unusual in national constitutions. It was seen as a matter of central importance to the CPC, and underlines its faith in the efficacy of the independence *Constitution*, as it believed the Code could "avoid the kind of corruption too often seen abroad, that stems from the failure to put the public and national interest before personal advantage".[4]

As for the directives to the judiciary to develop an "indigenous jurisprudence" (s 21) and to apply the National Goals and the Basic Social Obligations as far as it is able (above), this reflects the concern of the CPC that the judiciary "must take full account of the goals of the society in which they live".[5] Finally, quite apart from the National Goals and Directive Principles and the Basic Social Obligations, there are other apparently unenforceable "in principle" statements included as guides to governments and courts; for example, provision on the numbers of days that the National Parliament should meet each year (s 124).

---

[2] Ibid, p 2/2, paras 10-11.
[3] Ibid, p 15/1/2.
[4] Ibid, p 1/4/22, and see also pp 3/1-3/3.
[5] Ibid, p 8/1.

Extensive subject matter and detail

The *Constitution* makes provision on numerous matters that are normally either left to ordinary statutes or rejected as imposing unreasonable fetters on the state, some of which are dealt with in chapters included in this volume. In addition to the programmatic material already mentioned, these include provisions in respect of: an Ombudsman Commission with a remarkably wide jurisdiction (Chapter 13 by David Cannings and Chapter 14 by Gregory Toop); an especially circumscribed role for a ceremonial head of state (Chapter 7 by Jill Cottrell and Yash Ghai); creation of constitutional office-holders separate from and with a high degree of independence from the three traditional arms of government (Chapter 15 by Regan); decentralisation of significant levels of powers, funding and personnel to provincial and local-level governments (Chapter 11 by Ghai and Regan); financial arrangements for the National Government; arrangements for treaty-making (Chapter 18 by Eric L Kwa) and other aspects of foreign affairs (Chapter 17 by Edward P Wolfers); a system of unwritten law similar to the English common law, but intended to give some primacy to "custom" (Chapters 9 and 10 by Owen Jessep and Regan); natural justice (Chapter 8 by Michael A Ntumy); aspects of land matters (Chapter 21 by R W James); and detailed provisions on citizenship (Chapter 16 by Graham Hassall). The considerable detail often provided on matters normally covered by ordinary statute contributes to the *Constitution* being one of the longest in the world.

Changing the Constitution

The concern that the *Constitution* should not be easily changed reflects the high degree of legitimacy derived from consultation with the people. The *Constitution* contains complex provisions on amendment (ss 13 to 17). Among other things, they provide for two separate votes of the Parliament separated by at least two months, and varying "prescribed majorities" that must be met in those votes for particular provisions to be changed. What might be called "core" provisions of the *Constitution* require "a three quarters absolute majority vote": that is, more than three-quarters of the number of seats in the Parliament (s 17(3) and Sch 1.2(1)).

A "home-grown" Constitution?

Before independence there was considerable interest in the *Constitution* being "home-grown", an expression used by Chief Minister Michael Somare in his June 1972 statement to the pre-independence House of Assembly concerning the setting up of the CPC.[6] There were two separate but nevertheless related ways in which the expression was used, in that the CPC discussed the need for the *Constitution* to be "legally, as well as politically, "home-grown".[7]

"Politically home-grown" was the main sense of the expression used by the CPC, meaning that it was "seeking to build a constitutional framework uniquely suited to Papua New Guinean needs",[8] and as a result was not following any particular foreign precedent. By contrast, the expression "legally home-grown" involved important symbolism, in that the severing of colonial ties should be emphasised by the *Constitution* being "autochthonous": it should derive its legal authority

[6]Ibid, p 15/1/2.
[7]Ibid, p 15/1/3.
[8]Ibid, p 1/2/10.

from within Papua New Guinea, from the people rather than through a formal transfer of power from the departing colonial authority.[9]

Although discussion by lawyers tends to focus on the legal sense of "home-grown", the political aspect remains relevant. Even though the *Constitution* provides for a modern state, and most elements in it can be found in other national constitutions, it nevertheless does provide a unique mix of characteristics intended to respond to the wishes of the people distilled into the vision of the CPC (see Chapter 2 by John Momis). In this sense the *Constitution* can still be said to be autochthonous.

Availability and use of the views of the constitution-makers

Discussion about the aims of the CPC gives rise to mention of another unusual aspect of the *Constitution*: the accessibility of, and the constitutional requirement for the judicial use of, the reasoning that underlies it. In many other former colonies such reasoning is buried in such minutes and other records as were kept of constitutional conferences, often held in London, Paris or Brussels. Such records are often quite inaccessible, and are seldom easily related to particular provisions of the independence constitution. In addition, of course, in a majority of post-colonial states records of the pre-independence constitution-makers were quickly made irrelevant by coups and other forms of fundamental constitutional change.

By contrast, in Papua New Guinea 20 years on, the detailed arguments for the inclusion of most aspects of the constitutional arrangements are to be found in a readily accessible form in the Final Report of the CPC.[10] Further, despite some 16 amendments the fundamental scheme of the independence *Constitution* remains intact, meaning that the CPC's Final Report remains relevant to anyone interested in understanding why much of the *Constitution* is as it is. More importantly (at least for lawyers and judges), and to some degree reflecting the high degree of legitimacy acquired by the efforts of the constitution-makers, the *Constitution* requires that not only the CPC's Final Report but also other basic documents relevant to the making of the *Constitution*[11] should be used by the courts, whenever relevant, to interpret or apply the *Constitution*.[12]

ABOUT THIS BOOK

This book results from a conference held to examine the operation of the Papua New Guinea *Constitution* in its first 20 years. Organised by the Faculty of Law, University of Papua New Guinea, and the National Institute for Continuing Legal Education, the conference was held over three full days, from 28 to 30 March 1996. It was attended by about 250 people each day, with participants including the Chief Justice and most members of the National Court, some 15 of the original constitution-makers, numerous lawyers and academics, representatives of non-governmental organisations, and members of the public. The constitution-makers included members of and advisers to both the CPC and the pre-independence government. This unusual

[9] Ibid, pp 15/1/1-15/2/13. See also the discussion in C J Lynch, "The Achievment of Independence in Papua New Guinea" (1980) 11(3) *Journal of Pacific History* 175.

[10] Above n 1.

[11] The documents include records of proceedings that resulted in some changes to the recommendations of the CPC, including the records of debates both on the CPC's Final Report in the pre-independence House of Assembly and on the Draft Constitution in the National Constituent Assembly. For discussion of the documents available to the courts see A J Regan and E P Wolfers, "Aids to Interpretation of the Constitution - Some Preliminary Thoughts" (1986) 14 *Melanesian Law Journal* 153.

[12] Section 24 of the *Constitution*. For discussion of the intention of this provision and its use by the courts, see Regan and Wolfers, above n 11.

combination of people presenting and discussing papers made for a remarkably vibrant and interesting conference, and contributed directly to the quality of the chapters in this book.

The conference had several aims. One of the most important was to evaluate the operation of the *Constitution* by reference to the goals and vision of the constitution-makers. Because so many of the key figures in the constitution-making process had been relatively young in the early 1970s, most of them were still alive in 1996. Indeed, many of them were still active in public life. As a result, the conference organisers made it a priority to gather as many of them as possible to participate in the conference. Unfortunately, the limited funding available for the conference (as well as pressure of other commitments for some of the constitution-makers) made it impossible to include them all. Those who attended made invaluable contributions, in the form of both the papers presented by several of them and participation in discussion panels and debate about papers presented by other participants.

A second goal was to better understand the workings of the *Constitution*. To this end, papers were presented on numerous aspects of its operation. A third goal was to contribute to debate about assessing the overall impact of the *Constitution* in Papua New Guinea.

The book is not a record of the conference. It does not include many of the over 40 papers presented, nor most of the rich debate in both panel discussions and comments on papers presented. Limited space was the main reason why it was not possible to include all papers. Bearing in mind the aims of the conference (above), and the need to meet the high editorial standards of the series of books in which this volume is being included, the editors selected papers for inclusion on four main criteria; namely, that they:

(a) dealt with an aspect of the *Constitution* about which little or nothing had been published elsewhere, or where the paper shed new light on a subject dealt with elsewhere; or

(b) contained important background information, or otherwise interesting material, not readily available elsewhere; or

(c) contained interesting or controversial arguments about aspects of the *Constitution*, or contrasting arguments that contributed to debate; or

(d) contained personal reflections on events and legal developments of historical importance.

Further, papers were omitted either if they did not deal principally with the *Constitution* or its origins, or if they dealt primarily with the political situation in 1996 rather than with the *Constitution.* Finally, some papers that were not presented at the conference have been included on the basis that they meet the criteria applied to the selection of other papers (see Chapter 4 by Ghai, Chapter 15 by Regan, and Chapters 9 and 10 by Jessep and Regan).

An edited transcript of a panel discussion by the 15 constitution-makers who attended the conference is included. Editing of the original transcript had to be severe, both because the quality of the original was variable, and because a large part of the more than half a day of discussion recorded in it related to contemporary politics in the lead up to the 1997 national elections, rather than to reflections on the constitution-making process or the subsequent operation of the *Constitution*.[13]

While it is not possible for this book to provide a comprehensive coverage of constitutional issues, it does provide a range of perspectives, including:

(a) the views of some constitution-makers on aspects of the constitution-making process (Chapter 1 by Sir Michael Somare, Chapter 2 by Momis, Chapter 3 by Bernard Narokobi, and the transcript of the discussion of a panel of 15 constitution-makers in the Appendix);

(b) assessments of the overall impact of the *Constitution* (Chapter 4 by Ghai, Chapter 5 by Sir Arnold Amet, Chapter 2 by Momis and Chapter 3 Narokobi); and

(c) analysis of the operation of particular aspects of the *Constitution*, ranging from analysis of provisions that are not particularly unusual - for example, the chapters on separation of powers (Chapter 12 by Ntumy), the executive (Chapter 6 by James Baker) and human rights (Chapter 19 by B D Brunton) - to those on less common subjects for a national constitution such as the chapters on women (Chapter 20 by Tiffany Twivey) and the environment (Chapter 22 by Meg Taylor).

Reflecting the focus of the conference on the aims of the constitution-makers, a link between all of the papers on the substantive provisions of the *Constitution* is an emphasis on the extent to which the aims of the CPC have been met in the first 20 years.

The book states the law in Papua New Guinea as at the time of the conference (March 1996).

TOWARDS EVALUATION OF OUTCOMES: SOME CONCLUSIONS FROM THE 1996 CONFERENCE

In various ways, the remaining chapters in this book seek to evaluate the outcomes of the first 20 years of operation of the *Constitution*. Most do so in relation to specific aspects of the *Constitution*. Others (notably Ghai, Amet, Momis, and Narokobi) consider both the broader outcomes and the reasons for those outcomes.

At the end of the conference that gave rise to this book, I made some summary concluding remarks, attempting the perhaps impossible task of pulling together some of the many "threads" emerging from the many papers presented, but more particularly seeking to summarise the rich discussion generated by three days of debate about the goals, performance and outcomes flowing from the operation of the *Constitution* in its first 20 years. While matters discussed at the conference went beyond the material covered in this book, that summary may nevertheless provide a helpful context for the reader of the selected papers presented in this volume:

> "The CPC had a clear vision, both of what Papua New Guinea could be as a country, and of what the right sort of independence constitution could do for Papua New Guinea. At the same time the CPC also accepted that there were limits to what constitutions could

[13] The transcription was made by trainees being prepared to work as part of a transcription service for the National Judicial System. The tapes were inadvertently wiped soon after the transcription was made. A copy of the original transcription is held by the writer, and a further copy is being placed in the New Guinea Collection in the Michael Somare Library, University of Papua New Guinea, Waigani, NCD, Papua New Guinea.

do, that in the end it is not just the contents of a constitution that determine its effectiveness, but also the interaction of a constitution with a range of other things, including the political and economic forces that shape the environment in which it operates and the people that implement the constitution and run the institutions and systems that it provides for. The CPC anticipated that there would be problems in running a post-independence Papua New Guinea, and so tried to build much in to the *Constitution* that took account of the political and economic forces it expected to be at work, and of simple human frailty. Many aspects of the problems of Papua New Guinea today that were discussed at this conference [and in the chapters in this book] involve things that the CPC anticipated.

It cannot be denied, however, that the CPC had a highly idealistic view of the *Constitution*. Indeed, the CPC struggled to get that approach accepted as against the more pragmatic view of the *Constitution* held by the government. The CPC's vision of the *Constitution* shaping the nation for the better and setting directions for future development was of limited interest to a government focused mainly on achieving the goal of independence and getting the basic institutions of government established. Ultimately the *Constitution* emerged as a sort of compromise between these two views. While neither view predominated absolutely, and while CPC members still tend to feel that the changes that government made to their proposals greatly weakened the *Constitution*,[14] undoubtedly the CPC shaped the *Constitution* far more than the government. A key issue, then, is whether the CPC was unrealistic in its idealism.

More than most national constitutions, that of Papua New Guinea sets goals for the state and for the people. It also seeks to distribute power in various ways. It distributes power vertically: between the National Government and provincial and local-level governments. It distributes power horizontally: between the institutions at the national level, several of which are guaranteed a high degree of independence from the traditional three main arms of government (legislature, executive and judiciary) with a view to their acting as a check on the three main arms. It seeks to promote political and bureaucratic leadership committed to the constitutional goals and to the welfare of the people.

Various assessments are commonly made of the impact of the *Constitution* in its first 20 years in public debate in Papua New Guinea, and that was the case with the discussion at this conference. Generally people are proud of the *Constitution*'s contribution in helping to keep the country together. The assessment is more difficult when its impact is measured against the high hopes for Papua New Guinea held by the CPC and others in the lead-up to independence. When issues such as limited "development", corruption and mismanagement come up, there is sometimes heated debate about the role of the *Constitution*. There is probably wide acceptance of the view that the CPC was not entirely realistic about the capacity of a constitution to change society and to shape the direction taken by the state, but this view takes different forms.

One approach is that the *Constitution* is quite adequate, but that it is the leaders who have failed to give effect to it. Another is that the *Constitution* is too weak and did not try to do enough, either because the CPC vision was undermined by the government's rejection of key recommendations, or because the CPC itself failed to understand the true extent of

[14]See, for example, Chapter 2 by Momis, and the views expressed by some CPC members in the edited transcript, which appears as the Appendix.

the problems ahead and the need for even more stringent limits on government and leaders than it recommended. A variation on this second approach was suggested in discussion at this conference, to the effect that in focusing on the rule of law and the rights of individuals the *Constitution* placed too many limits on the executive arm of government, thereby preventing it from governing effectively, and did not do enough to secure the rights of groups, thereby weakening the foundations of traditional society.[15] But most discussion at this conference did not support the view that the *Constitution* did not attempt to do enough, or that it is too narrow.

It is worthwhile attempting to sum up some of the positives and negatives in terms of outcomes. Concerning the positives: the *Constitution* did redistribute power. It brought relative stability compared with most post-colonial countries. Most political conflict is managed within a constitutional framework that is accepted by all. Although there is corruption, it is widely believed to be less than it would be without the Leadership Code and the Ombudsman Commission and the various other mechanisms for accountability. Limits on the executive government are generally accepted. The human rights regime may not be perfect but the system for enforcement of rights is accepted by government, which pays up, for example, when the courts say the police have burnt villages in contradiction of people's human rights. On the negative side, enforcement of rights is limited in practice. There is an excessive concentration of power in the executive. There is probably too much power concentrated at the centre, without being balanced by strong sub-national centres of power (as was envisaged by the CPC). There is rampant corruption despite the Ombudsman and the Leadership Code. Rapid economic and social change is undermining traditional societies, and there is little to suggest that the state is based on Melanesian values as the CPC envisaged.

As for the assessments - that the *Constitution* is perfect and the leaders bad, or that the Constitution is too narrow - I suggest that both are deficient. We need to take a wider view, and be fairer to both the constitutional fathers and present leaders in trying to understand what has happened in the first 20 years. History shows that all state structures tend to be deficient in actual operation, that they seldom work as intended and that there is a tendency in human beings once they are in power to abuse power. Why did the CPC want to build in such extensive checks and balances? In large part it was to try and prevent the sorts of abuses seen in all other political systems. Perhaps the CPC was idealistic to think that their particular mix of checks on excesses of power would work any better than any other attempted elsewhere. There are political and economic forces at work - both globally and within Papua New Guinea - that the law and the *Constitution* have limited ability to control.[16] Further, while there have been basic forces and pressures militating against the CPC's vision of the *Constitution*, there has been little evidence of political forces being mobilised to support the goals of the CPC. Perhaps the fairest assessment might be that the CPC set its expectations for the *Constitution* higher than was realistic, overestimated the ability of law to produce the outcomes it desired, and underestimated the need for the political mobilisation that might have improved the chances of more of the goals of the *Constitution* being met. Further, there is so far little

[15]T Deklin, "Constitutional Changes and Modus Operandi: the Papua New Guinea Style", paper presented at the conference on *Twenty Tears of the Papua New Guinea Constitution*, Port Moresby, 28-30 March 1996.

[16]For further discussion of these issues, see Chapter 4 by Ghai.

evidence that by setting its goals so high the CPC caused harm.[17] For example, while the Leadership Code may be somewhat "out of step" with the public morality of Papua New Guinea 20 years on, it also seems to have contributed to some limits on corruption without leading to undermining of the *Constitution* by those adversely affected by the operation of the Code.

The basic message from discussion at this conference was not one of despair. There was little support for radical constitutional change. Perhaps surprisingly, if anything the message was that "more of the same" is needed. The constitution-makers in the 1972 to 1975 period were a group of human beings struggling to find the best way to set up human institutions that would work, that would provide a framework for future development for the people. Most discussion at the conference did not denigrate that view or the outcomes of the efforts of the constitution-makers. Indeed many saw a need for today's leaders and the people of Papua New Guinea generally to engage in much the same sort of struggle. Specific proposals made at this conference included: much improved general education of people about the *Constitution*; greater empowerment of the people at the local level; making the Parliament a more effective and assertive body through such things as a preferential voting system, a more effective parliamentary committee system and so on; and more resources so as to improve the effectiveness of accountability bodies such as the Ombudsman Commission. Of course, these proposals are remarkably similar to many made by the CPC, and in the light of the assessment I have just made of the impact of the *Constitution* in its first 20 years, perhaps there should be question marks about whether or not these prescriptions are realistic.

At the same time most at the conference agreed on the need to be open to constitutional reform. The CPC itself wanted built into the *Constitution* institutionalised review and reform processes, because it recognised that there would be difficulties in making the whole constitutional system work as expected. But whatever reform processes are in place, the general feeling from discussion here was that such processes need to be open and highly consultative, sensitive to the wishes of the people in much the same way as the CPC was. Concern was expressed about the possibility that non-consultative review processes and constitutional changes resulting from them might be dominated by leaders mainly concerned about their own interests. This view perhaps reflects acceptance of the view that the *Constitution* not only continues to reflect the views of the people as expressed to the CPC, but also that those views continue to be relevant. Further, the concerns expressed about reform processes suggest that many people believe that legitimacy built upon wide-spread public acceptance of the *Constitution* continues to be important and that fundamental change without wide popular consultation may result in a dangerous lack of legitimacy for the *Constitution*.

These views expressed by so many attending this conference suggest that the vision of the constitution-makers of the first half of the 1970s still resonates in Papua New Guinea 20 years after independence."

[17] This is a conclusion, however, that will perhaps require more consideration over the next few years.

CONSTITUTION-MAKING

Chapter 1

REFLECTIONS ON CONSTITUTION-MAKING

SIR MICHAEL SOMARE

> "WE, THE PEOPLE, do now establish this sovereign nation and declare ourselves, under the guiding hand of God, to be the Independent State of Papua New Guinea . . . AND ACTING through our Constituent Assembly on August 15th 1975 HEREBY ESTABLISH, ADOPT and GIVE TO OURSELVES this Constitution to come into effect on Independence Day, that is 16 September 1975."

Most people will recognise these words, which form part of the Preamble to Papua New Guinea's *Constitution*. I have chosen to open my remarks with this quotation because there can only be one reason for this conference. If we have gathered here simply to celebrate our actions of 20 years ago or to record our regret about what might have been, I suggest we would be wasting our time. The value of the conference lies in its ability to contribute to moving our nation forward and to making use of our past actions as a springboard to the next century.

Since 1995, in the belief that our nation needs radically to alter its *Constitution*, the Constitution Review Commission (CRC) has engaged in analysis of varying forms of government around the world. I would draw the attention of the CRC to the portion of the Preamble of the *Constitution* that I have just read. It contains no suggestion that our existing *Constitution* was granted to us, or that it was forced upon us, nor that it was anything other than a home-grown product. Papua New Guinea was different to other colonial territories where independence constitutions were drafted in Marlborough House in London, or in Paris, or elsewhere. Our *Constitution* was home-grown, home-written. We, the people, established this nation. We did it through a Constituent Assembly and we gave ourselves this *Constitution*. That action was not taken lightly. Many of us here today will recall that the *Constitution* was the result of the most exhausting consultative process with the citizens of this country that has ever taken place. The Constitutional Planning Committee (CPC) set up a process of face-to-face discussions. It involved 500 discussion groups, each of 20 members. Later the CPC visited almost every subdistrict in Papua New Guinea and held public meetings attended by a total of more than 60,000 people. More than 2,000 written submissions and verbal opinions flooded in from all sides.

The current CRC, in its determination to reconstruct that which remains solid, will do well to compare that organised and effective process of consultation with its own hasty and ill-prepared approach to our people.

The CPC was established as a direct result of the April 1972 elections which enabled me, as leader of the Pangu Party, to form a coalition government. When our House of Assembly met in June of that year, I urged the establishment of the CPC because I wanted to ensure that independence, when it finally came, would be true independence, approved by our own people and reflected in a constitution of our own making.

As Chief Minister I was the ex-officio Chairman of the CPC, which was made up of 15 members drawn from the House of Assembly. It is important to remember that this was a bi-partisan committee and it represented nearly all areas of the country. John Momis was officially my deputy, but in fact he was the working Chairman. The late Sir John Guise was a member, as was Sir John Kaputin, then Minister for Justice. We had some consultants, a word at that time devoid of the more negative meanings it has developed recently. They were there mainly as a source of information and to carry out research. Bernard Narakobi, then a practising lawyer, was one of the consultants, and Ted Wolfers (now Professor of Politics at Wollongong University) was the most senior of the Australian advisers. The CPC also made use of consultant lawyers and political scientists experienced in public law and administration of developing nations.

Even before the establishment of the CPC, the House of Assembly had been concerned about constitutional development for Papua and New Guinea. The previous House of Assembly, elected in 1968, had established a Constitutional Development Committee (CDC). It was headed by John Guise, who agreed for some of us to travel to parts of Africa and the Pacific to look at the constitutions of various countries. We were concerned to understand how those constitutions were drawn up, who did it for them, the format of the consultative process, and so on and so forth. One group, headed by the late Paulus Arek, went to various parts of the Pacific. I was part of the group that went to Africa. I was especially interested in Tanzania and in the African socialism being developed there because I believed in some kind of socialism (indeed, people call me socialist, although I have since become more of a campaigner for social change). We went to Uganda. We went to Ghana. We could not get to Nigeria because a coup d'état was happening there, so we were told at the airport that we could not enter the country. As a result we had to turn to Entebbe in Uganda where at that time, in 1971, Corporal Idi Amin was firing at the Kampala Hotel and Foreign Ministry. So these were some of the experiences we had when developing our *Constitution*. While travelling then, our aim was to find the constitutional arrangements most suitable for Papua New Guinea. We came back with many great ideas.

By contrast with the previous CDC, the CPC decided we should not rely on models from elsewhere: instead, we must write our own constitution. It must be home-grown, developed in consultation with the people. The people must decide what they want for their constitution. As a result, the CPC did not travel to other countries.

I believe the CRC is doing exactly what we did, going to other parts of the world to try to find out how they wrote their constitutions and to determine the best kinds of arrangements. But I think that we did the job already, in the first half of the 1970s. It is there. We have a proven constitution. We have tried it, we have made it work; and it has worked very successfully.

It is important to remember that after April 1972 the elected representatives in the House of Assembly felt that they were in reality the government. We began to initiate policy. Until then it had been the Australian administration officials, both here and in Canberra, who had made all the decisions for Papua New Guinea. Now, suddenly, we could see the road ahead of us and we were beginning to have the powers we needed to walk that road. Perhaps we were fortunate in the newly-appointed Australian Minister for External Territories, Andrew Peacock. He was then a young man who showed a very real interest in what we were trying to achieve. Peacock made no secret of his support to me, John Momis, John Guise and the Opposition Leader at that time, the late Sir Tei Abal. When Peacock made his first trip to Port Moresby, he immediately addressed the task of separating the new Papua New Guinean Administration from Canberra and moving power into the hands of the House of Assembly. This had direct relevance to the development of the *Constitution*. Les Johnson, who was to be the last colonial administrator of Papua and New Guinea, was supportive, and set up a special legal and constitutional unit to assist in the transfer of power. That unit and my own private advisers worked closely together. In the process, the government's lawyers became the source of ideas that balanced the work of the CPC.

It is true that there were many differences and even sharp arguments between the CPC and the government, and particularly between me and the CPC. Part of the reason for the different views was that some of us from the old school (and I was one of them) were trying to compete with the people from the new school like Momis and Kaputin and the rest of them. Some of us believed that the *Constitution* should be small, that there was a lot that should not be included. As in the United Kingdom, much could be dealt with by conventions, and would not have to be spelt out in a constitution. On the government side we wanted a very small report from the CPC, but the CPC saw things very differently. Although there were a lot of arguments, like good Melanesians we were able to reach compromise on many issues. An example of an area of disagreement was the debate on the Head of State. Should we have a constitutional monarchy, or should we have a republican constitution? Should the Head of State be elected? One school of thought said the Head of State should be elected by Papua New Guinea as a whole. Another view was that the Sri Lanka model should be followed, so that the President is elected from Parliament and then becomes an Executive President. So, although there were a lot of arguments and discussions about how we should do it, our Melanesian conscience made us believe that we should write a constitution that is effective and that will safeguard the interest of Papua New Guineans. That is why we opted for what we have today.

In its *Final Report*, tabled in the House in 1974, the CPC made the following observation, which provides an insight into the thinking underlying the development of the *Constitution*:

> "We see the planning of our own constitution as a vital aspect of the process of self-determination. It is not just the matter of our people determining that they should govern themselves. We have the opportunity of determining *how* we shall govern ourselves. To answer this question, we must know what philosophy of life we wish to live by, what social and economic goals we wish to achieve, what kind of society we wish Papua New Guinea to be."[18]

In other words, we had an opportunity, which many developing countries never had, of devising our constitution in-house and taking into account what our own people wanted. We were not writing a constitution to last for 12 months. We were not drawing together some cardboard imitations that would see us through to independence. We were totally committed to providing a constitution that: first, reflected the wishes of the people: secondly, provided a structure for the government and administration; and thirdly, gave notice of the nation's political ideals. At its most basic, we decided we should have a constitution made by Papua New Guineans so that in

[18] CPC, *Final Report of the Constitutional Planning Committee 1974: Part 1* (Port Moresby: Government Printer, 1974), p 1/3.

the future, when it is contested, people will say, "yes, we had the ideas, we wrote the *Constitution*, and so it's entirely up to us to keep it or to change it".

The CPC prepared two interim reports, and then submitted its final report to me as Chief Minister, in August 1974. I have already indicated the government did not necessarily agree with some of the CPC judgments on the fundamental issues. So in the same month, the government published a document entitled *Government Paper: Proposals on Constitutional Principles and Explanatory Notes,* which indicated where we disagreed and why, and proposed alternatives. The basis for the proposals was a proposed minority report of the CPC which I prepared with others, mainly Sir John Guise, but eventually decided not to submit. Debate in the House of Assembly on the two sets of proposals then followed for about five months, from late 1974 to March 1975. I had moved a motion to have the CPC's *Final Report* as amended by the House of Assembly resolutions forwarded to the legislative draftsman as drafting instructions for the proposed constitution. After lengthy debate, that motion was carried but with many amendments. A number of drafts of the *Constitution* were prepared, with a fourth draft being considered by the Constituent Assembly (which was constituted by the members of the House of Assembly) from May 1975. Sir Barry Holloway was the Presiding Officer of the Constituent Assembly as well as the Speaker of the House of Assembly. The Constituent Assembly adopted the *Constitution* on 15 August 1975. The Australian Government passed the *Papua New Guinea Independence Act*, with Royal Assent being given to that Act on 9 September 1975.

At the same time, from mid-1975, a secession movement was developing, with Bougainvilleans wanting to separate from the rest of Papua New Guinea. There were also secessionist grumbles about Papua breaking away. There was a Mataungan problem in East New Britain. There were bitter debates about these matters. One of the things that made us write our own constitution was the desire to include every district (from independence provinces) in the new Papua New Guinea. We thought it would be far better to have a constitution which reflects the real feelings of people, gives them some autonomy and gives them the responsibilities to run their own affairs. We thought that by adopting our own constitution quickly and declaring independence, we could contain secessionist feelings and make these people feel an integral part of our one home-grown constitution, adopted in our Constituent Assembly.

The *Constitution* has served Papua New Guinea very well, and continues to do so. There may be a need for review and for changes. But you cannot change the whole set of fundamental beliefs that were enshrined when the founding fathers were thinking about what type of constitution Papua New Guinea should have. I am not suggesting that the *Constitution* should be set in cement and never altered or amended. Rather, alterations should be made only where there is a clear need for change; where the *Constitution* is actually hindering the progress of the nation's development.

We determined, as I have explained, that Papua New Guinea should have a home-grown constitution, one which reflected as far as possible the wishes of the people. I therefore have no intention of standing to one side while we are straight-jacketed into a "new-age" constitution, thrown together as a result of a few flying visits overseas and a highly exclusive seminar. Constitutions are not intended to change with the fashion. They are meant to provide a nation and its people with a framework to guide their development, define their obligations and secure their freedoms. I believe it is imperative that the Parliament remember that.

Chapter 2

THE CONSTITUTIONAL PLANNING COMMITTEE AND THE CONSTITUTION

JOHN MOMIS

INTRODUCTION

The House of Assembly approved the setting up of the Constitutional Planning Committee (CPC) in June 1972. Three months later the members of the Committee and its terms of reference were approved by the House of Assembly. In his wisdom, Sir Michael Somare, then known as the Chief Minister (or "The Chief") asked me to be the Deputy Chairman of the CPC. This was an important strategic move in that it convinced the then Opposition that the CPC and its terms of reference were credible and honourable.

I would like to pay tribute to Sir Michael Somare's unique capabilities and qualities as a leader. He chose to listen to all sectors of the community of Papua New Guinea in trying to evolve a new system of government and in trying to evolve a strategy which would put into place the National Goals and Directive Principles which the CPC worked out during its exhaustive consultations with the people of Papua New Guinea. Without his very able and wise leadership, Papua New Guinea would not have achieved independence in the manner that it did. It would not have adopted a constitution that leaves many constitutions in the world not only for second place, but for dead!

The members of the CPC came from various backgrounds and party affiliations. It was not easy to mould a united team committed to finding an effective way of creating a united nation. It had to be done in a way that was not at the expense of the people's participation; not at the expense of restricting the rights of the people to dissent from certain government policies. Instead we had to find a way of creating a system that would accommodate the diversity and various views of the many sectors of the community and in so doing create a common thrust towards nationhood.

The CPC was officially a committee of the government. But, in its method of operation, the CPC made itself more into a committee of the House of Assembly. This was because we believed that we were not there merely to rubberstamp prefabricated ideas either from Canberra or – with due respect to the Chief – from the executive government. We believed that the constitution we were developing must belong to the people and that the CPC, comprised as it was exclusively of members of the legislature (then the House of Assembly), had a serious responsibility to listen to the aspirations and the basic needs as expressed by Papua New Guineans.

The CPC listened very carefully to the people and then reached decisions. The people provided the raw material for the CPC's work. We were fortunate that we had good consultants, both expatriate and Papua New Guinean nationals, who had the technical expertise to assist the CPC members in refining the raw material provided by our people. We believed that if you wanted to give the right prescription, the right treatment, the right solutions to people's problems, you had to find out from them what the problem was. It was no use coming up with all kinds of prefabricated answers: perfect answers to the wrong questions. We had to listen to the people. I can say honestly that the CPC did that, even though it was sometimes frustrating and took a lot of time. We listened and we were convinced of what the people were trying to tell us. And only then did we feel that we were in a position to prescribe the right medicine.

Consequently, despite pressure to make international trips, to go gallivanting around the world to seek views of outside countries, we did not take one overseas visit. In contrast to what the Constitutional Review Commission is doing in 1996, we made many, many visits to the villages and attended many consultative meetings with members of the public.

I wish to emphasise that the CPC was not responsible for the drafting of the *Constitution* as we have it today. We disagreed with the way it was drafted. In fact, we believed that the lengthy nature of the *Constitution* could have been avoided if we were allowed to choose our own legal draftsman. However, as de facto chairman of the CPC, I do accept in full the spirit of the *Constitution* as enshrined and expressed in the National Goals and Directive Principles. To a certain extent the CPC disagreed strongly with the then executive government's approach, which we believed unduly limited a golden opportunity which independence offered for Papua New Guineans to leave their mark on the most basic law of our human existence.

We believed that the *Constitution* should not be perceived as purely a sterile legal instrument to effect the transfer of power from Canberra to Port Moresby. We believed that the *Constitution* should be much more than a legal instrument. It should be a charter, a vision of the aspirations of Papua New Guineans. It should contain the vision of what Papua New Guineans wanted to work towards when breaking the umbilical cord that, until then, connected them to mother Australia. The Australian administration was providing services to the people of Papua New Guinea. But that was at the expense of the people's right to determine the kind of society they wanted. We refused to compromise on this issue. We felt that independence provided the opportunity for us to bring about qualitative change and not just quantitative change. We were not just interested in effecting change from Canberra to Port Moresby while continuing to operate in the same old way.

We were interested in questions such as:

(1) What sort of government?

(2) What sort of society?

(3) How are we going to distribute power?

(4) Who will exercise power?

(5) Will there be protection for the rights of our people?

Of course, most of the people were still living in the villages and did not understand the complexities that were to be included in the *Constitution*. We paid special attention to the fact that certain sectors of the community had least access to power and therefore deserved to be specially protected. Consequently, we recommended very important sets of rules to be included in the *Constitution*: the provisions for our rights and obligations.

Even though the Basic Obligations are contained in the *Constitution* they are not enforceable in law. Instead they are intended as guides for the leaders and members of the judiciary. They are intended to help determine cases and issues against people who are working against the National Goals and Directive Principles to our *Constitution*.

THE NATIONAL GOALS

There are five National Goals and Directive Principles to our *Constitution*.

The first National Goal is Integral Human Development. Development should not be viewed as merely economic or physical, or in terms of multi-storey buildings. It is not just development of the country or of its resources. Rather it should be development of all Papua New Guineans as human beings. This includes their rights to participate in the process of development and in the process of governing themselves. Belief in the importance of this kind of development is based on our belief as a Christian country that a person should not be a mere recipient: should not be just an object of people's efforts to provide services. In fact, the person is both subject and object of the human process of developing himself or herself. As Christians we believe that the person is central. Situations must be created for the person to create, to evolve, and to change things to make this society, the situation of Papua New Guinea, better for all of our citizens.

The second goal of the *Constitution* is Equality and Participation. Consequently, in many of our recommendations, we insisted that people must be given equal opportunities and services. So the provision of education and other services must be done on an equitable basis. People must be given equal opportunity to use their talents and their energies to liberate themselves from attitudes that may be detrimental to full realisation of their human potential. And people must be allowed to participate. People are not to be treated as mere recipients of goods and services, for as recipients they could easily become dependent on the handouts from leaders who really do not believe in allowing them to share in power.

The third goal is National Sovereignty and Self-reliance. We viewed this goal to be very important because we had seen that in many other independent Third World countries leaders literally prostituted the resources and the people by succumbing to pressures from multinational corporations and from other people who were only interested in what they could make out of the countries in question. So we insisted that leaders must not sell their country. They were to be prohibited from use of public office to promote the enhancement of their own private political or economic interests or their roles as agents of foreign interests. I think today this country is going through a very difficult time, not because we have a bad constitution, not because Papua New Guineans are bad, not because this is a poor country. Rather the problems are arising because we have leaders who are being allowed by their constituents to sell this country as part of their own personal selfish interests, whether political or economic.

The fourth goal concerns Natural Resources and Environment. Twenty years ago the CPC was talking about this essential goal of development at a time when many of our so-called First World nations did not think much about these issues. Papua New Guinea was way ahead of many countries. We were talking about the need for sustainable human development. We were concerned that the resources of the country must not be destroyed, for they belong not only to the present generation, but to future generations. We have been proven right by what the many more established or older democracies are now talking about in relation to exploitation and development of resources. The *Constitution* protected and called upon leaders and the people not to destroy their resources. One of the root causes of today's Bougainville problem has been the failure of multinational corporations and governments to adhere to this very worthy goal of our *Constitution*: the need for sustainable development.

Goal number five is Papua New Guinean Ways. It is about the need to adapt; the need to use acceptable and appropriate ways and means and institutions of Papua New Guinea. We should not simply emulate what may be good for Africa, China or the United States. We are a people with our own culture, our own will and the potential to learn and work out ways and means of running our own country.

Some armchair critics and academics have been critical of the CPC, saying that we failed to come up with traditional or customised institutions. I think these people are talking through their hats. We must understand, however, that the CPC was being dragged in opposite directions by those who wanted to keep Papua New Guinea as a museum piece and by those who wanted to throw Papua New Guinea headlong into the so-called modernised world. We did not agree that either option was relevant for Papua New Guinea. We did our best to come up with a pragmatic mix between those two extremes in order to propose something that would be workable for our country. The vision, as enshrined in the National Goals and Directive Principles, clearly shows what the people of Papua New Guinea want as a society for ourselves. The CPC did not have the time or the technical expertise to be devising institutions and practical administrative policies at that time. But we felt it was adequate that the *Constitution* provide guidance to those who would later devise institutions - for example, local-level government bodies - and policies for future management. We had done our job by clearly spelling out the kind of society we wanted: one that was egalitarian, based on our ways, respected the rights of people and encouraged people to accept responsibility for development and for national unity.

DECENTRALISATION

One of the important subjects in the CPC's terms of reference was the question of decentralisation. Decentralisation was an issue not just because of Bougainville. It is true that at that time there were secessionist movements in Bougainville, in East New Britain, in Papua and even in some parts of the Highlands. As Sir Michael Somare has discussed, we had to find a framework that could accommodate this diversity. However, the CPC recommendations on provincial government were not made purely for pragmatic reasons. We were not forced to take the decentralised approach just because we had to contend with the secessionist movements. We also did it because we believed that only a decentralised form of government would allow people to participate meaningfully and effectively. As people are endowed with the important faculty of volition or willpower, they have to be given flexibility within the system of government to participate creatively, dynamically and responsibly.

We did not believe that human beings were merely fit to be recipients, as decided upon by a highly centralised and bureaucratised government such as the Australian colonial administration. Even though it may have seemed to deliver perfect or efficient services, it was de-humanising people, in that it made people so dependent on centralist bureaucrats. In the process, it created a situation conducive to the sort of dictatorial and national security ideology that had been prevalent in South America and some of our Asian neighbours to the north. So the CPC decided to use the opportunity to be creative and to find a way of creating a society and a system of government which was appropriate and relevant to the real needs and aspirations of Papua New Guineans. Of course, Papua New Guineans are communal people, with an integrated and holistic approach to life. The CPC recommendations on provincial government aimed to take full account of the complex reality of Papua New Guinea.

LEADERSHIP CODE

Another important subject that the CPC dealt with was the Leadership Code. This caused a lot of controversy, both during the debate on the *Constitution* and subsequently. The Chief Minister then also believed that, unless we had leadership that was legally and morally required to account for what it did or did not do, then even the best system of government would not work. Hence there was the need for the Leadership Code and the Ombudsman Commission. Sapos yu baim gutpela Mercedes Benz kar tasol, sapos draiva i spak na longlong nabaut, dispela kar bilong yu bai bam. (You can buy a good motor vehicle, but if the driver is drunk and drives badly, your car will crash.) I think that is the problem in this country today. We still have good systems. We have a good judiciary. We have a legislature (although I do not know whether it is good or bad). But, draiva paol, draiva i spak (the driver is confused, drunk) and consequently we have a lot of problems. In the final analysis, unless you have a leadership that is morally committed, that believes in principles, that rejects mediocrity and corruption, then our present problems will get worse.

INVESTMENT CODE

The other important thing that the CPC dealt with was the Investment Code. I come from Bougainville, the province which had the first large-scale mining experience in this country. I was asked by Sir Michael Somare to be the Deputy Chairman of the CPC even though I had no legal training. My only training relevant to foreign investment was a little bit of schooling in the school of life gained by working in Kieta and observing what Conzinc Riotinto Australia (CRA) was doing in Bougainville. CRA was convinced that it had all the answers for this country, and it convinced the government of the same thing. But even though the CRA operation at Panguna was a technological feat, it failed precisely because it did not listen to the people. It was an enclave development that generated a lot of revenue for our budget, but it failed completely and dismally to take into account the human dimension of development. I think the current problems of ongoing violent conflict in Bougainville are a direct result of that failure. It was concern about the potential for such problems that led the CPC to believe that, despite the lack of local capital and technical expertise, the people of Papua New Guinea must be given a stake in all major projects, whether they be government, business or community projects. We believed that was the most effective way of giving them a role, of tying them in, in a responsible way, and ensuring that they did not have the excuse to stand aside and throw stones at any project. We were very concerned about the proposed laws on residency requirements for acquiring citizenship because we knew there was already a process of stratification in this country where some people were becoming rich at the expense of others. We were concerned about the need to equalise opportunities. We wanted to come up with systems that engaged people meaningfully in this attempt to equalise. We recognised that would be a difficult task. That was why we were concerned that it should not be too easy for expatriates to become citizens and then use their already privileged positions to further aggravate the gap between the rich and the poor.

HEAD OF STATE

The CPC did not agree that we should have the Queen as Head of State. We could see no real historical or pragmatic reason for it. We also had an ideological basis for our rejection of this proposal by the government. Our *Constitution* was to be autochthonous, with the power to come from the people. It would be contrary to this principle if we had the Queen as the Head of the Government of Papua New Guinea, and the Parliament as the Queen's Parliament. We believed the Parliament should belong to the people, and that therefore the people, through their elected representatives, should elect or appoint their Head of State.

THE CONSTITUTION AND THE FUTURE

The question often asked now is whether our home-grown *Constitution* has achieved its aims. I think a better question would be whether the people and their leaders are succeeding in adhering to the noble goals and principles of our *Constitution*. The *Constitution* is an instrument; a charter. It is the people who are endowed with the faculties of willpower and intellect who should use these two faculties to help them to work towards the achievement of the vision of the type of society that the people through the CPC and the government at the time were offering as appropriate for Papua New Guinea.

The CPC was under a lot of pressure because we did not have to struggle or fight physically with Australia to convince them that it was time that they allowed us to have our independence. The Chief Minister had already decided that we should get independence, and I was one of his most ardent supporters on that issue, even before I entered politics. Now I am not too sure whether we did the right thing. But we took the plunge, and the time for blaming the colonial power is over. I think we have to take the bull by the horns now and work up enough moral courage and political will to put this country on the rails again. I think we also have to develop the ideological commitment for the kind of society which the *Constitution*, through the National Goals and Directive Principles, has spelt out for us. My fear is that if we do not, then Papua New Guinea will come out as second best. When we were developing the *Constitution*, the CPC argued about the need to develop Papua New Guinea in line with the Eight Aims of the Government which Sir Michael had introduced in 1972.[1] We had to introduce small-scale industries and develop the informal sector. What has happened to those ideas? We have six huge mines now and for the life of me, I do not know who is benefiting. It is obvious that our people are becoming poorer and poorer. At the same time they are frustrated by a definite experience of political powerlessness in the face of the reforms required by economic rationalism. Unless we address this problem by involving the people in an integrated approach, I think we will have ever-increasing problems. We may be creating yet another banana state in this very richly endowed country with very poor people.

[1]CPC, *Final Report of the Constitutional Planning Committee 1974: Part 1* (Port Moresby: Government Printer, 1974), pp 2/1-2/2.

Chapter 3

THE CONSTITUTIONAL PLANNING COMMITTEE, NATIONALISM AND VISION

BERNARD NAROKOBI

INTRODUCTION

I started formal schooling at the age of 12. Hence, I was not able to complete my university studies until I was 28. Soon after that, in 1972, I had the distinct and rare honour to be nominated by the late Sir John Guise, and then Chief Minister Michael Somare, to serve as a legal consultant to the Constitutional Planning Committee (CPC). I did not have a hand in the making of the *Constitution*, only a finger. My role was to help prepare some position papers, offer legal advice and generally be around to assist.

In this chapter, I comment on the constitution-making process, with particular reference to CPC members and advisers, the emerging nationalism which informed the work of the CPC, and the broad vision which the CPC developed for Papua New Guinea and which informs the *Constitution.*

THE CONSTITUTIONAL PLANNING COMMITTEE

The CPC was a mixed bag of politicians, all of them members of the House of Assembly. The key political figures included John Momis, John Kaputin, John Kaupa and Anton Parao. Sixteen members served on the Committee. Membership was broadly representative of regions, political parties (major political parties were Pangu Pati, the National Pati, United Pati, Peoples Progress Party and the Mataungan Association), interest groups and a spectrum of opinions, ranging from radical to conservative.

From among the Huli of Tari in the Southern Highlands came the Honourable Matiabe Yuwi. He was a practical, pragmatic man, short, stout and well built, with a small moustache. He had basic education and spoke typical Highlands Pisin. He was patient, tolerant, cautious and conservative. He was convinced Papua New Guinea was nowhere near ready for independence, and so did not want independence too soon. But he was a true democrat, ready to go by the majority wish.

Anton Parao was among the most well educated Highland leaders. He had been educated in Enga and East Sepik districts. Although he was a member of the Opposition United Pati, he was a progressive conservative. He understood both the pressure of the coastal leaders to become independent and the reluctance of men like the late Sir Tei Abal, leader of the Opposition and of the United Pati, to delay or defer independence. In supporting independence, Parao lost Abal's favour and later lost elections.

Then there was John Kaupa, who would sometimes enter the conference room, drunk, chewing betelnut and smoking at the same time. He hated expatriates, wanted independence, but had to contend with his Highlands colleagues who did not want independence so soon. He, Kaputin and Momis did most of the swearing and fighting with the white colonialists.

John Momis and John Kaputin had both had long, often bitter-sweet encounters with the colonial masters that had resulted in their holding a common conviction: get rid of them. Both were from the islands. Momis was a Catholic priest. Part New Ireland and part Buin, he had been born in Salamaua. Momis had been kicked out of the Madang seminary, later completing his studies in Australia. As a young priest he had gone back to Bougainville where his caring and tolerant American Bishop had placed him in charge of education. It was there that he developed a hatred for multi-national colonialism and its exploitation of the people.

John Kaputin was a Matupit man, a true Tolai, who had developed a long love-hate relationship with colonialists through rugby football, his outspoken role with the Mataungan Association and his work with the New Guinea Development Corporation. This background gave him a unique ability to compare and contrast the vices of western civilisation with what we had in Papua New Guinea.

The Committee was backed by Michael Somare who, in 1972, had become the Chief Minister. Although he was the official chairman of the CPC, it was the deputy chairman, John Momis, who became the full-time, effective and working chairman. John Kaputin was, in fact, the effective deputy to Momis.

Other active members of the Committee included: Sinake Giregire of Goroka; McKenzie Daugi of Oro; Stanis Toliman, a Tolai representing Bogia Open; Angmai Bilas of Riwo, Madang; Paul Langro of Lido, West Sepik; Tony Ila of Gulf representing Lae Open, Morobe; Naipuri Maina of South Fly; Pika Kasau, the youngest MP at the time, representing Manus; and Tei Abal, who was later replaced by Anton Parao; and Paulas Arek (who died in September 1973).

John Guise and Michael Somare rarely attended the meetings as they were both in the executive government of the Administrator's Council. They were busy preparing for the transition to independence.

There were also a number of other advisers who did much to help the CPC. They included John Ley, a hard-working Australian Government lawyer from Canberra; Yash Ghai, that tireless academic lawyer from Kenya; Ted Wolfers, a friend of Papua New Guinea; and David Stone, a New Zealand historian. There were also other overseas consultants. Seaea Avosa from Gulf Province was the often-abused executive officer to the CPC, who often bore the brunt when things went wrong.

Other key advisers involved in the constitution-making process were Joe Lynch, the legislative draftsman, and various advisers to the government, including Ili Tarua, Buri Kidu (then a young lawyer) and Tos Barnett, another lawyer.

From the start, a decision was made that the CPC should be made up only of indigenous members of the House of Assembly, and that it would mould a constitution from home, without travelling overseas to seek views. Instead the CPC travelled extensively within Papua New Guinea, holding hundreds of public meetings. In the process, it experienced difficulties and tensions. In Mendi, some CPC members had a near brawl with a member of the House of Assembly, the late Ron Neville. At Kainantu we were thrown out of a hotel because some of us did not wear shoes.

Momis had his papers stolen at one point, and there was some concern that this might have been the work of "spies" from Canberra!

EMERGING NATIONALISM

The *Constitution* was prepared against the backdrop of Mataungan nationalism, Papua Besena, the Kabisawali Movement of the Trobriand Islands, nationalist pressures in Bougainville and a broad elite pressure for independence for Papua New Guinea on the one hand, and massive conservatism of the immobile rural masses on the other hand. Mataungan nationalism was a major exception to the rural immobility rule. The murder of Jack Emmanuel on the Gazelle Peninsula in August 1971 had driven home to many Australians that their time was up. Anti-colonial, anti-business and anti-foreigner sentiment actually forced many Australian and Chinese businesses to close up and go home in the years immediately preceding independence.

The CPC was vocal and outspoken. It had an immense distrust of the use of state power. It feared bureaucratic despotism, and spoke strongly against centralisation. English legal tradition and constitutional conventions had no part in the thinking of the Committee and would have no place in the constitutional scheme envisaged by the CPC. Nothing was to be left to executive discretion and everything was to be defined by a detailed written constitution.

Initially the support given to the CPC by the government was outstanding. The Chief Minister's office created a Government Liaison Office (known as the GLO). In every province and district of Papua New Guinea there was a government liaison officer, well equipped with educational aids. These officers in turn set up constitutional planning and discussion groups. They received published discussion papers with questions for views to be given after discussions. There were extensive discussions over a period of almost three to four years.

Discussion papers on the legislature, the executive, the judiciary, citizenship, the kind of government the people wanted, human rights, the Leadership Code, the Ombudsman and others were discussed by the CPC, adopted and sent out to the people for debate and response.

Despite the tensions of the time, and much to the credit of the Australian colonists, the making of our *Constitution* was left to us to determine. This positive "hands off" attitude facilitated the peaceful enactment of our independence *Constitution* and the peaceful pulling down rather than tearing up of the Union Jack with the Southern Cross.

To achieve independence under a written constitution became a head chasing the tail exercise. The CPC and the "home rule" executive government under Chief Minister Somare both reversed their positions on the need for speed in the transition to independence. Initially it was the CPC that pushed hard for immediate independence. But when, by 1974, independence had become inevitable, a bitter debate developed between the CPC and Somare and his government. By then it was Somare who pressed for early independence. But the CPC position now argued that independence was no longer the key issue. Rather it was the quality or the kind of Papua New Guinea society that was now at stake. As a result, the CPC argued, it was necessary to delay independence until the colonial laws and the public service were sorted out and the quality of independence was settled.

Tensions between the CPC and the government became intense. Twice, the date for independence was altered. CPC advisers came under intense suspicion from the government. Mr John Ley was almost deported.

In mid-1974, the CPC was forced to make its report and wind up its activities. The expatriate advisers and staff were forced to leave Papua New Guinea. (John Ley left without any formal farewell.) I was transferred to the newly created Law Reform Commission.

THE VISION

Although not so young, I was not an old man when it happened. The members of the CPC were not old men either. Perhaps the main thing we shared in common was that we were excited, tickled, motivated, and inspired by what we were involved in. We wanted to see an egalitarian society with justice, equality, fair play and opportunity for all. We believed deeply in human dignity, equal worth and social obligations. We saw enormous opportunity in Papua New Guinea's villages and saw real "darkness in neon lights".[19]

We gave due recognition to the colonial heritage. Much good had been deposited by the colonial tidal wave but at the same time it had caused much destruction. Our task was not to throw out the bath tub with the baby, but to save the baby. We sought to enable and enrich our cultural heritage by what we could learn from outside. We wanted to build a modern Papua New Guinea on our solid ancestral foundations.[20]

What did the framers of the *Constitution* have in mind as the role of this document?

For the CPC, the *Constitution* was to play a central role in the development of both the individual and the nation. Development was seen as a total process of liberation. Liberation was not just a political slogan, but a theological perspective based to a large extent on the Latin American theology of liberation, and intended to be a guide to political and economic action. In this perspective, humankind is a fallen angel, but (as outlined in the *Book of Genesis*) humankind is also made in the image of God and must liberate itself from all forms of sin and slavery. The incarnation of God in Christ and his resurrection confirms the duty to liberate humanity from all forms of oppression. Humanity everywhere is engaged in a process, a struggle for liberation against all forms of oppression and slavery. We are called to struggle against structures of sin. As a result, politics is a noble enterprise, worthy of human participation.

This perspective rings loud and clear in the *Constitution*; through the Preamble (especially the National Goals and Directive Principles and Basic Social Obligations), the provisions on human rights and the general push for an open, participatory system of government. The liberation struggle was an affirmation, without force or violence, of what political struggles for freedom are all about, everywhere.

---

[19] CPC, *Final Report of the Constitutional Planning Committee 1974: Part 1* (Port Moresby: Government Printer, 1974), p 2/14/116. This was a phrase I coined based on inspiration from reading Mahatma Ghandi's writings.

[20] The CPC put it this way: "The process of colonisation has been like a huge tidal wave. It has covered our land, submerging the life of our people. It leaves much dirt and some useful soil, as it subsides. The time of independence is our time of freedom and liberation. We must rebuild our society, not on the scattered good soil the tidal wave of colonisation has deposited, but on the solid foundations of our ancestral land": ibid, p 2/13/98. Again, I am deeply grateful for the unique role history gave me to pen the above sentences that are now so often quoted.

The dream of the CPC was to transform society, not by the sword of the warrior, but by the double-edged sword of the rule of law. If that was the goal, a key question was how we were to root or base the *Constitution*. What was to be the source of its authority?

Our solution was not to use a Westminster statute or a Canberra enabling code, nor to seek authority by reference to some ancient or contemporary monarch. Instead, we envisaged that the people collectively, under the guiding hand of God, were to be the source of all power, authority and justice, which was then to be exercised on behalf of the people by various agents of power, who were to be accountable to each other and to the people. These views came through in the CPC proposals for the Preamble, and despite some significant modifications later made by the government to those proposals, they are still reflected in the text as adopted (discussed later).

Such views also came through in other provisions. For the CPC it was imperative that leaders were to be unquestionably incorruptible. To avoid outright corruption, or even mere immoral activities, there was to be a strict Leadership Code and an Investment Code. Leaders were to serve one and only one master: Papua New Guinea Incorporated. In this regard the CPC was influenced strongly by then President Nyerere of Tanzania. Unfortunately, the strict code proposed by the CPC was opposed by the government under pressure from the People's Progress Party, the present Leadership Code being much milder than the CPC had wanted.

The Ombudsman Commission was to be set up, not as a strict law enforcement body, but as an institution that would act as a watchman, a go-between, a mediator between the people and the powers that be. The Commission would use its moral influence to stop leaders from doing wrong things, preventing maladministration and facilitating honest and open government. Only the worst cases would be prosecuted.

The CPC opposed outright the role of the Queen as the Head of State. This view was particularly remarkable, bearing in mind the strong conservative forces of the day. This position was abandoned, however, in the Constituent Assembly when Sir Tei Abal and the Chief Minister supported the Queen of England as the Head of State for Papua New Guinea. But she was to be a strictly ceremonial head with absolutely no discretionary powers and represented by a Governor-General.

The CPC insisted that people's participation was a prerequisite to democracy and development. Although the CPC proposals on decentralisation in the form of provincial government were dropped from the draft *Constitution* in July 1975, the CPC's strongest advocates for decentralisation, Messrs Momis and Kaputin, together with Bougainvillean leaders such as Leo Hanett, later forced the inclusion of a chapter on provincial government in the *Constitution* through adoption of the first amendment in 1976.

NATIONAL GOALS AND DIRECTIVE PRINCIPLES AND BASIC SOCIAL OBLIGATIONS

Perhaps the clearest statement of the vision of the CPC is to be found in the National Goals and Directive Principles and the Basic Social Obligations. They make it clear that the preoccupation was not so much with political power, but with the building up of the "right kind of society". Our central concern was: "What kind of society will PNG become?"

In part the National Goals and the Directive Principles were intended to expand on the Eight Aims - the Eight Point Improvement Plan - that Chief Minister, Mr Somare, had introduced as government policy in December 1972, again greatly influenced by Tanzanian experience. But beyond that, Momis and I held the view that a modern constitution should not just be another dry, soulless document for lawyers only. Instead, it should state the kind of society we wanted for our people, and propose a set of ethical values that would inspire decision-makers and the general population alike. The CPC believed that "leaders and people must know where we want to go before we can decide how to get there".[21]

By and large, the other consultants and advisers chose not to make an input into developing the CPC position on these values. They took the view that only the Papua New Guinea citizens should articulate what they believed was best for Papua New Guinea. I commend them for their understanding.

In framing these goals, we were keenly aware of the similar goals in the constitutions of India and Indonesia. We also looked at the statement in the constitution for the State of California on the conservation of the environment in the formulation of the National Goal No 4 on Natural Resources and Environment.

The inclusion in the *Constitution* of the five National Goals and the Directive Principles associated with each of them clearly reflects the vision of the CPC for Papua New Guinea, a vision that reflected the spirit of the times. It was as if an artist or photographer had captured the spirit of hope and tension prevailing at that time. The colonial era was fading into the grey, orange and brown yesterday, and the bright red clouds of a Papua New Guinea dawn were emerging. As Sir John Guise often said, we were now daring to walk on ground on which even the angels of heaven had not yet dared to tread. We were to set sail upon uncharted waters, with the National Goals as our guiding stars.

The first goal - Integral Human Development - is a statement of a moral or philosophical view of development. Here again we derived much inspiration from the Latin American theology of liberation and hope, and from church social teachings. Development was not an end product for an accountant to count how many kina and toea had been made. It was a process of improvement: materially, spiritually and socially. Development ought to promote a balanced, well-adjusted and sound human atmosphere. As Kaputin would often say, development was not a sweet cherry waiting to be picked and eaten; instead, it was a continuous struggle against the odds.

The emphasis often well articulated by Momis was on the human person. In the CPC view, the person should not be the object of development but rather the subject, an active participant in human improvement. We tried to reflect perhaps one of the greatest mysteries of Judeo-Christian foundations. In this perspective man is born to pursue perfection, just as the Father in heaven is perfect. Man is not just a product of history. Man is a co-creator, a co-worker, with God and therefore an active participant/partner. After the angels, humanity is a masterpiece, only not like the Mona Lisa, existing as an object in the great halls of art galleries, but rather a vital artist, continuously shaping the environment.

The other four National Goals reinforce this profound vision for the people of Papua New Guinea. The second goal - Equality and Participation - sought to press further the issue of

[21] Ibid, p 2/1/4.

development with a human face. The entire system of politics and government was to be guided by the belief that all persons are born with equal dignity and self worth. Accordingly, citizens must not be treated with contempt. They must not become bystanders and observers but, rather, must be deeply involved in decision-making. Men and women must have equal opportunities.

The third National Goal - National Sovereignty and Self Reliance - is also part of the same drive for identity and real independence. The CPC was not so naive as to believe that any nation could be completely self-reliant. Rather, interdependence was the order of the day. However, the CPC wanted freedom from over-dependence on foreign aid and foreign influences. The best way to achieve national sovereignty and self-reliance was to link these values with straight, strong and incorruptible leadership.

Turning to the fourth goal - Natural Resources and Environment - conservation and sustainability are key words in today's ecological battle. How wise and inspired it was for the founding fathers to adopt this goal as a constitutional star to guide development. From memory, this goal was almost original, although in part influenced by the Californian conservation program and Californian State Constitution.

In retrospect, more should have been written to elaborate on this great goal. It has its beginnings in biblical perspectives as well as the ancient Melanesian wisdom of reverence for nature. The instruction in the *Book of Genesis* is for us to manage wisely our resources, not to destroy them. Reading Chapters 1 and 2 of *Genesis* would have you believe that the Garden of Eden was indeed Papua New Guinea. For it was in the country in the east that the garden was created. All kinds of beautiful trees grow there. The tree that gives life is the sago-coconut tree and the stream flowing through it is none other than the mighty Fly-Sepik system. The country of Havilah is none other than Papua New Guinea. Pure gold is found in that country.

More generally, conservation and replenishment do not involve "doing nothing" to the wilds. Rather, the issue is sustainable use, wise use, of our heritage. We must have in mind our great grandchildren when we deal with our resources.

The fifth goal – Papua New Guinean Ways - calls upon us all to make use of our Melanesian values in the process of liberation from our past, both colonial and cultural. This is necessary in our political and economic processes. This is not a call to be backward: the goal is quite consistent with also pressing for the same excellence in sciences and mathematics as in any other country. The point is that we are Melanesians. It is our Melanesianness in all its richness and diversity that will make us a great people.

Decentralisation also has its roots in Melanesian ethnic diversity and popular participation. Economic participation has its roots in Melanesian family unit participation in economic self-reliance. Melanesian values have strong roots in long histories of still vibrant diversity in languages, autonomy, architecture, law, music, song, dance, health and education. Our ethnic diversity is our source of strength.

Not many modern constitutions have a set of National Goals, less still a list of Social Obligations. Our *Constitution* has both. The Social Obligations are set in the same mould as the National Goals and their Directive Principles. For example, the fourth Social Obligation - protection of Papua New Guinea and the safeguarding of "national wealth, resources and environment in the interests not only of the present generation but also of future generations" - is similar in wording to the fourth National Goal. The second and third Basic Social Obligations involve "active participation in the development of the national community as a whole" and the use of opportunities "to participate fully in the government of the Nation". They echo the second and third National Goals: equality and participation and national sovereignty and self-reliance.

The idea underlying the Basic Social Obligations was that human rights are one side of a coin. Social or civic duties or responsibilities represent the other side of the coin. The CPC took the view that these goals could be realised if all citizens felt the moral conviction to implement them. Human rights could best be experienced if the people felt the responsibility to respect others in the exercise of their rights.

The Obligations are constitutional, political, social and economic in nature. They are intended to instruct everyone to be a responsible citizen, accepting our roles in the unending process of development of the self, the family and the wider world. Economic Obligations are intended to encourage all of us to avoid selling our national heritage for quick personal gain. The CPC did not fear any foreign military dominance. It feared foreign economic dominance.

CONCLUSIONS

In retrospect, I ask myself, did we set our goals too high? Why are we so poor in a country so rich? Why are we so insecure in a country well secured and endowed with gold, oil, copper, gas, fish, timber, sunshine, water and many, many more resources? Why are we strangers, beggars in our own land? Why do we have so much unemployment, yet we have so much land and water?

The CPC sounded warnings about these things 20 years ago. These warnings have been ignored. Much of what we feared would happen, has in fact happened.

Still, 20 years from independence, our *Constitution* still operates. The standards it embodies are still the benchmarks for considering how we develop. We can confidently say that in many ways our *Constitution* has served us well. We should be suspicious of anyone who attempts to undermine the *Constitution* and all its vision for an open and vibrant democracy.

The CPC has left legacies in other ways. The period between 1972 and 1975 was an intense period of exciting dialogue, debate and consultation. It was a great era, full of tension and a groaning for a new birth. This intense, open and honest debate helped shape Papua New Guinea's present-day open society, committed to open, participatory democracy. It helped shape a *Constitution* that has lasted 20 years. A tradition of non-violence, peaceful transition from one group of members to another group of members in and out of government has been created. Needless to say, those of us who had a finger in the making of the *Constitution* are enormously proud of, and grateful for, the privilege. We can only hope and pray that the traditions of consultation and peaceful transition will be carried on beyond 2020.

OVERVIEW AND ASSESSMENT

Chapter 4

ESTABLISHING A LIBERAL POLITICAL ORDER THROUGH A CONSTITUTION: THE PAPUA NEW GUINEA EXPERIENCE

YASH GHAI*

HISTORICAL BACKGROUND

One of the central concerns of this chapter is the potential of a constitution to mould the social and political system of a newly independent country, in particular its role in establishing a liberal, democratic polity. This has been widely perceived to be the task of most independent constitutions arising out of the decolonisation of Western imperial systems since the end of World War II.[22] Papua New Guinea provides an instructive subject for study: its *Constitution* is outstanding for its liberalism and the attempt to establish a democratic order; yet few countries could be regarded as less promising candidates for a liberal democracy for reasons such as the strong persistence of traditional cultures, the country's difficult and fragmented terrain, its low literacy rates, and the parochial loyalties that displace national sentiments.

Papua New Guinea, previously administered by Australia as part colony and part trust-territory, became independent in September 1975 under a constitution that was designed largely by its own parliamentarians. The history of Papua New Guinea and its people is estimated to go as far back as 5,000 years,[23] the population consisting of a large number of linguistic and clan groups (nearly 800 languages appear to have been spoken). The size of the groups varied from just a handful of people up to about 1,000. There was no common political authority over them: each group was what we may call "stateless", with political functions subsumed in social relations. Like other Melanesian societies, there was a high degree of egalitarianism and little social stratification. Leadership ("big man") status was achieved by special skills, such as oratory talents or success in warfare, and sustained through gifts and exchanges.[24] Exchanges were important for other reasons as well: they created bonds of reciprocity and increased the scope of relations with outsiders. This egalitarianism does not seem to have extended to women, however, who were socially and economically subordinated to men, were often married into other communities (voluntarily or otherwise), and were subjected to violence.

The main forms of livelihood were agriculture and fishing. Since tools were simple and specialisation limited, resources were not concentrated in individuals or families but were accessible to all members of a community. For the most part land was not individually owned; in

*This chapter was originally published as an article in (1997) 28 *Development and Change* 303. It is reproduced here with the kind permission of the author and the editors of that journal. The chapter is the text of a public lecture at the 21st Waigani Seminar in Port Moresby on 28 August 1995. The author is grateful to Anthony Regan and Peter Larmour for comments on a draft of the lecture.

[22] However, these perceptions are not shared by all, particularly frequently not by nationalist leaders who see a liberal constitution as a price to be paid for independence. For an exploration of this issue in the African context, see Y Ghai, "Constitutions and the Political Order in East Africa" (1972) 21 *International and Comparative Law Quarterly* 403.

[23] J D Waiko, *A Short History of Papua New Guinea* (Melbourne: Oxford University Press, 1993), Ch 3.

[24] M D Sahlins, "Poor man, rich man, big-man, chief: political types in Melanesia and Polynesia" (1963) 5 *Comparative Studies in Society and History* 285; A Strathern, *A Line of Power* (London: Tavistock Publications, 1984).

any case it was not made into a commodity. As in many pre-capitalist societies, land was more a matter of social relations than an object in itself. Disputes did of course arise among members of a community, but there appear to have been well-developed techniques for their settlement, with an emphasis on mediation, and peace was generally maintained within communities.[25]

However, the same cannot be said of relations *between* communities (speaking mutually incomprehensible languages). These were often marked by tensions and conflicts, and frequently resolved by warfare. The consequent tendency towards community self-sufficiency and social exclusiveness was reinforced by mountainous topography, especially in the northern part of the country, where warfare appears to have been more intense. This also had a profound effect on mobility, of which there seems to have been little.

This situation survived for a long period, and was still intact when the European colonisation began towards the end of the 19th century. In 1884 Germany, seeking to expand its colonial empire, annexed the northern part of the country (as New Guinea); this led to pressures on Britain from Australia to annex the southern part (as Papua). Australia formally took over the administration of Papua from Britain in 1906, having already established its presence there. As a result of both its ambitions and the tropical needs of its domestic economy, the German colonisation was more active and intense, leading to stronger European settlement and the development of plantations. With the start of World War I, however, Australia occupied New Guinea, and in 1921 it secured a mandate from the League of Nations to administer it. The administration of the two parts became increasingly, but never completely, integrated, until the final stages of decolonisation. Inevitably colonialism brought big changes in the traditional lifestyle of indigenous communities. But there were also remarkable continuities, even in the face of capitalist penetration into their mode of production.

Much of the period up to World War II was concerned with establishing colonial administration and the rudiments of a capitalist economy. For various reasons economic development was slow: Australia's own climate and topography were suitable for the type of agriculture that might have otherwise been promoted; there was discrimination against non-Australian enterprises; Australia itself was a British neo-colony; and for a variety of political, administrative and economic reasons, there was a preference for the conservation of the traditional indigenous economy.[26] The pace of change speeded up in the post-war period. Restrictions on indigenous economic activity were relaxed, opening the path to cash cropping, particularly coffee in the highlands. More efforts were made at social development, with education, health and community organisations. Some important developments took place in the mineral sector, most notably the opening of the vast copper mine on the island of Bougainville by Rio Tinto Zinc, a British multi-national operating through a subsidiary in Australia (and in many ways initiating early forms of nationalist protest).

These changes had various consequences for indigenous societies. There was some integration into the world economy, not just as consumers of foreign products as in the early days, but also as exporters, particularly with the growth of the mining sector. Domestically, the penetration of capitalism into the rural areas led to the development of social differentiation, with "big men" and others able to take advantage of new opportunities by the exploitation of communal institutions,

[25] P Fitzpatrick, *Law and State in Papua New Guinea* (London: Academic Press, 1980), pp 101-104.
[26] Ibid, Ch 3.

especially land and co-operative forms of labour, so that a symbiotic relationship grew up between capital and tradition. However, by the time of independence the differentiation was incipient, and on the whole Papua New Guinea was a relatively classless society (with only a small working class). Land, for the most part, remained embedded in communal relations and obligations, despite the efforts of colonial authorities to encourage individual landholding. (Just over 2 per cent of land was alienated to foreign settlers). Custom also held strong in most other areas, with one major exception: there was wide-scale conversion to Christianity. For a long time missions had a monopoly over provision of education and, inevitably, the education they offered emphasised the bible. Custom and Christianity did not always mix easily: indeed the tension continues even now.

The numerous clans came under a common colonial administration and a uniform system. They were increasingly affected by the growing and highly centralised state apparatus. Contacts among them increased, as the demands of capitalist enterprises required a mobile labour force, and the capacity of traditional systems to care for all diminished. Urban centres grew, as did a lingua franca, Pidgin. While the apparatus, and even the symbols, of statehood developed, a sense of nation did not. Administrative and capitalist penetration was uneven. Anti-colonial movements were few and were easily contained. There were no political parties virtually until independence, and even these were stimulated by its imminence. Incipient forms of political identity related to administrative boundaries established by the colonial government, giving rise to regional movements where the effects of the new economy were most marked, but even these boundaries were not congruent with the clan, which continued to provide the primary form of identity. Independence was stimulated more by the colonial authorities, especially with Gough Whitlam's accession to power in Australia, than by local pressures. Once it came, independence posed new challenges of national integration, modernisation, dealing with the outside world, and coping with rapid change in a largely traditional society.

The transition in Papua New Guinea society is therefore not a simple change from clan to state or tradition to modernity. Instead, the process can be viewed as a complex interweaving, in which change is mediated, to some extent, through traditional practices. The inevitable conflicts between tradition (largely clan-based) and the modern (as represented in the institutions of the state and the market economy) have adversely affected the capacity of both to cope with the problems of transition. Put simply, traditional values and practices have lost the capacity to provide coherence within the society, while the state institutions have not acquired either that capacity or the capacity to guarantee to its citizens physical or emotional security.

In the circumstances it is somewhat surprising that the country has been able to mark the 20th year of its independence by celebrating the uninterrupted rule of the *Constitution*. This achievement is the more remarkable since the *Constitution* establishes a tight balance of powers among various state institutions and a strict regime of the Rule of Law. One can turn the proposition around and say that the achievement is due precisely to this balance and the strict regime, but we would do well to remember the old adage that a constitution which cannot bend will break. Of course the *Constitution* has been bent, both formally and in practice.

THE GENESIS AND ORIENTATION OF THE CONSTITUTION

The making of the Papua New Guinea *Constitution* has been marked by several unusual features.[27] In the first place, the process was left almost entirely to the local people through a Constitutional Planning Committee (CPC) comprising local parliamentarians, with the colonial power having little say in the process. The CPC's function was to submit constitutional proposals to the National Constituent Assembly. The government had little hand in formulating the original proposals. Although Michael Somare, then Chief Minister, was the formal head of the CPC, he played almost no role in its deliberations or decisions. The CPC's decisions were therefore singularly free from the constraints and anxieties of statecraft. The CPC was able to impose as many restrictions on the state and to expand the scope of liberty as widely as it desired. The impulse towards these tendencies grew as the CPC, under the de facto chairmanship of John Momis, established its own identity and autonomy, and as the ideological distance between Konedobu (the seat of government) and Waigani (the offices of the CPC) increased. It is not fanciful to suggest that the CPC began to see itself as the Opposition, holding fast to the true purpose of independence in the face of what it regarded as the capitulation of the government to the will of Canberra. The broadly-based consultations that the CPC held with the people throughout the country, and the high moral ground it increasingly sought to occupy, gave it visibility and legitimacy that were denied to the government as the latter engaged in various regional problems.

The CPC did not have things its own way in all matters, however. At an early stage, proposals for controls over foreign capital were successfully attacked during a debate in the House of Assembly. Decentralisation proved another bone of contention: both Canberra and Konedobu were suspicious of it, and the Chief Minister was eventually prevailed upon to seek the removal of the mandate for decentralisation in the Constituent Assembly. The CPC proposals for dispensing with a Head of State were also rejected, in favour of a constitutional monarchy. It was only the admirable organisational and lobbying skills of the members of the CPC, forming itself into a Nationalist Pressure Group, that enabled it to overcome repeated challenges to many of its other proposals in the Constituent Assembly. In spite of these setbacks, however, the resulting *Constitution* did bear the stamp of the philosophy of the CPC.

The CPC saw the function of the *Constitution* as charting a new course for the organisation and development of Papua New Guinea and its institutions. It found itself with a virtual carte blanche, not only for the reasons mentioned, but also because of the paucity of ideas and platforms on independence from other sources including intellectuals or political parties. There was, in fact, widespread, popular anxiety about the difficulties that independence would bring. The CPC saw the allaying of these worries as one of its functions, and it achieved this partly through a forward-looking approach, highlighting the promise and potential of self-rule. The CPC was not always consistent, however. It was suffused with a nationalism – anti-colonial, anti-foreign, anti-bureaucracy – that had little resonance in the country. Anti-foreign feelings are most clearly reflected in the provisions on land and citizenship (and restrictions on the freedom of expression

[27] J Goldring, *The Constitution of Papua New Guinea* (Sydney: Law Book Company, 1978); C J Lynch, "The Achievement of Independence in Papua New Guinea" (1980) 11(3) *Journal of Pacific History* 175.

of non-citizens),[28] while anti-colonial feelings are demonstrated in the wish to establish an autochthonous constitution, drawing both its legal validity and legitimacy from domestic sources, and anti-bureaucratic sentiments are shown in the desire to refashion the state. Its anti-foreign sentiments, sometimes quite virulent in its deliberations, if not quite so dominant in the text, were out of place within its general humanistic approach, and contrasted with another influence present, that of liberation theology, introduced by John Momis, a Catholic pastor much influenced by the efforts of progressive priests in Latin America. It was also inspired by "populism", a belief in the capacity of the people to make "correct" decisions and to hold the government accountable.

The CPC was more consistent in its view of the design of the state, a view driven in large part by its vision of the political society. The primary function of society was "integral human development", which it defined as "nothing less than the unending process of improvement of every man and woman as a whole person".[29] That goal was to be achieved less through material progress than through the empowerment of individuals and communities. Public participation at all levels of government was one means towards that end, the centrepiece of which was to be the restructuring of the state through wide-ranging decentralisation. The CPC was also inspired by the vision of an equal and just society: equity between regions and between sexes. This fundamental goal was to be reached through national sovereignty and self-reliance, and in particular the use of "Papua New Guinean ways":

> "We must rebuild our society, not on the scattered good soil the tidal wave of colonisation has deposited, but on the solid foundations of our ancestral land. We must take the opportunity of digging up these political and social organisations. Wherever possible, we must make full use of our ways to achieve our national goals. We insist on this, despite the popular belief that the only viable means of dealing with the challenges of economic development is through the efficiency of Western techniques and institutions."[30]

Independence was liberation, the flowering of the genius of the people: "We must place an unswerving trust in Papua New Guineans and their wisdom."[31] With the end of oppressive colonialism would come the New Jerusalem: participation, consultation and consensus, and, inspired by tradition, the willing sacrifice by leaders of their privileged position for the common good would replace the tyranny of an alien bureaucracy. The CPC had an enormous faith in the indigenous political process. Fortunately it was not completely mesmerised by its own, typically South Pacific rhetoric or mystification. If it trusted the political process, it did not necessarily trust politicians, and it realised that the political process too could degenerate into petty squabbles, opportunism and abuse of authority unless adequate safeguards were built around it. The Papua New Guinea *Constitution* thus included an unusual number of safeguards.

These safeguards included tight control over rapacious and corrupting foreign capital (although, as mentioned above, some of the proposals in this area were successfully opposed by the allies of

---

[28] See *Constitution*, s 46(1)(b).
[29] CPC, *Final Report of the Constitutional Planning Committee: Part 1* (Port Moresby: Government Printer, 1974), p 2/3/14.
[30] Ibid, p 2/13/98.
[31] Ibid, p 2/13/100.

capital). There was also to be tight regulation of the finances, activities and foreign links of political parties. Politicians, like other public leaders, were to be subject to a comprehensive code of conduct designed to prevent abuse of office and to maintain the dignity of public institutions. The *Constitution* would entrench the fundamental principles of democracy, and vest the responsibility for their implementation in independent commissions, the Electoral Commission and the Boundaries Commission. The courts would resolve electoral disputes. Parliament would be vested with a range of powers, embroidering on the Westminster system, to ensure the accountability of the government. Parliament's own power (and derivatively that of the government) was circumscribed by an extensive Bill of Rights protecting individual liberties and freedoms. A number of independent institutions were established to ensure accountability of public bodies and the redress of grievances of citizens, particularly the Ombudsman Commission.

If the potential of democratic politics was one overriding theme of the *Constitution*, another was the Rule of Law. It is often assumed that democracy and the Rule of Law are cut from the same cloth, but this is a modern fallacy. Democracy is based on "people power", while the Rule of Law exists to curb such power.[32] Democracy demands an open-ended process and discretionary powers, while the Rule of Law needs a closed and clearly regulated process, substituting rules for discretion. Rights are central to the Rule of Law: the relationship between rights and democracy can be problematic. It is true that certain kinds of rights may be prerequisites to democracy. It is also true that certain kinds of rights may be better protected in a democracy than in other political systems. But the logic of rights is different from the logic of democracy. The former are individual-centred (even when they concern social rights), while democracy is majority-oriented. The scope of rights is drawn from the nature of the human person, the scope of democracy from the general will. Rights serve to limit state power, while democracy might be the justification for its expansion. Rights may be said to be rational and purposive (and indeed ideological), while democracy is frequently messy and manipulative, oppressive of minorities and careless of individuals.

If the CPC did not see the contradictions between democracy and the Rule of Law, it did perceive the tensions between them and used one to balance the other. Consequently the *Constitution* is particularly strong on the Rule of Law. It provides for an independent judiciary (although it makes the mistake of limiting the tenure of judges which, whatever its historical reasons, is unjustified today).[33] It has an impressive Bill of Rights and strong mechanisms for their enforcement. It ensures the fair and impartial administration of criminal justice through vesting prosecutorial powers in the independent Public Prosecutor. It facilitates access to courts and legal advice through the independent office of the Public Solicitor. It arms the Ombudsman Commission with considerable responsibilities and powers to enforce fair administration and honest public life. It authorises various agencies to seek the considered opinion of the Supreme Court on the interpretation of the *Constitution* in order to test the legality of legislation or official policy or administrative acts.

---

[32] Y Ghai, "Human Rights and Governance: The Asia Debate" (1993) 15 *Australian Yearbook of International Law* 1.

[33] See s 2 of the *Organic Law on the Terms and Conditions of Employment of Judges*: this provision was justified on the ground of avoiding the lengthy tenure of expatriate judges or inadequate local judges.

The *Constitution* has thus travelled a considerable distance from "Papua New Guinean ways". All that seems to remain are the pious Fifth National Goal and Directive Principle, "to achieve development primarily through the use of Papua New Guinea forms of social, political and economic organisations", and the direction to the Parliament and the judiciary to develop an indigenous jurisprudence, in particular by incorporating custom (see ss 20 and 21 and Sch 2). We are now in the world of Western constitutionalism: the separation of powers, democracy, limited government, the independence of the judiciary. The CPC became a captive of the system whose logic it was so keen to negate: the state. In its search for a "home-grown" foundation, or autochthony, the CPC was confronted with problems of constitution-makers elsewhere: how to transfer or translate the principles and institutions of small-scale societies (even assuming they were homogenous) onto the national scene. Enlarged boundaries, and the state within them, are the abiding legacies of colonialism which entrap constitution-makers. The CPC did a heroic job of getting out of the trap, trying in various ways to humanise and democratise the state, to circumscribe its powers and to increase its accountability, to encourage power sharing. But stripped of its rhetoric, the *Constitution* is about the state: about its institutions and how others relate to them. That the *Constitution* should deal with public power and its exercise is scarcely surprising; nor is it surprising that the CPC should fall back upon well-tested ways to tame the state (liberation, or indeed mainstream, theology not providing a coherent theory of the state, being concerned with issues of state and religion, or the superiority of religious doctrine).[34] The CPC was also hedged in by limitations: the virtual absence of civil society outside small rural communities, the continuing pull of ethnic loyalties and affiliations, the absence of political parties or national movements or ideologies, the incomprehension of the apparatus of the state, the uncertain and uneven penetration of capital, and so on. It was thus on a shallow foundation that the CPC sought to build a most ambitious constitution.

As with other independence constitutions, a major function of the Papua New Guinea *Constitution* was to replace foreign authority as the basis of the state. It also tried to democratise and humanise the colonial state. It became the foundation of the state and the symbol of an incipient national unity for a multitude of peoples and islands. It even tried to provide a national ideology. In that way it gave greater legitimacy to the state. But it provided for a different kind of state: democratic, participatory and humane. Its mission was to tame the colonial Leviathan, its vision of development being human rather than material.

[34] D Held, *Models of Democracy* (Cambridge: Polity Press, 1987), pp 36-41.

The resulting *Constitution* shows a heavy programmatic bias. The CPC was well aware of the task, and the *Constitution* not only set up an agenda but also provided signposts, if not actual instructions, on how to flesh out details and implement provisions. The legacy of the CPC was not only a lengthy and detailed *Constitution*, but an even heavier tome in the form of its Final Report, which was accorded the status of a Testament by the *Constitution* (s 24)[35]. But the *Constitution* could not institutionalise the CPC (undoubtedly to the regret of some of its members!) and was left to the tender mercies of the state that it so bravely tried to tame, with the rapid re-emergence of bureaucrats from the woodwork, the predation of politicians and the assaults of aid agencies with their conceptions of development, all pulling in the direction of strengthening state structures and minimising popular participation. Moreover, the *Constitution* rapidly fell into the hands of professional politicians whose raison d'etre was the apparatus rather than the purposes of the state. The question remained: would the logic of the *Constitution* prevail over that of the post-colonial state?

In terms of its structure, the *Constitution* broke every rule in the book of that well-known constitutionalist of the French Revolution, the Abbé Sieyes (as annotated by Edward McWhinney).[36] His first rule was to keep the constitution short. It is neither a municipal ordinance on sewers and drains, nor a master planner's detailed blueprint for a new community welfare program. His second rule: keep the language clear and non-technical. It is intended to be read by ordinary citizens, and not simply by constitutional specialists and Supreme Court judges. Other rules include: avoid flights of oratory; keep the constitution neutral, or at least open-ended in political ideological terms. It should never try to act in vain or to legislate the politically or socially impossible. Do not try to solve too many specific, purely temporary and short-range problems, as the constitution must endure for ages. A pre-condition for any politically viable exercise in constitution-making is a prior political consensus - on the part of the society for which the constitution is intended, or at least its dominant elite - as to the main goals and values. Then there are the extra-constitutional rules that effectively condition or limit the application of a constitutional charter: let the draftsperson beware and avoid self-indulgence, for it is not her or his constitution.

The first report of the CPC did pay homage to some of these rules. It argued for a short constitution and warned against a preoccupation with immediate problems. It was, however, inevitable that the CPC would break the Abbé's rules: it was unable to rely on an existing consensus and had to fashion one; it needed to preserve national unity and thus accommodate immediate problems of particular communities. It embodied various historic compromises such as those over land, where the compulsory acquisition procedures were muddied so that plantations could be transferred to the new elite intact instead of being broken up and returned to custom owners. It wanted to chart the social and economic future of the country, providing it with a vision. It believed in social engineering and the efficacy of the law. It wanted to harness social forces to the values of the *Constitution* rather than let the *Constitution* become hostage to them. The *Constitution* was to be an instrument, in addition to being a framework (the Abbé would have

[35] At its publication, the CPC's Final Report (above n 8) was widely considered to be the most radical and systematic political tract in the South Pacific. It influenced political discourse for some years following independence. Courts frequently refer to it in the interpretation of the *Constitution*, as authorised by s24. But it is now clear that politicians and governments are uncomfortable with its vision, which is inconsistent with their predilections, and although the penchant of Papua New Guinean intellectuals for rhetoric and oratory provides some sustenance to the Report, less is heard of it today.

[36] E McWhinney, *Constitution Making: Principles, Process, Practice* (Toronto: University of Toronto Press, 1981).

preferred the latter). The length was an indication of the CPC's mistrust of government, even indigenous government.

As it eventually emerged from the pen of the draftsman, C J Lynch, the *Constitution* has the character of a primer, describing a liberal democracy and indicating how it might be achieved. It attempts to cover practically the whole of the legal and administrative machinery of government, and codifies (and modifies) constitutional conventions to avoid misunderstanding, especially as it was evident that these were not generally understood. It is full of definitions, perambulatory statements and guidance.[37] Furthermore, contrary to the advice of the Abbé, Lynch apparently did see the primary addressees of the *Constitution* as being constitutional specialists and Supreme Court judges, as well as bureaucrats and politicians. Indeed, the task of redesigning (and managing) the state according to its provisions would fall upon these persons, many of whom were barely conversant with the principles and rules of the political system that the *Constitution* aimed to establish. (There is in any event a high degree of romanticism in the notion of people going about their everyday life studying and chanting verses from the *Constitution*: there are other ways in which popular knowledge of and respect for the *Constitution* must be stimulated.)

The wording of the *Constitution* also indicates a perception that the system that it intended to create did not exist, but had to be called into being, and that its values had to be internalised by those in charge of the state. In other words it was not superstructural, but was an attempt to design society from above, through the exercise of political power. Thus the *Constitution* of Papua New Guinea falls between the extremes of a constitution of a liberal democratic state and that of a communist state. The liberal constitution has grown out of and reflects society and economy; there is an organic link between it and social forces. The constitution therefore corresponds to social reality and amendments are made only when society feels ready for change. The constitution's function is to provide stability and a framework for political competition.

The socialist constitution was less a framework than an instrument: technically of the proletariat but in practice of the communist party. Its mission was not stability but the transformation of society. Decisive power was political, hence the eminence of the state: the constitution offered no constraints. Nor was the socialist constitution static, since social forces change with the advance towards socialism, and indeed communism provides a teleological view of history (towards the classless society) to guide the development of society and constitution. For a long time, however, the constitution acted partly as a camouflage of the site and exercise of power.

The Papua New Guinea *Constitution* is a liberal constitution, yet it is different from the constitution of a liberal state. It is more aspirational, less well connected to reality. It has a much greater task: to mould society to its imperatives. The *Constitution* provides a grand vision and a public morality, and at least for the latter it provides some machinery - the Leadership Code and the Ombudsman Commission - but it was not built on existing morality. On its own, the *Constitution* has little effect on the development of social forces; they may or may not grow in such a fashion as to support its philosophy.

[37] For a fascinating essay on the styles and purposes of drafting constitutional instruments, see C J Lynch, "Styles in the Drafting of Some Pacific Constitutions" in Y Ghai (ed), *Law, Politics and Government in the Pacific Island States* (Suva: Institute of Pacific Studies, University of the South Pacific, 1988), pp 202-241.

The Papua New Guinea *Constitution* is like a socialist constitution in that it too is "top down"; it is instrumental and aspirational (although it is also pluralistic). It does not directly transform the material basis of society as a socialist constitution would seek to do, by re-organising property and production. The CPC was partly correct in diagnosing problems of the market economy, but its preoccupation with the influence of foreign forces blinded it to the dynamics of domestic capitalism. Although this may be understandable, in the end it did not really come to grips with material forces or their probable trajectory, although it identified correctly the problems of political corruption. Its grand vision remained abstracted from material conditions of the country, and it relied primarily on the political process for its achievement.

CONSTITUTIONALISM: A THEORETICAL FRAMEWORK

The *Constitution* has had a profound effect on the development of politics in Papua New Guinea. Elections have been held regularly and changes of government consequent upon votes of no confidence have followed peacefully. One can say (with some reservations: see below) that a basic purpose of the *Constitution*, the establishment of the Rule of Law, has been achieved. However, given the tension between opportunism and principle, and given the fact that politicians have been less than happy with several aspects of the *Constitution* (such as the Leadership Code and the Ombudsman Commission), how does one explain the survival and even persistence of the *Constitution*? Answering this question may provide some insight into Papua New Guinea's post-independence constitutional experience.

I have argued elsewhere that the Rule of Law is possible in societies where there is a congruence of economic and political power,[38] although such congruence does not necessarily guarantee the Rule of Law. In this situation the constitution can to an extent be regarded as superstructural; that is, it supports the forces that dominate in society, particularly those with economic wealth. These forces are able to deploy their power over others through the economic and social systems, through the processes of production, employment practices and other uses of financial resources, and do not need to rely overtly on political or state power.

The Rule of Law is problematic in societies where economic and political power do not coincide. This has been the case in most ex-colonies at independence. Politicians who gain access to the apparatus of the state initially have little independent economic base, either as individuals or as a class. As the state becomes for them the primary instrument of accumulation, corruption is endemic, woven into the very fabric of the state. Pressures towards corruption arise not only from economic greed, but also from the imperatives of political survival, since the primary basis of a politician's support is generally not the party or another political platform, but clientage, sustained by regular favours to one's followers. Independent political control and accountability over that apparatus are unacceptable to the ruling regime. The state therefore becomes authoritarian. This may be termed the logic of the post-colonial state. The pervasiveness of executive power weakens institutions of control and accountability. In these circumstances rules are bent to the interests of politicians and bureaucrats or are applied selectively, so that the Rule of Law becomes problematic. In more extreme versions of this development, where a dictator or a

[38] Y Ghai, "Constitutionalism and the Problematic of the State in the Third World" in D Greenberg et al (eds), *Constitutionalism and Democracy: Transitions in the Contemporary World* (New York: Oxford UP, 1993).

powerful president emerges, lending the state a "patrimonial" character, with highly personalised authority, the Rule of Law may disappear: the top levels of bureaucracy become an extension of the presidential household; the judiciary is undermined to the extent that justice is seen to flow from the president, and personal petitions replace writs under the law.

Those who are familiar with Papua New Guinea may feel that parts of this description apply here, but clearly the more extreme version does not. Papua New Guinea cannot be called a patrimonial state since no dominant leader has emerged and the public service still retains some autonomy, although Ministers do tend to regard their departments as personal fiefdoms. Papua New Guinea has avoided the extreme scenario outlined above and has remained a relatively open society. Athough not all of its standards have been reached, the *Constitution* has established a remarkable vitality, given its high ambitions and the context within which it was imposed.

THE CONSTITUTIONAL EXPERIENCE OF PAPUA NEW GUINEA

The essence of all constitutions is how they define power and provide for access to it. This is particularly true in Papua New Guinea where so much reliance was placed on the political process. Its centrepiece is the Westminster model of access to and exercise of power, although it has been modified in some important ways: the Head of State is almost completely ceremonial, playing no role in the appointment or dismissal of the Prime Minister or the dissolution of Parliament. Such functions are given to Parliament to emphasise popular sovereignty but also to increase the effectiveness of the legislature vis-à-vis the executive in order to reverse the trend towards the executive dominance over the legislature in parliamentary systems. But the modifications also recognise the lack of a firm party system and the dangers under such circumstances of relying on conventions regarding the Head of State.

Although the *Constitution* carefully modifies and codifies conventions, these are conventions about the relationship between the executive and the legislature and fail to capture another dimension of the parliamentary system: the responsibilities of the member of Parliament to her or his constituency, standards of public morality, party solidarity, the pursuit of policy and general welfare. The Papua New Guinea variant of the Westminster system has become largely procedural: it has more to do with access to and removal from power and less and less to do with public purpose in the exercise of power. It has tied itself to certain underlying political realities of Papua New Guinea, giving a fascinating insight into the manner in which the Westminster system has unfolded in the South Pacific.[39]

Parliamentary politics

In general a parliamentary system relies upon well-established political parties. As the government has to command the support of a majority of Parliament, and to manage its parliamentary business, it is necessary to have organised and reliable support. Similarly, for the Opposition to maintain a sustained attack on the government and to offer itself as an alternative, it needs the organisation and consolidation of its support base. Just as the structure and policies of

[39] Y Ghai, "Systems of Government" and "Political Consequences of Constitutions" in Ghai, above n 16.

political parties become the major influences on the nature of many parliamentary systems, the *absence* of a well-established party system in Papua New Guinea (as in some other South Pacific states) has greatly influenced the operation of government and Parliament. There would appear to be both social and structural reasons for the relative absence of parties. Structurally, the system of elections based on "first-past-the post" (the plurality system) plays a role; in single member constituencies, the candidate with the largest number of votes wins. Although such a system is supposed to encourage two major parties (since it tends to discriminate against minority interests), in Papua New Guinea it has led to a proliferation of parties, or more accurately, to a lack of effective parties. This is because such a system can also help independents: it encourages a multiplicity of candidates, since only a small percentage of votes may suffice for victory. It is not unknown for candidates with a support of less than 5 per cent of voters to win an election. Unlike most systems of proportional representation which require an effective organisation of parties, in the plurality system as it has operated in Papua New Guinea, a candidate can succeed without the assistance of parties. (The escalation of campaign costs may compel some to seek a party endorsement, but then the party may be willing to officially endorse or have informal understandings with more than one candidate in the same constituency, given the importance of numbers and the fluidity of politics.) The CPC rejected both preferential voting (which had applied in Papua New Guinea during the colonial period) and proportional representation, as being too complicated. The latter was also thought to be dependent on the existence of well-established parties, thus overlooking the possibility that proportional representation could in fact lead to the development of parties.[40]

The plurality system has worked in this way in large part because of social forces. The arrival of independence before the emergence of nationalism denied politicians the opportunity to use anti-colonial protest as an instrument to fashion national parties; such protest as there was remained local, embedded in the cultural matrix of a particular community. Independence set in motion a process for the scramble for power, for which ethnicity provided the most ready base. Elections have been dominated by local, not national, issues; it is more important to be recognised as a local "big man" than as a leader of a party.[41] Politicians are more dependent on the support of these "big men" than they are on the party. The low level of urbanisation, physical distances and difficulties of terrain aggravate the effect of the lack of financial resources and managerial skills for mobilisation and party organisation. Furthermore, politicians who might have skills for this find their time committed to government or party manoeuvres, which (as I shall discuss below) the rules for the dismissal of government encourage. This suggests another factor behind the lack of party solidarity: the limited notion that power is to be used not for public policy but for personal aggrandisement. In the political marketplace, where parliamentary membership has become a commodity, every MP wants to carry a personal price tag. This has lent itself to the development of a practice whereby "parties", in order to secure the votes of successful candidates, literally highjack them, isolating them from rival groups and plying them with liquor until the opening of Parliament and the election of the Prime Minister.

The lack of firmly based parties with an ideological agenda, the predominance of parliamentarians who have no clear allegiance to a party, and the high turnover of

[40] CPC, above n 8, pp 6/15/101-6/16/109.

[41] On the concept of "big man", see M Godelier and M Strathern (eds), *Big Men and Great Men: Personifications of Power in Melanesia* (Cambridge: Cambridge UP, 1991), and Sahlins, above n 3; for their role in politics, see Strathern, above n 3.

parliamentarians (more than 50 per cent in each election) that results from a multiplicity of candidates in an ethnically deeply fragmented society, combine with constitutional rules for the formation and dismissal of government to produce a highly unpredictable and unstable government. The requirement for the formation of government - the support of a majority of parliamentarians - means that "parties" emerge after rather than before elections: parties are more important for forming government and staying in power than for elections. They are therefore best regarded as parliamentary groups rather than parties: certainly they do not have the structure or popular base of a party. For the same reason, "coalitions", which have become a necessary condition for formation of government, are formed after rather than before elections due to MPs and parliamentary groups not wanting to miss any opportunities of office. Consequently, the issues involved in party solidarity or coalition-building are not those of consensus or the pursuit of policy so much as personal access to power. The pursuit of personal power has led to the most unlikely of bedfellows, liberating parliamentarians from any pre-election commitments or allegiances. Because party links and ideologies are weak and the power base of MPs is ethnic and not policy oriented, these shifts of allegiances involve neither anguish nor sanctions.

These circumstances would in any event produce instability or at least uncertainty, but in Papua New Guinea the situation is aggravated by the rule for the dismissal of government. Dismissal is on a vote of no confidence which, for the first four years of the normal five-year term of a particular Parliament, requires the nomination of an alternative Prime Minister (s 145). The Prime Minister who loses the vote has no right to ask for dissolution. Prime Minister Sir Julius Chan has commented on this rule.[42] Since MPs do not have to seek re-election after a vote of no confidence (as would be the case in most parliamentary systems), the rule produces in them a certain recklessness in moving no confidence motions. The Prime Minister has constantly to negotiate with individual politicians and groups, to maintain her or his majority:

> "[W]ith many political groupings representing regional and other interests, any government has to depend on the support of a number of separate groups. This means that in order to stay in office the Prime Minister of the day has to spend a quite disproportionate amount of his time and energy keeping individual politicians 'happy'."[43]

He goes on to point to the unfortunate consequences, the first of which is political corruption. The second is that:

> "the Prime Minister has little leeway to do his real job, which is to think about the good of the country as a whole, to look ahead, to make rational choices and to pursue consistent policies designed to benefit ordinary people in the longer term."[44]

Thirdly, politics are conducted in an atmosphere of perpetual day-to-day crisis.[45] Sir Michael Somare, the first Prime Minister who was ousted by a vote of no confidence moved in favour of

---

[42] J Chan, "Experience with Papua New Guinea's Constitution: A Prime Minister's Reflections" in Y Ghai, above n 16.
[43] Ibid, p 247.
[44] Ibid.
[45] Ibid.

his deputy, Sir Julius Chan, has also highlighted this as a major factor behind political instability.[46]

Although there is undoubtedly an element of truth in their criticism, the influence of "no confidence" motions may have been exaggerated. In parliamentary systems where the Prime Minister has the right to ask for dissolution (in India, for example), he or she may still spend a great deal of time placating her or his parliamentarian supporters. There is no reason to believe that a Prime Minister is keener to go to the country than parliamentarians (except when a motion has been successfully carried, and he or she has nothing to lose), although the threat of dissolution that the Prime Minister wields may be more significant than the dissolution itself. The way in which the rules for no confidence motions have been operated may be a symptom rather than the underlying cause of the malaise of politics in Papua New Guinea.

However, it is clearly hard to follow any consistent policies in the circumstances outlined by Sir Julius Chan. Moreover, each ministry becomes a site of profit and patronage, and consequently a kind of fiefdom. It is therefore not surprising that the collective responsibility of the Cabinet is weak. Policy issues are seldom negotiated when coalitions are formed and may or may not emerge in the course of administration. The Cabinet has not been particularly effective in resolving differences. In order to strengthen their position or win popularity, Ministers tend to air their differences in public, thereby imposing further strain on Cabinet unity and cohesion. It is not easy for the Prime Minister to enforce collective responsibility through dismissals of Ministers, for the future of the government itself may be placed in jeopardy. Parliamentary groups are based on personalities or regions and there are "coalitions in waiting" ready to embrace breakaway groups. Paradoxically a Prime Minister is able to maintain the unity of the coalition or the Cabinet only by tolerating open dissent within its ranks.

The consequences of this state of affairs are not always what one might expect; for example, given fluid coalitions and factions, Parliament could influence and discipline the executive; Parliament would be able to exact responsibility from individual Ministers; there would be a fair equilibrium in the balance of power between the Parliament and the Cabinet; or, indeed, Parliament may tend to assume the direction of executive functions (with analogies respectively with the operation of the parliamentary system in Britain in the 18th and 19th centuries and the French system until the Fifth Republic, with the Gaullist *Constitution* representing a clear shift from Parliament to the executive).[47] However, parliamentarians have not seized upon the instability or weakness of government to impose their own will. Executive functions still remain with the Cabinet or Ministers, even though they may not be carried out with vigour. This is partly because the executive has the assistance of public servants while parliamentarians have shown less interest in policy than in personal advancement. Parliamentarians, on the whole, have not displayed much skill in exploiting parliamentary procedures to embarrass the government or win concessions. In recent years parliamentary committees have virtually ceased to operate. There have been few adjournment motions, critical parliamentary questions or policy debates, but there have been motions of no confidence, indicating that their purpose is not accountability. Instead,

[46] M Somare, "The Challenges of Independence - My Yesteryears Vision of Papua New Guinea", Keynote Address for the 21st Waigani Seminar, Port Moresby, 28 August 1995.

[47] M J C Vile, *Constitutionalism and the Separation of Powers* (Oxford: Oxford UP, 1967).

parliamentarians have concentrated on acquiring a share in the executive (leading to "politics of intrigue"). The powers of the executive to summon and prorogue Parliament have been frequently used to delay or disperse meeting; it has preferred safety to the enactment of policy. Parliament has failed to be the main instrument of public accountability as the CPC had hoped and anticipated. Public accountability, such as it exists, has been achieved through other institutions, which will be discussed shortly.

At one stage it seemed that political instability (and shifts in administration) were of little consequence. Changes of government were seldom based on policy disputes, the incoming government cheerfully carrying on with the legislative and administrative agenda of its predecessor. As in post-war Italy, the public service provided continuity, as did the concerns and the influence of the international aid agencies. However, it may be that political instability is no longer so innocuous, and the present economic and social problems facing the country may not be unconnected with the inability of governments to formulate and pursue consistent and long-term policies, just as Sir Julius Chan had feared some years ago. There seems to be little capacity to focus on any particular problem for any sustained period, even an important issue like the Bougainville crisis.[48] There is little consistency of policy, and the government appears to react rather than to plan or anticipate.

Sir Julius and others have suggested constitutional reforms to deal with these problems. His own preference would be to give the Prime Minister the right to dissolve Parliament on a vote of no confidence, so that if Parliament is not willing to sustain a government it should face the voters. He would also like to give a government that survives a vote of no confidence one year's "free run" thereafter.[49] A different kind of constitutional amendment was made in 1990, which now gives a new government some respite: it is safe from a no confidence motion for the first 18 months. (If these 18 months immediately precede the last year of Parliament, this effectively offers protection for two-and-a-half years.) There is already an original constitutional rule that if a motion of no confidence is successfully moved in the last 12 months of a Parliament, Parliament stands dissolved (s 105). Under these circumstances, MPs would be most reluctant to support a no confidence motion; and in fact none has been moved. The combination of these rules gives the government a high security of tenure.

The public service

The relationship between Ministers and public servants is also affected by these developments. At independence civil servants were more experienced than Ministers, and able to form policy. There now appears to be a shift: on a recent visit I was told by more than one departmental secretary that they rarely see Cabinet submissions from other departments (or in one case, of his own department) and do not, as a rule, brief Ministers before the National Executive Council meets. Departmental submissions to the Cabinet are frequently drawn up by outside private interests. This supports the view that ministries have become fiefdoms and the politics of semi-patrimonialism have replaced collective responsibility. These developments have undoubtedly

[48] The Bougainville "crisis" refers to attempts by some dissidents (calling themselves the Bougainville Revolutionary Army) to secede from Papua New Guinea. When the attempts were promoted by armed violence, the government retaliated by sending in troops, which tortured and murdered many innocent people. After several years of negotiations the problem remains unresolved. It is perhaps the biggest problem that the country has faced since independence, but the capacity or even the willingness to solve it are woefully inadequate.

[49] Chan, above n 21, p 248.

weakened the capacity of the state to make and implement policy. They may not be unconnected with a constitutional amendment in 1984, which reduced the status and powers of the Public Service Commission. The independent Public Service Commission originally had a firm control over the public service, not just as regards recruitment, promotion and dismissal but also the establishment and general management of the public service. These latter functions are now vested in the government.

Devolution and provincial government

Some executive stability is undoubtedly desirable but there are other urgent problems too, such as the capacity to make and implement policy, and public accountability. In this context an examination of the fortunes of provincial government is rewarding. The CPC had argued strongly for a significant decentralisation of power to provinces (as an essential part of its agenda to restructure the colonial state) and proposals for this were contained right up to the fourth (and penultimate) draft of the *Constitution*. It is unnecessary to relate the circumstances that led to their removal,[50] but it is relevant to point out that the amendments were necessary to bring the secession of Bougainville to an end and thus ensure territorial integrity. The amendments went beyond the original provisions in giving greater powers to the provinces. This was just as well, since it is very probable that the original provisions (and the proposals that would have been implemented under them in an Organic Law)[51] would have failed to ensure effective decentralisation because of a lack of adequate conceptualisation of powers and insufficient guarantees of financial resources to provinces (and would have been even more complex than the system established in 1976).

In keeping with most constitutional amendments that are designed to increase the authority of national politicians or the executive, the 1995 amendments relating to provincial government involve a major restructuring, providing key roles for national parliamentarians. The changes are complex, and beyond the scope of this chapter, but my analysis would be incomplete without some reference to the amendments since they highlight two continuing constitutional preoccupations in Papua New Guinea: the role of decentralisation and the personalised nature of politics. Perhaps the CPC erred in placing such a heavy reliance on the devolution of power, both to restructure the state and to increase local participation. Except in a few provinces, provincial governments were bureaucratic, allowed for little public participation in the affairs of the province, and became corrupt. They sought to imitate central government, down to the black cars. The provinces did, however, provide sites of alternative power; to some extent they acted as a check on the central government, and facilitated a new group of representatives.[52] It is largely for this reason that they incurred the wrath of national government and parliamentarians. They were seen by national parliamentarians to have too much power and too much money; particularly too much money, which in their view should have gone to the national parliamentarians. The criticisms which were brought against provincial government – overgovernment, corruption, waste, inefficiency, lack of accountability – could be levelled on a greater scale against national governments and parliamentarians themselves.

[50] Y Ghai and A J Regan, *The Law, Politics and Administration of Decentralisation* (Boroko: National Research Institute, 1992); J Ballard, "Policy Making as Trauma" in J Ballard (ed), *Policy Making in a New State: Papua New Guinea 1972-77* (St Lucia: University of Queensland Press, 1981).

[51] Somewhat unusually, the constitutional laws of Papua New Guinea are contained in the *Constitution* and a series of Organic Laws. The proposal to have Organic Laws was first made in order to keep the principal instrument brief, although in this it was not successful.

[52] For a balance sheet, see Ghai and Regan, above n 29, especially the concluding chapter, and Y Ghai and A J Regan, "Decentralisation: 1976-1995", Chapter 11 in this volume.

National governments gave provincial government little chance to develop and improve. All the powers of intervention and obstruction that were allowed to the national government under the *Constitution* and the *Organic Law on Provincial Government* were used, mostly in arbitrary and unreasonable ways. The spirit of co-operation and consultation that underlay the Organic Law was completely ignored by the government and national parliamentarians. The politics of patronage and clientage, and the corruption that feeds them, simply did not permit that state resources be siphoned off to provinces when they could be used instead to prop up national politicians. As recently as June 1995 parliamentarians passed constitutional amendments and a new Organic Law taking the resources away from provincial politicians and giving these to themselves.[53] The amendments were presaged by earlier provisions to support MPs against their provincial rivals. To compensate MPs for the decline in their role in local affairs (and particularly their access to development funds) after the establishment of provincial government in 1976, two funds were created by the national government: the sectoral development fund, to which MPs could apply for agricultural or transport projects in their constituencies, and the Electoral Development Fund which gave each MP a discretionary grant for projects in her or his constituency. It has been estimated that about K100 million a year are dispensed in this way, giving each MP something like K4 million over the life of Parliament to nurse his or her constituency: a fine instance of the institutionalisation of the politics of clientage.[54]

Accountability

The CPC's expectation that the political process would generate responsibility and accountability has patently not materialised. Provincial government provides a good illustration. Parliament was cast in the role of the fundamental protector of provincial interests against central government arbitrariness, particularly with regard to the suspension of a provincial government. Far from being a neutral umpire, however, Parliament was highly partisan and countenanced wide-scale abuse of the powers of suspension. The Premiers Council was another political institution that was to negotiate agreements between the provinces and the national government, and to settle inter-governmental disputes. The national government treated provincial views with total disdain (and instituted the National Public Expenditure Plan around the time of the *Organic Law on Provincial Government* leading virtually to the disestablishment of the National Fiscal Commission provided for under that law).

The provinces turned to the courts for protection. This was quite ironic given that the CPC had been so emphatic that, as far as possible, courts should be kept out of inter-governmental relations to encourage mediation and conciliation and to prevent legalism.[55] In some important instances the courts defended provinces against the most egregious abuses of power: on the question of the appointment of a provincial secretary (*SCR No 1 of 1984; Re Morobe Provincial Government v*

[53] Under the new *Organic Law on Provincial Governments and Local-Level Governments*, drawn up with "bipartisan" parliamentary support, national parliamentarians constitute provincial authorities, and the regional member of the province is the Governor. They thus gain access to significant financial resources and ample powers of patronage. Little thought appears to have been given to conflicts of interests and political disagreements between a Governor and the Centre; it is a singularly ill-thought out piece of legislation.

[54] This is not the only self-serving amendment passed by parliamentarians. As well as the establishment of the 18 months' "honeymoon" period for new Prime Ministers (already mentioned), another amendment overrules a decision of the Supreme Court in 1982 that a required deposit of K,1000 for elections is unconstitutional (15th amendment, 1991), a device to help sitting MPs. Parliament has also amended the *Constitution* whereby it may *increase* budgetary proposals for allocation of parliamentary salaries - a break from normal Westminster financial rules (10th amendment, 1988).

[55] CPC, above n 8, pp 10/22/194-10/23/96.

Papua New Guinea [1984] PNGLR 212); on the suspensions of government (*Papua New Guinea v Kapal* [1987] PNGLR 417; *SCR No 3 of 1986; Reference by the Simbu Provincial Executive* [1987] PNGLR 151), and on the calculation of unconditional grants to provinces (*SCR No 1 of 1990; Re Enga Provincial Government* [1990] PNGLR 532).

In other areas too the judiciary's record has generally been commendable. It has delivered a number of positive decisions in favour of human rights, although there have been some restrictive decisions as well. It is impossible to review the case law briefly because it is voluminous, but through its opinions on constitutional references it has upheld the Rule of Law. As illustrations, it has supported those seeking to enforce the *Constitution* (*SCR No 4 of 1980; Re Petition of M T Somare* [1981] PNGLR 265); protected prisoners from degrading treatment by prison staff (*Amaiu v Commissioner of Corrective Institutions* [1983] PNGLR 87); ruled against the validity of collective punishments (*SCR No 1 of 1981; Re Inter-Group Fighting Act 1977* [1981] PNGLR 151); and declared the most draconian provisions of the *Internal Security Act* 1994 unconstitutional (*SCR No 3 of 1993; Re Internal Security Act* [1994] PNGLR 141). It has also supported the freedom of movement (*Re Vagrancy Act* [1988] PNGLR 1) and upheld a number of safeguards in the administration of the criminal law. Insofar as it lies within its power, it has tried to keep the political process open and honest; and in the most blatant case of the abuse of the parliamentary process - when a Prime Minister tried to evade the rule against motions of no confidence by resigning and being re-elected in questionable circumstances - the Supreme Court upheld the spirit of the *Constitution*, reversing an unthinking decision of the National Court (*Haiveta v Wingti (No 3)* [1994] PNGLR 197). On the other hand, while the Supreme Court has frequently urged a "purposive" interpretation, it has taken a narrow view of some provisions, as in relation to the Leadership Code (*In re Joseph Auna* [1980] PNGLR 500 and *Karo v Ombudsman Commission* [1995] PNGLR 547), the meaning of the phrase "according to law" (*Avia Aihi v The State* [1981] PNGLR 81) and the rights of non-citizens (*Premdas v Papua New Guinea* [1979] PNGLR 329; *Perryman v Minister of Foreign Affairs and Trade* [1982] PNGLR 339). It has made little use of the interesting and useful provision that invalidates harsh, oppressive, disproportionate or unreasonable executive action (s 41), equating it, wrongly, with common law principles, and has been ambiguous in the application and development of the rules of natural justice as mandated by the *Constitution* (ss 59-60).

Citizen judges of Papua New Guinea were asked to shoulder responsibility for the integrity of the judicial and political systems at a very difficult time when, in 1979, the then Prime Minister Michael Somare, in defiance of the courts, released his Minister of Justice from her sentence for contempt of court, prompting a mass resignation of expatriate judges. They rose to the challenge with great courage and competence. Much credit must go to the late Chief Justice Sir Buri Kidu and his Deputy Sir Mari Kapi for restoring the morale and effectiveness of the courts. Other independent authorities, particularly the Ombudsman Commission and the Public Solicitor, have also contributed greatly to ensure justice, prevent the abuse of power and facilitate access to courts. They have suffered from a lack of resources, and in the case of the Commission, from a weak and faulty Leadership Code. Nevertheless these independent institutions, along with the judiciary, are the redeeming features of Papua New Guinea's constitutional system. They have prevented the decline of the executive and Parliament into total irresponsibility and unaccountability. They have attempted to enforce constitutional standards of public morality, and have supported the protection of human rights. However, even these institutions have played a questionable role in the atrocities that accompanied what is now called the "Bougainville Crisis", doing little to ensure that the perpetrators of the atrocities were brought to account. Many of the serious violations of human rights took place within the law enforcement system (by the police and custodial services), as well as by the army. The legal profession, as in so many other countries, has cultivated its own self-interest in making money at the expense of its public duties and responsibilities.

CONCLUSIONS

By way of conclusion, a brief balance sheet might prove useful, followed by an attempt to explain some salient features in that balance sheet. On the credit side, the *Constitution* has survived and with it the political and legal system that it established. The *Constitution* provides the framework for national politics. Papua New Guinea is an open society, where most rights are protected. No-one can accuse the various governments since independence of being tyrannical, and no dictator has emerged to undermine the constitutional order. Elections have been held regularly, and have been conducted competitively and fairly. Changes of governments have followed peacefully. The press is free. Despite the aims of the notorious "anti-terrorist" legislation of 1993 (the *Internal Security Act*), there is no preventive detention. To a significant degree, the Rule of Law has been maintained.

On the debit side, almost none of the national goals have been achieved. There is no gender equality; indeed, women are highly exploited, in the economy and in the household, and are often victims of violence. There is not a single woman in Parliament today, and relatively few in senior positions in government or the private sector, even at the 20th anniversary of independence. There is still very limited public participation in the affairs of state; provincial governments in most cases have been no better than central institutions. Public accountability, particularly through the political process, has fared little better. Corruption is now of endemic proportions: one might call this an "achievement" of independence, since it is my impression that there was little of it before.

National sovereignty has been somewhat battered, and national unity is fragile. A solution to the Bougainville crisis continues to elude the government, and the changes in provincial government have added to the strains on national unity. Self-reliance is no longer fashionable. The dependence on external funding and other forms of assistance has increased, particularly now with the country's financial crisis, and in spite of extensive exploitation of the country's rich natural resources. There is little progress towards - indeed there may be regression away from - the goals of equity and equality, both as regards regions and as regards individuals and groups. Public policy concerns do not embrace the alleviation of poverty or the equalisation of opportunities. One result is a horrendous breakdown in law and order.

The *Constitution* requires government and citizens to have control over the bulk of economic enterprises and production and to provide a strict control of foreign investment.[56] Instead, privatisation, dictated by foreign institutions, is in vogue. Successive governments have pursued big projects, primarily in minerals and forestry, and have surrendered the economy to foreign corporations. In their wake have come the degradation of the environment and the destruction of communities. In this pursuit of mega-projects, "Papua New Guinean ways" are dying a sure and painful death.

[56] National Goal No 3, in the Preamble to the *Constitution*.

In looking at this balance sheet, one first has to explain an apparent paradox: the *Constitution* "works" but its primary goals are subverted. I have already mentioned that the *Constitution* did not change the material conditions that might have facilitated the achievement of the national goals it espoused. The CPC left that largely to the political process, but it is the political process that has largely subverted most national goals. The idealism of the CPC did not necessarily represent the aspirations of the elite. As Peter Fitzpatrick has said: "dominant internal class elements were interested in some purchase on the existing system that sustains them. They were not interested in radically changing it".[57] The ideological provisions were effectively ousted by a competing (though less overt) ideology in the *Constitution* - centrality of the state apparatus and the market economy - reinforced by the continuation of political, economic and military links with the former metropolitan power.

As I have indicated, the whole parliamentary system is now lubricated by cash. Candidates, unable to count on party organisation or the loyalty of supporters to win elections, rely on monetary or other material incentives to win votes. Reciprocity and ethnic ties have become the basis of politics. Politics are an investment: a clan will contribute significant sums, often exceeding K500,000, to the campaign of its candidate, in the expectation of subsequent rewards. The obligations to members of the community are thus woven into state politics, so that state roles cannot - any more than state resources - be separated from communal exchanges. The Electoral Development Fund and the sectoral grants have institutionalised these forms of dispensation. Governments cannot maintain their cohesion through common purpose, but must rely on patronage and trade offs. Some of the cash to maintain this system may come from private resources, but the bulk of it comes from the state. In the absence of significant indigenous entrepreneurial economy activity, the plunder of the state takes the form of the abuse of public political office. The lure of ministerial office is especially strong in the South Pacific, yet few qualifications are necessary for such public office. The politics of survival concentrates the politician's mind on the personal appropriation of public resources: clearly public accountability is anathema to such pursuits. Because of ties of kinship and the clientele basis of politics, state plunder does not tend to lead to accumulation that might, in time, provide the springboard for economic independence, class formation, and some separation of the state from daily depredations of politicians.

Thus the political system adheres less to democratic values or parliamentary procedures than to traditional notions of leadership and kinship. Most parliamentarians are content with support of kin and the clan. Morality that is relevant to the success of a candidate is clannish rather than public: the state is remote and its plunder increases rather than diminishes the value of the local MP. Conviction in state courts does not necessarily tarnish a politician's reputation. It is a world in which an impartial and efficient bureaucracy cannot fit: and, indeed, it has not. The dynamics of Papua New Guinea politics rests more firmly on the model of the "bigman" than that of a conscientious MP holding weekly surgeries. To secure clan support, a politician has to enter into traditional exchanges and reciprocity: today, this is done through the medium of money. The clan's contribution to a candidate's expenses is a modern form of the large moka, a communal exchange: the reciprocity is wantokism.[58] Electoral violence, which is increasing, also takes the

[57] Fitzpatrick, above n 4, p 206.

[58] Andrew Strathern (above n 3, p 68) has captured the trajectory of politics as follows:

form of clan fights.[59] In that unintended sense, by sticking to traditional notions of authority and leadership, the *Constitution* has indeed achieved the adoption of "Papua New Guinean ways"!

However, accumulation is taking place selectively, based on plantations in the Highlands or real estate in northern Australia, and the children of the political elite are being educated abroad, which will no doubt consolidate emerging class formation. This process may in time change the relationship between politics and economics, and alter the mode of the appropriation of the benefits of the state.

If one component of the matrix within which the *Constitution* has operated is the clan, another is its seeming opposite: international capital. The state has relied heavily on foreign investment and in particular on mega-mineral projects. There is no general legal or administrative regime for these big projects: each has to be individually negotiated over a long period. This facilitates the granting of special concessions and, with it, the possibilities of bribes. There is consequently a tendency to disregard the national interest. Additionally, weakened by political compromises and intrigues that have become the hallmark of all governments in Papua New Guinea, the state lacks the capacity to deal with the problems that these big projects cause. The devastating effects of the projects on the lives of the people and their environment serve to mobilise them politically, encourage resort to courts and, in at least one case, promote self-determination. Unable to deal with them politically, the state tends to rely on coercion (as in Bougainville) or doubtful legal procedures (as in the *8th Ok Tedi Supplemental Agreement*, which seeks to limit the jurisdiction of the Supreme Court over the claims of landowners). It also increases the reliance of the state on foreign investors (and their lawyers who are unable to appreciate the social dynamics of the project), and indeed becomes something of a hostage to them, particularly given that the government is also a shareholder in the projects. It is not surprising that the state system has of recent years appeared to be so out of control.

Why has no strong man appeared in Papua New Guinea? Or, in other words, why has the Rule of Law survived? Strong men usually either appear from the military barracks and rely on armed force or they ride on the back of a powerful party. Sir Julius Chan has given us a hint as to why a strong Prime Minister is unlikely to emerge from Papua New Guinea's parliamentary system. The emergence of a strong man is further discouraged by other factors: the absence of a dominant tribe or ethnic group; the dispersed nature of the country; the vitality of many small clans or tribes; the difficulty of operating for long periods through pure coercion. There have been one or two ill-planned attempts at a coup, but it is surprising that no politician has seen fit to overcome these problems, or parliamentary hurdles, by establishing a strong, well-organised mass-based political party: Gramsci's Modern Prince. He or she would have to create an appropriately broad ideology, but that should not be difficult, given the present predicaments and the still incipient class distinctions. At the moment parties play no significant role in the integration of the country. As in colonial days, this is still left to the bureaucracy. Even the most senior politicians stick to a narrow parochial, geographic base.

"Politics has become 'commoditized'. In the 1960s candidates asked for votes on the grounds that they were 'good men' or 'strong men', well known for their ability to act as negotiators and thus to obtain general benefits for their electorate. During the 1970s there was growing emphasis on material wealth, on the prominent membership of development corporations, and the swinging of block votes behind these. In the 1982 elections a fully commoditized model emerged: candidates would buy votes and sitting MPs would use their sectoral funds covertly, in order to do this. This commoditization, then, reflects the growing importance of money as such in the economy of Highlands societies [the subject of Strathern's study], money which is gained from growing coffee, and thus from changes in the system of basic production."

[59] Strathern, above n 3; S Dinnen, "Fighting with Votes: Violence, Security and the 1992 National Election in Papua New Guinea" (1993) 5(2) *Current Issues in Criminal Justice* 130.

As to the Rule of Law, it is necessary to make the preliminary point that Papua New Guinea's record is not as good as is often assumed.[60] There are violations of the law, grave ones in the Bougainville crisis, and the violators include the police in the ordinary work of investigation. Papua New Guinea's record of social and economic rights is appalling: massive violence against women, declining standards of health and nutrition, high levels of illiteracy, environmental degradation. Many of these are the consequences of political corruption (and the result of lack of interest in policy issues). The incidence of political corruption is evidence of deviations from legal norms and procedures. That the violations of the law are not more widespread may not be because the government or Parliament are solicitous of rights: the denial of resources to the judiciary, the Ombudsman Commission, the Public Prosecutor and the Public Solicitor is evidence of the lack of such solicitude. The fact that all major political leaders have accepted defeats in elections or motions of confidence may be attributed to the weakness of politicians or the inability of their parties to override others or to take control of the state through alternative means. At present all of them have a stake in the system of elections and the rules for the formation of government.[61] In contrast to many developing countries, the system has ensured a regular change in Prime Ministers and Ministers, so the key actors are willing to wait for their turn rather than upset the applecart. Meanwhile they are sustained by their electoral and sectoral development grants.

It may also be worth reflecting on why the Rule of Law is threatened in other developing countries. It becomes necessary to resort to coercion only when there is a falling out among political leaders or when there is effective opposition to the government from the public or special groups. Sometimes there are serious conflicts between different social or economic classes or between significantly large ethnic or religious groups. Strategies of development may require heightened control or regulation of labour or special groups (like women or indigenous peoples), creating social tensions. Political corruption may provoke grave disquiet and lead to challenges to those who are engaged in it. These differences are mobilised and aggravated by socially active groups. Some of these factors are indeed present in Papua New Guinea, but so far the mobilisation of discontent has been muted. Combined with the elite consensus on the constitutional framework, this enables judges to discharge their tasks with impartiality. That the discontent is no longer entirely muted is evident from the periodic crises in Bougainville, the first region to become the victim of state development strategy. Other mineral and forestry projects have already begun to create discontent. Public opinion is becoming anxious at the exploitation of natural resources from which they seem to secure no benefits. Various provincial politicians are upset at the dismantling of the system under which they achieved some purchase on political power. The reaction of the government so far to these developments does not augur well for the future of the Rule of Law. Is the *Internal Security Act*, with its massive invasions of rights and freedoms under discretionary executive powers, the portent of the future?

This chapter has looked at post-independence developments through the perspectives of the *Constitution*, but there is limited mileage in this strategy. The *Constitution* does not control the unfolding of social forces, although it may nudge them in one direction or another. Nor does the *Constitution* encompass the whole range of forces that determine the country's development: some of the most potent of them, such as large corporations or external governments that have such a major influence, are not captured by it. The hurly-burly of parliamentary and executive

---

[60] United Nations Centre for Human Rights, *Report of a Needs Assessment Mission to Papua New Guinea* (Geneva: UNCHR, 1995).

[61] A J Regan, "Limiting State Action: Some Comparative Perspectives on Constitutionalism, Participation and Civil Society in Papua New Guinea", paper for the 21st Waigani Seminar, Port Moresby, 28 August 1995.

politics may be marginal to the processes of change. The operation of the *Constitution* is more reflective of these autonomous changes than determinative of them. We thus run against the limitations of constitutions. At best a constitution can set up institutions and give them resources and competencies, but it can seldom infuse them with particular values. It is especially hard to determine the dynamics of politics or the conduct of parties. It is somewhat easier to prescribe legal roles (although not dictate outcomes), since they come with a long tradition of procedures, values embodied in numerous cases binding on courts, and rigorous professional training (although that same tradition also handicaps the profession and courts from developing a custom-based indigenous jurisprudence). However, the *Constitution* can rarely operate against the tide of social and economic change.

Chapter 5

REFLECTIONS OF THE CHIEF JUSTICE

SIR ARNOLD AMET CJ

INTRODUCTION

On 15 September 1995 Papua New Guinea celebrated the 20th anniversary of the attainment of its political independence from Australian administration. That date also marked the 20th year of the operation of the *Constitution* that was adopted by the Constituent Assembly and came into operation on 16 September 1975.

The passing of 20 years provides a fitting and unique occasion for all the interested agencies, institutions, leaders and ordinary citizens to gather to reflect upon the development and operation of the *Constitution* in its many facets: on the achievements and successes as well as areas that may not have been so successful. This may give some guidance to the appropriate authorities to consider possible improvements and modifications.

We are very fortunate to have still alive and active in public life and leadership many of the constitution-makers and the founding fathers of our *Constitution*. Several of them make interesting and useful observations in contributing to this volume.

The task for the implementers and interpreters of the *Constitution*, such as members of the legal and judicial community, becomes all the more enriching when we are able to listen to the views and aspirations of the *Constitution* founders. This experience helps us to find life in the *Constitution*.

Many of us have had the opportunity to grow up with the *Constitution* from its adoption, implementation and application, to where we are today. In my 20 years of working life I have endeavoured to understand the ideological and philosophical aspirations of our founding fathers embodied in the Constitutional Planning Committee (CPC) Report, the National Goals and Directive Principles and the *Constitution*. My own experience with the *Constitution* has been a most challenging, dynamic and rewarding one. My career path has been fairly narrow, commencing and progressing through the ranks of the Public Solicitor's Office to ultimately being its head and then joining the judiciary 13 years ago. In the two areas of my working life - as a lawyer and as a judge - the discharge of my professional responsibilities has evolved primarily from the *Constitution*. My exposure to the *Constitution* has not been exhaustive and comprehensive by any means, with many areas remaining to be visited.

I propose to make some general remarks and observations on the implementation, application and operation of the *Constitution* in relation to several different institutions and areas.

FOREIGN MODELS

A basic observation concerns the fact that after the consultative and planning processes, which culminated in the adoption of the *Constitution*, the laws and the institutions adopted or established by the *Constitution* were all of foreign origin. The three principal arms of government - the legislature, the executive and the judiciary - were all inherited largely from our immediate past-colonial experience. The bureaucratic infrastructure was quite simply adopted from the Australian model, which understandably was our only source of experience. The legal and judicial regimes adopted were similar to pre-independence arrangements. Initially, most members of the legal profession and the bench were largely non-Papua New Guineans. Likewise, in the bureaucracy the heads and senior administrators at that time were mostly non-Papua New Guineans.

A process of localisation has expanded since independence (except in a few areas, such as the judiciary). But the training and experience of most Papua New Guineans who have assumed responsibilities and leadership in government institutions have been largely based on the introduced models.

My fundamental view is that, with the exception of the legislature and the executive, there have been some fundamental inconsistencies and conflicts in the operations of the inherited public sector institutions since independence. The result is that inherited philosophies and concepts are constantly in conflict with the aspirations and philosophies that underlie the *Constitution.* These aspirations and philosophies were intended to create a new socio-political and economic order at independence.

Over the years since independence, the institutions that were inherited and adopted then have outgrown their usefulness. The constitutional aspirations that were enshrined in the National Goals and Directive Principles and that required modification and change of attitudes and beliefs in order to transform those institutions so that they would conform with the aspirations of the constitutional directives have been found wanting. The institutions and structures based on foreign principles have had great difficulty in responding to social change in Papua New Guinea. As a result, National Goals Nos 3 and 5 (National Sovereignty and Self-reliance, and Papua New Guinean Ways) were never given effect.

Contrary to those National Goals, the process of utilising and resorting to introduced models and value systems continues. This I believe is true in the legal profession and judiciary and, more generally, in the private and public sectors more generally.

LEGAL AND JUDICIAL SYSTEMS

I have often expressed my view that our inherited legal and judicial systems, with all of their entrenched rules of practice and procedure, are largely foreign to our people. We are required under National Goal No 5 to redirect our attitudes and institutions of government towards Papua New Guinean forms of participation and decision-making. National Goal No 5 is in the following terms:

> "We declare our fifth goal to be to achieve development primarily through the use of Papua New Guinean forms of social, political and economic organisation.
>
> We accordingly call for:
>
> (1) a fundamental re-orientation of our attitudes and the institutions of government, commerce, education and religion towards Papua New Guinean forms of

participation, consultation and consensus, and a continuous renewal of the responsiveness of these institutions to the needs and attitudes of the people; and

(2) recognition that the cultural, commercial and ethnic diversity of our people is a positive strength and for the fostering of a respect for, and appreciation of, traditional ways of life and culture, including language, in all their richness and variety, as well as for a willingness to apply these ways dynamically and creatively for the tasks of development."

Together with Sch 2, this goal provides ample scope for developing fundamental change. Schedule 2 provides for the recognition of custom as the basis for the underlying law. The principles and rules of the common law of England are to be part of the underlying law where they are consistent with the constitutional laws and are applicable or appropriate to the circumstances of the country from time to time. They do not form part of the underlying law if they are inconsistent with custom. Part 3 of Sch 2 also directs the National Judicial System and, in particular, the Supreme and National Courts to formulate appropriate rules as part of the underlying law. There have been continuing efforts and increasing opportunities in the superior courts to apply these provisions, but the record of the courts in the 20 years since independence has not been as impressive as it ought to be.

In 1992 at the conference on the "Future of Customary Law in Papua New Guinea", I said the same things. My view remains largely the same: that some improvements are being made, but by and large the attitude remains the same. I quoted from a 1973 speech by John Kaputin, the then Minister for Justice, who described the law, as utilised by the Australian authorities, as:

> "an instrument of domination and oppression by the ruling classes . . . an instrument of colonialism and a means whereby the economic dominance of the white man was established over us."[62]

The then Chief Minister Michael Somare also stated in 1973 that:

> "we are facing, at this very moment, the need to devise a system of laws appropriate to a self-governing, independent nation. The legal system that we are in the process of creating must ensure the orderly and progressive development of our nation. But, in addition, it must respond to our needs and values. We do not want to create an imitation of the Australian, English or American legal system. We want to build a framework of laws and procedures that the people of Papua New Guinea can recognise as their own - not something imposed on them by outsiders. There is great scope for imagination and creativity in making the law responsive to the needs of the people, and I put this challenge to all of you who are concerned about the future of our nation: how can we build a legal system that will truly serve the peoples' needs?"[63]

The same caution was echoed by the CPC when it said:

> "This ability to accept new ways is evident in the manner in which our people are quietly accepting the demands of a modern nation. There is the danger, however, that in so

[62] J Kaputin, "The Law: A Colonial Fraud" (1975) 10(1) *New Guinea and Australia, The Pacific and South East Asia* 4-5.

[63] M Somare, "Law and the Needs of Papua New Guinea's People" in J Zorn and P Bayne (eds), *Law Bilong Ol Manmeri* (Port Moresby: UPNG Press, 1975), p 14.

doing, we as a people and as a nation might become borrowers only. There is the danger that we might discard our ways or place them in subservience. No matter how hard we try to copy foreign ways, we will always end up being second rate unless we make full use of our own traditions and institutions to achieve our national goal."[64]

These cautions and sentiments remain true. We continue to depend on foreign common law principles and precedents (mainly from Australia and Britain) in developing the underlying law and also in interpreting statute law, without relying on the perspective and intentions of our home-grown *Constitution*. In doing so we are in danger of abdicating our judicial and legal sovereignty to inappropriate principles and decisions originating from foreign jurisdictions.

Of particular concern are the rules of practice and procedure that the legal and judicial regimes have inherited. These rules make access to legal process by the vast majority of Papua New Guineans difficult, costly and most often impossible. This is another area where continual resort to foreign precedents render nugatory the aims of National Goal No 5, which calls for a fundamental re-orientation of our attitudes and the institutions of government towards Papua New Guinean forms in the tasks of development.

I believe that the rules of practice and procedure, both in the lower courts and in the superior courts, should be overhauled to conform with National Goal No 5. There is some consideration under way amongst the judiciary and the legal profession to review these rules to make appropriate recommendations and modifications so that they accord meaningfully with this particular aspiration.

CONSTITUTIONAL INSTITUTIONS

Other constitutional institutions, such as the Ombudsman Commission, the Public Solicitor, the Public Prosecutor, the Auditor-General, the Public Services Commission and the Police Commissioner also need some review. Their experience since independence has been one of insufficient resources to perform their responsibilities adequately. The Ombudsman Commission, the Public Solicitor and the Public Prosecutor all continue to be under-staffed and under-funded.

Consequently, the effectiveness of these institutions is considerably diminished. There are also some minor areas of adjustments to be made in terms of their full and effective independence from the executive bureaucracy in the areas of finance and administration and support staff.

The same concern can be expressed in respect of the judiciary. If funding is inadequate to enable the provision of resources and personnel, the judicial and administrative functions and responsibilities of the judiciary are considerably limited in actual application.

There are also issues concerning moves to limit the powers of some constitutional offices. In 1986 the Public Services Commission, for instance, had its powers considerably diminished by an amendment to the *Constitution* (*Constitutional Amendment No 8 - Public Service Commission*).

[64] CPC, *Constitutional Planning Committee Final Report: Part 1* (Port Moresby: Government Printer, 1974), p 2/13.

HUMAN RIGHTS

The ability of the judiciary to invoke its inherent powers to protect human rights has so far been minimal even in relation to reported incidents of violations. This can be attributed in large part to the continued operation of the inherited adversarial system and the limitations in the court's resources. In recent years some administrative efforts have been made to facilitate the filing of complaints in a simplified form. But the record of processing these complaints has remained poor due to the lack of adequate machinery, resources and personnel. Partly because of this limitation on the part of the judiciary, the creation of a Human Rights Commission has now been endorsed and is, hopefully, in the process of being established.

DEVELOPMENT OF NATURAL RESOURCES

The harvesting, exploitation and development of renewable and non-renewable natural resources has received comparatively little judicial attention in the 20 years since independence. As a result, National Goal No 4, which addresses natural resources and the environment, has received little judicial attention. Only in recent years, with increased economic activities affecting the land, the environment and natural resources generally, has litigation dealing with such matters reached the courts. It is an area of increasing concern and interest by the resource owners, leaders and members of the community in general. It is an area where the courts are likely to play an increasing role.

ACOUNTABILITY

One of the biggest areas of concern in the constitutional processes is the need to balance the exercise of power with responsibility and accountability. After all, institutions and offices are vested with such powers and responsibilities by the *Constitution* on behalf of the people. My general observation is that the impact of the checks and balances intended to ensure responsible discharge of powers and responsibilities is almost non-existent in many public sector institutions. A major part of the problem concerns abuse of powers, including actions taken in excess of powers. Such problems apply not only to chief executive officers of government institutions, but also to subordinate managers and even rank and file officers. Actions in excess of power and lack of accountability have led to the general perception not only that our system of government is ineffective and inefficient in delivering goods and services to the people, but that our leaders lack accountability and are corrupt.

Evidence of this breakdown in accountability comes from the increasing number of applications for judicial review involving allegations of mismanagement and wrong exercise of power and authority. Increasing litigation over administrative and inter- or intra-governmental agency disputes is also indicative of abuse of proper authority and power.

The constitutional and legal machinery intended to ensure accountability remains in place in many instances. But my experience is that many leaders lack the integrity and willpower to allow such machinery to operate effectively. It may be that these leaders are implicated in corruption and consequently are compromised.

These concerns apply as much to the institutions of the disciplined forces as to any others. In my experience, the efficiency and accountability of officers and members of these institutions have declined markedly. They are the subject of continuous public and media commentary. Some of the contributing factors have to do with lack of resources, logistics and infrastructure generally. Many quite simply have to do with lack of discipline and leadership, integrity and insufficient openness to accountability processes.

CONCLUSION

I conclude by reiterating the view that the basic constitutional structures adopted at independence have outgrown their usefulness. They are incapable of sustaining the socio-political stresses and challenges that now impact upon them. Having been inherited from our colonial administrators they now need to be modified, adjusted and varied to conform with the aspirations of the new nation state as enshrined in the National Goals and Directive Principles and the body of the *Constitution*.

The National Goals and Directive Principles should not be seen as mere rhetoric. They are meant to reflect the living realities, aspirations and visions of a vibrant, dynamic and evolving society. The leaders and members of constitutional institutions such as the judiciary, the legislature, the executive and the bureaucracy, as well as the members of the legal profession, are directed to observe and give life and meaning to these goals and principles.

There needs to be a fundamental re-orientation of our attitudes and the institutions of government with a continuous renewal of these institutions to be responsive to the needs and aspirations of our people as envisaged by National Goal No 5. This change must conform with Papua New Guinean cultural and traditional ways of life. In many of our institutions of government and industry we have become far too formalistic and westernised. We have estranged these institutions from the very people they were intended to serve.

In the discharge of powers and responsibilities vested in us, we have become selfish and power-hungry and have abused positions of responsibility. We are not being accountable to the people through the *Constitution*. As a result we are not rendering services promptly and efficiently. After 20 years, if the people who are the source of all authority and power remain dissatisfied and aggrieved, then as the custodians of the constitutional power and authority of the people we have failed in that responsibility.

As its head, I am conscious of the awesome responsibility mandated upon the judiciary, primarily by the National Goals and Directive Principles and Sch 2 of the *Constitution*. I am not complacent. I believe there is much that needs to be done in the next 20 years. I believe that relative to the length of time that has passed and the opportunities offered, and the clear directive and mandate vested in the judiciary and the legal profession under the *Constitution*, the judiciary and legal systems have performed poorly.

THE EXECUTIVE

Chapter 6

THE EXECUTIVE AND THE COURTS

JAMES BAKER

INTRODUCTION

In determining the shape of the executive branch of government the Constitutional Planning Committee (CPC) opted for the Westminster model of an executive answerable to the legislature.[65] Many of the conventions associated with the operation of the Westminster system were embodied in substantive law in the *Constitution*, which therefore specifies in detail the workings of the system as well as the actual operation, role and functions of the executive.

The concept of "the executive" includes, in constitutional terms, the Head of State, the National Executive and the National Executive Council (NEC), the Ministry and the Prime Minister and the functions and powers of each of these institutions. The relationship between the executive and the legislature and the exercise by the executive of its constitutional powers were areas of concern to the CPC.

The CPC wanted to ensure that the executive remained accountable to the legislature and for that reason provided for: the Prime Minister to be elected by the Parliament; motions of no confidence in the Prime Minister, a Minister or the ministry; permanent parliamentary committees; and ultimate financial control by the Parliament over the raising and expenditure of funds.[66]

CPC RECOMMENDATIONS ON THE EXECUTIVE

There are some differences between the recommendations of the CPC on the executive and the final form of the provisions in the *Constitution*. Two major areas of difference are in respect of the actual procedure for the operations of the NEC and the position of the Head of State.

NEC procedures

The CPC recommended that there be a Cabinet, to be called the NEC, to carry on the executive government of the country. It considered that the procedures to be followed by the NEC should be prescribed by law; that is, they should actually be included within the *Constitution*.[67] This unusual proposal was not fully implemented in the *Constitution*, which says that the procedures of the NEC are determined by it, subject to any Organic Law or Act of the Parliament (s 149(5)). The CPC proposal for a secretariat to service the NEC was adopted, but the detail as to NEC functions was not.

The rationale for the CPC proposal on NEC procedures was that the prescribing of procedures would prevent abuse of power. Through legislating procedures, such as the quorum required for a

[65] CPC, *Final Report of the Constitutional Planning Committee: Part 1* (Port Moresby: Government Printer, 1974).
[66] Ibid, Ch 7.
[67] Ibid, pp 7/7-7/9.

meeting, voting on decisions, and the time within which submissions were to be presented, the CPC hoped to ensure that decisions were made "collectively". Further, decisions would not be set aside at the whim of an individual Minister or department because there would be follow-up and implementation through the NEC secretariat. The CPC envisaged that the secretariat would constitute a check through a rigorous implementation process. The CPC did draw back from the possibility that NEC procedures might be litigated in the courts and specifically made them non-justiciable. Evidently, the CPC was concerned that a powerful Prime Minister might act unilaterally and that the concept of a Cabinet of Ministers operating collectively might not be well understood or accepted.

These proposals do not follow any particular precedent since the typical Cabinet within an executive does not rate many mentions in the legislature. For example, in the United Kingdom the cabinet is hardly referred to in legislation and its procedures are administratively determined.

It is noteworthy that the *Constitution* appears to give Parliament the option to make NEC procedures justiciable, since s 153(2), while providing that the question of whether the procedures prescribed for the NEC have been or are being complied with is non-justiciable, makes that provision subject to any Constitutional Law or Act.

The Head of State

The CPC presented the arguments for and against a separate Head of State and concluded that there needed to be only one body in which the executive power should be vested.[68] The emphasis is on collective decision-making by an NEC that includes all the Ministers. At the same time, however, the CPC recognised that in the future there might arise an "inner Cabinet" comprising only some of the Ministers of the government, but it warned against the NEC taking on only a formal role and not being involved in the process of policy making.

In relation to the issue of a separate Head of State, although the *Constitution* provides for such a position, the CPC had its way in the sense that the Head of State has no powers to act except on the advice of the NEC.

Checks on the executive

The CPC was concerned to ensure that there were appropriate checks on the executive, and they saw the legislature as the main instrument for this purpose. In this respect then, their approach was to follow the Westminster model, in which the executive is answerable to the Parliament through motions of no confidence and other aspects of the parliamentary process. Of course, in reality, in the Westminster system the legislature ceases to provide any real check so long as the government of the day commands a majority in the Parliament. Any scrutiny by the Parliament is therefore often only notional. The CPC considered that having the Prime Minister chosen by the Parliament and having Ministers appointed from amongst the Parliament amounted to checks on the executive. The CPC said in relation to the Parliament:

> "We believe that while the executive must be given every opportunity to provide strong leadership in reshaping our new nation to meet the needs and aspirations of our people, it

[68] Ibid, pp 7/1-7/2.

> is important also that this leadership does not become autocratic so that the legislature becomes a mere rubber stamp. The legislature should not be seen as a rival to the executive arm but rather as a full and constructive partner. It can then help to ensure the overall effectiveness of government by keeping the executive accountable to the people."[69]

The CPC envisaged a situation where many parties existed and a possible Prime Minister might have to gather support from a number of those parties, but it considered that its proposal for the election of the Prime Minister allowed "for a maximum of flexibility".[70] The CPC also recognised that it could not legislate for the political process.

In light of the CPC appreciation that there might be a number of parties in the Parliament, it seems curious in hindsight that the CPC saw its recommendation for the removal of the Prime Minister through a motion of no confidence after a period of only six months to be a measure "to ensure some stability in government".[71] Evidently the CPC underestimated the capacity of Parliament for changing the Prime Minister, and thought that motions of censure, rather than motions of no confidence, would be brought. Perhaps the CPC thought that the Westminster conventions of conduct by the executive in the face of censure motions would apply in PNG and that motions of no confidence would be rare.

Apart from motions of no confidence and censure motions, the *Constitution* attempts to impose further accountability on Ministers through the system of parliamentary committees. The *Constitution* establishes permanent parliamentary committees, the chairmen of which may not be Ministers. Importantly, s 120 provides that the chairman and deputy chairman of each such committee are to be granted full access to each Minister having responsibilities relevant to the work of that committee. As well, the chairman and deputy chairman are to be given access to the relevant departmental head and are entitled to be briefed and consulted on major policy issues. The CPC devoted considerable attention to identifying the nature and composition of parliamentary committees, which it saw as helping to make the Parliament an effective body. The CPC saw for the Parliament "a more constructive role than is usually provided for it, particularly in a Westminster-type system of government and its variations".[72]

Now that the *Constitution* has been amended to extend the no confidence grace period to 18 months,[73] the ability and capacity of the Parliament to act as a check on the executive may well focus less on attempting to oust the Prime Minister and more on exercising the power to question policy and amend and propose legislation. For example, the recent government legislation on the provincial government system provoked a number of Opposition amendments. The Opposition was in a strong position to have its amendments accepted by the government because the government needed the support of the Opposition to achieve the high majorities required for the passage of the legislation.

It remains to be seen whether the recent enactment of legislation providing for parliamentary committees will tempt the members of those committees to exercise their undoubted constitutional powers to be consulted and briefed.

---

[69] Ibid, p 6/1.
[70] Ibid, p 7/4, para 27.
[71] Ibid, p7/6, para 45.
[72] Ibid, pp 6/9-6/10.
[73] See *Constitutional Amendment No 14 – Motions of No Confidence* (1991).

The CPC also saw Parliament as having ultimate control over public finances through the annual budget process. The provisions in the *Constitution* that were recommended by the CPC appear to have diminished this "ultimate" control, in the sense that the power of the Parliament actually to change financial legislation is circumscribed by s 210(2), which prevents the Parliament from increasing or re-allocating "the amount or incidence of", or from changing "the purpose of any proposed taxation, loan or expenditure". In this respect, therefore, the CPC had to recognise that "the detailed management of the economy should remain the responsibility of the executive".[74]

ISSUES OF EXECUTIVE POWER AND THE COURTS

The courts have been concerned with the exercise of the constitutional power to change the head of the executive government in a number of cases. These are the cases concerned with motions of no confidence and the election of the Prime Minister.

As to the actual exercise of the constitutional executive power, the executive has had to deal with challenges in two cases concerning the powers of Ministers over public servants and the age of appointment of public servants. The position of the Head of State and the status of the NEC have also been examined in the courts.

Motions of no confidence and the appointment of a Prime Minister

Given the frequency of motions of no confidence up to the time of the change to the *Constitution* extending the grace period from six months to 18 months, it is surprising that there have been relatively few cases concerned with the motion and with the appointment of the Prime Minister by the Parliament. The cases do, however, show that on this pre-eminently political issue, after an initial hesitation, the courts have been willing to examine events in the Parliament and make rulings as to winners and losers rather than stepping aside from the fray as the common law would require. As well, the cases show that decisions of the Parliament, reached on political grounds, will not be accepted by either government or Opposition if there is the chance of having a third party, namely the court, make the decision. This may reflect a number of things, such as: the acknowledged complexity of the *Constitution*, so that only the court can determine the "correct" answer; the importance of being in government rather than Opposition, so that all means of remaining in office must be exhausted; or the perception that such issues ought to be decided by an impartial third party because the law provides for such matters and it is the task of the court and no-one else to interpret the law.

The first case on motions of no confidence was one of the earliest cases in Papua New Guinea constitutional law: *Constitutional Reference No 2 of 1976* [1976] PNGLR 228. This was a reference by Parliament to the question of whether a motion of no confidence could be moved during the life of the first Parliament. It is appropriate to note that this was the first reference under s 19 to come before the Supreme Court. The court had no great difficulty in answering the question in the negative. It is interesting to note that at this early stage in constitutional development two members of the court referred to the provisions of the CPC report in their decisions.[75]

---

[74] CPC, above n 1, p 9/2.

[75] *Constitutional Reference No 2 of 1976* [1976] PNGLR 228 at 232 per Frost CJ; at 238 per Saldanha J.

In the second case, in 1977, Mr James Eki Mopio MP challenged the appointment of the Prime Minister in the case of *Mopio v Speaker of the National Parliament* [1977] PNGLR 420. In this case the Supreme Court appeared reluctant to adjudicate on matters dealt with in the Parliament, notwithstanding s 134 limiting the non-justiciability of parliamentary proceedings by the introductory words "except as specifically provided by a Constitutional Law". It is suggested that this case cannot now be said to be the law in view of the comments of the Supreme Court in *Haiveta v Wingti (No 3)* [1994] PNGLR 197 (see below).

The court essentially avoided answering the very pertinent issue put to it by Mr Mopio by accepting the argument put by counsel for the Parliament and supported by the Principal Legal Adviser that the issues related to procedures in the Parliament and those matters were non-justiciable. Had Mr Mopio been legally represented, the case may well have taken a different turn.

The third case is *Haiveta v Wingti (No 3)* [1994] PNGLR 197. Before discussing that case it is worth noting that there have been a number of cases dealing with motions of no confidence in provincial governments.[76] In most of these cases the court has held the internal procedures of the legislatures to be non-justiciable.

In the case of *Haiveta v Wingti*,[77] the National and Supreme Courts had to deal with a novel approach to the procedure for election of a Prime Minister. The facts were that on the evening of Thursday, 23 September 1993 Paias Wingti, the then Prime Minister, gave notice of his resignation as Prime Minister to the Governor-General. On that same evening the Governor-General purported to accept the resignation and then wrote to the Speaker notifying him of the resignation. On the morning of Friday, 24 September 1993, when Parliament sat, the Speaker advised the House of the resignation. He notified members that, in accordance with the *Constitution*, s 142(3), the first matter of business must be the election of a new Prime Minister. He then called for nominations. Mr Wingti was the only person nominated. A vote was taken and he was elected Prime Minister.

The central issue before the Supreme Court on appeal, after the National Court had upheld the resignation and re-appointment, was whether the election on Friday, 24 September 1993 had taken place on the "next sitting day" as required by s 142(3) of the *Constitution*. The court ruled that the "next sitting day" meant the date after Parliament was notified of the resignation, and that accordingly the purported resignation and re-appointment were invalid.

In terms of parliamentary control over the executive, the case demonstrates that the executive was able to put itself into a position where the Parliament was helpless to check its actions. No prior notice of the resignation or intending re-appointment was given to the Opposition and the then government commanded a majority in the Parliament. In this case, the novel approach taken to resignation and subsequent re-election of the Prime Minister, as well as the fact that the Parliament was taken completely by surprise by the strategy adopted, meant that the Parliament had no effective method of responding. Accordingly, only the *Constitution* could assist the

[76] See *SCR No 2 of 1987; Reference by Seeto* [1987] PNGLR 31; *Rova Maha v Kipo* [1994] PNGLR 445; *Kaguel Koroka v Kapal* [1985] PNGLR 117; *Hagai Joshua v Aron Meya* [1988-89] PNGLR 188; *Eichorn v Ninikin* [1988-89] PNGLR 222; *Koraea v Sepoe Karava* (1989) N791; and *Salan Ere v Enga Provincial Government* (1994) N1284.

[77] The various judgments in this case are reported as follows: *Haiveta v Wingti (No 1)* [1994] PNGLR 160 (Sheehan J in the National Court); *Haiveta v Wingti (No 2)* [1994] PNGLR 189 (Supreme Court); and *Haiveta v Wingti (No 3)* [1994] PNGLR 197 (Supreme Court).

Parliament and the Opposition, and only the court could say whether what had occurred was correct.

In terms of the relationship between the executive and the Parliament the case is of great importance. It is also significant in terms of the way in which the court now sees its role in the interpretation and application of the *Constitution* generally. In respect of the latter, the Chief Justice expressed himself as follows):

> "In Papua New Guinea it has come to be accepted that the judiciary is the guardian of the *Constitution*."[78]

After enumerating provisions which confer powers on the courts to enforce the *Constitution*, the Chief Justice went on to say:

> "These comprehensive provisions charge the judiciary (the National and Supreme Courts) with the power and duty to ensure that the provisions of the *Constitution* are observed by all the instrumentalities of government, including the legislative, executive, or for that matter, the judicial."[79]

The Chief Justice also noted later:

> "Judicial interpretation and pronouncement are as important as the decisions and policies of the executive and the legislature. When the judiciary makes a decision and pronounces it, it is laying down a standard for the community. The judiciary, therefore, cannot divorce itself from the consideration of public national interest."[80]

In this statement the court clearly recognises the overwhelming importance of its role as interpreter of the *Constitution*. This statement is the result of 20 years of constitutional interpretation and constitutional dispute settlement. It states explicitly what the court had come to understand over the years. That is to say, that the court would have to make decisions that have the same effect as a policy decision of the executive or the Parliament, and the court, in the constitutional sense, and not the executive or the Parliament was the final guardian of the national interest.

The basis for the court's decision in holding the re-appointment invalid is the need for the executive to be accountable to the legislature. It was argued on behalf of Mr Haiveta that the court should give effect to the spirit of parliamentary democracy and the accountability of the executive to Parliament. Of further significance, therefore, is the emergence from this case of the recognition accorded by the court to the rights of Parliament.

In defining the rights of Parliament and therefore its role in accountability, the court included a requirement that there be "fairness and justice" by the executive in its dealings with the legislature. Some members of the court clearly saw the procedure of resignation and re-appointment of the Prime Minister as an abuse of power by the executive. It was an abuse because it did not conform with notions of fairness and justice which the court has consistently upheld in all its decisions, both constitutional and otherwise. The Chief Justice asked: "What is

---

[78] [1994] PNGLR 197 at 206.
[79] Ibid.
[80] Ibid at 207.

the interpretation that will best achieve a sense of fairness and justice?"[81] In so doing, the court was giving effect to s 158 of the *Constitution*, which states:

> "In interpreting the law the courts shall give paramount consideration to the dispensation of justice."

As the Deputy Chief Justice expressed the issue:

> "There can be no justice where all parties are not given an equal opportunity in electing the Prime Minister."[82]

If the court continues to apply this principle of justice and fairness in constitutional interpretation, then it is surely giving effect to s 158 of the *Constitution* and to the recommendations of the CPC. In so doing, the court will presumably be prepared to interpret the *Constitution* in a purposive and non-literal manner.

In a more recent case, *Kaseng v Speaker of the National Parliament* [1995] PNGLR 481, the Supreme Court appears again to have followed this fairness and justice approach, in that the majority held that the circulation of amendments to the *Constitution* and the *Organic Law on Provincial Governments and Local Level Governments* for less than the required period of 30 days did not breach the *Constitution*. The court noted the overwhelming support for the amendments in Parliament, and said that the fact that there had been circulation of the amendments 21 days before introduction into Parliament was substantial compliance.

Ministers and public servants

It seems that the CPC was concerned at the future relationship between the executive and the public service, no doubt due to the dominant role played (at the higher levels) by a mostly expatriate public service during the period to independence. The CPC noted three basic principles in its recommendations:

(1) the need to be served by loyal and impartial officers appointed on merit;

(2) the need for management control by the executive; and

(3) the need for coordination between the public sector and the statutory bodies and policy and personnel matters.

The CPC saw the public service as vital to the success of the development process and determined that it would need to be "moulded to suit the needs of change and development".[83] This explains in part the recommendation that Ministers be given power to lay charges against public servants,[84] but the CPC also saw this procedure as being a check against Ministers bringing unwarranted and unsubstantiated charges.

The *Constitution* contains some fairly elaborate provisions on the public service, on appointments to it and on the relationship between the public service and the executive. The role of the Public

[81] Ibid
[82] Ibid at 221.
[83] CPC Report, above n 1, p 12/3.
[84] Ibid, p 12/4.

Services Commission (PSC) has of course been changed following amendments to the *Constitution* in 1986.

It is perhaps therefore not surprising that a major case during the early years after independence sought to have the powers of Ministers over a particular departmental head, and therefore over departmental heads, generally delineated by the Supreme Court. The case was *SCR No 1 of 1982; Re Bouraga* [1982] PNGLR 178.

The brief facts of the case were that Mr Bouraga, who was the Police Commissioner and the Head of the Department of Police, had been charged with a series of disciplinary offences by the PSC. The offences related to his refusal to give advice to his Minister, to brief the Minister, and to provide information to him. A board of inquiry was set up to hear these charges and the board referred three questions to the Supreme Court which, squarely raised issues relating to the power of the Minister to discipline his departmental head.

The court found that the PSC had no power to discipline the Police Commissioner, relying, among other matters, on the appointment power in s 193 of the *Constitution*, and the provisions of Sch 1.10(4). Of interest is the court's discussion of the relationship between a Minister and the departmental head. In this respect the court focused on the difficult provisions of s 148(2) of the *Constitution*, a section which demonstrates the necessity never to underestimate the subtlety of the drafter of the *Constitution*.

The court explained that s 148(2) of the *Constitution* dealt with the "political responsibility" of a Minister, a term not expressly defined by the *Constitution*, but which the Chief Justice said related to the responsibility of a Minister for the executive government.[85] Kapi J went so far as to identify quite precisely the matters that comprised the political responsibility of a Minister. The court said that s 148(3) did not give the Minister any power to direct or control in relation to his political responsibility, and that such powers had to be looked for elsewhere in the *Constitution* or in Acts.[86] Kapi J also pointed out that, whilst Ministers may make only requests of their departmental heads, this does not render them powerless because the NEC has the power to remove a recalcitrant departmental head from office.[87] The judgment of Pratt J is noteworthy in the manner in which he attempts to put the relationship between the Minister and the departmental head on a commonsense basis, pointing out that there is an expectation that requests for information and briefing by Ministers need not be put in the form of directions and should be complied with.[88]

Since that decision there have been no similar challenges concerning directions given by Ministers to their departmental heads. The decision may therefore be said to have settled that particular issue, although issues such as the dismissal of a departmental head for cause, through the laying of disciplinary charges, are still brought before the courts.

In the context of the CPC recommendations, their concern as to the Minister and departmental head relationship was borne out and the Supreme Court entered the debate. Perhaps if the *Constitution* had been plainer in its terms, the case would have been avoided. It seems clear that a statement in the *Constitution*, taken out of context, that nothing in a particular provision gave a Minister any power of direction or control did create a belief that Ministers had no such powers.

[85] [1982] PNGLR 178 at 185-87.
[86] Ibid at 196-97.
[87] Ibid at 197.
[88] Ibid at 202 and 206-208.

The powers of Ministers over the public service and its machinery were again tested in the case of *National Executive Council v Public Employees Association* [1993] PNGLR 264, but this time the protagonist was not the public service or a member of it but the Public Service Union. (It should be understood, however, that behind the union was a group of public servants who objected to a senior appointment on the same grounds as were relied upon by the union.)

The issue in the case was the retirement age for public servants, the NEC having appointed a Mr Lucas to a departmental head position after he had attained the retirement age. On appeal, the court had no difficulty in affirming the decision of the National Court that the appointment was invalid. The case shows the willingness of the executive to pursue its decisions through the legal process, and the ability of the public service to act as a check on the activities of the Cabinet even to the extent of bringing a matter before the court.

The NEC and the Head of State

The status of a decision made by the NEC was one issue arising out of the litigation between the Water Board, the National Capital District Interim Commission and the State in *Water Board v NCDIC and the State* (1990) N864. In this case, counsel for the NCDIC sought to call the Secretary of the NEC to answer questions relating to decisions of the NEC. The court indicated that whilst it had an inherent power to review judicial acts:

> "It could be improper for this court to allow general far-ranging questions of the Secretary, NEC on matters of executive policy. It will only cause confusion and appear to impinge on the executive workings of this government. It is not a valid exercise of the powers of this court to summons witnesses in this case to enquire into the executive workings of the Council."

The court might well have added that there is an acknowledged degree of confidentiality in the workings of government and particularly in the case of Cabinet deliberations. The *Constitution* explicitly recognises this in s 51 by permitting reasonably justifiable secrecy in respect of records of meetings and decisions of the NEC.

> "In *Kila Wari v Ramoi and Dibela* [1986] PNGLR 112, the Supreme Court considered the provisions of the *Constitution* dealing with the NEC and its function of giving advice to the Head of State and s 86(4) of the *Constitution.*"

In the proceedings, the appellants were members of the board of the Post & Telecommunications Corporation who believed that action was to be taken under the relevant legislation by the Head of State on advice to terminate their appointments for cause. The appellants sought to head off this action by applying for an injunction in the National Court. The National Court refused the injunction and the board members appealed.

In its decision, the court noted that the Minister had been wrongly joined in the proceedings since the advice as to termination was to be given to the Head of State by the NEC and not by the Minister alone. The court said that it was not possible to grant an injunction against the Head of State personally, even though the *Constitution* did not prohibit actions being brought against the Head of State. The reason was that he had no independent discretion and the *Constitution* provided that such claims should be brought against the state. The Deputy Chief Justice discussed the nature and extent of the protection given by s 86(4) of the *Constitution*, holding that the advice given to the Head of State by the NEC is not subject to review by the courts unless the advice can be shown to be inconsistent with an Act, or ultra vires, or inconsistent with the provisions of the *Constitution*.[89] Amet J put the matter as follows:

> "The executive power of the people in reality is vested in the National Executive Council, which in many instances acts through the Head of State. In my view therefore, whenever the National Executive Council performs an executive act through the Head of State, or put another way, when the Head of State performs an executive act upon advice from the National Executive Council, he is in fact acting on behalf of the people of Papua New Guinea who are collectively known by their corporate name as 'The State'."[90]

On the issue of the meaning of s 86(4) of the *Constitution*, he drew a distinction between the advice given to the Head of State and the final decision, pointing out that s 86(4) did not protect against a challenge but only prevented the question of what advice was actually given being litigated.[91]

CONCLUSION

The above cases have raised procedural and substantive issues relevant to the position of the executive within the system of government. They show the court carrying out its role of explaining the meaning and effect of some of the complex concepts and expressions of the *Constitution*. The CPC envisaged that the court would be involved in this process of clarifying the constitutional laws and, in view of the number of institutions recommended to be created with legal powers, said:

> "It is inevitable that doubts will arise as to the respective powers and functions of these bodies."[92]

One wonders, however, whether the CPC really envisaged the full extent to which the burden of resolving issues between the centre and the provinces, between the Parliament and the executive, and between the executive and the public service would have to be undertaken by the courts.

The CPC said that "true participation in our societies requires consultation and consensus",[93] and the *Constitution* calls for "Papua New Guinean forms of participation, consultation and consensus" and for "our leaders . . . to make all of their decisions in the national interest".[94]

The argument can be made from a review of the above cases that the executive and those institutions with whom it has to deal have not developed mechanisms for internal dispute resolution but have continued to rely on the court to adjudicate disputes. It might also be said that the role of the court in terms of the national interest has grown in importance as the political process has been unable to resolve issues internally.

---

[89] (1990) N864, pp 118-19.
[90] Ibid, p 121.
[91] Ibid, p 122.
[92] CPC Report, above n 1, p 8/13.
[93] Ibid, p 1/4.
[94] See the National Goals and Directive Principles to the *Constitution*.

Chapter 7

THE HEAD OF STATE IN PAPUA NEW GUINEA

JILL COTTRELL AND YASH GHAI

INTRODUCTION

In 1972, when Papua New Guinea was about to become independent, the Constitutional Planning Committee (CPC) went shopping, as it were, for an independence suit. In theory it would have found a number of models in the pattern books. Each model in these pattern books has a certain core set of characteristics, but can potentially be produced with a number of variations, some of which are more matters of style than substance, but others of which can make a real difference to the way government functions. Of course, no country is obliged to adopt the fashion of any other country, and the Papua New Guinea *Constitution* has a number of innovations.

Among the fundamental issues which must be borne in mind in a country such as Papua New Guinea, two points are of particular relevance here: Is it going to have a Head of State separate from a Head of Government? And is the country going to be a monarchy or a republic? These are not totally unconnected questions: a newly independent country would not be envisaging a king or queen with real governmental powers (in the modern world only Tonga has such a system and even there the King has limited powers and there is a Prime Minister), so a decision to be a monarchy would necessarily involve having a Head of Government separate from the monarch. But having no monarch does not mean that one has no separate Head of State. Many republics, including India and the Irish Republic, have both a President and a Head of Government, with largely ceremonial functions vested in the former, while what might be described as the "French model" incorporates a President and a Prime Minister, both with substantive governmental functions. That scheme is found in Sri Lanka and, at the time of Papua New Guinea's quest for a constitutional form, in the Soviet Union. The United States system of the Executive President, Head of State and Head of Government combined in one was another available pattern, later to be adopted in some Pacific Island states such as the Federated States of Micronesia. The system is substantially different from another which combines in one person the two roles, namely the "parliamentary presidential" system adopted in Kiribati and Marshall Islands, though not until some time after Papua New Guinea's independence. In the last type of system the President is a member of the legislature, but is also Head of State, and his or her selection involves an element of direct election by the people.

In the course of time all these patterns, except the French, came to be represented in the independent states of the Pacific. Of the Melanesian countries (the others being the Solomon Islands, Vanuatu and Fiji), all opted for separate Heads of State, three with Westminster-style parliamentary systems with the Queen as Head of State, and Vanuatu with a President and Prime Minister, but within the broad Westminster system. In the mid-1970s only Fiji was already independent. It had a "standard model" Westminster system with the monarch represented by a Governor-General, and a Prime Minster who was a member of Parliament and the leader of the largest party. This was, and still is in fact, the model in Australia and New Zealand, and in most other independent small island states, which were generally found at that time in the Caribbean.

The CPC, however, in a move described as showing a "refreshing lack of respect for the useless trappings of tradition",[95] recommended against the adoption of any Head of State for the newly emerging nation of Papua New Guinea. The CPC set out its arguments[96] as follows:

> "3. It is important in a constitution to say where executive power lies. In accordance with the practice of most of our societies, in which decisions are made by a group, we propose that the executive power of Papua New Guinea be vested in the National Executive Council. This is the name we have chosen for the group of Ministers who, collectively, will administer the country and be responsible for this work to the National Parliament.
>
> 4. In reaching this conclusion, we have given consideration to other possibilities - especially the more usual practice of vesting executive power in one person. We believe that this would be contrary to the customs of most of our people. Also, it has usually occurred elsewhere for historical reasons that have little or no relevance at all to the circumstances of the present day . . .
>
> 7. The case for a separate Head of State is sometimes associated with the view that too much power should not be placed in the hands of the elected Head of Government. We have found that this view is widespread among our people; it has influenced the great majority who have expressed an opinion on the matter to reject the idea of Papua New Guinea having an executive-type president. We share this view. However, we believe that in order to avoid a concentration of power in one man, it is neither necessary nor desirable to establish a new separate Head of State to act either as a representative of, or as a substitute for, a king or queen . . .
>
> 9. Two things are thus quite clear. A separate Head of State has little relevance to the cultural heritage of our people, and, in any case, the existence of such a person can be no real safeguard against too much power being exercised by the Head of Government. To guard against that possibility, we recommend that there be collective leadership in the executive - as was suggested to us by people in various parts of the country - and that a truly effective legislature be established.
>
> 10. We have not overlooked other arguments that are sometimes put forward in favour of a separate Head of State. One of these is that a Head of State helps to symbolise national unity. We recognise that this may be true of nations which have their own king or queen, but this has often been achieved only after a long period, perhaps centuries, during which the people as a whole have come to forget the regional or foreign origins of the royal dynasty, and the battles or wars that gained it ascendancy. There is no historical basis for anything of this nature in Papua New Guinea. Moreover, experience elsewhere in the Commonwealth indicates that a Governor-General acting for the Queen is unlikely to be an acceptable alternative. In few of those nations comparable to our own has such an arrangement lasted for long.[97] Furthermore, were we to opt for a presidential substitute, we would be creating an additional institution which, having no

[95] J Goldring, *The Constitution of Papua New Guinea* (Sydney: Law Book Company, 1978), p 48.

[96] CPC, *Constitutional Planning Committee Final Report: Part 1* (Port Moresby: Government Printer, 1974), pp 7/1-7/2.

[97] The countries to which the CPC referred were presumably those in Africa and Asia where, it is true, the arrangement did not endure: examples of countries that became independent with the Queen and a Governor-General include Pakistan, Sri Lanka, Nigeria and Ghana. Looking back, little has changed since 1975. In the Pacific only Fiji, for reasons connected with the 1987 coups, has ceased to be a monarchy, though presumably it is only a question of time before Australia follows suit. In the Caribbean, the islands which were monarchies in 1975 have remained so.

> traditional roots, would need to gain acceptance among our diverse peoples. It is quite possible that the installing of a titular or ceremonial President would have a divisive rather than a unifying effect in Papua New Guinea.

The government, and indeed the Opposition, found this "too radical".[98] They apparently clung to the notions that the CPC had rejected: continuity, mediation and symbolism.

THE POSITION AND POWERS OF THE HEAD OF STATE

So Papua New Guinea entered independence with the Queen as Head of State, though represented for all purposes (save those connected with the appointment or removal of the representative) by a Papua New Guinean Governor-General.[99] Whenever the *Constitution* or other legislation refers to the Head of State, it effectively means "Governor-General", again except where the Act in question refers to appointment or removal. No doubt the Governor-General will keep the Queen informed of events in Papua New Guinea, especially those in which he or she is involved as her representative, but the issue of whether the Governor-General is actually acting in accordance with her wishes cannot be inquired into in a court, nor by the Ombudsman or anyone else (Sch 1.21(b)). The Governor-General must be a Papua New Guinea citizen who is "a mature person of good standing who enjoys the general respect of the community" (according to s 87(1)), though no court may inquire into whether these qualities are actually possessed (s 87(2)).

The Governor-General may not hold any office or position, or engage in any calling, unless this is approved by the Queen acting in accordance with the joint advice of the National Executive Council (NEC) (the Papua New Guinea Cabinet) and the Ombudsman Commission (s 87(3)). If the appointee is a member of Parliament at the time, the member's seat is automatically vacated (s 104(2)(a)). The purpose of these restrictions is to ensure that the Governor-General can genuinely symbolise the entire nation and, as the involvement of the Ombudsman Commission indicates, be free from possible conflicts of interest. The Governor-General's salary is protected from reduction during the term of office, unless consent is given (s 96(2)). These terms of service are intended to ensure that the Governor-General can live with dignity and without temptation. The *Organic Law on the Terms and Conditions of Employment of the Governor-General* provides that the Governor-General is to have rent-free accommodation, at least one vehicle, domestic staff and a free telephone, and the pension is to be 70 per cent of the Governor-General's salary from time to time (even in the event of dismissal from office). The Organic Law also provides that the salary is not to be less than that of the Speaker (a provision no doubt welcomed by Sir Kingsford Dibela, who had been Speaker before becoming Governor-General in 1983). Nonetheless, it seems that at least one Governor-General found that his salary was lower than in the private sector, and that the sorts of demands made on his hospitality meant that he was actually worse off than before appointment to this high office.

---

[98] Goldring, above n 1, p 48.

[99] During the first 20 years the Governors-General were Sir John Guise, Sir Tore Lokoloko, Sir Kingsford Dibela, Sir Ignatius Kilage, Sir Vincent Serei Eri and Sir Wiwa Korowi. The knighthood bestowed on each by the Queen is traditional for Governors-General.

Appointment

The Governor-General is appointed essentially on the nomination of Parliament, and serves for a term of six years, under s 91, though this may be extended by Parliament during a national emergency, by virtue of s 246. Under s 88(2) of the *Constitution*, the nomination is to be by simple majority in an "exhaustive secret ballot". Details of the procedure are laid down in the *Organic Law on the Nomination of the Governor-General*. According to s 9, if there are more than two nominees, there will be successive ballots, with the candidate with the lowest number of votes being eliminated each time, until one receives a majority of votes. Even if there is only one nominee, members of Parliament must vote (s 7). After the election, the NEC advises the monarch of the decision. Section 87 of the *Constitution* permits a second term only if there is a two-thirds majority vote, and there is no possibility of a third term. During the first 20 years, apparently no-one has sought a second term.

Removal

The Papua New Guinea provisions on removal of the Head of State are the most elaborate among the Pacific constitutions. Section 93(2) contemplates the removal of the Governor-General for incapacity, by a process involving the Speaker, Parliament, the NEC and the monarch. Section 93(1) provides for "dismissal" by the monarch at the behest of the NEC acting either on its own initiative or "in accordance with" a decision of Parliament. The parliamentary decision must be by an "absolute majority", which means more than half of the total number of seats, regardless of how many are present and voting on the occasion (Sch 1.2). It is not clear whether the NEC must accede to the will of Parliament, as there are no criteria and there is very little special procedure specified under s 93(1). If "in accordance with" when used in reference to the Head of State means that he or she must comply (as we shall see shortly), then it presumably means the same when used of the NEC. In effect, it seems that either the NEC or the Parliament may decide to advise the dismissal, but if the NEC wishes to suspend her or him first then the decision must be turned over to Parliament. Interestingly, no grounds are specified for removal, only for the possibly less serious penalty of suspension. Only once has removal of a Governor-General apparently been a live possibility: it seems that had Sir Serei Eri not resigned, he would have been removed under the s 93(1) procedure. The background is discussed below.

THE POWERS AND FUNCTIONS OF THE HEAD OF STATE

Though the government just before independence was unable to stomach the CPC's innovative proposal to have no Head of State, it endorsed a *Constitution* that gave the Governor-General a good number of functions, but virtually no freedom of action. He or she is in effect a rubber stamp for the NEC or, much less often, for others.

The requirement to act on advice

Section 86(2) of the *Constitution* stipulates:

> "[I]n the exercise and performance of his privileges, powers, functions, duties and responsibilities the Head of State shall act only *with, and in accordance with*, the advice of the National Executive Council, or of some other body or authority prescribed by a Constitutional Law or an Act of the Parliament" (emphasis added).

The expression "with, and in accordance with" advice is the most emphatic provision in any Pacific constitution, and it effectively leaves no room for the independent exercise of discretion.[100] It means that the Governor-General (and the Queen in those limited situations where she acts personally) must do as advised, and he or she cannot act in the absence of advice. Any piece of legislation which permitted the Head of State a sphere of action "in his or her deliberate judgment" (to use the phrase commonly used in those constitutions which do confer some independence of action) would be unconstitutional, and any Act that failed to include the "acting on advice" formula would be construed as requiring the advice of the NEC.[101] As mentioned earlier, a failure on the part of the Governor-General to comply with advice is grounds for suspension from office, to be followed by a meeting of Parliament to decide whether the dismissal process should be invoked (s 94).

The only provision that, at first sight, appears to give any discretion to the Governor-General is s 245(5), which relates to a refusal to release a detainee in times of emergency: "Where in his opinion it is necessary to do so in the interests of national security or public order." However, it also, somewhat paradoxically, gives the power to refuse to release the detainee to the Head of State "acting with, and in accordance with, the advice of the NEC". One must conclude that even s 245(5) gives no real freedom of action to the Head of State, and that the phrase "where in his opinion" is meaningless. If the NEC advises the Head of State to act, he or she must, and if it does not, he or she must not! The word "may", which also appears in that section, and in many other sections, also carries no implication of any choice on the part of the Head of State.

Inquiring into the advice

Section 86(4) provides that "the question, what (if any) advice was given to the Head of State, or by whom, is non-justiciable", which means that the issue of whether the advice was given cannot be taken to court. Suppose a Governor-General suddenly decided to act without the requisite advice: does this mean he or she could get away with it? The Supreme Court held in the case of *Kila Wari v Gabriel Ramoi* [1986] PNGLR 112 that s 86(4) did not prevent the courts entertaining an action challenging an act of the Head of State on the grounds that, for example, it was unconstitutional. The rationale was that to challenge the act was not the same as inquiring into the advice. A court may hold invalid any regulations published by the Head of State which are ultra vires the statute under which they were made, even if the action had been taken, as

[100] E P Wolfers, "Discretion, Politics and Governors-General: Some Comparisons between Papua New Guinea and Australia" (1977) 49(2) *Australian Quarterly* 75.

[101] The only exception contemplated relates to the Governor-General being required to consent to the alteration of her or his terms of service under s 96(2) of the *Constitution*.

would presumably be the case, on advice. This was established in *Minister for Lands v Frame* [1980] PNGLR 433. A litigant could not say, "but the advice the Head of State was given was to do something different". And if the only reason the act of the Head of State was unconstitutional was that there was no advice, it would surely be more difficult to challenge the act, for one could not do so without raising the question of the lack of advice. The draftsman of the provision has implied[102] that it could just be argued that it does not preclude a challenge on the ground that no advice was given. However, he also says that the incorporation of the words "if any" was intended to make it clear that the provision covered the matter of the existence as well as the content of advice. The High Court in the Solomon Islands contrasted the two provisions in the case of *Kenilorea v Attorney-General* [1983] SILR 61. It was held that while in Papua New Guinea the existence of advice could not be inquired into, in the Solomon Islands it could: the draftsman had apparently chosen not to embrace the absence of advice in the Solomon Islands provision.

In the case of *The State v Independent Tribunal; Ex parte Sasakila* [1976] PNGLR 491, the Governor-General had dismissed a Minister and member of Parliament following certain proceedings before a tribunal set up under the *Organic Law on the Duties and Responsibilities of Leadership* (the Leadership Code). The real complaint was about the decision of the tribunal (and its consequent recommendation to the Governor-General). If that advice was non-justiciable, in the sense that it could not be inquired into, there would be no remedy for injustice. The Chief Justice was clearly right to say that s 86 hardly seems appropriate to the proceedings of an independent tribunal, the proceedings of which could presumably be challenged by an order of certiorari. Perhaps the best way to put the point was that it was the determination of the tribunal that was being challenged and not the advice to the Governor-General. This involves drawing a distinction between the decision of the tribunal and the advice to the Head of State. But it could be argued that the outcome of the tribunal's deliberations is the advice, which is rather the view taken by Kapi J when dissenting in the *Frame* case (above).

Thus the absence of advice would not lead to the Governor-General being held to have acted unconstitutionally. But the presence of advice is no guarantee of not being held to have acted unconstitutionally. The advice given may be to do something that is in violation of the law or the national *Constitution* with the result that the Governor-General may be held to have acted unlawfully. In *Supreme Court Reference No 3 of 1986; Reference by Simbu Provincial Executive* [1987] PNGLR 151, the NEC, at a time when the Simbu provincial government was suspended, advised the Head of State to amend the provincial *Constitution* to provide for new elections to be fixed by the Head of State on the advice of the NEC. The Supreme Court decided that the power to amend the provincial *Constitution* did exist. However, Barnett J did say that:

> "Subject to hearing full argument . . . it seems to me that the Head of State, acting on advice, acted unconstitutionally in amending the Simbu Provincial *Constitution*."[103]

---

[102] C J Lynch, "Styles in the Drafting of Some Pacific Constitutions" in Y Ghai (ed), *Law, Politics and Government in the Pacific Island States* (Suva: University of the South Pacific, 1988), p 222.

[103] [1987] PNGLR 151 at 182.

In some constitutions, if the Head of State does not act when called upon to do so, the act is deemed to have been done after a certain time has elapsed. There is no such provision in the Papua New Guinea *Constitution*, with the result that a contract would not be effective if the Head of State did not sign it, for example. The absence of any deeming provision means that the only effective way for the NEC to resolve the issue (if the Governor-General is adamant) is either to be patient or to take the perhaps drastic step of dismissing the Governor-General, or to exercise the power of suspension. Then the Speaker will act in the place of the suspended Governor-General (s 95). It would be possible for the Parliament then to decide that, the particular issue having been dealt with, the suspension could be lifted (s 94(3)(b)).

Limited functions in connection with Parliament and formation of government

Appointment of Heads of Government, dissolution of Parliament and signing of legislation are perhaps the most significant functions performed by Heads of State in most systems. They are also those that potentially give rise to the greatest controversy. But the Head of State in Papua New Guinea has either no role or no discretion in any of these.

Appointment of the Prime Minister is the duty of the Governor-General, but there is no room for any discretion here. Section 142(2) of the *Constitution* clearly stipulates that he or she must act in accordance with a decision of the Parliament. Similarly, the Prime Minister must be dismissed by the Head of State if Parliament passes a motion of no confidence in the Prime Minister or in the ministry. Under s 142(5)(c), the formal removal of the Prime Minister in the case of medical unfitness is also carried out by the Governor-General, though again "in accordance with a decision of the Parliament". The Governor-General also appoints and dismisses Ministers as stipulated under s 144(2). However, under s 146(2), the Ministers can resign only to the Prime Minister. The Head of State, acting in accordance with the advice of the Prime Minister, also fixes the number of Ministers as provided for under the *Organic Law on the Number of Ministers*.

The Head of State does not prorogue or dissolve Parliament. The only functions of the Head of State in connection with elections are provided for under s 105(2), namely to fix the period within which elections are to be held (acting on the advice of the Electoral Commission) to issue the writ for a general election as provided for under s 72 of the *Organic Law on National Elections*,[104] and to issue a writ for a supplementary election if no candidate is elected.

The functions of the Head of State in connection with the legislative process are very limited. In most countries with a formal Head of State, even a merely ceremonial one, the signature of the Head of State is a requirement for the enactment of legislation. But in Papua New Guinea this role has been given to the Speaker under s 110(1) of the *Constitution*. However, s 110(3) contemplates the possibility of provisions which allow the Head of State to direct that a statute be

[104] This Organic Law has now been replaced by the *Organic Law on National and Local-level Government Elections* (1996).

remitted to Parliament for the consideration of amendments proposed by the Head of State. It is a prerequisite to Parliament passing legislation, raising taxes or authorising loans or public expenditure that it be recommended by the Head of State (s 210). Moreover, the Head of State has power to make Constitutional Regulations under s 258 and Emergency Regulations under s 231 of the *Constitution*. The Head of State is one of the authorities empowered under s 19 to apply to the Supreme Court for an opinion on the interpretation of a point of constitutional law. But all the powers mentioned in this paragraph are to be exercised in accordance with the advice of the NEC.

The armed forces

Papua New Guinea also departs from the common pattern of making the Head of State head of the armed forces. Section 201(1) of the *Constitution* expressly states that there shall be "no office of Commander-in-Chief of the Defence Force, whether honorary or otherwise". It goes on to say that control of the force is to be in the hands of the NEC, through the relevant Minister. However, there are contexts in which a role is given to the Head of State, rather than to the Prime Minister or the Minister concerned. For instance, under ss 202(c)(ii) and 204, if the forces are to be used domestically to restore public order they must be called out (and recalled) by the Head of State acting in accordance with the advice of the NEC. Similarly, the force can only be used on active service or sent out of the country (other than for training or to enforce a law) at the behest of the Head of State acting in accordance with the advice of the NEC. By virtue of s 205, these provisions do not apply when the force is acting in response to an attack.

Pardons

Section 151 of the *Constitution* stipulates that the Head of State acting on the advice of the NEC may grant pardons or commute the sentences of a convicted prisoner or a detainee. However, the NEC cannot advise the Head of State to take that step unless it has received and deliberated upon a report from the Advisory Committee on the Power of Mercy, established under s 152 and the *Organic Law on the Advisory Committee on the Power of Mercy*.

The appendix at the end of this chapter sets out the powers of the Governor-General derived from the *Constitution* and the Organic Laws. In each case the legislation sets out on whose advice the Governor-General is to act. It is usually that of the NEC. Other legislation may also confer functions upon the Head of State, and the expression "acting on advice" is then usually used, as in s 11 of the *Post and Telecommunications Act*. Section 3(1) of the *Interpretation Act* provides that this expression means "acting with, and in accordance with, the advice of the NEC".[105]

The Head of State as symbol of the nation

Presumably when the government decided to keep the institution of Head of State it had in mind that the Governor-General would symbolise the nation. The Queen is not effectively in a position to do this, but to some extent the Governor-General may; though, as we have seen, not as Commander in Chief of the Armed Forces. The Governor-General does appoint and swear in Ministers, appoint judges and many other office bearers, receive certain official reports (such as that of the judiciary), receive visiting foreign dignitaries, receive the credentials of newly

[105] See *Kila Wari v Gabriel Ramoi* [1986] PNGLR 112.

appointed ambassadors and sign certain contracts. There is also the delivery of the speech on the opening of the annual session of Parliament, setting out the program of the government of the day. Although all these acts are performed without any exercise of free will on the part of the Governor-General, the representative is embodying the state of Papua New Guinea in doing them.

The guardian of the Constitution?

In many constitutions with a ceremonial Head of State, one of the relevant functions is as "guardian of the *Constitution*". This may have two aspects. The minimum would be the "right to warn": the possibility of advising the government, in an elder "statesman-like" fashion, if it seems to be going astray. In some constitutions, there would be the possibility of refusing to take advice, or even of having the discretion to refer to the courts' legislation which the Head of State thinks might be unconstitutional. In Papua New Guinea, however, where the Head of State must act "in accordance with" the advice of the NEC, there is no scope for the Head of State to decline to take the advice, even if it is thought to be unconstitutional. This places the Head of State in an uncomfortable position. The *Constitution* clearly intends that he or she should exercise no independent will, yet the Head of State is subject to some risk of being said to have acted unconstitutionally by following the advice of the NEC; just as the representative would have acted unconstitutionally by failing to do so! A Governor-General who refused to act on the advice of the NEC could be suspended, and then dismissed at the request of Parliament, even though the act in question was unconstitutional. No doubt the Governor-General could go to court to establish the legitimacy of the refusal, but this could not prevent the dismissal.

The Governor-General can advise the government if the action which it proposes seems undesirable. For the Governor-General to be able to advise the government effectively, however, the representative would need to know what is proposed before things develop to the stage when the signature is required, and not all government actions will require the Governor-General to act. Is there a "right" on the part of the Governor-General to be informed about government policies and decisions? In some systems it is conventional, if not constitutionally required, for the Head of State to be informed on a regular basis by the Head of Government. In Papua New Guinea, the only explicit right to be informed (or more accurately, the only duty on the part of Parliament or the NEC) is provided by s 97, and concerns acts and advice specifically related to the Head of State. Any more general informing of the Governor-General about government policy, or listening to the vice-regal counsel, is left to courtesy or convention.

Liability of the Governor-General

We have seen that the Governor-General may be suspended, and ultimately dismissed, for refusing to act on advice, and even dismissed for no reason at all. Is he or she subject to any other form of accountability? The Leadership Code does not apply to the Governor-General (s 26), the only leader not subject to it. There is no express provision in the *Constitution* protecting the Governor-General from civil or criminal liability for official actions. Despite this, the Supreme Court has held that the representative cannot be sued personally. Possibly the absence of any specific provision on this point can be traced to the fact that the CPC did not recommend any Head of State at all. Since the Head of State has no personal power, the court held it inappropriate for her or him to be sued in person for official acts. According to the *Kila Wari* case any action which is in essence complaining about an act of the Head of State should be brought against the state and not against the Head of State.[106]

THE CONSTITUTION IN ACTION

So Papua New Guinea became independent with a Governor-General whose role was supposed to be to offer an element of continuity (a, perhaps, mediating role in case of intra-governmental disputes), an element of gravitas and wise guidance, and a dignified presence representing the country to the outside world. How has this worked in practice?

Warning and guiding

There is an expectation that comment on government policy will be made only in private, and that in public utterances the Head of State will either seek the prior approval of the government or restrict the subject matter to non-controversial issues. This tradition, it must be said, has been honoured as much in the breach as the observance by some Pacific Heads of State, but generally the Governors-General of Papua New Guinea have been less outspoken in public than, for example, some Presidents of Vanuatu.

Nonetheless some Governors-General have found it difficult to stay aloof from party politics. The first holder of that office, Sir John Guise, felt the limitations of the office keenly. He insisted on his right to be informed and to advise. Indeed, he stepped beyond this role to criticise the government publicly, and he was known to be unavailable when his signature was required for something of which he disapproved. To no small extent these difficulties no doubt flowed from the political connections, and ambitions, of the particular Governor-General. He had stood as a candidate for Prime Minister against Somare and lost. He ultimately resigned to re-enter politics in 1977, finally leaving Parliament in 1982.[107] It has been suggested that Michael Somare, first Prime Minister of Papua New Guinea, declined the Governor-Generalship precisely because of its limited role: "He will well remember how painful his old rival, the late Sir John Guise, found the powerlessness of the position".[108]

In 1990 the Governor-General (Eri) provoked a vigorous debate about the appropriateness of public expression of vice-regal views when he came out as personally favouring the abolition of provincial government.[109] The interesting point is that this was perceived as unusual. In 1993 Sir Wiwa Korowi launched what seems to have been a personal criticism of the environmental standards of the Ok Tedi copper mine, saying "people living along the Fly River are being forced to eat fish poisoned with cyanide".[110]

Another area where Governors-General have occasionally been tempted to exceed their limited official role is in relation to honours, the function of the Governor-General being only to forward the list to Buckingham Palace. In 1975 Sir John Guise suggested he had the right to vet the list of nominees coming from the NEC, which incurred the justified ire of the Prime Minister.[111] And

---

[106] Ibid.
[107] See generally Wolfers, above n 6.
[108] (April 1993) *Islands Business Pacific*, p 33.
[109] Y Saffu, "January–December 1990" in C Moore and M Kooyman (eds), *A Papua New Guinea Political Chronicle 1967-1991* (Bathurst NSW: Crawford House, 1998), p 493.
[110] BBC Summary of World Broadcasts, 26 August 1993, found on lexis.com visited 25 November 2000.
[111] J Griffin, "'July–December 1975" in Moore and Kooyman (eds), above n 15, p 256.

nearly 20 years later Sir Wiwa Korowi insisted on the government inserting some names on the list to receive Queen's Birthday Honours.[112]

Trying not to be a rubber stamp

Sir Serei Eri portrayed himself as trying to act as guardian of the *Constitution* and upholder of fairness in public life in the events that led to his resignation. Most onlookers at best attributed his actions to misplaced loyalty; that is, loyalty to a friend rather than to the country or the office which he held. The *Pacific Islands Monthly* reported:

> "Sir Serei Eri has had successful careers as an author, teacher and diplomat, but he is likely to be remembered for his role in Papua New Guinea's recent constitutional crisis."[113]

A Leadership Tribunal found Ted Diro, the then Deputy Prime Minister, guilty of 81 charges of corruption and recommended his dismissal. But when the papers arrived on Sir Serei's desk, he failed to sign them. He left the papers on the desk and went to consult the political party that he had founded and of which Diro was a member. He stated in a letter to the chairman of the Leadership Tribunal:

> "I have a very real and strong conviction that nothing must be done to upset the united Papua New Guinea and the peaceful and harmonious co-existence of all the various tribes that we now enjoy. I believe that the dismissal of the Hon Edward Diro CBE, OStJ, MP, would cause immense social and political upheavals and therefore reject this first part of your recommendation."

The Governor-General's fall from grace amounted to more than a hesitation to consign a friend to political oblivion, for he had earlier written to the Chief Justice, Sir Buri Kidu, asking for the charges against Diro to be dropped. This earned him this rebuke:

> "When I took my oath as Chief Justice 13 years ago, I promised to uphold the *Constitution* and the Law of Papua New Guinea. You did the same when I swore you in as Governor-General of Papua New Guinea. Your letter on the third instant is an attempt to induce me to breach my oath of office. It is not my intention to violate my oath of office."

The government is said to have recommended to the Queen that Sir Serei be dismissed as Governor-General, but he resigned before the dismissal could be carried out, following a conversation with the Prime Minister and the Attorney-General, the Cabinet Secretary being called back from his flight to London to deliver the request for dismissal to the Queen.[114]

[112] *Australian Financial Review*, taken from Reuters Textline, 15 June 1993.

[113] J Grubel, (1991) 61(11) *Pacific Islands Monthly* 10.

[114] For accounts of these events, see R Callick, "Why the Governor-General went with Diro" (October 1991) *Islands Business Pacific* 64; and "Governor-General quits, ending Papua New Guinea constitutional crisis", *Agency-France Presse* (1 October 1991), found on lexis.com 25 November 2000.

The constitutional rubber stamp

In 1994 the courts of Papua New Guinea were called on to decide the constitutionality of the acts of the Governor-General in appointing as Prime Minister Paias Wingti. On 21 September that year Parliament began its session, and on 23 September the Prime Minister, Paias Wingti, resigned. On 24 September, the Speaker announced the resignation to Parliament. The Speaker then called for nominations for the position of Prime Minister. Only one nomination was received; that of Paias Wingti. The members of the Opposition walked out in protest, and Mr Wingti was elected unopposed. The Governor-General then appointed Mr Wingti as Prime Minister.

This apparently pointless manoeuvre only makes sense in the light of the constitutional provision to the effect that after election a Prime Minister has 18 months during which he or she cannot be the subject of a no confidence motion. In the eyes of the Opposition, the resignation and re-election were a blatant manipulation of the *Constitution*, designed to make Mr Wingti secure in his position until closer to the next general election due in mid-1997. Hence, the Opposition's walkout and its action in the National Court.

The Opposition accused the Governor-General and the Speaker of having acted in collusion with Wingti. The Leader of the Opposition said the Governor-General had had plenty of time to notify the Opposition of the resignation and that:

> "His failure to do so has created a constitutional crisis which requires him to step down as the Queen's representative."

The Governor-General, Sir Wiwa Korowi, insisted that he had no choice because he was "very simply a constitutional rubber stamp who has no executive powers of veto".[115]

The case came first before Sheehan J in the National Court. The Attorney-General was also included as a nominal defendant for the Head of State. Although the plaintiff clearly hoped to prove to the court that there had been collusion as he had alleged to the press, the decision actually turned on a very narrow point of fact and constitutional interpretation. This "coup", as the press called it, thus went before the National Court, and was set aside on appeal by the Supreme Court, without the behaviour of the principal actors being directly inquired into by the court.[116]

The *Constitution*, in s 142(3), says that when a Prime Minister is to be appointed, the question of the appointment is to be "the first item of business . . . *on the next sitting day*" (emphasis added). "Next after what?" is the issue on which this case ultimately turned. Sheehan J held in *Haiveta v Wingti (No 1)* [1994] PNGLR 160 that the Prime Minister had resigned on 23 September (thereby rejecting evidence of certain nocturnal letter writing activities, which the Opposition said showed that the resignation actually took place in the early hours of 24 September). The "next day" was therefore 24 September. Even if, as the plaintiff also contended, the day in question was to be the next after that on which Parliament was informed of the resignation, that information had been conveyed to Parliament when the Speaker was told of it, which was also on 23 September.

---

[115] Press release published in *the PNG Post-Courier*, 5 October 1993, quoted by I Omar, "Parliament, the Executive and the Court in Papua New Guinea" (1996) 70 *Australian Law Journal* 313 at 314.

[116] *Haiveta v Wingti (No 3)* [1994] PNGLR 197.

The Supreme Court held that the question of the resignation is first raised when the Speaker informs the House of the resignation, not when the Speaker hears of it. This event took place on 24 September, and the "next day" ought therefore to have been 25 September. This conclusion was reached in the light of the constitutional structure that places the responsibility for the choice of Prime Minister in the hands of Parliament, which must be given proper opportunity to carry out that responsibility.

The consequence of this ruling was that the appointment of Wingti on 24 September was invalid. This did not mean that Wingti was declared not to be the Prime Minister. Rather, he was declared to be still the Prime Minister because after resignation the Prime Minister remains in office until his or her successor is appointed. No successor having been validly appointed, Wingti remained Prime Minister but not, of course, in circumstances which bestowed upon him the 18 months post-election immunity from votes of no confidence.

This is a remarkable decision. Most notably it is a courageous decision. It was certainly not inevitable on a reading of the *Constitution*.[117] The decision leaves open the question of what was the appropriate course of action for the Governor-General. Does the fact that the Governor-General is to act only on advice mean that he or she is obliged to act against her or his conscience? If required to act thus, should not the Head of State either resign or act instead according to conscience, leaving it then to the NEC to resort to suspension or dismissal?

PROSPECTS FOR THE FUTURE

In its first *Interim Report* in 1979, the General Constitutional Commission reported that public opinion was divided between those who favoured the retention of the Queen and those who wanted a republic.[118] The former opinion was supported by considerations such as: "Papua New Guinea should show respect to the Queen for looking after the country until independence and until now"; "The Queen will come to our aid in times of difficulties such as war"; "Our country is still too young to be left alone". Those favouring a republic considered that: "Since we are independent we should not be attached to the Queen, who is outside our country"; "Since she has no effective powers it is expensive for such a young and underdeveloped nation as Papua New Guinea to keep the Queen".[119] However, by the time the Commission came to write its *Final Report* (1983), it stated that "the present ties with the Queen of England being our Head of State has received little support from our people".[120] In endorsing the people's view that Papua New Guinea should "make a clean break with its colonial umbilical cord and establish its own Head of State",[121] the Commission considered that an indigenous President "is eminently suitable to the peculiar and distinctive circumstances of our nation and that will enhance our national identity, pride and sovereignty".[122]

The Commission also made recommendations on the nature of the office and functions of the President. Consistent with its stance on severing the link with the British monarchy, it saw the President as the symbol of national unity, whose official residence was to be in the style of local

[117] Omar, above n 21 (p 322) suggests that the decision was in fact in error as it involved ignoring s 134 of the *Constitution*, to the effect that the question whether the procedures of Parliament have been complied with is non-justiciable. He cites *Mopio v The Speaker of the National Parliament* [1977] PNGLR 420, also concerning the appointment of the Prime Minister.
[118] General Constitutional Commission, *Interim Report* (Port Moresby: 1979).
[119] Ibid, p 28.
[120] General Constitutional Commission, *Final Report* (Port Moresby: 1983), pn93.
[121] Ibid.
[122] Ibid, p 85.

architecture, "an important and sacred house . . . through which national sovereignty, pride and unity will be found".[123] The President was to be "the source of our national development ideologies, in line with the National Goals and Directive Principles as the father of our Nation", and was to encourage the growth of "genuine Papua New Guinea development philosophy, as well as national pride and confidence".[124] The Commission would have had the Head of State continue to act on the advice of the executive, although it recommended a slight departure from the present purely ceremonial role of the Governor-General, in relation to the dissolution of Parliament. During the first two decades after independence, various other voices suggested that the notion of a foreign Head of State, represented by a Governor-General, should be abolished. For example, in 1991, Bernard Narakobi, then Attorney-General, urged the move to a republic,[125] and such suggestions have surfaced at intervals.

WHAT ARE THE OPTIONS FOR THE FUTURE?

In a sense the choices faced by Papua New Guinea are the same as those it faced 20 odd years ago. But the choices can be made in the light of the experience of those years, experiences that throw some light upon the constitutional provisions and upon the reasonable expectations of people in public life.

One might say it has been 20 years in which faith in all institutions has been seriously eroded. Respect for the monarchy is no longer what it was. Talk of republicanism in Britain has been more audible in the last few years than at any time since perhaps the 17th century. By no means have all of Papua New Guinea's Governors-General proved able to rise above politics and personality in the way which would be necessary for the institution to play the sort of role the government and Opposition purported to anticipate in 1975. On the other hand, as Ghai has said elsewhere,[126] Papua New Guinea's politicians have also failed to live up to expectations. If the CPC believed that there should be no Head of State because the political process, and in extremis the courts, should be decisive, could they have had in mind the sorts of politicians, and the sort of political process, which the people of Papua New Guinea have been forced to endure?

Republicanism

What would be gained by Papua New Guinea becoming a republic? The question as to whether Papua New Guinea should become a republic goes beyond the scope of this chapter, which is concerned with the position of the Head of State. Of itself, being a republic would not necessarily make a great deal of practical difference. In Australia, where there is serious discussion of the possibility of republicanism, it would not be possible to replace the Governor-General with a President and expect to find no difference. But in Papua New Guinea it would be perfectly possible to replace the Governor-General with a President with precisely the same powers, or lack of powers. It is true that in order to do away with any Head of State it probably would be necessary for Papua New Guinea to become a republic. But being a republic does not mean having no Head of State.

---

[123] Ibid, p 103.
[124] Ibid, p 95.
[125] *Agence-France Presse* (14 August 1991), found on lexis.com visited 25 November 2000.
[126] See Chapter 4, "Establishing a Liberal Political Order though a Constitution: The Papua New Guinea Experience" by Y Ghai.

It is likely that Papua New Guinea will decide whether to become a republic on the basis of whether or not it is still appropriate for the Head of State to be a foreign and distant monarch of another country, rather than for any reason immediately related to the amount of power which it is desired to give to the Head of State. There are 15 other Commonwealth countries of which the Queen is still Head of State. These include Australia and New Zealand: but for how much longer? Both these countries, particularly Australia, have come to feel a certain strain in the situation of the Queen with her multiple Crowns. The problem is more acute, in one sense, for a country such as Australia, which has some pretensions to a world role. Australians have become conscious that, especially when travelling abroad, the Queen may be called upon to express views that are those of the British Government, but never those of the Australian Government unless they happen to coincide. This is probably less of a difficulty for Papua New Guinea, which would rarely see itself as having a world role.

On the other hand, Australia is likely to experience the presence of the Queen more often than Papua New Guinea. Any sense of symbolic significance is much more likely to be experienced as real when the Head of State is actually present, and actually acting as the Head of State, which she can actually do in Australia, in the sense that she may open Parliament or sign legislation.

Can the Queen ever play, for good or ill, a real role in the political life of the country? Could she, for example, restrain the excesses of the Governor-General in circumstances in which a President would be less inhibited? Or can she back up a Governor-General who is taking a stand in which he or she might falter as a "stand-alone" Head of State; that is, a non-executive President? In short, is the Governor-General or the Queen somehow more powerful than a ceremonial President?

On balance, the answer is probably "no". It has been suggested that in Fiji at the time of the first coup, the Queen gave some support to the Governor-General, Sir Penaia Ganilau. Later suspicions were, however, to the effect that the Governor-General was sympathetic to the coup leaders. One might say that the Queen's support camouflaged what was really going on. Could she have dismissed Sir Penaia and reinstated the Prime Minister? She might have done the former, but by what practical means could she have done the latter? And is it really desirable for a monarch who has for so long acted only on advice suddenly to take such drastic action, even in a good cause? And anyone who nurtures some hope that the Queen might be able to exercise in any other realm the sort of quiet influence which she is believed to wield in Britain should not ignore the great difference in her experience of British politics and that of any other country.[127] Anyway, one imagines that no such hopes and illusions tempt Papua New Guinea politicians.

Enhancing the power

Whether Papua New Guinea continues to have a Governor-General or switches to a system of non-executive President, it would be possible to enhance the powers of that office. There are some who feel that in such a situation as Wingti created in 1993, it might actually have been desirable for the Governor-General to have some power. Omar also suggests a constitutional amendment to give the Governor-General some minimal discretionary power for such

[127] V Bogdanor, *The Monarchy and the Constitution* (Oxford: Clarendon Press, 1995).

circumstances.[128] If the Governor-General was in cahoots with the Prime Minister in such a situation, such discretion would, of course, avail nothing!

It may be true that politicians no longer command the sort of faith they had at independence, which may make a strengthening of the potential check represented by a Governor-General/President more appealing. On the other hand, the two major crises which have faced the Governor-Generalship in Papua New Guinea should be kept in mind here. When one Governor-General denied he had any freedom of action, some said he ought to have acted; when another Governor-General did act independently, the critics said he should have acted without using any discretion! In 1993 it was the courts that, albeit by an act of creative interpretation, stepped in to uphold the spirit of the *Constitution*. The inactivity of Korowi does not really seem to have resulted from lack of power, but from lack of will. It can be argued that he already had a power, indeed a duty, to decline to act unconstitutionally.

One possible area for enhancement might be to give the Head of State the power to refer matters of dubious constitutional legitimacy to the court, as is possible in Vanuatu. Is this a valuable power? It is already the case that anyone whose interests are affected by legislation that is arguably unconstitutional may attack it if the case comes to court, and possibly may bring a pre-emptive action to determine the constitutionality of the legislation. Indeed, it is possible, by court action or constitutional provision, to give the power to take hypothetical issues to court to determine constitutionality. Is there any virtue in giving such a power to the Head of State? If the power is desirable, it might more appropriately rest with the Ombudsman, as is already the case under s 19 of the *Constitution*.

If, as had tended to be the case, the Governor-General has been a political appointment, could one rely upon the representative using such a power in an independent and impartial way?

If there were a real desire to enhance the Head of State's powers in this or any other way, it would presumably be an argument in favour of republicanism, for it would be less offensive, even if only symbolically so, to give such powers to someone who was in no way the representative of a colonial monarch.

Powers should not be considered in isolation from appointment. It may be unfortunate that not all Governors-General have found it easy to be detached in political terms. It would be more unfortunate if the Head of State were to have real power, and yet not be detached. It is not easy to see how such greater detachment could be achieved. Papua New Guinea already gives the power to nominate the Governor-General to Parliament and not simply to the government of the day. If it were really desired to give some genuine powers to the Head of State, perhaps appointment, or at least nomination, might be given to some sort of electoral college consisting only partly of politicians?

Doing away with the Head of State

But if the desire were to adopt the proposals of the CPC, two decades later, what would be involved? If we look at the powers, or more accurately functions, given by the *Constitution* to the Governor-General, where might they be bestowed if the Governor-General ceased to exist?

---

[128] Omar, above n 21, pp 317-18 and 323.

As we have seen, the overwhelming majority of the functions of the Governor-General are to be exercised on the advice of the NEC. There would seem to be no reason why these functions could not be performed by the Prime Minister, or some other relevant Minister, also acting on the decision of the NEC as a whole. In matters involving the army it might sometimes be the Minister with responsibility for the armed forces, though if it is a question of declaration of war perhaps this should be reserved to the Prime Minister. The only issue would be to ensure that this is not carried out by the Minister in question without an NEC decision. It might not be possible to allow for challenge on the basis that no NEC decision had been made: this would create problems of Cabinet secrecy. But a Minister who carried out some function without NEC backing would presumably not last long in government. And even now, it is in theory possible for such a Minister to convey to the Governor-General "advice" which is in fact personal, rather than that of the NEC. Unlike some constitutions, that of Papua New Guinea already vests the executive power in the NEC: to give it the formal function too is only to recognise reality.

The appointment of the Prime Minister, which depends upon parliamentary support, cannot be something which is carried out by the Prime Minister. But there is no reason why it cannot be the function of the Speaker (as in some countries) to declare someone elected as Prime Minister, leaving no role for the Head of State. The Speaker already signs legislation into law. The most appropriate Minister could perform other functions which are currently the formal responsibility of the Head of State; for example, the presentation to Parliament of the annual report of the judges on the national judicial system (s 187). Consent to entering into a treaty, currently formally given by the Governor-General on the advice of the NEC (s 117) could be given by the NEC alone.

CONCLUSION

The Governor-General is given so small a constitutional role that there is very little impact that he or she can have on the nation, unless possessed of personal qualities such as to transcend the limitations of the constitutional role. The almost total absence of discretion reflects the fact that there was no expectation that the representative would play any significant role in a political crisis, and indeed it does not seem that any Governor-General has been able to play a positive role in the crises that afflicted the country during its first two decades. One might almost say that Governors-General have been of interest only when they have, as it were, broken the rules. A time may come when the role of the Governor-General may come into more prominence as, for example, the position of the Head of State did in 2000 in Fiji and in the Solomon Islands, as a result of the elected government in each country being paralysed by coup or insurrection. But thus far it is hard to believe that, the expense aside, the decision of the government to reject the recommendation of the CPC and to have a Head of State after all has actually made any difference to the country.

APPENDIX

Powers of the Head of State under the *Constitution* and Organic Laws, and on whose advice they are to be exercised

Power	Provision	On advice of	After consultation with or report from etc
To appoint the Chief Justice	s 169(2)	NEC	Minister responsible for National Justice Administration
To appoint members of Boundaries Commission, Administrator of Public Broadcasting, Commissioner of Police	s 193	NEC	Public Service Commission (PSC) and Permanent Parliamentary Committee
To appoint the Secretary to the NEC, Commander of the Defence Force, certain public officers	s 193	NEC	
To appoint the Auditor-General	s 213	NEC	PSC and Public Accounts Committee
To appoint Ombudsman Commissioners	s 217(2)	Ombudsman Appointments Committee	
To set up a tribunal to consider dismissal of CJ	s 179	NEC	
To dismiss CJ	s 179	NEC	
To suspend CJ	s 182(1)(a)	NEC	
To give directions to the Public Prosecutor on matters of national security or international relations	s 176(3)(b)	NEC	
To grant pardons	s 151	NEC	After NEC considers a report from the Advisory Committee on the Power of Mercy
To appoint a person to receive Declarations of Loyalty	s 250	NEC	

To substitute for non-citizens appointed to statutory office a different oath or declaration or exempt him/her from the requirement entirely	s 251(1)	NEC	
To declare war	s 227	NEC	
To give consent to treaties (or authorise Ministers to perform this role)	s 117(2)(a) and (b)	NEC	
To approve a citizen serving in the armed forces of another country, thereby exempting the former from automatic loss of citizenship	s 70(1)(e)	NEC	
To declare the territory of Papua New Guinea	s 2(1)	NEC	
To call out Defence Force in support of the civil authorities	ss 202(c)(ii) and 204(1)	NEC	
To order Defence Force on active service or out of the country	s 205	NEC	
To declare a state of emergency	s 228(1)	NEC	
To revoke such a state of emergency	s 229	NEC	
To make emergency laws (known as Emergency Regulations) to the extent necessitated by the state of emergency, and only while Parliament is not meeting, or during the first 24 hours of its sitting	s 231(1)	NEC	
To alter such Regulations	s 236(2)(a)	NEC	
In case of internment without trial, to release internees	s 245(1)(g)	NEC	If tribunal finds wrongful detention

To refuse to release internees	s 245(5)	NEC	
To fix times for reporting to Parliament by the Minister for Provincial Affairs on the working of the provincial government system	s 187(j)	NEC	
To fix times for reporting by the Ombudsman Commission to Parliament, and by Judicial & Legal Services Commission	s 220 *Organic Law on the Judicial and Legal Services Commission,* s 11	NEC	
To receive reports on provincial affairs and of Ombudsman Commission for presentation to Parliament	ss 187(j) and 220		
To make regulations prescribing matters to carry into effect various Organic Laws	*Organic Law on the Duties and Responsibilities of Leadership*, s 41; *Organic Law on the Judicial and Legal Services Commission*, s 14; *Organic Law on National Elections,* s 243; *Organic Law on the Ombudsman Commission*, s 37	NEC	
To make laws for province while provincial government suspended	*Organic Law on Provincial Governments,* s 97	NEC	
To appoint members of Internment Tribunal, and their terms of service, Electoral Commissioner	*Organic Law on the Internment Tribunal*, ss 2(2) and 3; *Organic Law on the National Elections*, s 4(2)	NEC Electoral Commission Appointments Committee	
To appoint members of National Fiscal Commission	*Organic Law on the National Fiscal Commission*, s 76	NEC	Specified provincial and local government officers
To fix conditions of employment of members of Judicial and Legal Services Commission	*Organic Law on the Judicial and Legal Services Commission*, s 4	NEC	Parliamentary Salaries Tribunal and PSC
To fix conditions of employment of Electoral Commissioner	*Organic Law on National Elections*, s 9	PSC	

To fix conditions of employment of members of Boundaries Commission	*Organic Law on National Elections*, s 26	NEC	PSC
To fix conditions of employment of the Ombudsman Commission	*Organic Law on the Ombudsman Commission*, s 6	NEC	PSC
To fix conditions of employment of members of the Public Service Commission	*Organic Law on the Public Service Commission*, s 4	NEC	
To fix conditions of employment of judges of the National Court	*Organic Law on the Terms and Conditions of Employment of Judges*, s 3	NEC	PSC
To grant leave of absence to Electoral Commissioner	*Organic Law on National Elections*, s 12	NEC (not specified)	
To accept resignation of Electoral Commissioner, Ombudsman Commissioners	*Organic Law on National Elections*, s 13; *Organic Law on the Ombudsman Commission*, s 9	NEC (not specified)	
To grant provincial government	*Organic Law on Provincial Government*, s 6	NEC	After resolution in Parliament and provincial *Constitution* adopted

THE LEGAL SYSTEM

Chapter 8

THE NEMO JUDEX PRINCIPLE OF NATURAL JUSTICE

MICHAEL A NTUMY[*]

INTRODUCTION

An essential requirement of the judicial process is that judges should be impartial and neutral in relation to the subject matter and parties of a dispute, and should also be in a position to apply the law objectively without any bias. This procedural requirement is based upon the principle of nemo debet esse judex in propria causa (no-one can be judged in his own case), one of the two fundamental principles of natural justice.[129] The nemo judex principle, which operates as a safeguard against legal bias, has been extended to administrative officials as well. Basically, the principle has the following requirements:

(1) No person shall be a judge in his or her own cause.

(2) Justice must not only be done, but must be seen to be done.

Section 59 of the *Constitution* of Papua New Guinea invokes this principle, also known as the rule against bias (or the bias rule), in the following general terms:

> "(1) Subject to this *Constitution* and to any statute, the principles of natural justice are the rules of the underlying law known by that name developed for control of judicial and administrative proceedings.
>
> (2) The minimum requirement of natural justice is the duty to act fairly and, in principle, to be seen to act fairly."

For reasons of economy, the *Constitution* appropriately does not elaborate on defining the rules of natural justice, the circumstances under which they apply and the procedural requirements to meet "the minimum requirement . . . to act fairly and, in principle, to be seen to act fairly". Instead, s 60 of the *Constitution* places a duty on the judicial system to develop the rules of natural justice in a way that responds to the particular needs and circumstances of Papua New Guinea.

Acting on this constitutional direction, the courts have laboriously laid down the rules of the underlying law applicable to natural justice in Papua New Guinea. This chapter discusses the rules developed by the courts with regard to the bias rule. From the outset, it should be observed that the nemo judex principle has not featured prominently in the Papua New Guinean courts. In view of the negative connotations of alleging bias against a judge, the paucity of cases in this area of the law may be evidence of the maturity and integrity of the judiciary.

---

[*] I wish to thank Mr and Mrs Rannells of the Law Library, UPNG, for reading the first draft of this chapter and making very useful suggestions for improvement.

[129] The second principle is the right to a fair hearing. This principle requires that a person may not be condemned unheard or, more generally, that all parties should have the opportunity to present their case.

LEGAL BIAS

Legal bias may be manifested in two different forms; namely, actual bias and an appearance of bias. In *Boateng v The State* [1990] PNGLR 342, one of the few cases in which an allegation of bias was brought against a judge, the Supreme Court alluded to these two forms when it stated that the facts of the case did not raise an issue of actual bias, but merely the principle that "not only must justice be done, but it must be seen to be done". Although the court did not elaborate on the point, it is an important distinction that is always made in the application of the rule against bias.

Actual bias

Actual bias usually flows from pecuniary or proprietary interest. Hence, whenever a person has "any direct pecuniary or proprietary interest in the subject matter of a [judicial or quasi-judicial] proceeding" there is an irrebuttable presumption of bias.[130] In such a case, there is an automatic disqualification of the person from adjudicating or assisting in adjudicating on a case on the ground of bias. If the interest of the person is discovered after the case has already been heard, then the decision of that person may be challenged on appeal on the ground of bias. Generally, judges by their training and disposition normally disqualify themselves from sitting on cases in which they may have a direct pecuniary or proprietary interest. It is, therefore, rare to hear about a charge of actual bias against a judge. Perhaps for this reason, to my knowledge, there are no decided cases on this issue in Papua New Guinea or in any other common law jurisdiction.

Appearance of bias

The rule against bias also requires that a person be disqualified from acting in a judicial or quasi-judicial capacity on the ground of personal interest, other than pecuniary or proprietary interest, in the subject matter of the proceeding, provided there is an appearance of bias.[131] The type of interests that may give rise to an appearance of bias include a close or intimate personal relationship with one of the parties of the case and the expression of hostility towards one of the parties or a group to which the party belongs. These types of interests, however, do not lead to an automatic disqualification. On the contrary, there is a rebuttable presumption of bias, and the person alleged to have an interest is given the chance, in a separate hearing, to rebut the presumption of bias. If the presumption is successfully rebutted, the person may be permitted to continue to sit on the proceedings. On the other hand, if the rebuttal is unsuccessful, then the person is disqualified and any decision already made by that person is impeached and quashed on the ground of bias.

To disqualify a person on the ground of appearance of bias, the English courts have developed three tests, which are selectively applied depending upon the discretion of the court. These tests are the "reasonable suspicion" test, the "real likelihood of bias" test, and the "reasonable man" test.

---

[130] *R v Camborne Justices; Ex parte Pearce* [1954] 2 All ER 850 at 853 per Slade J.
[131] Ibid.

The reasonable suspicion test

The reasonable suspicion test is based upon the oft-quoted dicta of Lord Hewart CJ in *R v Sussex Justices; Ex parte McCarthy* [1924] 1 KB 256. In this case the deputy clerk to the justices, a solicitor who sat with the justices and retired with them, had had his firm act for one of the parties in prior civil proceedings. Although the clerk did not take part in the deliberations of the justices, the decision of the court was struck down on appeal on the ground of bias. In quashing the decision, Lord Hewart CJ said that it:

> "is of fundamental importance that justice should not only be done, but should manifestly and undoubtedly be seen to be done. The question therefore is not whether in this case the deputy clerk made any observation or offered any criticism which he might not properly have made or offered; the question is whether he was so related to the case in its civil aspect as to be unfit to act as clerk to the justices in the criminal matter. The answer to that question depends not upon what actually was done but upon what might appear to be done. Nothing is to be done which creates even a suspicion that there has been an improper interference with the course of justice."[132]

The reasonable suspicion test received its greatest support in *Eckersley v Mersey Docks & Harbour Board* [1894] 2 QB 667 where Lord Esher MR adopted and elaborated upon it as follows:

> "When the proposition sought to be established on behalf of the plaintiffs is examined, it comes to this, that the disputes ought not to be referred to the engineer because he might be suspected of being biased, although in truth he would not be biased. It is an attempt to apply the doctrine which is applied to judges, not merely of the Superior Courts, but to all judges - that, not only must they be not biased, but that, even though it be demonstrated that they would not be biased, they ought not to act as judges in a matter where the circumstances are such that people - not necessarily reasonable people, but many people - would suspect them of being biased."[133]

Although this test has been followed in several other judgments and continues to be applied up to today, it has been criticised by many judges and scholars.[134]

The real likelihood of bias test

The real likelihood of bias test is concerned with the type of interest, other than pecuniary or proprietary interest, that may give rise to an appearance of bias as a question of fact. It is determined by reference to the circumstances of the case and the real likelihood that a person may, in fact, be or might have been biased. As Lord O'Brien CJ expressed it in *R v Queen's County Justices* [1908] 2 IR 285:

---

[132] [1924] 1 KB 256 at 259.

[133] [1894] 2 QB 667 at 670.

[134] In *R v County Cork Justices* [1910] 2 IR 275, Lord O'Brien CJ rejected this test because it "goes too far. It makes mere suspicions of unreasonable persons a test of bias". See also Slade J's observation in *R v Camborne Justices; Ex parte Pearce* [1954] 2 All ER 850 at 855 that the dictum "is being used as a warrant for quashing convictions or invalidating orders on quite unsubstantial grounds and, indeed in some cases, on the flimsiest pretexts of bias". Commenting on the test, Devlin LJ in *R v Barnsley Licensing Justices* [1960] 2 QB 167 suggests that there is no need for the courts to inquire into what sort of impression might be left on the mind of the public generally. In his view, what is important is for the courts to satisfy themselves that there was a real likelihood of bias.

> "By 'bias' I understand a real likelihood of an operative prejudice, whether conscious or unconscious. There must, in my opinion, be reasonable evidence to satisfy us that there was a real likelihood of bias. I do not think that the mere vague suspicions of whimsical, capricious, and unreasonable people should be made a standard to regulate our action here. It might be a different matter if the suspicion rested on reasonable grounds - was reasonably generated - but certainly mere flimsy, elusive, morbid suspicions should not be permitted to form a ground of decision."[135]

In *R v Rand* [1866] LR 1 QB 230, trustees who sat on a case, the result of which could benefit not themselves but the beneficiaries, were held, on the basis of this test, not to have an interest that would give the appearance of bias. According to Blackburn J, who is credited with the original expression of the test, the test requires that:

> "Whenever there is a real likelihood that the judge would, from kindred or any other cause, have a bias in favour of one of the parties, it would be very wrong in him to act."[136]

The real likelihood of bias test was also applied by Slade J in *R v Camborne Justices; Ex parte Pearce* [1954] 2 All ER 850 at 855 where, after reviewing the reasonable suspicion test and the reasonable man test, he concluded:

> "[T]he right test is that prescribed by Blackburn J in *R v Rand*, namely, that to disqualify a person from acting in a judicial or quasi-judicial capacity on the ground of interest (other than pecuniary or proprietary) in the subject matter of the proceeding, a real likelihood of bias must be shown. This court is, further, of opinion that a real likelihood of bias must be made to appear not only from the materials in fact ascertained by the party complaining, but from such further facts as he might readily have ascertained and easily verified in the course of his inquiries."

This dictum by Slade J has been interpreted to mean that the real likelihood test requires something more than a mere possibility or suspicion that a close relationship may give the appearance of bias. According to this rather high standard, there must be something positive said or done between the judge and one of the parties to the case that is directly connected with the particular proceedings, prior to the commencement of the proceedings or during the proceedings.

The reasonable man test

The reasonable man test has been put forward by some judges who, in principle, agree with the reasonable suspicion test and yet, out of caution, avoid the epithet "suspicion". Instead, they substitute "suspicion" with "man" in order to inject an element of objectivity.

Swift J formulated the question that forms the basis of the test in *R v Essex Justices; Ex parte Perkins* [1927] 2 KB 475 at 490. He said:

---

[135] Cited by Slade J in *R v Camborne Justices; Ex parte Pearce* [1954] 2 All ER 850 at 853.
[136] [1866] LR 1 QB 230 at 233.

> "It is essential that justice should be so administered as to satisfy reasonable persons that the tribunal is impartial and unbiased. As Lord Hewart CJ said in *R v Sussex Justices; Ex parte McCarthy* [1924] 1 KB 259, 'Nothing is to be done which creates even a suspicion that there has been an improper interference with the course of justice'. Might a reasonable man suppose that there had here been such an interference with the course of justice?"

In *Cottle v Cottle* [1939] 2 All ER 535, Mr Cottle's mother-in-law clearly asserted that she would like the case to come before a particular judge who was her friend. Following this test, Bucknill J found that, on the basis of the available evidence, a reasonable person might form the impression that Mr Browning (the chairman of the Bench) could not give an unbiased hearing. He stated the test in the following words:

> "The test which we have to apply is whether or not a reasonable man, in all the circumstances, might suppose that there was an improper interference with the course of justice."[137]

By comparison, the reasonable man test seems closer to the real likelihood test than to the reasonable suspicion test. The difference between it and the suspicion test is that it purports to be based on reasonable facts rather than mere suspicion. Consequently, the application of this test requires that the whole question of an appearance of bias be viewed from the impression a reasonable person may gather from the facts of the case and the surrounding circumstances. In this respect, although slightly less objective than the standard required by the real likelihood test, it is much closer to it than the reasonable suspicion test.

APPLICATION OF THE PRINCIPLE IN PAPUA NEW GUINEA

The leading authority in Papua New Guinea on the rule against bias is *Boateng v The State* [1990] PNGLR 342. In this case, the appellant appealed his conviction of rape on several grounds, one of which was that the trial judge ought to have disqualified himself from presiding over the trial as it appeared that his wife was a friend of the prosecutrix. The court noted from affidavit evidence that the judge's wife attended the hearing of this case on a number of occasions, sat together with the prosecutrix and was seen on numerous occasions conversing with the prosecutrix outside the courthouse when the court had been adjourned.

The court went to great lengths to explain that there was no allegation of actual bias, no suggestion of bias on the part of the trial judge, no question about the propriety of his conduct of the trial, nothing wrong with the judge's wife attending and observing court proceedings, and no indication that the judge's wife might have influenced the decision of the husband. In the words of the court:

> "Whether or not a judge's wife actually influences the outcome of the case is important, but it is not the point here. The point here is the reaction of a reasonable man or woman knowing the relevant facts that justice might have miscarried because of such association in or in the precincts of the court.

[137] [1939] 2 All ER 535 at 541.

> Justice requires that there be complete absence of any inference or impression that a judge or his family have, by personal association with parties or witnesses, influenced the outcome of a case. However impeccable a judgment or decision of a judge might be, the appearance created by such association in the mind of a reasonable man that justice might not have been done to a party cannot be remedied by denials, however true, that such association had no effect on the outcome of the case.
>
> In the National Court, all trials, civil and criminal, are entertained by judges sitting alone. It is therefore, crucial to a fair trial and the actual appearance of a fair trial that spouses of judges not be seen in court or within the precincts of court, associating with witnesses or parties in cases being tried by their husbands or wives."[138]

Having clarified these points, the court proceeded to determine whether the judge had an interest that would give the appearance of bias. This was done by reference to one of the common law tests for determining an appearance of bias.

Relying on *R v Liverpool City Justices; Ex parte Topping* [1983] 1 WLR 119, an English authority, the court quoted what it regarded as pertinent to the case as follows:

> "Would a 'reasonable and fair-minded person sitting, in a court' and knowing all the relevant facts have a 'reasonable suspicion that a fair trial' for the appellant 'was not possible'?"[139]

According to this test, the court found that any reasonable and fair-minded person who knew what was stated in the affidavit evidence would have "a reasonable suspicion that justice had miscarried in this case". It therefore quashed the decision of the trial judge and ordered a re-trial of the case by another judge.

It is instructive to note that the Supreme Court in this case applied the reasonable suspicion test. The court did so without making any reference to the existence of the other two tests. Hence, it is not clear as to whether the court was making a choice of the tests or not since there is no indication that it was aware of the other tests.

In *Kavali v Hoihoi* [1984] PNGLR 182, when the issue of bias was raised, Bredmeyer J appropriately considered the three tests, albeit with varying degrees of clarity. The circumstances leading to this case were as follows. The appellant (a Minister of the State) and a second defendant were tried by the District Court for an offence (drinking liquor in a moving vehicle) under s 6(1) of the *Liquor (Miscellaneous Provisions) Act* (Ch 313). During the trial, counsel for the appellant was barred from the court on account of certain remarks made to the magistrate. During the counsel's absence, the second defendant, a law graduate, made a no-case submission on their behalf. The magistrate ruled that the second defendant had no case to answer and discharged him, but found that the appellant had a case to answer. On the date appointed by the court for the continuation of the trial against the appellant both he and his lawyer failed to appear in court. The prosecution then applied for the case to be adjourned and a warrant to be issued for the appellant's arrest. The court refused to grant the application and proceeded to receive

[138] [1990] PNGLR 342 at 346.
[139] Ibid.

submissions from the prosecution and convicted the appellant. After convicting the appellant, the magistrate said:

> "As far as evidence by prosecution's witness there was enough evidence to convict Mr Kavali. The only element of the charge disputed by the defence was that the consuming of liquor was proved beyond any reasonable doubt. *Had defence evidence were [sic] available it could not have caused any doubt*."[140]

On appeal against the conviction and sentence imposed by the trial court, the appellant argued, among other things, that the trial magistrate erred in law in failing to disqualify himself from the proceedings for likelihood of bias. The argument on this ground of appeal was in two parts.

The first part alleged that the above stated ground for refusing the prosecution's application showed actual bias toward the appellant. Bredmeyer J overlooked the obvious error in the reference to actual bias, and found that the trial magistrate's statement revealed "bias or prejudice" against the appellant. However, he considered the statement as irrelevant to the decision to convict because it was not made during the trial or at the close of the prosecution case, but after the conviction of the appellant. The judge explained further why, in his view, the statement had no effect whatsoever on the conviction. He reasoned as follows:

> "I will assume in favour of the appellant that, although unstated at that time, the magistrate held the same view at the close of the prosecution case. But because he did not reveal that view and because no evidence was called by the defendant, and because there was no question of weighing up the prosecution and the defence evidence, in my view it cannot be said that there was a real likelihood or a reasonable suspicion that the magistrate convicted the defendant because of his prejudice. It was as if the prejudice was compartmentalised in the magistrate's mind; the prejudice was there but the magistrate did not use it to decide the case."[141]

Bredmeyer J's reasoning highlights the importance of the choice of test to be applied in determining an appearance of bias. Clearly, although unstated, the test applied here is the real likelihood of bias test, the most objective of all the three tests. The interesting question is whether the judge in this case would have come to the same conclusion if he had applied any of the two other tests, particularly the reasonable suspicion test. This question was somewhat addressed by Bredmeyer J in relation to the second part of the argument alleging bias.

The second argument was that the trial magistrate's antipathy towards the appellant's counsel, which resulted in barring him from the court, may have carried over to the appellant. Before making a ruling on this point, Bredmeyer J made a quick reference to the relevant tests in other common law jurisdictions. He found that in England, although there is a conflict as to whether the test is real likelihood of bias or the reasonable suspicion of bias, the preferred one seems to be the former. In his view, this was expressed by Lord Denning as follows:

> "There must be circumstances from which a reasonable man would think it likely or probable that the justice . . . would, or did, favour one side unfairly at the expense of the other."[142]

140 [1984] PNGLR 182 at 187.
141 Ibid at 188.
142 In *Metropolitan Properties Co (FGC) Ltd v Lannon* [1969] 1 QB 577 at 599.

Despite the view of Bredmeyer J, the conflict in England, as demonstrated above, is not only between the real likelihood of bias test and the reasonable suspicion of bias test. The conflict also extends to the third test, namely the reasonable man test, which, incidentally, is what Lord Denning's dicta would seem to support. The judicial practice in England, as indicated above, shows that different judges have applied different tests.[143] This suggests that there is no rigid rule as to which test applies and judges are free to exercise their discretion.

With regard to Australia and New Zealand, Bredmeyer J found that there is a definite preference for the reasonable suspicion test.[144] This conclusion was derived from the following quotation, which was approved by the High Court of Australia in a joint judgment:

> "Those requirements of natural justice are not infringed by a mere lack of nicety but only when it is firmly established that a suspicion may reasonably be engendered in the minds of those who come before the tribunal or in the minds of the public that the tribunal or a member or members of it may not bring to the resolution of the questions arising before the tribunal fair and unprejudiced minds."[145]

Having found that there is no uniform rule regarding the choice of the test of bias, Bredmeyer J surprisingly resolved that it was not necessary in the case to decide which test was appropriate for Papua New Guinea. This was because, in his view, in many cases the two tests will produce the same result. Consequently, he decided to apply both tests.

Bredmeyer J then reviewed the material facts of the case and found that there was sufficient evidence to justify dismissing the no-case submission and to support a conviction. He also found that there were good and proper reasons for proceeding with the trial in the absence of the appellant and his counsel, and noted that it was the absence of the appellant and his counsel rather than any enmity that led to the decision to continue and conclude the hearing of the case. On the basis of these findings, he held:

> "I cannot see how a party or a member of the public would think that there was a real likelihood of bias or a reasonable suspicion that the enmity that existed between the magistrate and counsel led to the magistrate rejecting the no-case submission on behalf of Mr Kavali on 2 March or led to the conviction on 6 July."[146]

On appeal to the Supreme Court, the decision of Bredmeyer J was reversed in *Kavali v Hoihoi* [1986] PNGLR 329. Woods J ruled that the magistrate erred by closing his mind to any evidence that the defendant might have been able to produce if he had sought to do so. In his words:

> "[T]he words of the magistrate, 'had defence evidence were [sic] available it could not have caused any doubt', must be read as being his thinking when he made the decision, and quite clearly suggest a blocking out by the magistrate in his mind of any possible defence the defendant could produce thereby suggesting that the defendant would not get a fair and unbiased hearing."[147]

---

[143] Indeed, it is not unusual that even in the same case different judges adopt different tests in support of their judgment. See, for example, *R v Essex Justices; Ex parte Perkins* [1927] 2 KB 475 where Avory J adopted the real likelihood test while Swift J applied the reasonable man test.

[144] [1984] PNGLR 182 at 188.

[145] *R v Watson; Ex parte Armstrong* (1976) 136 CLR 248 at 262.

[146] [1984] PNGLR 182 at 189.

[147] [1986] PNGLR 329 at 337.

Similarly, Barnett J ruled:

> "At the time he decided to reject the prosecutor's application to adjourn and to issue a bench warrant the magistrate had already been exposed to all the facts on which the state of mind disclosed in his reasons was based. It indicates a significant bias and certainly gives rise to a suspicion of bias (as actually found by the National Court judge on appeal). I cannot agree with the learned appeal judge that such bias did not raise a real likelihood or suspicion that the magistrate convicted the appellant because of that bias. Once the appellant failed to appear, the magistrate had first to decide if he was consenting to the trial proceeding in his absence. If so, the magistrate had then to decide if he should proceed ex parte or adjourn and have him arrested and brought in. If he had already decided that no defence the appellant might bring forward could possibly raise a doubt in the magistrate's mind then that mind is closed, and that is bias. In those circumstances the decision to proceed ex parte was not a proper exercise of discretion as it was influenced by bias and, of course, it did lead to conviction."[148]

In addition to the fact that Bredmeyer J's decision was reversed, it is also important to point out that his view that the application of the reasonable man test and the reasonable suspicion test produce the same result is not entirely accurate. The appearance of bias may be viewed from five different angles:

(1) from the viewpoint of the judge against whom the objection is raised;

(2) from the viewpoint of the court hearing the application;

(3) from the viewpoint of the fictional "reasonable man", which is virtually the same as (2) above;

(4) from the applicant's viewpoint; and

(5) from the viewpoint of the general public.

According to these different viewpoints, it is clear that, while the reasonable man test obviously comes within the scope of (2) and (3) above, the reasonable suspicion test combines (4) and (5). As explained earlier, the reasonable man test is based on reasonable facts and views bias from the impression a reasonable person may gather from the facts of the case and the surrounding circumstances. This test is, therefore, purportedly an objective test. The reasonable suspicion test, on the other hand, does not lay any claim to objectivity and is merely concerned with the sort of impression, objective or otherwise, that might be left on the mind of the general public. The application of either test, therefore, is quite unlikely to yield the same results. It may be added that the application of the third test, the real likelihood of bias test, which is strictly based upon very precise objective criteria, will also lead to an entirely different result.

Hence, if the reasonable man test were applied to the two arguments in the *Kavali* case, it is conceded that it could produce the results obtained by the court. However, if the reasonable suspicion test were applied, the court could have come to a different conclusion, since it would have been irrelevant as to whether the trial magistrate's statement actually had any effect on the decision to convict or not. As long as it was possible for some members of the public to perceive, whether objectively or not, that the "compartmentalised prejudice" may have been operative, that

---

[148] Ibid at 339.

would have been enough to support a finding that the trial magistrate could not have given an unbiased hearing. Similarly, if it was possible for some members of the public to perceive that the trial magistrate's hostility towards the appellant's counsel may have influenced the decision to reject the no-case submission and to convict the appellant, the application of the reasonable suspicion test would support a finding of sufficient interest to disqualify the trial magistrate. Finally, if the real likelihood of bias test had been applied, since the trial magistrate's statement was made after the conclusion of the trial, it arguably could not be said to have influenced the decision to convict the appellant. However, the expression of hostility towards the appellant's counsel most likely would have met the requirements of this test.

These different implications of applying the various tests may be supported by reference to Bredmeyer J's decision in *Agai v Yarume* [1987] PNGLR 124, where he rejected the argument that the fact that the prosecutor and the presiding magistrate in a criminal case came from the same province raised a reasonable suspicion of bias in favour of the prosecution. Even though Bredmeyer J purported to follow the test laid down in *Kavali v Hoihoi*, namely whether there is a real likelihood of bias or reasonable suspicion of bias, it may be inferred from his own words that he did not apply the reasonable suspicion test. Referring to an analogical situation, he said:

> "To say that the magistrate and victim are from the same province, that they live in a small town, and that therefore I can infer that they know each other well, see each other often socially etc, is not proof. It is not evidence."[149]

Indeed, the application of the reasonable suspicion test would have required the magistrate to disqualify himself from hearing the case as long as it was possible for the defendant or any member of the public to form an impression or merely suspect that the defendant could not obtain a fair hearing because of the wantok (from the same clan, tribe, group or having the same interest) relationship between the prosecutor and the presiding magistrate. This, as the court rightly observed, would have brought the administration of justice to a standstill.

In view of the profound implications that the application of the different tests have, it was quite crucial and would have been beneficial for future purposes if Bredmeyer J had made a ruling on the appropriate test for Papua New Guinea. Incidentally, since this issue was not raised on appeal before the Supreme Court, it was not addressed by that court either.

AN APPROPRIATE TEST FOR PAPUA NEW GUINEA

In *Diro v Amet* [1995] PNGLR 411, Hinchliffe J addressed the question of the appropriate test for Papua New Guinea. The case arose out of a Leadership Tribunal hearing concerning allegations of misconduct against the plaintiff. During the hearing, counsel for the plaintiff made an application to the tribunal that the chairman, Amet J, should disqualify himself from sitting on the tribunal because of his close relationship with Mr Barnett, a former judge and presiding commissioner over the Commission of Inquiry into Aspects of the Papua New Guinea Forestry Industry. The charges against the plaintiff were based upon the recommendations of the Commission. It was undisputed that Amet J's family and the Barnett family were practising Christians who attended the same church; that the former had helped the latter with their marital problems; and that the majority of the charges that the plaintiff was facing before the tribunal

[149] [1987] PNGLR 124 at 126.

arose out of Mr Barnett's findings in the said inquiry. According to affidavit evidence, Mr Barnett's wife revealed that her husband had always expressed hatred towards the plaintiff, had sworn to "pin" and "kill" him, and was continuously briefed by Amet J, the Chairman, about the proceedings of the tribunal. After hearing submissions from both counsel appearing before it, the tribunal ruled that the application be dismissed and that the tribunal should continue as constituted. The plaintiff then brought an action seeking to have the tribunal's decision reviewed by the National Court.

The main issue before the court was whether a fair-minded person would have a reasonable suspicion, in view of all the material placed before the tribunal, that the plaintiff might not have a fair hearing before a tribunal chaired by Amet J, the first defendant in this case. The determination of this issue turned on the question of the appropriate test in Papua New Guinea for disqualifying judges from sitting on proceedings on the ground of bias.

Relying on *Kavali v Hoihoi*, counsel for the plaintiff and the defendant submitted that since the issue had not been decided, the law in Papua New Guinea regarding the proper test for determining when a judge should be disqualified on the ground of bias was not settled. Hinchliffe J, however, rejected this submission and ruled that the question had been decided in *Boateng v The State* [1990] PNGLR 347, when the Supreme Court applied the reasonable suspicion test and stated that that test was pertinent to the case. In his view:

> "Although the Supreme Court did not discuss the two tests and specifically stated which test (if either) was appropriate for Papua New Guinea, it is clear that it applied the 'reasonable suspicion' test and I am of the view that that is the test that we should now apply in Papua New Guinea."[150]

On the basis of this view, Hinchliff J purported to apply the reasonable suspicion test to the facts of the case and found that, notwithstanding the fact that the allegations of Mr Barnett's hostility towards the plaintiff were based upon hearsay evidence:

> "a reasonable and fair-minded person who has sat and listened to the proceedings in the tribunal and is aware of all the contents in all the affidavits would have a reasonable suspicion that a fair hearing for Mr Diro was not possible before the first defendant."[151]

The decision of the tribunal to refuse the plaintiff's application that the chairman of the tribunal should disqualify himself from further participation in the tribunal proceedings was, therefore, quashed.

Assuming that the ruling in this case settles the law in Papua New Guinea regarding the appropriate test for determining when a judge should be disqualified on the ground of bias, then the law as it stands today is that the appropriate test is the reasonable suspicion test. The application of this test in the *Diro* case, however, seems to deviate from the strict application of the test. It may be recalled that the reasonable man test is based upon reasonable facts and considered from the viewpoint of the court hearing the application or the viewpoint of the fictional "reasonable man". The reasonable suspicion test, on the other hand, is based upon the mere suspicion of the applicant and general public and does not necessarily concern itself with

---

[150] [1995] PNGLR 411 at 420.
[151] Ibid at 426.

objectivity. However, by taking into account what "the reasonable and fair-minded person", "the reasonable and fair-minded Papua New Guinean" and "a reasonable man" would think under the circumstances, Hinchliffe J, while ostensibly applying the reasonable suspicion test, seems to have blended this test with elements of the reasonable man test as well.[152]

It is possible that Hinchliffe J may have been led into this confusion by the imprecise way in which the legal issues before the court were framed. Instead of asking the objective question of whether or not there was sufficient evidence to support a finding that the chairman of the tribunal had an interest in the case that gave the appearance of bias, Hinchliffe J accepted the leading question as to whether or not a fair-minded person would have a reasonable suspicion that the plaintiff might not obtain a fair hearing before the chairman of the tribunal as the legal issue before the court. This latter statement does not only beg the question as to which test is the appropriate one, but it also blends elements of the two tests.

Of course, this confusion may not have had any impact on Hinchliffe J's decision. This is because it is conceivable that, by applying the reasonable man test, "the reasonable and fair-minded Papua New Guinean", whether well versed in the law of evidence or not, and whether he appreciates fully the meaning of hearsay evidence and its weight or not, could still have made a reasonable judgment on the basis of reasonable facts and reached the same conclusion as the court. Indeed, in my opinion, the process by which Hinchliffe J reached his decision seems to have followed this exact approach. Otherwise, there would have been no need to consider the viewpoint of "the reasonable and fair-minded person", or "the reasonable and fair-minded Papua New Guinean". On the other hand, even if the reasonable suspicion test were applied, the applicant or a member of the general public, whether present at the tribunal or not, and whether aware of all the contents in all the affidavits or not, could still have formed an impression just from hearing some of the allegations against the chairman of the tribunal that the chairman could not have given an unbiased hearing to the plaintiff. In these two instances, while the end result may be the same, the processes of reaching the result are distinctly different. It is this difference in approach that underscores the question of the appropriate test.

Before leaving this case, it is pertinent to comment on another significant aspect of the Hinchliffe decision. The court's attention was drawn to a ruling of the tribunal that stated, inter alia, that the plaintiff had "succeeded in manufacturing a suspicious association between Mr Barnett and Justice Amet", and the plaintiff's counsel had "somehow by the concoction of the imagination scurrilously and offensively attempted to impute some malicious motive to this quite ordinary friendship between judicial colleagues, extended by church association and help in marital problems".[153] Referring to this statement as "a serious error" on the part of the tribunal, Hinchliffe J ruled:

> "[A] reasonable and fair-minded person, after hearing what I have just learnt, would have a reasonable suspicion that a fair hearing from now on, because of what was said about the plaintiff and his counsel, was not possible."[154]

On the basis of this ruling, he extended the prohibition order, which precluded the first defendant from further participation in the tribunal, to the two other members of the tribunal. In his view,

[152] This approach, however, is not unusual; cf Swift J's approach in *R v Essex Justices; Ex parte Perkins* [1927] 2 KB 475 which, apparently, also combined the reasonable man and the suspicion tests.

[153] [1995] PNGLR 411 at 426.

[154] Ibid at 429.

this was a logical necessity because the statement referred to as an error was the ruling of the tribunal as a whole.

The significant thing about this decision is that it removes entirely the lingering suspicion in the minds of some skeptics that it is not possible or likely that a fellow judge would take such firm action against other members of the bench (in this case, a judge of the National and Supreme Court and two senior magistrates) in the interest of fairness and justice. Ironically, depending upon the test applied in this instance, the fact that the ruling of the tribunal was held to have given rise to an appearance of bias has an interesting repercussion. If it was the reasonable man test, then Hinchliffe J's decision may be viewed as a serious indictment of the tribunal for it means that the fact that the members of the tribunal were likely to be biased would not be based upon mere suspicion, but on reasonable facts. On the other hand, if the test applied was the reasonable suspicion test, then the decision may simply be an implementation of s 59 of the *Constitution*, which requires that judges act fairly and, in principle, be seen to act fairly so that "nothing is to be done which creates even a suspicion that there has been an improper interference with the course of justice".[155]

CONCLUSION

It has been said that it would be wrong to view bias from the viewpoint of the judge against whom the allegation of bias is made because the judge is, in fact, the real respondent. Also, to be absolutely certain, some people have argued that to assess bias from the viewpoint of the court hearing the application may be incorrect. This is because it would lead to the requirement of a high standard of proof since the judge deciding the issue would, in effect, be a "brother" judge, and, for that reason, it would be difficult to rule out completely the possibility of "brotherly sympathy". These reminders may justify the adoption of the reasonable suspicion test as the appropriate test for Papua New Guinea. This test is based upon the viewpoint of the applicant and the general public and seems to be in harmony with the constitutional directive that judges must act fairly and, in principle, be seen to act fairly. While endorsing and fully maintaining the integrity of the principle behind the reasonable suspicion test, nevertheless, it is also important to bear in mind the following observation of Slade J:

> "[T]he continued citation of [the reasonable suspicion test] in cases to which it is not applicable may lead to the erroneous impression that it is more important that justice should appear to be done than that it should in fact be done."[156]

[155] *R v Sussex Justices; Ex parte McCarthy* [1924] 1 KB 256 at 259.
[156] *R v Camborne Justices; Ex parte Pearce* [1954] 2 All ER 850.

Chapter 9

DEVELOPING A COHERENT UNDERLYING LAW – INTEGRATING CUSTOM AND COMMON LAW IN PAPUA NEW GUINEA: PART ONE

OWEN JESSEP AND ANTHONY J REGAN

INTRODUCTION

Among the many unusual features of the Papua New Guinea *Constitution* are its detailed provisions about the underlying law, which is the law other than that made by or under authority of legislative bodies.[157] Under Schs 2.1 and 2.2 the primary elements of the underlying law are the principles of custom and English common law "adopted" under those schedules, with common law rules giving way where "in their application to any particular matter they are inconsistent with custom". However, where there are no applicable rules of either custom or common law the courts may develop their own rules under Sch 2.3. Further, Sch 2.4 enjoins the judiciary to ensure that the underlying law "develops as a coherent system in a manner that is appropriate to the circumstances of the country from time to time". The emphasis on custom in the underlying law is consistent with the views of Papua New Guinea's constitution-makers about breaking with the colonial past and emphasising Papua New Guinean ways.

Much of the extensive commentary on the development of the underlying law has focused upon the limited extent to which custom has been integrated, and the continued heavy reliance of the courts upon the common law. The courts have been criticised for failing to develop a coherent underlying law system.[158] However, there is much in the constitutional provisions about custom and the common law that contributes to the difficulties of that task. Although Schs 2.1 and 2.2 talk simply of custom and the common law being "adopted" as part of the underlying law, the Schedules contain complex rules that courts must refer to before either custom or common law principles are in fact applied in any particular case. Further, once applied, the Schedules create considerable uncertainty about the extent to which any such principle operates as a precedent in subsequent cases.[159]

This chapter examines the rules on adoption of custom and common law - rules that constitute major limitations on the adoption of both custom and common law - and several of the key issues that have arisen in their interpretation. Despite more than 20 years of judicial explanation and reflection, there is a great deal that is still unclear and controversial about these provisions. It is

[157] All legal systems have a role for law that has not been made by the legislature, including such elements as custom, executive directions and judicial decisions. This is true even of the civil law systems. In most cases, however, such matters are not provided for in national constitutions, but rather are matters of practice or ordinary legislation

[158] See, for example, B Sakora, "Judicial Law-making under the Papua New Guinea Constitution" in P Sack (ed), *Pacific Constitutions* (Canberra: ANU, 1982), pp 257-70; D Weisbrot, "The Impact of the Papua New Guinea Constitution on the Recognition and Application of Customary Law" in P Sack (ed), *Pacific Constitutions* (Canberra: ANU, 1982), pp 271-90; J Zorn, "Common Law Jurisprudence and Customary Law" in R James and I Fraser (eds), *Legal Issues in a Developing Society* (Port Moresby: UPNG, 1992), pp 103-27; J Nonggorr, "Development of Customary Law: Replacing the Customs Recognition Act" (1993) 21 *Melanesian Law Journal* 49; J Nonggorr, "The Development of an 'Indigenous Jurisprudence' in Papua New Guinea: The Past Record and Future Prospects" in J Aleck and J Rannells (eds), *Custom at the Crossroads* (Port Moresby: UPNG, 1995), pp 68-83; A Amet, "Severing the Umbilical Cord from the Common Law" in J Aleck and J Rannells (eds), *Custom at the Crossroads* (Port Moresby: UPNG, 1995), pp 62-67; T Deklin, "The Future of Papua New Guinea Customary Law: Rot Wei?" in J Aleck and J Rannells (eds), *Custom at the Crossroads* (Port Moresby: UPNG, 1995), pp 34-42.

[159] See, however, the point made in n 65, below.

also unlikely, we think, that the main causes of confusion and uncertainty will be removed in the near future. It is possible, in fact, that the very notion of the underlying law as defined in Sch 2, with its peculiar mixture of extremely specific and very generalised aspects, is itself essentially incoherent. If this is so, then the problems will not be resolved by judicial activity alone.

CONSTITUTIONAL AND STATUTORY PROVISIONS

By s 9 of the *Constitution*, the laws of Papua New Guinea consist of the *Constitution* and Organic Laws, Acts of the Parliament and Emergency Regulations, provincial laws, laws made or adopted by or under the *Constitution* or any of the above laws, and the underlying law. Under s 20, until an Act of the Parliament otherwise declares and provides for its development, the underlying law and the manner of its development shall be as prescribed by Sch 2 of the *Constitution*.

The wording of Schs 2.1 and 2.2 is sufficiently important to set out in detail:

> "Sch 2.1. Recognition, etc, of custom.
>
> (1) Subject to Subsections (2) and (3), custom is adopted, and shall be applied and enforced, as part of the underlying law.
>
> (2) Subsection (1) does not apply in respect of any custom that is, and to the extent that it is, inconsistent with a Constitutional Law or a statute, or repugnant to the general principles of humanity.
>
> (3) An Act of the Parliament may -
>
> (a) provide for the proof and pleading of custom for any purpose; and
>
> (b) regulate the manner in which, or the purposes for which, custom may be recognized, applied or enforced; and
>
> (c) provide for the resolution of conflicts of custom.
>
> Sch 2.2. Adoption of a common law.
>
> (1) Subject to this Part, the principles and rules that formed, immediately before Independence Day, the principles and rules of common law and equity in England are adopted, and shall be applied and enforced, as part of the underlying law, except if, and to the extent that -
>
> (a) they are inconsistent with a Constitutional Law or a statute; or
>
> (b) they are inapplicable or inappropriate to the circumstances of the country from time to time; or
>
> (c) in their application to any particular matter they are inconsistent with custom as adopted by Part 1.
>
> (2) [refers to the Royal Prerogative]
>
> (3) The principles and rules of common law and equity are adopted as provided by Subsections (1) and (2) notwithstanding any revision of them by any statute of England that does not apply in the country by virtue of Section Sch2.6 (*adoption of pre-Independence laws*).

(1) In relation to any particular question before a court, the operation of Subsection (1)(b) shall be determined by reference, among other things, to the circumstances of the case, including the time and place of any relevant transaction, act or event.

Schedule 2.3(1) states that where "there appears to be no rule of law that is applicable and appropriate to the circumstances of the country", the courts (and, in particular, the Supreme Court and the National Court) have a duty to "formulate an appropriate rule as part of the underlying law". In doing so, the court is to have regard to:

(a) the National Goals and Directive Principles and Basic Social Obligations set out in the Preamble to the *Constitution;*

(b) the Basic Rights in the *Constitution*;

(c) analogies to be drawn from relevant statutes and custom;

(d) legislation and case law from countries with similar legal systems to that of Papua New Guinea;

(e) relevant decisions of Papua New Guinean courts at any time; and

(f) "the circumstances of the country from time to time".

By Sch 2.4, the courts, and especially the Supreme Court and the National Court, have a duty:

> "to ensure that, with due regard to the need for consistency, the underlying law develops as a coherent system in a manner that is appropriate to the circumstances of the country from time to time, except in so far as it would not be proper to do so by judicial act."

Part 5 of Sch 2 (Sch 2.8–Sch 2.12) sets out the rules of judicial precedent under which courts are bound by decisions of courts higher in the judicial hierarchy. Those rules apply to judicial decisions on the underlying law. As discussed later in this chapter, however, because the adoption and applicability of both custom and common law under Sch 2 may vary according to time and place, particular rulings on the underlying law may have limited value as precedents.

Three matters arising from these provisions of Sch 2 are of particular relevance to our analysis of custom and common law concern: first, the definition of "custom"; secondly, the legislation envisaged by Sch 2.3 (as to proof and pleading of custom etc); and thirdly, the place of the underlying law in the hierarchy of laws of Papua New Guinea.

As to the first matter, in Sch 1.2, the term "custom" is defined to mean:

> "the customs and usages of indigenous inhabitants of the country existing in relation to the matter in question at the time when and the place in relation to which the matter arises, regardless of whether or not the custom or usage has existed from time immemorial."

As to the second matter, Parliament has not since independence passed any Act as contemplated in Sch 2.1(3). However, the pre-independence *Native Customs (Recognition) Act* 1963 has been adopted, "subject to any Constitutional law", as an Act of the Parliament by virtue of Sch 2.6 of the *Constitution* and is now Ch 19 in the Revised Laws. While that Act does deal with the subject matter envisaged by Sch 2.1(3), it was developed many years before independence, at a time when custom was not accorded the same respect and status as is inherent in the constitutional scheme. Indeed, the terms of the Act indicate only a qualified acceptance of custom. It may only be "taken into account" in certain kinds of cases, and some provisions perhaps indicate that custom is not necessarily regarded as law;for example, s 5(g) permits custom to be taken into account in a case involving a transaction intended to be "regulated wholly or partly by custom and not by law". Nevertheless, in the absence of a statute tailored to the expansive role of custom envisaged by Sch 2.1(3), it has generally been assumed that the *Customs Recognition Act* (Ch 19) is the main relevant Act of Parliament, despite the fact that it imposes considerable limits on the circumstances in which custom can apply (as discussed further below).[160]

For the purposes of this account, it will be helpful to set out here the terms of ss 3(1), 4 and 5 of this Act:

> "3. Recognition of custom.
>
> (1) Subject to this Act, custom shall be recognized and enforced by, and may be pleaded in, all courts except so far as in a particular case or in a particular context -
>
> (a) its recognition or enforcement would result, in the opinion of the court, in injustice or would not be in the public interest; or
>
> (b) in a case affecting the welfare of a child under the age of 16 years, its recognition or enforcement would not, in the opinion of the court, be in the best interests of the child.
>
> . . .
>
> 4. Criminal cases.
>
> Subject to this Act and to any other law, custom may be taken into account in a criminal case only for the purpose of -
>
> (a) ascertaining the existence or otherwise of a state of mind of a person; or
>
> (b) deciding the reasonableness or otherwise of an act, default or omission by a person; or
>
> (c) deciding the reasonableness or otherwise of an excuse; or
>
> (d) deciding, in accordance with any other law whether to proceed to the conviction of a guilty party; or
>
> (e) determining the penalty (if any) to be imposed on a guilty party,
>
> or where the court thinks that by not taking the custom into account injustice will or may be done to a person.
>
> 5. Civil cases.

[160] See, for example, PNG Law Reform Commission, *The Role of Customary Law in the Legal System* (Port Moresby: Government Printer, 1977), p 9. The *Village Courts Act* 1989 also deals with situations where custom may apply, but is not relevant to the matters considered in this chapter.

> Subject to this Act and to any other law, custom may be taken into account in a case other than a criminal case only in relation to -
>
> (a) the ownership by custom of or of rights in, over or in connexion with customary land or -
>
> (i) any thing in or on customary land or -
>
> (ii) the produce of, customary land,
>
> including rights of hunting or gathering; or
>
> (b) the ownership by custom of rights in, over or in connexion with the sea or a reef, or in or on the bed of the sea or of a river or lake, including rights of fishing; or
>
> (c) the ownership by custom of water, or of rights in, over or to water, or
>
> (d) the devolution of customary land or of rights in, over or in connexion with customary land, whether -
>
> (i) on the death or on the birth of a person; or
>
> (ii) on the happening of a certain event; or
>
> (e) trespass by animals; or
>
> (f) marriage, divorce or the right to the custody or guardianship of infants, in a case arising out of or in connexion with a marriage entered into in accordance with custom; or
>
> (g) a transaction that -
>
> (i) the parties intended should be; or
>
> (ii) justice requires should be,
>
> regulated wholly or partly by custom and not by law; or
>
> (h) the reasonableness or otherwise of an act, default or omission by a person; or
>
> (i) the existence of a state of mind of a person,
>
> or where the court thinks that by not taking the custom into account injustice will or may be done to a person."

The Act also makes provision in respect of conflict of custom (s 7), allowing the court to adopt that system of custom, or make such other order, having regard to the "ordinary rules of the underlying law" (modified as may be necessary), as the justice of the case demands.

Finally, as for the place of the underlying law in the hierarchy of laws of Papua New Guinea, both the use of the word "underlying" and its position at the end of the list of categories of law in s 9 suggest that it is intended to be at the bottom of the hierarchy. However, there is no reference to the underlying law in ss 10 and 11: the main provisions on the hierarchy of laws in the body of the *Constitution*.[161] Rather, Schs 2.1 and 2.2 deal with the issue by stating that neither custom nor

---

[161] Curiously, in an article about the underlying law, the draftsman of the Constitution cites ss 10 and 11 to support the proposition that the "underlying law must be subject to the Constitution and other Constitutional Laws and to all other statute law": C J Lynch, "The Adoption of an Underlying Law by the Constitution of Papua New Guinea" (1976) 4 *Melanesian Law Journal* 37 at 44.

common law is adopted to the extent that either is "inconsistent with a Constitutional Law or a statute".[162] There may also be a hierarchy within the underlying law, in the sense that custom might be regarded as in a sense superior to common law (an issue we return to below).

ORIGINS: WHY CUSTOM AND COMMON LAW?

The Papua New Guinea *Constitution* is in many ways a programmatic document, and as a result our understanding of particular sets of provisions can be enhanced by insights into the aims of the constitution-makers. But while the *Constitution* (s 24) encourages reference to the key documents concerning its development, there is little in those documents with direct relevance to the provisions of Sch 2 on the underlying law. Indeed it appears that the term "underlying law" and the complex arrangements in Sch 2 were developed quite late in the constitution-making process, after the Constitutional Planning Committee (CPC) had submitted its *Final Report*, and well into the parliamentary and public debates on that report. There are, however, several aspects of the CPC's *Final Report* that clearly informed the development of the underlying law provisions.

First, concerning the central role for custom envisaged by the *Constitution*, the CPC emphasised the need for reliance on "Papua New Guinean ways",[163] making that the fifth of the five National Goals that shape the *Constitution* and are intended to provide national policy. That goal requires development to be achieved "primarily through the use of Papua New Guinean forms of social, political and economic organizations". Guiding principles directed towards achievement of that goal include "traditional villages and communities to remain as viable units". Recognition of custom and its integration into modern life - inclusive of modern law - was an obvious concomitant of the fifth National Goal. The CPC saw Village Courts as providing "a suitable means of developing our traditional judicial institutions and of significantly influencing the evolution of the imposed court system *and the common law which it applies*"[164] (emphasis added). Consistent with its views on Papua New Guinean ways, in its discussion of the judiciary the CPC made it clear it wanted the law to be based on Papua New Guinea values: for example, it opposed appeals to courts outside Papua New Guinea on the basis that this "would perpetuate the incorporation in our legal system of values alien to our own".[165]

Secondly, the CPC seems to have assumed that the common law would continue to apply in post-independence Papua New Guinea, but subject to review of appropriateness to the needs of the country. This approach is clear in both the CPC views on village courts (above) and its proposals on the need to achieve a break in the pre-independence chain of legal authority through arrangements for autochthony.[166] These arrangements included provision for all pre-independence law to be repealed and adopted under the authority of a *Constitution* adopted by a representative Papua New Guinean body without legal authority from the colonial power. While the CPC would have preferred that only laws in conformity with the new *Constitution* would be adopted under it, as a practical measure it was necessary to allow time for the review of existing law. Hence it proposed that a new Law Reform Commission have two years from the coming into effect of the *Constitution* to review pre-independence laws in order to recommend repeal or

[162] There is no such provision concerning underlying law rules made by judges under Sch 2.3, perhaps because such a requirement may be implied from the inconsistency rules in respect of custom and common law as the possible sources of the underlying law that must first be inapplicable before Sch 2.3 applies.

[163] CPC, *Final Report of the Constitutional Planning Committee: Part 1* (Port Moresby: Government Printer, 1974), pp 2/12-2/15.

[164] Ibid, p 8/3/21.

[165] Ibid, p 8/3/24.

[166] Ibid, pp 15/1/1-15/2/16.

amendment of those not consistent with the new *Constitution*, and especially with the National Goals and Directive Principles and the Fundamental Human Rights provisions.[167] The common law was to be included in this brief.[168]

In an article published in 1976 the draftsman of the *Constitution* (C J Lynch) indicated that the requirements of the autochthony arrangements were a major consideration behind the unusual step of including complex provisions on the underlying law in the *Constitution* (rather than in ordinary statute law).[169] As a result, the CPC proposal for leaving it to the Law Reform Commission to recommend repeal or amendment of the common law was not implemented (although the *Constitution* does give the Law Reform Commission a role in reviewing the underlying law: see Sch 2.14).

There was debate among lawyers and policy makers about what the underlying law should comprise, some wanting just one or another variant of the common law, some wanting just custom, and others wanting a combination of custom and common law. Custom had to be included for "legal, political and practical reasons"[170] that had given rise to "the principle of 'home-grownness'".[171] In the interests of achieving a single national legal system as envisaged by the *Constitution* (s 155 and Sch 2.9), it had to be made part of any underlying law rather than a separate element.[172] However, custom "did not seem at the moment capable of covering the necessary field", in that it did not have clear rules covering the wide variety of situations that the common law had already developed.[173] As a result, a combination of custom and the already established common law system was needed.

It having been decided to include the common law, the decision on the variant of the common law to be used –(that is, the common law of England immediately prior to Independence Day) was based on its apparent advantages over the main alternatives. As a result of the differing laws on reception of the common law into the separate territories of Papua and New Guinea, there was no distinct unified Papua New Guinean common law to be adopted. There was also no single Australian common law (there being differences in the common law relevant to the *Constitution* of the Commonwealth and the common law regimes of the Australian States). Although many supported adoption of the common law "at large" (that is, "the common law considered as a single system applicable with minor modifications in various parts of the world")[174] there were dangers of situations arising where there would be "drastically different 'common law' rules on a given point in different 'common law' jurisdictions".[175]

Once it was decided that the common law of England was to be adopted, the final main issue was whether to adopt it as it existed from time to time, or to adopt it at a fixed time with a cut-off date. The main objection to the former approach was that it would have involved treating post-independence "English decisions (at least at the highest level) as being either binding or tantamount to binding"[176] on post-independence courts in Papua New Guinea, thereby offending the autochthony principle. Hence a cut-off date just prior to independence was chosen. It was

[167] Ibid, p 5/2/15.
[168] Ibid, p 15/2/16.
[169] Lynch, above n 5, p 44.
[170] Ibid, p 45.
[171] Ibid, p 54.
[172] Ibid.
[173] Ibid, p 45.
[174] Ibid.
[175] Ibid, p 47.
[176] Ibid, p 48.

agreed that in the interests of flexibility, and as with most examples of reception of the common law into a colony or post-colonial state, provision should be made for evaluation of the appropriateness of common law rules to the circumstances of Papua New Guinea. That evaluation was to relate not to the cut-off date for adoption, but to the date of the events leading to the litigation.[177]

LIMITATIONS ON THE ADOPTION OF CUSTOM UNDER SCH 2.1

Restrictions in Constitution and in Customs Recognition Act (Ch 19)

The constitutional and statutory provisions outlined above are part of a constitutional framework that limits the adoption of custom in any particular case. The reason is that under Sch 2.1(1) the adoption, application and enforcement of custom is made subject to subss (2) and (3) of Sch 2.1. Subsection (2) and the legislation for the purposes of subs (3) (the *Customs Recognition Act*) contain six main possible grounds that may be used to refuse to adopt as part of the underlying law a custom that otherwise appears to be relevant in a particular case.[178] These six grounds (three from the wording of Sch 2.1 of the *Constitution*, and three from s 3 of the *Customs Recognition Act*) are the following:

(1) inconsistency with the Constitution;

(2) inconsistency with a statute;

(3) repugnancy to the general principles of humanity;

(4) resulting in injustice;

(5) contrary to the public interest; and

(6) contrary to the best interests of a child under 16 years of age.

It is not possible here to examine each of the (often overlapping) six grounds in detail. Some relatively simple examples of decisions or judicial statements under each heading can, however, be given to illustrate the complexity of the tasks involved in adopting, applying and enforcing custom in any particular case.

Before discussing those grounds, it should also be noted that not only may s 3 of the *Customs Recognition Act* (Ch 19) be used to place significant limits on the operation of ss 4 and 5 of the Act,[179] but the terms of the latter sections (set out above) tend to restrict the application of custom. Those sections state specific circumstances (in relation to criminal cases) and certain kinds of cases (in relation to civil cases) as the only situations where custom may apply. Although both sections also contain broader enabling clauses permitting a court to apply custom where justice requires it, the wording suggests that a court would need to hear argument before turning

[177] Ibid, p 49.

[178] There is a possible additional ground that might arise by virtue of the wording of Sch 2.3(1) or Sch 2.10(1)(b)(ii), to the effect that a custom that is not disqualified under any of the established grounds might nevertheless not be "applicable and appropriate to the circumstances of the country". This issue, however, has yet to receive judicial consideration.

[179] See PNG Law Reform Commission, above n 4, pp 56-57.

to custom in any case other than those listed in the sections. If a narrow interpretation is taken of ss 4 and 5, there could then be considerable limits on the ability of a court to apply custom. For example, it could be argued that in most criminal cases there would be little basis under s 4 for considering the application of customary rules concerning evidence. This would, however, be contrary to the suggestion in the Supreme Court decision of *Uniss Kamugaip v The State* [1985] PNGLR 278 at 280 that a court considering reliance on common law principles concerning compellability of a spouse as a witness should first consider whether or not there was an applicable rule of custom. Although it is not possible to pursue this point further here, it is arguable that the Supreme Court, by not considering the wording of s 4, was incorrect on this point.

Inconsistency with the Constitution

The main necessity for this ground for not adopting custom relates to the place of the underlying law in the hierarchy of laws. Several examples will be given. In *State v Kule* [1991] PNGLR 404, a defendant who had pleaded guilty to murder wished to have taken into account, in mitigation of sentence, that he was obliged by custom to make compensation by handing over one of his young daughters to the relatives of the deceased. Doherty J[180] refused to recognise such a custom on several grounds, including that it was a practice analogous to slavery or servitude, and thus prohibited by s 253 of the *Constitution.* In *Re Wagi Non* [1991] PNGLR 84, a husband had left his wife and her four children in the care of his relatives while he travelled to another province to seek employment. After he had been absent for some years without making contact with them, the wife began a new relationship. On complaint by the husband's relatives, she was subsequently imprisoned for failure to meet a Village Court compensation order. She was freed by the National Court, on the basis that the custom in question infringed the equality provisions of s 55 of the *Constitution.* A similar result, on similar reasoning, was reached in a case involving a widow who outraged her deceased husband's relatives by beginning a new relationship: *Re Kepo Raramu* [1994] PNGLR 486. In *Re Willingal* (1997) N1506, Injia J refused to accept a custom whereby an unwilling woman was to be given in marriage as part of a complicated compensation settlement between two kin groups. A custom of this sort, according to the court, was objectionable on many grounds, including that of being in breach of the prohibition against discrimination contained in s 55,[181] and also amounted to a breach of her right to freedom under s 32 of the *Constitution.*[182] The court's general approach to the issue appears in the following passage:

> "The traditional customs of the people of Minj like the rest of PNG have existed from time immemorial and they serve complex value systems which only they themselves best know. It is not easy for any outsider to fully understand the customs and the underlying values and purposes they serve. Any outsider including the modern courts must not be quick to extract those customs and their values and pass judgments on their soundness or otherwise . . . But it is clear to me that the framers of our Constitution and modern day legislators were thinking about a modern PNG based on ethnic societies whose welfare and advancement was based on the maintenance and promotion of good traditional customs and the discouragement and elimination of bad customs as seen from the eyes of an ordinary modern Papua New Guinean. No matter how painful it may be to the small

[180] [1991] PNGLR 404 at 406-7.
[181] (1997) N1506, pp 48-49.
[182] Ibid, pp 47-48.

ethnic society concerned, such bad custom must give way to the dictates of our modern national laws."[183]

Inconsistency with a statute

Turning now to statutes, the general problem involved in determining when a custom is inconsistent with a statute will be discussed later. In relation to criminal law, it is clear from the wording of s 4 of the *Customs Recognition Act* (Ch 19) that custom is not accepted in Papua New Guinea as a complete defence to a criminal charge, although it may sometimes be taken into account in determining sentence.[184] In civil cases, a relatively straightforward example comes from the case of *Re Willingal* (1997) N1506, mentioned earlier. There, Injia J found that the practice of forced marriage infringed the provisions of s 5 of the *Marriage Act* (Ch 280).[185] Another instance, perhaps more controversial, is that of *Mura v Gigmai* (1997) N1573, where Injia J held that to consider matters relating to payment of bride price in determining the future custody of a child of the marriage would be inconsistent with certain provisions of the *Infants Act* (Ch 278).[186]

Repugnancy to the general principles of humanity

Despite the lack of a clear judicial definition of this phrase, a number of decisions have applied the principle to deny recognition of customs relating to dispossession of land in tribal fighting, cannibalism, and payback killings or injuries.[187] More recently, the National Court has found that the general principles of humanity forbid the forced marriage of a woman (*Re Willingal* (1997) N1506, pp 50-51). Again, in *Re Kaka Ruk* [1991] PNGLR 105, Woods J held that the same principles invalidated a custom which prevented a wife from starting a new life by moving away from the husband's relatives, despite the husband's absence and failure to provide for her for some time.[188] A final illustration is the case of *Ubuk v Darius* [1994] PNGLR 279, in which the court applied this ground in refusing to countenance a Mailan (Siassi) custom that ensured automatic custody of children to the father, in the event of the breakdown of an informal relationship between the parents. In the words of Sevua J:

> "Whether one views it subjectively or objectively, the woman is a sex object. So where is the morality and value of humanity in this woman? . . . How does a woman in such a situation free herself from this seemingly sexual domination? I consider the Mailan customs repugnant to the general principles of humanity and, therefore, inapplicable to the present case. The applicant can gain no assistance from that customary law."[189]

---

[183] Ibid, pp 51-52 and 54-55. In the event, the court found it unnecessary (p 49) to consider whether the relevant custom also infringed other provisions in the *Constitution*, such as s 36 (freedom from inhuman treatment), s 42 (liberty of the person), s 49 (right to privacy), and s 52(1) (freedom of movement).

[184] For an example of where the court refused to take a custom of payback into account, see *State v Nerius and Tingas* (1982) N397.

[185] (1997) N1506, pp 47 and 49.

[186] (1997) N1573, p 7. For earlier discussion of the issue, see O Jessep and J Luluaki, *Principles of Family Law in Papua New Guinea* (Port Moresby: 2nd ed, UPNG Press, 1994), pp144-46.

[187] See, for example, *Wena Kaigo v Siwi Kurondo* [1976] PNGLR 34; *State v Aubafo Feama* [1978] PNGLR 301; *Aundak Kupil v State of Papua New Guinea* [1983] PNGLR 350; *Public Prosecutor v Apava Keru and Aia Moroi* [1985] PNGLR 78; and *Public Prosecutor v Sidney Kerua and Billy Kerua* [1985] PNGLR 85.

[188] [1991] PNGLR 105 at 107.

[189] [1994] PNGLR 279 at 283-84.

Resulting in injustice

A growing body of human rights jurisprudence in the National Court has in recent years also used the criteria set out in s 3 of the *Customs Recognition Act* (Ch 19) as alternative or additional grounds on which to object to customary practices, especially those which discriminate against women or children. The previously mentioned case of *Re Willingal* (1997) N1506, for instance, also referred to this provision, saying that it would be unjust for any woman from Minj to live under the threat of a forced marriage, while "men from Minj and other men and women in other parts of Papua New Guinea live, associate and marry freely".[190] In *Aundak Kupil v State of Papua New Guinea* [1983] PNGLR 350 at 361 enforcement of a customary claim for compensation to the exclusion of a common law claim for negligence was rejected as likely to promote injustice. (That case is discussed in detail later.)

Contrary to the public interest

For similar reasons, the same court in *Re Willingal* (1997) N1506 found that the custom of forced marriage of a woman would be contrary to the public interest.[191] This principle was also referred to as an alternative ground in *State v Kule* [1991] PNGLR 404 at 406, where the court refused to reduce a criminal sentence to reflect the fact that a child of the defendant was expected to be transferred by way of customary compensation to the victim's kin group. The principle was also a ground for rejection of the customary claim in *Aundak Kupil v State of Papua New Guinea* [1983] PNGLR 350 at 361.

Contrary to the best interests of a child under 16 years of age

As further indication of the frequently overlapping nature of the grounds in s 3 of the *Customs Recognition Act* (Ch 19), the court in *State v Kule* [1991] PNGLR 404 at 406 also used this ground to reject the custom whereby a young child was to be part of a compensation arrangement between the families of the defendant and the victim.

The universality doctrine: Must custom be common throughout the country?

So far, we have given some simple illustrations of the way in which the courts in Papua New Guinea have been prepared to apply constitutional and statutory provisions to restrict the application of custom or prevent its adoption in particular cases. We now turn to a judicial view that would, if applied generally, constitute a more far-reaching obstacle to the adoption of custom. This view was referred to and debated in cases up to 1981, but (with one exception) has received no judicial attention since then.

---

190 (1997) N1506, p 50.

191 Ibid.

The case law to 1981

In *Poisi Tatut v Chris Cassimus; Constitutional Reference No 1 of 1977* [1978] PNGLR 295, the plaintiff husband had brought an action for enticement, apparently based on common law, in the District Court at Rabaul. The magistrate formed the view that the common law action, having been abolished by statute in England in 1970, was not part of the underlying law under Sch 2.2 of the *Constitution* (see next section for discussion of this aspect). The case was therefore referred to the Supreme Court to determine what law should be applied pursuant to Sch 2.3.

By the time the case reached the Supreme Court, the dispute had virtually been resolved between the parties. Consequently, the court was denied the benefit of detailed argument on the issues. Saldanha J agreed with the magistrate that the common law action was not part of the underlying law, but pointed out that the magistrate had apparently overlooked Sch 2.1, by which custom is also part of the underlying law.[192] In the absence of evidence of custom (which Saldanha J expected could have been found), Saldanha J was unwilling to formulate a rule of law under Sch 2.3.[193] In any event, he concluded, Parliament was in a better position than the court to formulate new law on such a topic.

It seems as if Saldanha J regarded local custom as eligible to be applied under Sch 2.1, a result obviously consistent with the definition of "custom" in Sch 1.2, quoted earlier, which is quite specific as to place and time. Strangely, however, Prentice CJ took a markedly different approach, saying that "having regard to Sch 2.4", custom in Sch 2.1 must mean "custom obtaining throughout the country".[194] Further, since the evidence in the magistrate's court did not resolve the issue about the ubiquity of custom, either one way or the other, and hence it was not clear whether there was a relevant custom to be applied under Sch 2.1, it would not at this stage be appropriate for the court to intervene under Sch 2.3. For that matter, Parliament might be expected to act on the matter in the near future.[195]

Raine Dep CJ, unhelpfully, stated his agreement[196] with both of the other judgments, and in the result the magistrate was directed to enter a verdict for the defendant. It is therefore hard to know what part of the court's reasoning would have been regarded as binding in later cases.

Further difference of judicial opinion on the point is evident in the case concerning the sending of Papua New Guinea troops to Vanuatu for a peacekeeping operation. In *Supreme Court Reference No 4 of 1980* [1981] PNGLR 265, Michael Somare as leader of the Opposition sought to challenge the constitutional validity of a parliamentary decision and an Act of the Parliament approving the commitment of troops to Vanuatu.

The decision in this case dealt merely with the petitioner's standing to challenge the actions of the Parliament. By a majority of three to two (Kidu CJ, Kapi and Miles JJ; Kearney Dep CJ and Greville-Smith J dissenting), the Supreme Court held that the petitioner did have standing. The court reached this result by formulating a new rule of underlying law under Sch 2.3 to deal with

---

192 [1978] PNGLR 295 at 299-300.
193 Ibid at 300.
194 Ibid at 297.
195 Ibid at 298.
196 Ibid at 299.

standing, based on the petitioner's status as a member of the Parliament and as a citizen of Papua New Guinea.

Of interest to the present discussion is the court's approach to the meaning of "custom" in Sch 2.1. As a preliminary matter, four of the judges considered (and rejected) the petitioner's claim to standing based on his position as a "big man" according to custom. This claim was raised both in relation to Sch 2.1, as to whether there was a custom which enabled a "big man" to speak in any forum, and also in relation to Sch 2.3(1)(c), as to whether a new rule of underlying law should be declared by analogy with custom.

Kidu CJ refused to apply custom directly under Sch 2.1, because he felt that such a custom, if it existed, would breach the equality provisions of s 55 of the *Constitution*.[197] As to Sch 2.3(1)(c), Kidu CJ stated that evidence would be needed that the majority of the provinces of Papua New Guinea had such a custom.[198] In the absence of such evidence, he then turned to the other matters listed in Sch 2.3(1) to help him formulate the new rule of underlying law.[199]

Greville-Smith J, dissenting, observed that the petitioner had failed to establish evidence of any customary rights of leaders "of sufficient universality",[200] this comment apparently being directed to the application of Sch 2.1. Since the judge decided that the common law rules were adequate for the purpose at hand, and fatal to the application, he had little to say about the application of Sch 2.3.[201]

Miles J also found that the petitioner had not proved any relevant custom that could be applied and enforced under Sch 2.1. The evidence adduced related mainly to the rights of East Sepik "big men" in traditional forums, and did not resolve the question in the instant proceedings.[202] In discussing the proper approach to be taken by the court in regard to custom and the development of the underlying law, Miles J stated:

> "I would take a very liberal view as to the admissibility of evidence relating to custom. I expect that most courts in the country would need all available assistance to inform themselves on relevant custom, particularly if it be, as suggested in [*Poisi Tatut v Chris Cassimus; Constitutional Reference No 1 of 1977*] that it is only nationwide custom that is to be adopted as part of the underlying law under Sch 2.1.[203] . . . If a court is to adopt, apply and enforce a particular custom as a rule of law under Sch 2.1, it should only do so after it has fully informed itself as to the precise nature and extent of that particular custom. If analogy with custom is to be used to formulate a rule of law in accordance with Sch 2.3(1)(c), then it need not be 'proved' at all. It is clear that custom for the purposes of Sch 2.3 is quite different from custom for the purposes of Sch 2.1."[204]

---

[197] [1981] PNGLR 265 at 271. It is not clear which part of s 55 was being referred to by Kidu CJ in this comment. Section 55(1), so far as relevant, provides that "all citizens have the same rights, privileges, obligations and duties irrespective of race, tribe, place of origin, political opinion, colour, creed, religion or sex". If Kidu CJ had in mind differences based on "tribe" or "place of origin", a similar objection might arguably apply to many customs from most provinces; that is, that the customs are different to those found elsewhere. On the other hand, Kidu CJ might have been objecting to a custom pertaining to "big men" in contrast to women; that is, discrimination on the basis of sex. For a further comment on s 55 in relation to custom, see O Jessep and J Luluaki, *Principles of Family Law in Papua New Guinea*, (Port Moresby: 2nd ed, UPNG Press, 1994), p 17.

[198] Ibid at 272.

[199] Ibid at 272-74.

[200] Ibid ar 280.

[201] Ibid at 280-81 and 284.

[202] Ibid at 305.

[203] As noted, this was the view of Prentice CJ in the earlier case ([1978] PNGLR 295 at 297-98), although arguably Saldahna J took a different approach (at 300).

[204] [1981] PNGLR 265 at 304.

The most detailed discussion of Sch 2 appears in the judgment of Kapi J. He clearly rejected the requirement that custom under Sch 2.1 must always be common or widespread throughout the country. After referring to the definition of "custom" in Sch 1.2, he continued:

> "The first difficulty that arises is that the indigenous inhabitants of this country have different customs applying in various matters. Where parties come from the same custom area there is no difficulty as the custom would apply to both. However there is a difficulty when the parties before the court are from different custom areas or where the subject matter before the court is a national matter or a national issue. The question then arises as to what is the custom applicable . . . In my view before a custom is adopted and enforced as part of the underlying law under Sch 2.1 of the Constitution, it must be established that a custom which the court proposes to adopt as law is recognised and extends to both parties. In a case which involves an issue which has a general application to the whole country such as whether the leader of the Opposition has locus standi as in this case, it must be established that there is a custom which is common to all societies throughout the country. Custom as is referred to under Sch 2.1 of the Constitution is not created by the court but is discovered as a matter of fact and adopted as law."[205]

It will be seen that although Kapi J reached the same conclusion as Kidu CJ and Miles J, and the petitioner's evidence as to custom was not acceptable for the purposes of Sch 2.1 and was also insufficient to provide relevant analogies for the purposes of Sch 2.3, for Kapi J this was only because the issue at stake was a matter of national rather than local importance. It would consequently follow, on Kapi J's reasoning, that in any dispute of a local character, proof of merely local custom is all that would be required for purposes of Sch 2.1. Further, since Kapi J also indicated in a later passage his awareness of what is now s 7 of the *Customs Recognition Act* (Ch 19), which allows the court to deal with conflicts between two or more applicable customs,[206] the statement in the above passage that the custom must extend to both parties should accordingly be modified to take this into account.

Other views on universality

From the two cases discussed, it would seem that at least three judges (Prentice CJ, Miles and Greville-Smith JJ) supported the view that custom under Sch 2.1 should be common to the country. A similar point of view was put forward by the General Constitutional Commission in its 1983 *Final Report*. The Commission recommended as follows:[207]

> "3.18 Schedule 2.1
>
> We recommend that the reference 'custom' in Schedule 2.1 be clarified. Any custom which is proposed to be adopted under the schedule must be a custom that is recognised throughout Papua New Guinea as a matter of fact and should not include local custom or custom that applies only to some or certain parts of the country. Although the courts have recognised qualifications for custom that is to be adopted under Schedule 2.1, we make this recommendation, nevertheless, because it is not clear whether custom must be a custom prevailing throughout Papua New Guinea or not."

---

205 Ibid at 288.
206 Ibid at 289-90.
207 PNG General Constitutional Commission, *Final Report* (Port Moresby: 1983), p 297.

Unfortunately, the Report contains no explanation or discussion relating to this recommendation. Indeed, while consistent with the views of several Supreme Court judges, the Commission's view sits strangely with two other opinions it expressed: that insufficient materials and evidence on custom were being presented to the judges for consideration, and that little progress had been made towards a Papua New Guinea legal system more responsive to the customs and perceptions of the people.[208] That is to say, if the above recommendation was to be implemented, it is difficult to see how the Commission's other two complaints could ever be rectified. By contrast, the 1977 report of the Papua New Guinea Law Reform Commission - *The Role of Customary Law in the Legal System* - not only welcomed the diversity of custom,[209] but also clearly envisaged its localised application.

Universality: Demise or revival?

For a number of years after the *Somare* decision (*Supreme Court Reference No 4 of 1980* [1981] PNGLR 265), the issue of universality of custom under Sch 2.1 of the *Constitution* was not specifically raised before the National Court. Rather, in numerous cases the National Court has applied custom (or at least discussed its applicability) without reference to the universality principle. The numerous examples of such National Court decisions involving parties from the same custom group include *Aundak Kupil v State of Papua New Guinea* [1983] PNGLR 350 and *Pawa Kombea v Semal Peke* [1994] PNGLR 572. An example of a Supreme Court decision concerning a claim by customary landowners against an "outside" entity - the state - can be seen in *Madaha Resena v State of Papua New Guinea* [1991] PNGLR 174. (These cases are all discussed in some detail below.) Indeed it is fair to say that the universality doctrine was in practice disregarded and forgotten.

In 1996, however, the issue resurfaced. In *Kolta Development v Papua New Guinea Defence Force and the State* (1996) N1470, the plaintiff companies had been involved in running the Germania Club in Port Moresby. After a fight broke out at the club on the evening of 2 April 1993 between civilians and soldiers, further hostilities off the premises led to the death of a soldier. In retaliation, so the court found,[210] a group of soldiers left their barracks in the early hours of the next morning and burnt the club premises to the ground. The several plaintiffs subsequently sued the Papua New Guinea Defence Force and the state, claiming damages for the destruction of the club premises. The statement of claim was based both on custom and on the common law of negligence. While both aspects of the suit were ultimately unsuccessful, of interest here is the way in which the court treated the customary claim.

According to Salika J, the plaintiffs' case in custom was presented on the basis that the destruction of the property was to be regarded as a customary wrong, and since the identity of the individual soldiers responsible for the fire was not known, the group to which the individuals belonged was liable to pay compensation.[211] In other words, "the defendants are liable for the acts of destruction committed by its employees, namely the soldiers".[212] In support of their arguments, the plaintiffs presented evidence of custom from the Mt Hagen and Kairuku areas of Papua New

[208] [1981] PNGLR 265 at 278-79.

[209] The report notes that "customary law is a flexible system of law which may be different from place to place and from time to time": PNG Law Reform Commission, above n 4, p 17, note 3.

[210] (1996) N1470, p 3.

[211] Ibid, p 8.

[212] Ibid, p 7.

Guinea.[213]

In response, the defendants argued that the court was bound by the decision in the *Somare* case (*Supreme Court Reference No 4 of 1980* [1981] PNGLR 265), and that therefore the plaintiffs' claim must fail since they had only presented evidence of custom from two provinces. In substance, the court agreed and dismissed the plaintiffs' customary claim:

> "The position is that the plaintiffs must establish that the custom upon which they base their claim is prevalent or commonly practised in at least the majority of the provinces in the country . . . The *Somare* decision is a Supreme Court decision and is binding on the National Court . . . I am of the view that there is a lot of common sense in what the Supreme Court said in the *Somare Case* in respect of adoption of custom from a majority of provinces for the whole of the country, especially when there are so many varying customs in the country . . . [The plaintiffs] cannot simply call witnesses from only two provinces and assert that customs in those two provinces are common throughout the country . . . I therefore cannot apply the customs of two provinces to all the 19 provinces nationwide."[214]

In addition, the court went on to find other reasons for the failure of the customary claim. Having referred to the terms of ss 3 and 5 of the *Customs Recognition Act* (Ch 19), Salika J (somewhat surprisingly) concluded that to accept the notion of group responsibility or "no fault liability" relied on by the plaintiffs "would cause grave injustice and is not in the best interest of the public".[215] Further, in light of the definition of "custom" in Sch 1.2 of the *Constitution*, it was difficult to see how the customs of Mt Hagen and Kairuku could apply to the Papua New Guinea Defence Force and the State of Papua New Guinea, since those two defendants were not "indigenous inhabitants of the country". That is to say:

> "While it is accepted that customs do change over a period of time it has not been shown in this case that the customs of the Western Highlands and the Kairuku people in the Central Province extend to the defendants. If those customs are not used or practised by the defendants, why should those customs apply to the defendants."[216]

We cannot here examine all of the reasons given by Salika J for his decision, but it would seem that at least a major justification for rejecting the claim was the failure of the plaintiffs, as in the *Somare* case, to lead evidence of an appropriate nationwide custom. It may nevertheless be suggested, by applying the approach of Kapi J in the earlier decision ([1981] PNGLR 265 at 288), that the facts in *Kolta Developments* are very different to that of a customary dispute between parties from the same locality, or a dispute involving two or more systems of local custom. It may be accepted, at least hypothetically, that elements of custom could have some relevance even in a context involving corporations, commercial leases, beer, soldiers and a Chinese restaurant. Nevertheless, it is certainly not clear why Mt Hagen or Kairuku custom as such should automatically apply in Port Moresby, unless the parties themselves owed some allegiance to these relevant customs. Further, the question of whether a particular custom might be applicable to national organisations like the Papua New Guinea Defence Force or the State of Papua New

---

[213] Ibid, p 8.

[214] Ibid, p 10.

[215] Ibid, p 13. Although the court did not mention the point, it is also not clear how the plaintiffs brought their claim within the wording of s 5 of the *Customs Recognition Act* (Ch 19), except perhaps via the concluding words of the section ("or where the court thinks that by not taking the custom into account injustice will or may be done to a person").

[216] Ibid, p 14.

Guinea itself is a complex one, and raises issues analogous to the matter of national importance underlying the decision in the *Somare* case. On these facts, therefore, the earlier analysis of Kapi J may be equally apposite to require evidence of a more widespread and prevalent custom for purposes of Sch 2.1. This conclusion would not then compel anything like the same approach in other customary cases of merely local significance.

Differing judicial views on universality: summary

In summary, the position is that while minorities in two Supreme Court decisions (Prentice CJ in *Poisi Tatut* and Greville Smith J in *Somare*) supported the universality doctrine clearly, they were opposed by minorities with equally strong views (Saldanha J in *Poisi Tatut* and Kapi J in *Somare*). There was no clear majority for either view of the doctrine in *Poisi Tatut,* given that the third judge (Raine Dep CJ) apparently agreed with the (opposing) views of the other two members of the bench. The opinion of Miles J in support of the doctrine in *Somare* was apparently based on his assumption that *Poisi Tatut* supported the universality doctrine, and so his views do not provide a strong endorsement for the doctrine. From 1981 until 1996 the doctrine was ignored until applied by the National Court in *Kolta,* but this application was ostensibly based on the (erroneous) view that there was a binding ruling on the universality doctrine in *Somare.*

The subtlest analysis is that of Kapi J in *Somare*, where he suggests different approaches should be taken in three main sets of circumstances. First, where the parties in a case are from the same custom area, local custom should apply. Secondly, where parties are from different custom areas, custom may apply only if the same custom applies in both areas, or if not, the court may apply whichever custom (modified as may be necessary) suits the justice of the case (*Customs Recognition Act* (Ch 19), s 7). Thirdly, in cases involving issues of "general application to the whole country", custom should apply only if it is virtually universal. While there has not been a clear Supreme Court ruling on the point, in all post-1981 decisions, with the exception of *Kolta*, the approach of Kapi J appears to have been accepted.

Possible explanations for the universality doctrine

What explanation could there be for even the limited support that has been extended to this apparent doctrine of universality of custom under Sch 2.1? After all, it is a notion so obviously out of step with not only the definition of "custom" in Sch 1.2, but also the terms of s 5 of the *Customs Recognition Act* (Ch 19), both provisions being clearly directed to enabling the recognition of local custom in particular civil cases. If the universality doctrine did apply, how could Village Courts, and Local and even District Courts, be expected to continue to operate, since these courts are very frequently (and in the Village Courts constantly) called upon to resolve disputes arising from local custom?

One possibility is that the judges who insisted that custom should be common or at least widespread throughout the country were making assumptions about the later consequences of adopting custom as part of the underlying law in a particular case. That is to say, they may have felt that once custom was so adopted, it would thereafter as part of the underlying law be a binding precedent, applying automatically throughout the country, overriding any contrary custom (and also common law rules by virtue of Sch 2.2(1)(c)), and would thus be available to claimants in every province. For this reason, it may have been thought to be unjust to so adopt a custom that pertained in only one part of the country, since this would have the effect of inflicting it upon the rest of the country. If this suggestion has any plausibility, it must nevertheless be said at once that none of the judges favouring the "universality" requirement have made the point explicitly. Further, as will become clear in the later part of this chapter, it is also not the prevailing view as to how Sch 2.1 is supposed to operate. That is to say, rulings applying custom are not necessarily intended to stand as binding precedents.

CAN CUSTOM BE APPLIED OTHERWISE THAN AS PART OF THE UNDERLYING LAW?

Another possibility is that these judges felt that custom as applied in lower courts such as Village Courts or Local Courts, or as applied in any court by virtue of a particular statute, is somehow different in kind from custom as it is intended to be applied under Sch 2.1 of the *Constitution*. Ironically, given his support for the notion of local custom as generally sufficient for Sch 2.1 in the *Somare* case, just such a suggestion was made by Kapi J in *State v Robert Kupara* [1985] PNGLR 312. In that case, dealing with the relevance of the prior payment of customary compensation to the length of the sentence to be passed after a conviction for manslaughter, the court referred to s 4(e) of the *Customs Recognition Act* (Ch 19). By this subsection, custom may be taken into account in a criminal case for the purpose of "(e) determining the penalty (if any) to be imposed on a guilty party". Kapi J stated:

> "It can be seen from the circumstances I have discussed that the provision directs that a court may take into account custom in so far as it may give full explanation of the circumstances of the accused . . . As to whether or not custom is taken into account, it is limited by its relevance to these circumstances. This is altogether a different matter from recognising, enforcing or adopting custom as part of the underlying law under the *Constitution*. Custom may be taken into account on sentence without enforcing it as part of the underlying law. I discussed this in *Acting Public Prosecutor v Uname Auname* [1980] PNGLR 510 at 540-543. It follows from this reasoning that the *Customs Recognition Act*, s 3, and the *Constitution*, Sch 2.1 cannot be applicable. They are applicable where custom as such is adopted as part of the underlying law. This conclusion appears to be contrary to the reasoning of the Supreme Court in a recent decision, *Public Prosecutor v Apava Keru and Aia Moroi* [1985] PNGLR 78. The court there was considering the influence on an accused person to act in accordance with the custom of payback. Of course, I would be bound by that decision on custom of payback. However, I am here concerned with customary compensation."[217]

What Kapi J is suggesting here is that when custom is being applied by virtue of a specific statutory direction, it is not to be considered as part of the underlying law, and thus it is not necessary to go through the filtering process (that is, the six limitations mentioned earlier) contained in Sch 2.1 of the *Constitution* and s 3 of the *Customs Recognition Act*. So far as we are aware, this rather curious suggestion has not received support from any other decision. The reference by Kapi J to his own decision in *Uname Aunname* is also of little help, since Kapi J in that earlier passage ([1980] PNGLR 510 at 541 and 543, for example) appears clearly to

[217] [1985] PNGLR 312 at 315.

acknowledge the conditions for recognition of custom under what is now s 3 of the *Customs Recognition Act* (formerly s 6 of the *Native Customs (Recognition) Act* 1963) and Sch 2.1, and he does not suggest that custom can have any legal significance except by complying with those conditions. Further, given that the Supreme Court (Kidu CJ, Bredmeyer and Amet JJ) in *Public Prosecutor v Apava Keru and Aia Moroi* ([1985] PNGLR 78 at 82) specifically held that s 4(e) of the *Customs Recognition Act* is subject to s 3 of the same Act and to Sch 2.1 of the *Constitution*, the principle was directly applicable to the point which Kapi J was deciding. It is therefore impossible to see how Kapi J could have regarded the issue in his case as distinguishable.

In our view, Kapi J's suggestion must be rejected. First, it is inconsistent with the wording of Sch 2.1 itself, which gives no support to the idea of custom having any alternative legal significance, except as part of the underlying law. Secondly, with the exception of the Village Courts,[218] all courts in Papua New Guinea are bound by the terms of s 4 (in criminal cases) and ss 5 and 6 (in civil cases) of the *Customs Recognition Act*, as to the exclusive situations in which custom may be taken into account. The reasoning of Kapi J in relation to s 4(e) could equally be applied to all other subsections and paragraphs of ss 4-6, in which case the filtering mechanisms of s 3 and of Sch 2.1 would never become applicable. It is hardly surprising, then, that no other decision has pursued the same approach as that of Kapi J, and it is fair to conclude that *State v Robert Kupara* is a digression which will not be repeated. That is to say, it is the *Constitution* itself which gives custom its force and authority as part of the underlying law, and any statute which provides for proof of "custom", or the application of "custom" in a particular situation, or allows for claims based upon "custom" to be brought and determined in a particular court, can only be referring to custom as contemplated and recognised under Sch 2.1.

UNIVERSALITY: SOME CONCLUSIONS

It is notable that after *Somare* [1980] PNGLR 265 the universality doctrine virtually disappeared, with the exception of a brief re-appearance in the 1983 *Final Report* of the General Constitutional Commission, and then in the National Court decision of *Kolta Development v Papua New Guinea Defence Force and the State* (1996) N1470. So far as we know, no other cases have even mentioned the issue, and in many cases it has apparently been regarded as of no relevance; for example *Aundak Kupil v State of Papua New Guinea* [1983] PNGLR 350, *Pawa Kombea v Semal Peke* [1994] PNGLR 572 and *Madaha Resena v State of Papua New Guinea* [1991] PNGLR 174. The obvious implication is that the argument of Kapi J in the *Somare* case is now accepted by the majority of the National and Supreme Court judges. Thus, except in cases of "national importance", such as in the *Somare* case itself, custom under Sch 2.1 need not be of general application, but may be specific as to both locality and time. Whatever the requirements of generality or universality of custom when Sch 2.3 is being referred to (declaration of new rules of underlying law), no similar requirements or limitations are necessary to give proper effect to the provisions of Sch 2.1. Finally, if the gist of Sch 2.4 (need for uniformity in development of the

[218] See *Village Courts Act* 1989, s 57.

underlying law) can be said to be at all relevant to Sch 2.1, it will be satisfied if the courts pursue a consistent and uniform approach to the ascertainment and adoption of local custom in particular cases.[219]

[219] A point made some years ago by H McRae, "Reform of Family Law in Papua New Guinea - An Analysis of the Law Reform Commission's Working Paper No 9" (unpublished draft, 1979), note 22.

Chapter 10

DEVELOPING A COHERENT UNDERLYING LAW – INTEGRATING CUSTOM AND COMMON LAW IN PAPUA NEW GUINEA: PART TWO

OWEN JESSOP AND ANTHONY J REGAN

LIMITATIONS ON THE ADOPTION OF COMMON LAW UNDER SCHEDULE 2.2

We now turn to consider the role and importance of the common law as the second primary source of the underlying law of Papua New Guinea. Under Sch 2.2 of the *Constitution*, the adoption into the underlying law, and the application and enforcement of the principles and rules of English common law and equity (hereafter the common law), as at Independence Day, is subject to limitations. A common law rule that may otherwise be relevant to a particular case should not be adopted into the underlying law if any of the following limitations apply:

(a) inconsistency with the *Constitution*;

(b) inconsistency with a statute;

(c) inapplicability or inappropriateness to the circumstances of the country from time to time;

(d) inconsistency with the requirements of the cut-off date for adoption of the common law; and

(d) inconsistency with custom as adopted under Sch 2.1.

Of these limitations, the first two are relatively straightforward, relating as they do to the place of the underlying law in the hierarchy of laws, and have so far caused few problems for the courts.

Inapplicability or inappropriateness to circumstances from time to time

In deciding whether a common law rule is "inapplicable or inappropriate to the circumstances of the country from time to time" (Sch 2.2(1)(b)), a court dealing with any particular case is given assistance by Sch 2.2(4). In his 1976 analysis of the adoption of the underlying law, the draftsman of the *Constitution* outlined not only the broad aims (discussed in Chapter 9) but also the intended effect of those provisions. His analysis indicates that the provisions were intended to promote flexibility in the adoption (and application and enforcement) of the common law, taking account of changes in circumstances in relation to both time and place. This view is reflected in the wording of Sch 2.4, which according to Lynch:

> "relates applicability to the particular case, and hence recognises *geographical* as well as *temporal* applicability and inapplicability."[220]

[220] C J Lynch, "The Adoption of an Underlying Law by the Constitution of Papua New Guinea" (1976) 4 *Melanesian Law Journal* 37 at 61.

As the issues involved here are of some importance to questions about the role of the doctrine of precedent in relation to the underlying law discussed later in this chapter, they require brief elaboration. In relation to temporal applicability or inapplicability, "subsequent attraction" of a common law doctrine that was ruled inappropriate or inapplicable at the cut-off date is possible if lapse of time makes the doctrine applicable or appropriate. Similarly "subsequent rejection" is open in cases where a change of circumstances makes inappropriate or inapplicable a doctrine that was formerly appropriate or applicable.[221] More generally, Lynch talks of "dormant reception", in that "even though there is a fixed date of adoption, nonetheless there is adopted as at that date all the common law that, with changing circumstances, may later become relevant and appropriate".[222] In relation to geographical applicability or inapplicability, the idea is that appropriateness and applicability should take account of not just changes over time but also of "the fact that circumstances differ from place to place". That consideration leads to "a concept of applicability in the circumstances of the particular case".[223]

As to the "circumstances of the country from time to time" against which questions of applicability and appropriateness are evaluated under Sch 2.2, in Lynch's view that expression "must cover all relevant circumstances - physical, social, economic, legal and political".[224] As to the use of the words "inapplicable or inappropriate", Lynch was aware that the expression normally used in colonial statutes on reception of the common law was "inappropriate". In his view the addition of the word "inapplicable" added "flexibility",[225] but he did not elaborate.

Lynch accepted that uncertainty about the common law rules applying either at a particular time or in a particular case is a consequence of these provisions:

> "In this respect as in others, the *Constitution* as adopted represented a compromise between certainty (and concomitant rigidity and a degree of inappropriateness) and flexibility (with concomitant uncertainty). The general principle was relatively certain adoption and relatively wide adaptation by the courts."[226]

With evaluation required on a case-by-case basis, judicial reliance on a common law principle in a particular case does not ensure that it is necessarily a precedent that must be followed in subsequent cases. The question of applicability or appropriateness of a common law principle is always open. In many ways, therefore, the rules on common law are intended to operate in a manner similar to those concerning custom. Application and enforcement of rules from both sources of underlying law is intended to be determined on a case-by-case basis, taking cognisance of changing circumstances in relation to both time and place.

In fact, however, the provisions on applicability and appropriateness are seldom resorted to by the courts as required by Sch 2.2(1). When they are resorted to, there is little evidence that their intent (as elaborated by Lynch) has been understood. As to the extent of the use of the provisions, the general tenor of the complaint of a commentator, made a few years after independence, remains valid after more than 20 years of operation. Sakora noted that not only did courts seldom inquire into the possibility that custom might apply in a particular case, but that they also:

[221] Ibid at 50.
[222] Ibid at 51.
[223] Ibid.
[224] Ibid.
[225] Ibid at60.
[226] Ibid at 51.

> "invariably resort to the common law as their first step and once a particular principle or rule of the common law is discovered, its applicability is accepted as a matter of course. The real question as to whether or not a particular common law rule or principle, though applicable, is appropriate to the circumstances of PNG rarely warrants as much as a mention."[227]

There have been few cases where the courts have dealt with the issues of inapplicability and inappropriateness. Case-by-case evaluation has not occurred. Even in the 1990s, in the vast majority of cases where common law rules are considered or applied, the question of applicability and appropriateness is simply not mentioned.[228] There has been no development of principles that might guide the processes involved in such an evaluation. In most of the few cases where the issue is mentioned, it is dealt with in the most perfunctory manner. For example in *Wahgi Savings and Loan Society Ltd v Bank of South Pacific Ltd* (1980) SC185, Kapi J said:

> "It has not been argued in this case that the common law principles . . . are inapplicable or inappropriate to the circumstances of the country. I consider that these principles are applicable in the circumstances of the country."[229]

The cases where reasons have been given for either a positive or negative decision on applicability or appropriateness have been few and widely separated, and provide little evidence of the systematic evaluation envisaged by Sch 2.2.[230] Prevailing practice and some of its consequences are summarised by Amet J in *Madaha Resena v State of Papua New Guinea* [1991] PNGLR 174 at 190-91, where having observed that the applicability and appropriateness "pre-condition" to adoption of common law rules is very seldom applied, he noted that it was also not as easily applied as those concerning inconsistency with written law or custom:

> "[O]ften parties and courts pay lip service to this pre-condition . . . [W]hat theoretically takes place is a cursory consideration of the prevailing circumstances of the socio-economic and legal order in urban areas which often bear no real relevance to the circumstances of the majority of the indigenous inhabitants of Papua New Guinea. The inapplicability and inappropriateness pre-condition is applied to this status quo. No real consideration of the Preamble and the National Goals and Directive Principles of the *Constitution* is applied to the adopted English common law. Consequently, the courts . . . perpetuate the status quo of continued 'dependency' upon and 'subservience' to the Anglo-Australian common law and equity, the very danger which the CPC cautioned against."

---

[227] "Judicial Law-making under the Papua New Guinea Constitution" in P Sack (ed), *Pacific Constitutions* (Canberra: ANU, 1982), pp 265-66. Sakora's comments suggest a clear distinction between the concepts of "applicability" and "appropriateness", leading to two separate steps in the judicial process of evaluating a common law rule. Apparently the former would involve determining the general "fit" of the common law rule being considered, as to whether it was capable of being applied to the situation before the court. By contrast, the latter concept would involve the value judgments about suitability to the circumstances of Papua New Guinea. However, there seems little need for such a distinction. Irrespective of the wording of Sch 2.2(1)(b), a court has available for possible application all common law rules operating at the cut-off date. The comments by Lynch (above n 1, p 61) about the additional flexibility involved in the use of both the terms "inapplicable" and "inappropriate" indicate that there was no intention for Sch 2.2(1)(b) to be interpreted as Sakora suggests.

[228] For example, our review of cases reported in the 1995 volume of the *Papua New Guinea Law Reports* indicates that the issue was not raised in any case relying upon or referring to common law rules.

[229] (1980) SC185, p 21. For a more recent example where the issues have been dealt with in a similarly perfunctory manner, see *Pawa Kombea v Semal Peke* [1994] PNGLR 572 at 574, where Kapi Dep CJ said of a common law principle: "As there is no relevant custom and no issue was raised about the applicability and appropriateness of principles of common law, it will be adopted as part of the underlying law."

[230] See, for example, Prentice Dep CJ in *Paul Aika v Caspar Uremany* [1976] PNGLR 46 at 54-55, Saldanha J in *Jacob Prai and Otto Ondawame* [1979] PNGLR 1 at 9, and *State v Uniss Kamugaip* [1985] PNGLR 278 at 280-81.

Inconsistency with the requirements of the cut-off date in Schedule 2.2

A cut-off date exists, in that Sch 2.2 specifies that the common law adopted is that of England "immediately before Independence Day" (16 September 1975). Two distinct issues have arisen in the interpretation of the cut-off date provisions. The first issue concerns post-independence decisions of English courts modifying the common law as it stood at the cut-off date. The second concerns the effect on earlier English common law rules of pre-independence English statutes purporting to revise them.

Effect of English case law on the common law adopted in Papua New Guinea

It would be expected that one consequence of the cut-off date would be that the only decisions of the English courts with anything approaching binding effect under Sch 2.2 would be those made before Independence Day. Later decisions might well be referred to for their persuasive value when developing the underlying law (especially under Sch 2.3(1)(d)) but would not otherwise be relied upon. This view was propounded strongly by Kearney J in *State v Allan Woila* [1978] PNGLR 99 at 103. However, while the practice has been criticised by some judges,[231] it is far from uncommon for the courts to rely on post-independence decisions of both English and Australian courts, without first considering whether or not they are importable under Sch 2.3.[232] Further, in a number of cases Papua New Guinea courts have reached conclusions that can result in post-independence English decisions being treated as binding in Papua New Guinea. The issues have been analysed by Srivastava and Roebuck,[233] and so are merely summarised here.The Papua New Guinea decisions discussed by Srivastava and Roebuck all involved post-independence decisions of English superior courts that made significant changes to the common law as decided in pre-1975 English decisions. Each case turned on variations of one issue: whether the post-independence English decisions were supposedly correcting mistakes in the pre-independence common law, rather than developing it. Both Kapi J (in *State v Bisket Uranguae Pokia* (1980) N248) and Miles J (in *Vian Guatal v Papua New Guinea* [1981] PNGLR 230) took the view that post-independence English decisions that corrected mistaken pre-independence decisions should be followed in Papua New Guinea. In *Wahgi Savings and Loan Society Ltd v Bank of South Pacific Ltd* (1980) SC185, Kapi J, while not discussing explicitly the distinction between correcting errors and development of the common law, still took the view that:

> "[I]f after independence the House of Lords or any other competent court in England declares the decision of a lower court to be bad, the courts here would follow the decision."[234]

[231] See, for example, Kapi J in *Iambakey Okuk v Fallscheer* [1980] PNGLR 274 at 280, and Amet J in *Madaha Resena v State of Papua New Guinea* [1991] PNGLR 174 at 190-91.

[232] See *Wawa Trading Co Pty Ltd v Lie Tat Swie Lie* [1982] PNGLR 375, discussed by D K Srivastava and M J Le Brun, "Development and underdevelopment of the underlying law in Papua New Guinea: A critique of State v Kamugaip" (1985) 1(3) *Pacific Law Digest* 3 at 4-5. For a more recent example, see *Golue Pagau v MVIT* [1992] PNGLR 26 at 28, where Woods J followed post-independence English decisions that changed the law concerning calculation of damages in dependency claims arising in negligence actions.

[233] D Srivastava and D Roebuck, "The Reception of the Common Law and Equity in Papua New Guinea: The Problem of the Cut-Off Date" (1985) 34 *International and Comparative Law Quarterly* 850.

[234] (1980) SC185, p 19.

There are difficulties with these decisions. To begin with, in *State v Bisket Uranguae Pokia* the post-independence English decision was by the Privy Council on an appeal from Hong Kong,[235] and so strictly was not a decision binding even on English courts. More importantly, it is often difficult to see the distinction between correcting mistakes in and developing the common law, especially as the English courts have no need to make such a distinction when deciding cases (a point made by Miles J in *Vian Guatal v Papua New Guinea* [1981] PNGLR 230 at 244-45).

The practical problems involved were highlighted in *Vian Guatal*, during which the Papua New Guinea National Court adjourned for some time to await the outcome of a House of Lords hearing of an appeal from the decision of the post-1975 English lower court on the point of common law under consideration in the National Court (a bizarre situation for an autochthonous legal system, and one that could cause severe practical problems). The 1985 decision of the Supreme Court in *State v Uniss Kamugaip* [1985] PNGLR 278 illustrates other problems. Without referring to the relevant English cases, the Supreme Court stated a view of the common law principle on the compellability of spouses in criminal cases set down in a 1930 decision of the English Court of Criminal Appeal that had been overruled by the House of Lords in 1978, some years before the Supreme Court reached its decision in *Kamugaip.*[236] If the decisions in *Pokia*, *Wahgi Savings and Loan Society Ltd* and *Vian Guatal* are correct, and if the 1978 English decision can be said to be "correcting" the pre-independence common law decision, then the decision in *Kamugaip* may well be incorrect in neglecting to follow the 1978 English case.[237]

Srivastava and Roebuck note two possible arguments in favour of the approaches in *Pokia, Wahgi Savings and Loan Society Ltd* and *Vian Guatal.* First, it may be claimed that it would be "unthinkable to take the common law from England in an incorrect form when it has been corrected later".[238] The authors suggest, in answer to this hypothetical objection, that if an unsatisfactory common law rule is being considered for adoption under Sch 2.1, it can be modified by judicial development of the underlying law under Sch 2.3. It should be noted, however, that this will only be possible if in the particular case there is no applicable rule of custom, and if it has first been determined that the relevant common law rule should not be adopted (for example, because it is inappropriate or inapplicable to the circumstances of the country at the time). Only when that has occurred would Sch 2.3 permit examination of decisions of courts of countries with similar legal systems, including post-independence decisions of the English courts.

The second possible argument noted by Srivastava and Roebuck is that uncertainty would arise if it were necessary to wait for Papua New Guinean courts to use Sch 2.3 to propound rules of the underlying law correcting obvious mistakes in the common law. But, as the authors point out, such uncertainty is built into the constitutional requirements for the underlying law, which are directed towards development of a home-grown system of laws designed to meet the present circumstances of the country. The authors go on to suggest that the basic reason for the continued heavy reliance on the common law is the training of lawyers and judges. While that criticism is no doubt valid, we would also suggest that the complexity of the entire scheme of the underlying law in Sch 2 is an additional important factor.

---

[235] *Wong Kam-ming v The Queen* [1979]1 All ER 939, overruling *R v Hammond* [1941] 3 All ER 318.

[236] See *R v Lapworth* [1930] All ER Rep 340 and *Hoskyn v Commissioner of Police for the Metropolis* [1978] 2 All ER 136.

[237] The issues involved here are discussed in more detail in A J Regan, "Competence and Compellability of the Spouse of the Accused as a Witness in Criminal Proceedings in Papua New Guinea" (1997) 25 *Melanesian Law Journal* 87 at 102-107.

[238] Above n 48, p 856.

English statutory revisions of common law adopted in Papua New Guinea

As for situations where the English common law has been affected by a pre-independence English statute, Sch 2.2(3) states that the principles and rules of common law and equity are adopted under Sch 2.2(1) and (2):

> "notwithstanding any revision of them by any statute of England that does not apply in the country by virtue of Section Sch 2.6 (*adoption of pre-Independence laws*)."

The first case to consider the effect of a pre-independence statute on the reception in Papua New Guinea of the common law was the Supreme Court decision of *Poisi Tatut v Chris Cassimus; Constitutional Reference No 1 of 1977* [1978] PNGLR 295. There, the District Court magistrate in Rabaul formed the view that the common law action of enticement, having been abolished in England in 1970 by the *Law Reform (Miscellaneous Provisions) Act* 1970 (UK), was not part of the common law adopted under Sch 2.2 at independence. In the Supreme Court, following a reference from the magistrate, Prentice CJ and Saldanha J each agreed with the magistrate on this point,[239] and Raine Dep CJ concurred.[240]

Unfortunately, the judges in *Poisi Tatut* did not give any reasons for their conclusion and did not make any reference to the terms of Sch 2.2(3). It is possible that they had in mind the opening words of Sch 2.2, and considered that the statutory abolition (as opposed to revision of) the common law action meant that it did not form part of "the principles and rules that formed, *immediately before Independence Day*, the principles and rules of common law and equity in England" (emphasis added). Subsequent case law, however, has thrown doubt on the correctness of the holding in *Poisi Tatut* (1978), and highlighted two sources of ambiguity which arise from the wording of Sch 2.2(3). The first of these confusions is the meaning of the word "notwithstanding"; that is:

> "The principles and rules of common law and equity are adopted . . . notwithstanding any revision of them by any statute of England."

The second ambiguity concerns the meaning of the word "revision", and whether this includes, or is meant to be clearly distinguishable from, cases of "abolition", such as that dealt with in *Poisi Tatut* (1978).

The ambiguity concerning the first point, which is similar to some long-standing sources of controversy over the effect of earlier reception provisions in Papua and in New Guinea,[241] was

---

[239] [1978] PNGLR 295 at 297 and 299-300.

[240] Ibid at 299.

[241] See, for example, *Booth v Booth* (1934-35) 53 CLR 1 (High Court of Australia) and *Murray v Brown River Timber Company Ltd* [1964] PNGLR 167 (Supreme Court of Papua and New Guinea). For discussion, see especially R O'Regan, "The Common Law and English Statutes in the Territory of Papua and New Guinea" (1971) 45 *Australian Law Journal* 297, which appears in virtually identical form in Ch 4 of R O'Regan, *The Common Law in Papua and New Guinea* (Sydney: Law Book Co, 1971).

resolved by the Supreme Court in *The Ship "Federal Huron" v Ok Tedi Mining Ltd* [1986] PNGLR 5. It is not necessary here to discuss the complicated facts of the case, which turned on several distinct legal issues. In relation to Sch 2.2(3), the essential point was whether, following independence, common law principles of admiralty law were to be potentially applicable in Papua *with*, or *without*, taking into account any modifications effected by pre-independence English statutes. As the court (Kidu CJ, Pratt and Woods JJ) noted in a joint judgment, the word "notwithstanding" in Sch 2.2(3) could be read in this context to produce either result.[242] In the event, the court was impressed by the argument that the constitutional arrangements of 1975 represented "a deliberate plan executed to wipe the legislative slate clean at independence",[243] and went on to hold:

> "[A]fter very anxious thought we have . . . formed the firm view that it was not the intention of the Constituent Assembly to introduce statute law into this country by means of modification thereby to the principles of common law and equity . . . It seems slightly odd to us that a newly emergent sovereign nation should deliberately choose to import into its law a large number of statutes of completely foreign origin which were never specifically enacted in its own pre-independence legislatures. It seems a somewhat back-door method inconsistent with the particularity found elsewhere in the legislation of 15 September 1975 . . . [I]n using the term 'notwithstanding' in Sch 2.2(3) it was the intention of the Constituent Assembly to exclude statutory modifications to the common law."[244]

Turning now to the second ambiguity - the distinction between revision and abolition - the court in *Federal Huron* referred in a later passage to *Poisi Tatut* in the following terms:

> "This was a case involving the common law action for enticement brought by a husband against his wife's seducer. The action was entirely eradicated in the United Kingdom by the *Law Reform (Miscellaneous Provisions) Act* 1970 and consequently was not part of the common law by any interpretation of the word 'notwithstanding' at independence."[245]

Although this comment seems to indicate approval of the court's approach and decision in *Poisi Tatut*, it is noteworthy that this reference is made in a quite different context. The court was considering whether, when there is no relevant common law adopted under Sch 2.2, the gap could be filled by formulating an appropriate rule of the underlying law under Sch 2.3. Consequently, the passing mention to *Poisi Tatut* can hardly be taken as a specific endorsement of all aspects of that decision.

---

[242] [1986] PNGLR 5 at 18-19.

[243] Ibid at 20. On this point, the court referred to the views of Lynch (above n 1) and J Goldring, *The Constitution of Papua New Guinea* (Sydney: Law Book Co, Sydney), Ch 11.

[244] Ibid at 19 and 21-22. As the court noted (at 19), a similar view had been taken in the *Federal Huron* case at first instance by Bredmeyer J, and also by Kapi J in *Wahgi Savings and Loans Society Ltd v Bank of South Pacific Ltd* (1980) SC185, pp 17-18.

[245] [1986] PNGLR 5 at 33.

The correctness of the ruling in *Poisi Tatut* was later questioned in the Supreme Court decision of *Mt Kare Holdings v Wapula Akipe* [1992] PNGLR 60. There, as part of a complex dispute over the issue of a mining lease, several of the defendants sought to have the plaintiffs' action dismissed, on the basis of an arrangement between the plaintiffs and certain other parties which allegedly infringed the common law rules concerning champerty and maintenance; that is, the provision of financial support in return for a share of the proceeds of the litigation. At first instance Amet J refused to dismiss the action, holding that the common law rules had been abolished by statute in the United Kingdom by the *Criminal Law Act* 1967 (UK) (ss 13 and 14 of which removed both criminal and tortious liability), and hence were not part of the common law "immediately before Independence Day" under Sch 2.2(1).[246] As a second ground, the trial judge held that, in any event, the common law principles should not be applied under Sch 2.2 as they were inappropriate to the circumstances of Papua New Guinea.[247] On the first point, although the trial judge did not refer specifically to *Poisi Tatut*, he accepted the plaintiffs' argument that Sch 2.2(3) was not applicable, and hence the case of *Federal Huron* [1986] PNGLR 5 was not really relevant, because here the common law rules were "not simply revised, they were abolished completely".[248]

On appeal to the Supreme Court, the decision of Amet J was reversed. The whole court (Kapi Dep CJ, Woods, Hinchliffe, Konilio and Andrew JJ) held that the common law principles were still relevant under Sch 2.2, and were also not inappropriate to the circumstances of the country. Kapi Dep CJ and Andrew J delivered separate judgments; the other three judges expressed their agreement with both of these judgments.

In relation to the meaning of the term "revision" in Sch 2.2(3), Kapi Dep CJ stated:

> "The word 'revision' is not a term of art. It is derived from the root word 'revise'. The *Concise Oxford Dictionary* defines this as 'read or look over or re-examine or re-consider and amend faults'. The term 'revision' is used to describe the process by which the Parliament in England, through statute, reviews the principles of common law and considers bringing changes to them. In my opinion this process would include making changes either through modification and/or abolishment of the principles of common law. If a statute in England abolishes or modifies principles of common law, and that statute is not adopted under Sch 2.6 of the *Constitution*, the revision by the statute in England must be ignored . . . This conclusion is consistent with the decision of the Supreme Court in *The Ship 'Federal Huron' v OK Tedi Mining* [1986] PNGLR 5."[249]

Clearly, then, Kapi Dep CJ's conclusion is directly contrary to the holding of the Supreme Court in *Poisi Tatut*. Referring to the earlier case, Kapi Dep CJ was quite dismissive:

> "[T]his is not a good authority on the issue which has come before us in this case. That was a case in which this issue was not properly argued and the assumption in the reference was accepted by all parties as the correct proposition in law."[250]

---

246 Unreported, National Court, WS No 1067 of 1990, 25 October 1991, p 3.
247 Ibid, pp 3-4.
248 Ibid, p 3.
249 [1992] PNGLR 60 at 63.
250 Ibid at 64.

Andrew J, having examined the terms of ss 13 and 14 of the *Criminal Law Act* 1967 (UK), concluded that their effect was to abolish criminal and tortious liability for champerty and maintenance, whilst preserving other elements of the previous law, such as the rules whereby a contract involving maintenance or champerty might be treated as contrary to public policy.[251] Consequently, Andrew J held that the English amendments amounted only to a "revision" or "modification", rather than a complete "abolition", and on the authority of *Federal Huron* (1986) were therefore not to be adopted in Papua New Guinea.[252]

Although not strictly necessary for his decision, Andrew J also made some illuminating comments on the difficulty, if not impossibility, of distinguishing sensibly between types or degrees of statutory amendment of the common law.[253] As to *Poisi Tatut* (1978), Andrew J commented on the weakness of that decision as an authority on the supposed distinction between "modification" and "abolition", and also noted that the court in that case had not considered the meaning of the word "notwithstanding" in Sch 2.2(3). He continued:

> "Every statute which 'revises' or 'modifies' the common law would of necessity abolish a part of the whole body of law, and there is no logical distinction between a modification of the body of law as a whole and the abolition of a part thereof. I am in agreement with the submission . . . that the 'abolition' of one small rule is by definition a 'revision of the principles (plural) and rules (plural) of common law and equity'. It is true that the counter argument has weight, namely that whilst the draftsman considered that he needed a provision to deal with common law rules which had been revised by statute, he plainly considered that the reference to the common law rules as they stood 'immediately before Independence Day' took care of common law rules already abolished by statute. However, on the authority of *Federal Huron* . . . the statutory amendment is not adopted and the unaltered common law is what is in force in Papua New Guinea."[254]

The last sentence of this passage is rather cryptic, and may only be re-stating Andrew J's initial holding: that the rules relating to champerty and maintenance were only "revised" and not abolished in their entirety. Of the two opposed arguments dealing with the wider issue, however, Andrew J appears to have favoured the former.

Given that the other three judges agreed with both Kapi Dep CJ and with Andrew J, it is not easy to determine what parts of the decision are to be regarded as binding. It can be said, however, that the authority of *Poisi Tatut* is now very weak. Further, if it is accepted that abolition of a rule is equivalent to modification of the body of law of which the rule forms part, there seems little reason to give the word "revision" in Sch 2.2(3) an artificially narrow meaning. It might then be concluded that Sch 2.2(1) and (3) must be read together, and that to determine which common law rules and principles were in force "immediately before Independence Day", it is necessary to disregard via Sch 2.2(3) *all* changes introduced by English pre-independence statutes, however radical those changes may have been.

While the issue then is not completely free from doubt, the weight of recent authority supports the proposition that *Poisi Tatut* was wrongly decided, and that statutory "revisions", even extending

[251] Ibid at 68.
[252] Ibid at 69.
[253] Ibid at 68-69. For a related earlier discussion of the difficulty of distinguishing between degrees of statutory amendment, see the article and book chapter by R O'Regan, above n 22.
[254] Ibid at 69.

to the complete abolition of a cause of action, have no effect on the common law adopted in Papua New Guinea. Instead, the courts of Papua New Guinea have to consider the unaltered common law rules according to the criteria set out in Sch 2.2(1), namely consistency with the *Constitution*, with statute law, and with custom as adopted under Sch 2.1, as well as suitability to the circumstances of the country.

The implications of this view will obviously need to be considered carefully in future cases, especially in those areas of the common law that have been affected by English statutes passed long ago. As a simple example, would a court in Papua New Guinea dealing with a question of the law of real property, or the law of trusts, be expected to consider the relevance of the English common law prior to the passage of the *Statute of Uses* (UK) of 1535? In areas of English law where court decisions and statutory modifications have interacted for centuries (as in land law, succession law, criminal law, evidence law, and so on), it may in practical terms be quite impossible to locate the common law in a supposedly original and pristine form.

Relationship between custom under Schedule 2.1 and common law under Schedule 2.2

The issue of the relative superiority of custom and common law, in a situation where both sources of the underlying law appear to be applicable, has become a matter of some uncertainty. It might be expected that Sch 2.2(1)(c) makes the matter fairly clear, providing that the rules of common law should not be applied and enforced if "*in their application to any particular matter* they are inconsistent with custom" (emphasis added). On the face of it this provision should result in an otherwise applicable and enforceable common law rule being overridden in any particular matter by applicable custom. As custom varies considerably from place to place and as the principle of universality of custom has not been generally accepted, it seems likely that the intended effect of Sch 2.2(1)(c) is that custom should have precedence in any particular matter, but that where there is no applicable custom, the way is opened to the application and enforcement of common law. The result would be a limited precedence for custom.

However, a number of judicial rulings have left the relationship of custom and common law far from clear. Some judicial opinion seems to suggest that it may be possible for both a rule of custom and a rule of common law to have potential application, once each has met all the pre-conditions for adoption into the underlying law. At least three key issues arise from these decisions. First, does Sch 2 give custom precedence over the common law? Secondly, if custom does not have precedence then does a party in civil cases have a choice as between custom and common law causes of action, defences (and related matters)? Thirdly, if a party does have such a choice, what restrictions, if any, apply?

In the *Somare* case [1981] PNGLR 265, Miles J considered and rejected an argument that the wording of Sch 2.2 gave any priority to custom as against the common law. In particular he rejected the view that only where the court had already decided that there was no appropriate custom should it turn to consider whether there was any suitable common law rule to apply. He stated:

> "In my view a court in Papua New Guinea does not discharge its duty under Sch 2 of the *Constitution* without considering all the matters adverted to in Schs 2.1 and 2.2, and if necessary Sch 2.3. But this means little more than that a court in this country may not

apply the common law without due regard to whether it is inconsistent with a constitutional law or a statue, or custom, or inappropriate to the circumstances of the country. The order in which these various factors are taken into consideration cannot be of any consequence. The suggested requirement that a court must positively decide that custom is inapplicable before it can proceed to consider the common law carries with it the obligation to commence the case with a comprehensive inquiry into all possibly relevant custom. This would place a burden upon judges and lawyers which in the light of their present training and experience would be difficult to discharge, to say the least."[255]

Kapi J, however, thought that the form of wording used in Sch 2.2 was important:

> "The order in which these laws are listed under Sch 2 is not without significance. In a case where the underlying law of Papua New Guinea is in question or is an issue, the inquiry should always begin with the examination of custom which is applicable under Sch 2.1 of the *Constitution*. Custom which is adopted in accordance with Sch 2.1 of the *Constitution* is superior to common law because common law is only applicable to the extent that it is not inconsistent with custom as adopted under Sch 2.1 of the *Constitution* (Sch 2.2(1)(c) of the *Constitution*). The extent to which common law is applicable cannot be determined without determining what the custom says."[256]

Kidu CJ had little to say on the point made by Kapi J in the *Somare* case,[257] but made similar comments in the later Supreme Court decision of *State v Uniss Kamugaip* ([1985] PNGLR 278 at 280). In the latter case, counsel in a criminal case were reproved by the court for assuming that the only issue was whether the common law rules concerning compellability of spouses were applicable, without first having considered the relevance of custom on that matter under Sch 2.1.[258] In *Aisi v Hoala* [1981] PNGLR 199 at 202, Bredmeyer J said:

> "[U]nder the hierarchy of laws carefully established by the *Constitution* custom now occupies a premier place in the underlying law. By Sch 2 . . . custom is applied first to a problem and only if it is inapplicable, due to one of the circumstances specified in Sch 2.1, is the court to turn to the English common law and equity."

In comments on the role of the judiciary in the development of the underlying law, made in the judges' *Annual Report* for 1987, it was stated that of the two main sources of the underlying law "custom is the prime one", the common law being the "secondary source" that "applies provided it is not inconsistent with custom".[259]

---

[255] [1981] PNGLR 265 at 303-304.
[256] Ibid at 286.
[257] Ibid at 271.
[258] However, note the possibility - discussed elsewhere in this chapter - that this view may be incorrect, in that there is no basis for considering custom concerning rules of evidence in criminal cases under s 4 of the *Customs Recognition Act* (Ch 19).
[259] "The Judiciary and the Development of the Underlying Law", in *Annual Report by the Judges: 1987* (Port Moresby: mimeo, 1987), Appendix C, p 1.

Aundak Kupil (1983)

While the views just cited would suggest a clear preponderance of support for custom having precedence over common law, the position seems less clear as a result of views expressed in other cases, where issues about priorities and choices between customary and common law claims and remedies have received more detailed attention. Of these, the decision of Bredmeyer J in *Aundak Kupil v State of Papua New Guinea* [1983] PNGLR 350 contains perhaps the most careful and thoughtful analysis of the issues of inconsistencies and choice between custom and common law, in the context of a road accident case.

There, the two plaintiffs had sustained very serious injuries when the government vehicle in which they were travelling was involved in an accident. Both the plaintiff victims and the driver came from the Wahgi area of the Western Highlands. The driver was later convicted of dangerous driving. The plaintiffs brought a common law action for damages for negligence, suing the state as being vicariously liable for the actions of its driver. Before the trial began, the driver and his relatives paid customary compensation to the victims and their relatives. This compensation consisted of K2,400 each in cash, and a number of pigs and cassowaries, amounting to an overall total value in each case of about K5,500.

At the trial, the judge noted that the state in its defence had not argued that the payment and acceptance of the customary compensation amounted to a complete defence to the common law claim under Sch 2.2(1)(c), nor even that the common law damages should be reduced by the amount of customary compensation paid.[260] Nevertheless, the judge invited the state to address him on the significance of the payment of customary compensation in relation to the common law claim. This course was not objected to by the plaintiffs' counsel. A deal of evidence was then led concerning the relevant custom. In essence, this was to the effect that the same amount of compensation was generally payable whether or not the driver was at fault, and whether or not the victims were also to blame for their injuries. The compensation was paid collectively by the driver's relatives, and shared out among the victims' relatives. The main purpose of the compensation was to restore harmonious relationships between the two respective groups. Non-payment of compensation would lead to threats, and possibly fighting and death by way of retaliation from the victims' relatives.[261]

Faced with this evidence, the court then considered whether the Wahgi custom of compensation for road accident injuries should be applied via Sch 2.1 of the *Constitution*. Distinguishing between the payment of compensation, and the threats of retaliation if compensation were not forthcoming, the court found that the first part of the custom was in principle enforceable under Sch 2.1(2). The second part of the custom, in contrast, was inconsistent with several statutes and some sections of the *Constitution*, including the requirement of not being repugnant to the general principles of humanity.[262]

Bredmeyer J then referred to the "motor vehicle accident industry" in Papua New Guinea,[263] noting that for many years plaintiffs in Papua New Guinea had been bringing claims for road

260 [1983] PNGLR 350 at 354.
261 Ibid at 355-58.at 354.
262 Ibid at 359.
263 Ibid at 360.

accident injuries under the common law as supplemented by various statutes (for example, the legislation requiring compulsory third party insurance). The only real question then as to the applicability of the common law via Sch 2.2 was that of inconsistency with custom, for in effect the court regarded the prior payment of customary compensation as indicative of a claim based on custom.

Counsel for the state eventually argued that the customary and common law claims were inconsistent, and that the plaintiffs should be limited to the standard amount of customary compensation (proved to be about K10,000 in each case, plus pigs and cassowaries). Since the plaintiffs had actually received less cash than that standard amount (K2,400 each), they should only be able to claim the balance (about K7,600 each). Counsel for the plaintiffs, on the other hand, argued that the two claims were not inconsistent. First, they were between different parties: the customary claim involved the respective kinship groups of the plaintiffs and of the driver. Secondly, the claims were based on different aims and principles. Hence it was argued that the plaintiffs should be able to keep the full amount of both claims. If, in the alternative, the court decided that some reduction to the amount of common law damages was required, it should only be for the amounts of customary compensation actually retained by the victims, and not the other amounts shared out among the various relatives.[264]

The trial judge took an intermediate approach, appearing to conclude (without elaboration) that the customary and common claims were inconsistent. However, he rejected the view that the common law claim was precluded as a result of the inconsistency. Rather, Bredmeyer J stated that, in this instance, to enforce the custom to the exclusion of the common law claim would promote "injustice" and would not be "in the public interest" within the terms of s 3(1)(a) of the *Customs Recognition Act* (Ch 19).

On the first point, Bredmeyer J said that injustice would be caused because otherwise plaintiffs with similar injuries would receive different awards of damages. For instance, if the driver was an expatriate from France, or if the victim was a Tolai, in either case the Wahgi system of custom might not be able to be applied. Instead the defendant would be liable for, or the plaintiff victim entitled to, the common law assessment of damages.[265]

Secondly, to exclude totally the common law action would be contrary to the public interest, since the system of damages for road injuries, as bolstered by various statutory amendments, was well known, having been in operation throughout the country for more than 60 years. The Wahgi people pay compulsory third party insurance premiums and charges, as well as taxes to the state. Accordingly, Wahgi victims should not be either denied access to the insurance fund or be prevented from suing the state when its employees are at fault.[266]

As a final point, referring again to s 3 of the *Customs Recognition Act* (Ch 19), the trial judge said that it would not be unjust to either the plaintiff or the defendant (that is, the state) if the plaintiffs received both sets of damages. Nevertheless, it would be more in the public interest if customary claims in this area were ultimately discouraged (especially considering the negative aspects of threats and possible retaliation). Hence the damages at common law (which the judge then proceeded to assess) should be reduced by the total amount of compensation paid to each victim,

264 Ibid at 361.
265 Ibid.
266 Ibid at 362.

regardless of whether or not it had been retained by the victim or instead distributed to the victim's relatives.[267] A number of difficult issues arise from this interesting judgment. Before commenting further, however, it will be useful to refer to two more recent decisions which touch on the precedence question in the context of issues concerning "choice" between customary and common law remedies. To reiterate the main points, where both a claim under custom and a claim under common law appear to be applicable, does the customary claim take priority, or does the plaintiff in effect have a choice between the customary and common law remedies?

Madaha Resena (1990-91)

In *Madaha Resena v State of Papua New Guinea* [1990] PNGLR 22, the plaintiffs after lengthy proceedings under the *Land Titles Commission Act* had been confirmed as the customary owners of Fisherman's Island (near Port Moresby). They then commenced action against the state for various heads of common law damages arising from trespass, on the basis that the state had, about a century previously, wrongly taken over the island as waste and vacant land. The trial judge, Bredmeyer J, stated that he found the switch from a claim based on custom (that is, customary ownership of the land) to a remedy based on common law (that is, the claim of trespass to the customarily owned land) to be "very incongruous":

> "I do not think the plaintiffs can have it both ways, that they can choose the kind of law to give them the most advantageous claim. It seems to me that, logically, if their claim to the ownership of the island is based on custom, then their claim for compensation for the government's wrongful use of the island should also be based on custom. Applying s 5(g)(ii) and the final words of that section of the *Customs Recognition Act* I consider that this is a case of 'a transaction' which 'justice requires should be' regulated wholly by custom and not by the common law. And I consider that determining this claim by the common law would produce injustice to the state. I therefore propose to ignore the common law submitted to me and decide this case in accordance with the Motuan custom of the Tatana people."[268]

However, as no evidence of Motuan custom had been submitted to the court, the trial judge then proceeded via Sch 2.3 to develop the underlying law by applying his own views as to the appropriate heads and amount of damages (which appeared to be considerably less than would have been available at common law). The plaintiffs subsequently appealed to the Supreme Court ([1991] PNGLR 174).

In the Supreme Court, Amet J began by stressing the autochthonous nature of the Papua New Guinean *Constitution*, and the need to develop an indigenous jurisprudence.[269] He also referred approvingly to the opinion of Kapi J in the *Somare* case, that under Schs 2.1 and 2.2 custom is superior to the common law.[270] He continued:

> "If custom is adopted and applied under Sch 2.1, it becomes an underlying law principle. If a principle of common law is adopted and applied under Sch 2.2, it too becomes an underlying law principle. They become part of the development of a consistent and

[267] Ibid at 362-63.
[268] [1990] PNGLR 22 at 31-32.
[269] [1991] PNGLR 174 at 186-89.
[270] Ibid at 189.

> coherent system of our indigenous jurisprudence or underlying law. They do not remain separate systems of law. Upon adoption and application they become part of the 'underlying law' referred to in s 9(f) [of the *Constitution*].
>
> It was never, in my opinion, the intention of the [Constitutional Planning Commission] or the Constituent Assembly that there should exist a "dual system of law" applicable under Sch 2 of the *Constitution*. I do not believe that it was ever intended that litigants have a choice of law or remedy, nor do I think it was ever intended that there should be a different system of law for indigenous inhabitants and a different system for non-indigenous inhabitants."[271]

Amet J proceeded to complain that lawyers and courts in Papua New Guinea too often ignore custom and pay only cursory consideration to the circumstantial suitability test for common law, thereby perpetuating Papua New Guinea's dependency upon and subservience to Anglo-Australian common law and equity.[272] He then expressed his agreement with the views of the trial judge, that the plaintiffs were not able to change from a claim based on custom to seek a common law remedy in damages. He thought, however, that Bredmeyer J's resort to Sch 2.3 had been premature, because insufficient effort had been made to obtain evidence about the nature of Tatana custom where customary land rights had been infringed by trespassers.[273] He therefore held that the case should be returned to another National Court judge, for the purpose of inquiring into the relevant custom in relation to its potential adoption and application "as a superior source of underlying law pursuant to Sch 2.1".[274]

While Kapi Dep CJ agreed with Amet J as to the ultimate method of disposal of the case, he reached the result in a rather different way. To begin with, he pointed out that the trial judge had proceeded upon a false premise in saying that the plaintiffs had initially *chosen* to bring their claim under custom. In fact, the wording of s 15 of the *Land Titles Commission Act*, by providing for the Commission to be the exclusive forum, prevented the plaintiffs from proceeding in any other way.[275] Once title to the land had been determined by the Commission, Kapi Dep CJ continued, the separate issue of consequential relief for the plaintiffs was then to be determined according to Sch 2 of the *Constitution*. Just as statutes in some cases allow for a "dual system" of laws in Papua New Guinea (for example, marriage, custody of children, and inheritance of certain kinds of property can be dealt with either by custom or under statute), so Sch 2 contains, side by side, the two primary sources of the underlying law: custom and common law.[276] While customary law may normally be irrelevant for "non-indigenous inhabitants":

> "[a]s far as the 'indigenous inhabitants of the country' are concerned, they have their rights regulated by customary law as well as the common law . . . When the indigenous inhabitants of the county, such as the plaintiffs in this case, are considering their rights and the subject matter is regulated both by customary law as well as the common law, there is a choice of remedy. There is nothing under Sch 2 of the *Constitution* which would compel a litigant who is an indigenous inhabitant to litigate under the principles of custom."

[271] Ibid at 190.
[272] Ibid at 190-91.
[273] Ibid at 192.
[274] Ibid at 193.
[275] Ibid at 178-79.
[276] Ibid at 180.

As examples of the "choice of remedy" principle, Kapi Dep CJ then referred approvingly to *Aundak Kupil* (1983), and two cases from Kenya. In both of the East African cases,[277] the co-existence of customary claims for compensation with claims under the Kenyan *Fatal Accidents Act* was upheld by the court, together with the proviso that a plaintiff could not recover under both claims. Thus, in the case where the customary claim had been waived, the plaintiff could proceed with the claim under the Act. Alternatively, where compensation had already been accepted in full settlement of the customary claim, it was then not possible to bring a fresh suit under the *Fatal Accidents Act*.[278]

In a further development of his argument, Kapi Dep CJ then said that it was quite legitimate for the Fisherman Island plaintiffs to elect to sue for damages at common law. However, the filtering process of Sch 2.2(1) had then to be considered. Here, there was no indication that the *Constitution* or any other statute was relevant, nor that the claim was unsuitable to the circumstances of the country, but it would nevertheless be necessary to consider the question of inconsistency with custom:

> "This means that where a common law action is instituted as a matter of choice, if a custom which is applicable to any of the parties in the action is shown to be inconsistent with the common law action, the common law principle in the particular case cannot be enforced. It is the duty of counsel to ensure that this inquiry is made before principles of common law can be adopted and enforced as part of the underlying law."[279]

Hence, it appears that while a party would have a choice of cause of action - he or she can elect to sue under either custom or common law - ultimately there would be no choice as to the applicable law. The court would proceed to apply common law only if there was no applicable custom.

Since the trial judge had not applied sufficient attention to the question of Tatana custom, the matter would need to be returned for further inquiry on this point, for the purposes of Sch 2.2(1)(c). A related aspect of this inquiry would be whether any Tatana (Motuan) custom applicable to the plaintiffs would also be applicable to the defendant (the state). Clearly, the state did not come within the expression "the indigenous inhabitants of the country" (see the definition of "custom" in Sch 1.2). On the other hand:

> "Custom is capable of developing to extend to parties outside a particular customary area and it is also capable of developing to extend to modern properties or institutions."[280]

To conclude, should it turn out that any relevant custom, applicable to the defendant, was inconsistent with the common law action, then according to Kapi Dep CJ the common law action would have to be dismissed, and a fresh action under custom instituted instead.[281]

The third judge, Los J, echoed the terminology adopted by Kapi Dep CJ, as to "choice" of remedies, but shed no light on the inconsistency issue. He commented as follows:

---

[277] The two cases were *Mwaura s/o Kamau v Gatoto s/o Mwangi* [1962] EA 528 and *Nyokabu v Public Trustee* [1965] EA 530. Both cases are discussed in A Allott, *New Essays in African Law* (London: Butterworths, 1970), pp 246-48.

[278] [1991] PNGLR 174 at 180-81.

[279] Ibid at 182-83.

[280] Ibid at 184.

[281] Ibid at 183.

> "[T]here is a fundamental question that needs an answer: can I hold that there is now an enforceable duty under the Papua New Guinea *Constitution* to apply customary law instead of common law when, in a given situation, certain relevant principles under both laws are put through the constitutional screening in Sch 2 and they reach the other end with 'clean' status? . . . For the moment I consider that the *Constitution* has raised the status of customary law of the nation and has imposed a duty on the National Judicial System and other governmental bodies to develop, apply and continue to develop, the indigenous jurisprudence. But the fact that there is already a screening process in Sch 2 of the *Constitution*, I consider, is not intended to arbitrarily drop the common law in favour of the customary law . . . I conclude that, until such time as the Supreme Court decides on well-informed submissions, where there is no statutory law on a subject, the parties have a right to choose which law to apply."[282]

In the result, all the judges agreed that Bredmeyer J had been premature in resorting to Sch 2.3 to develop new rules of the underlying law, and the matter was referred back to the National Court to hear evidence as to any relevant Tatana (Motuan) custom.

Pawa Kombea (1994)

The final case to be mentioned is the National Court decision of Kapi Dep CJ in *Pawa Kombea v Semal Peke* [1994] PNGLR 572, where the plaintiff sued for damages at common law under a number of heads, including malicious prosecution, false imprisonment and defamation. After default judgment was signed, the matter came before Kapi Dep CJ for assessment of damages. He raised the matter of customary law, and repeated passages from his judgment in *Madaha Resena* as to the "choice" of remedies, subject to the priority of custom if inconsistent with the common law. He then adjourned the case to allow evidence to be obtained as to custom in the area of the Southern Highlands where both the plaintiff and defendant lived.

On the resumed hearing, Kapi Dep CJ expressed his satisfaction with the views of two experts (one village leader, and one Village Court magistrate) that "there is no custom which would be inconsistent with the actions taken in common law in this case".[283] The judge then proceeded to assess damages in accordance with common law principles, after summarising the legal position as follows:

> "The right time in which to raise the question of custom is at the outset, when a cause of action is instituted . . . If there is any custom which may be relevant, it should be pleaded to indicate whether or not it is inconsistent with the principles of common law and equity. If there is no custom which is relevant, that fact should also be pleaded.
>
> In my view, it is necessary to raise the question of custom in the pleadings in all actions which are based on the principles of common law and equity which are yet to be adopted as part of the underlying law to give effect to Sch 2.2(1)(c) of the *Constitution*."[284]

In the present case, custom was not pleaded, and when judgment was entered, it related only to the action brought in accordance with the principles of common law. As there is no relevant

[282] Ibid at 195-96.
[283] [1994] PNGLR 572 at 574.
[284] Ibid.

custom and no issue was raised about the applicability and appropriateness of principles of common law, it will be adopted as part of the underlying law.[285]

Custom and common law: the competing views

From the cases of *Aundak Kupil*, *Madaha Resena*, and *Pawa Kombea v Semal Peke*, it can be seen that there is a variety of judicial views as to the relationship between customary and common law claims under Sch 2 of the *Constitution*. Bredmeyer J in *Aundak Kupil* considered that the Wahgi custom dealing with compensation for road accident injuries was inconsistent with the common law claim for negligence. In that situation, although Sch 2 would normally give priority to the customary claim, Bredmeyer J decided for various reasons to apply the criteria in s 3 of the *Customs Recognition Act* (Ch 19) relating to justice and the public interest. As a result, he held that the Wahgi custom was not to be applied where it was inconsistent with the usual common law remedy (referring to the "motor vehicle accident industry" ([1983] PNGLR 350 at 360)). One aspect of the "justice" factor, according to Bredmeyer J, was that plaintiffs with similar injuries should receive similar damages. There were apparently no such competing considerations in the same judge's first instance judgment in *Madaha Resena*, where Bredmeyer J held, in contrast, that it was not open to the plaintiffs to choose a common law remedy in relation to a claim initially based on custom.

Amet J agreed with this approach in the Supreme Court decision in *Madaha Resena*, stating that it could not have been intended that plaintiffs should have a choice of remedies, or that the law applicable to indigenous inhabitants should be different to that applying to non-indigenous inhabitants. What is not clear, nevertheless, is how the holding in *Madaha Resena* will necessarily help to achieve Amet J's goal of a single underlying law for everyone in the future. The decision in that case makes the damages receivable by the plaintiffs depend upon the evidence of Tatana custom. But if a land trespass case were next to arise in the Wahgi district, for instance, damages would presumably depend upon the details of Wahgi (not Tatana) custom, and in a case where only non-indigenous inhabitants were involved, damages would presumably be assessed in accordance with common law principles. Further, where parties come from different custom areas, or one party is Papua New Guinean and the other is not, it is also not obvious on Amet J's approach which of the principles should apply. In this context it should therefore be noted that the opinions of Bredmeyer J (at first instance) and Amet J in *Madaha Resena* provide a contrast to the earlier view of Bredmeyer J in the *Aundak Kupil* case: that plaintiffs with similar claims or injuries should receive similar damages. (Or is the system of common law damages in motor vehicle cases to be seen as a special case?) That is to say, if the approach in *Madaha Resena* is taken, Papua New Guinean plaintiffs with analogous claims in different parts of the country will obviously receive differential amounts of compensation, according to the varying nuances of local custom.

Perhaps the answer is simply that Amet J does not necessarily envisage a single system of underlying law in terms of outcomes at the local level. After all, he has never shown support for the universality of custom principle. Rather, his concern is to see a more consistent system mainly in the sense that custom would be the preferred source of law to the common law. It nevertheless remains a mystery how the court would develop the underlying law in cases where there is no

[285] For comment on the last two paragraphs of this passage, see below.

applicable local custom, or where non-indigenous inhabitants are involved, matters about which Amet J expressed concern in *Madaha Resena.*

Turning to the views of Kapi Dep CJ, tentatively supported by Los J, it may be suggested that the idea floated of a "choice" of remedies is somewhat misleading, since this is immediately made subject to the proviso that if the customary and common law claims or principles or remedies are inconsistent, then custom should prevail (assuming no other Sch 2.1 disqualifications are applicable). If the possibility of choosing between the remedies disappears as soon as the remedies are discovered to be inconsistent, then in reality there is no choice at all. While Kapi Dep CJ's idea of what "inconsistency" means would at first sight seem clear, his emphasis on "choice" of remedy gives rise to some uncertainty that remains unexplored in his judgments to date. It is notable that the two East African cases, cited by him with approval in *Madaha Resena* [1991] PNGLR 174 at 180-81, in fact reflect a rather different notion of "choice". In each African case, the court asserted a genuine right to choose between remedies, subject to a prohibition on double dipping; thus receipt of customary compensation precluded a common law claim, and vice versa. This is certainly a different result to that contemplated by Kapi Dep CJ in *Madaha Resena* and in *Pawa Kombea.* It also appears different to the approach of Bredmeyer J in *Aundak Kupil.*

Returning to Kapi Dep CJ's concern with inconsistency, it is also not apparent why the customary law of defamation and false imprisonment (that is, customary ideas and practices relating to insulting words, and wrongful restriction of personal freedom), in that part of the Southern Highlands referred to in *Pawa Kombea*, was not inconsistent with the common law principles.[286] No details of the customary law, or for that matter of the elements of the common law claims, were given. The judge appears to have been simply satisfied by the assurances of two witnesses (neither of whom could be expected to have any particular knowledge of the common law), to the effect that there was no conflict. This may be compared with the more determined efforts of Kapi Dep CJ, Amet J and Los J in *Madaha Resena*, where the failure of the trial judge to locate and refer to any evidence of relevant custom was treated as a reason to return the case for further investigation on the point.

As a final comment on both *Madaha Resena* and *Pawa Kombea v Semal Peke*, it remains unclear what Amet J and Kapi Dep CJ have in mind when they talk of a principle of common law or equity becoming "adopted as part of the underlying law".[287] Presumably the word comes from Sch 2.1(1) and Sch 2.2(1), both of which talk of custom and common law each being "adopted" as part of the underlying law. But those provisions refer to bodies of principles that are adopted subject to the limitations we are discussing in this chapter. What is less clear is what being "adopted" means for a particular principle of the common law. When, and in what sense, does adoption occur, and does it involve the adopted principle necessarily having a binding effect in subsequent cases?

For example, in relation to the cause of action in *Pawa Kombea*, there have obviously been prior cases of defamation in Papua New Guinea in which the common law principles have been applied. But the whole gist of the main judgments of the Supreme Court in *Madaha Resena* is that the required process of checking for relevant customary law (law that may change over time, as contemplated in the definition of "custom" in Sch 2.1) should continue *in every new case as it arises*. In other words, the reference in *Pawa Kombea* to the court's adoption of the common law

[286] For that matter, might not the *Defamation Act* (Ch 293) also have been relevant (see below)?
[287] *Madaha Resena* [1991] PNGLR 174 at 190 per Amet J; *Pawa Kombea v Semal Peke* [1994] PNGLR 572 at 574 per Kapi Dep CJ.

principles "as part of the underlying law" seems to be limited to the particular case at hand, possibly with no significance at all for later cases. This view would be consistent with both the requirement of circumstantial applicability of the common law (see above), and the requirement that in its application to any particular matter the common law must not be inconsistent with custom (Sch 2.2(1)(c)).[288]

Returning now to the three questions identified at the beginning of this section, the first issue is whether Sch 2 gives custom precedence over the common law. The preponderance of judicial opinion seems to be that Sch 2 does have this effect. While controversy about choice of remedy has clouded the issue, perhaps the key point here is that ultimately Kapi Dep CJ and Amet J agree that custom has precedence. As to the second issue (that of choice of remedies), some judges support the view that parties have a choice between custom and common law actions, at least at the point of initiating and litigating an action. The consequences of such a choice are far from clear, however, in light of the fact that the choice apparently vanishes where there is inconsistency between applicable custom and common law rules (though as to the difficulties in determining inconsistency, see below). Finally, as to the third issue (namely, what restrictions, if any, apply in a situation of choice), as yet the position is far from clear.

The place of the common law in the underlying law: summary

There is much that remains doubtful about the status of common law as part of the underlying law of Papua New Guinea. First, the rules on applicability and appropriateness are not well understood and are seldom applied. Given full effect they would make application of the common law complex, as they would have to be applied on a case-by-case basis. What has been ruled appropriate and applicable at a prior point in time, or in a particular location, may not be so at a later time or in a different part of the country. Secondly, uncertainty about the particular rules of English common law that may be relevant arises because of the uncertainty of the tests used to determine the appropriate "cut-off dates" (both as to post-independence English case law developments, and as to pre-independence English statutory changes to the common law). Thirdly, the matter of the relative priority between customary law under Sch 2.1, and common law under Sch 2.2, is both controversial and ambiguous. Supreme Court decisions, unfortunately, have not so far clarified these issues. (Indeed, there is a striking, but so far unremarked, contrast in the case law between the view of at least some Supreme Court judges in the *Poisi Tatut* and *Somare* cases (only "universal" custom to be considered under Sch 2.1), and the Supreme Court's holding in *Madaha Resena* (particular local custom to be applied under Sch 2.1 in preference to the common law under Sch 2.2).)

[288] Difficulties involved in applying the doctrine of judicial precedent to the underlying law are discussed in the next section.

PROBLEMS FOR COHERENCE: INCONSISTENCY AND CUSTOM AND THE DOCTRINE OF JUDICIAL PRECEDENT

If the underlying law as defined in Sch 2 is to develop in a coherent manner, as envisaged by Sch 2.4, the many uncertainties identified in this discussion need to be addressed. In doing so, two matters of general application will also need attention, namely the difficulties in applying the concept of inconsistency to custom, and the problem of applying the doctrine of precedent to the underlying law.

Custom and inconsistency

A major cause of confusion, we think, is the difficulty of determining issues of *inconsistency*, especially as between custom and statute, and as between custom and common law. On the former point, it will be recalled that according to Sch 2.1 of the *Constitution*, custom cannot be applied and enforced as part of the underlying law if it is inconsistent with a statute. It then becomes a matter of statutory interpretation, in a particular instance, to determine whether the legislation is intended to affect the operation of custom. Is the purpose of the legislation to override the operation of custom, by covering exhaustively the relevant field of activity, or is it possible for custom and statute to exist simultaneously? Here, we can do no more than give a couple of examples of the problem.

As one illustration, if a Papua New Guinean couple make a statutory marriage under the *Marriage Act* (Ch 280), would it still be possible for the wife's relatives to bring a claim against the husband for customary payment of bride price? In *Peter v Mathew* (1995) N1365, Woods J noted in passing that "bride price is not a condition precedent to a marriage under the *Marriage Act*".[289] While this is undoubtedly true, the court was not being asked to deal with the question posed above. It might be arguable that there is no inconsistency between the *Marriage Act* and the custom of bride price, because the custom is not a mere "formality" relating to the celebration of marriage, but a practice which has implications for the future behaviour and expectations of the spouses, the relationship between their respective sets of relatives, the position and entitlements of their children, and so on.[290] It would follow that the husband or his relatives could not rely on the mere fact that the marriage was statutory to provide a complete defence to the claim for bride price. Whether the court would accept this argument might well depend on the specific details of custom introduced in evidence.

[289] (1995) N1365, p 5.

[290] For discussion of bride price, see O Jessep and J Luluaki, *Principles of Family Law in Papua New Guinea*, (Port Moresby: 2nd ed, UPNG Press, 1994), Ch 2.

Another example is that of customary defamation claims, in the light of the *Defamation Act* (originally passed in 1962, now Ch 293). According to its original Preamble, the purpose of this legislation was to "consolidate and amend the law of defamation". At the time, this presumably meant the introduced (common) law of defamation, and was not intended to have any application to customary claims. Certainly, Raine J in the pre-independence Supreme Court decision of *Taupa v Joel* (1974) SC822 saw no reason why a customary claim for defamation would not be possible. In contrast, Bredmeyer J in *Bole v Imbell* (1982) N354(M) rejected the possibility of a customary claim, saying that the "cause of action is given by the *Defamation Act* 1962, which being a statute overrides custom".[291] Interestingly, Kapi Dep CJ in the previously discussed case of *Pawa Kombea v Semal Peke* [1994] PNGLR 572, in which damages were awarded for customary defamation (among other injuries), made no mention of the legislation at all. The point of whether the statute operates to cover the field, in the sense of applying to all defamation claims, thus remains open for future determination.

The matter of inconsistency between customary and common law claims is rather more complex, given the number of levels at which conflict or inconsistency can potentially occur. It is also more pressing if the views of Amet J and Kapi Dep CJ in *Madaha Resena* gain ascendancy among the judges of the National and Supreme Court. This is because there can be inconsistency not simply in relation to "cause of action" in a broad sense, but also in regard to specific aspects or incidents of the claim. These aspects may include the precise type of remedy, measure of damages, choice of forum, relevant defences, rules of evidence, other procedural aspects, and time limits for bringing the action.[292] Of course, some of these matters may be regulated already by statute, but in other situations it may be difficult to determine whether "inconsistency" exists and, if so, how it can be resolved.

Even at the broader level of "cause of action", it is not always obvious when a customary claim and a common law claim are in conflict. While the judgment of Bredmeyer J in *Aundak Kupil* [1983] PNGLR 350 remains an outstanding example of judicial reasoning and creative interpretation of Sch 2 of the *Constitution*, it is noteworthy that the court did not elaborate on its reasons for its apparent view that the customary and common law claims arising out of the motor vehicle accident were inconsistent. The court did, however, say that it would not be in the public interest "for the plaintiff to get both forms of compensation".[293] Given that the evidence suggested that the customary claim involved different parties (the respective kin groups of the driver and the victims), and was based on both different principles of liability and of assessment of compensation,[294] it is interesting to speculate as to whether other judges would have reached the same conclusion. Or is the "inconsistency" here in fact a prohibition on allowing more than one type of claim from the same event or incident? Again, the reason for this conclusion is not apparent.

---

[291] (1982) N354(M), p 2.

[292] See A Allott, *New Essays in African Law* (London: Butterworths, 1970), Ch 7, for a discussion of some of these elements in the African context.

[293] [1983] PNGLR 350 at 362.

[294] See ibid at 354-58 and 362.

The doctrine of judicial precedent[295]

While there is a consistent emphasis on the goal of flexibility in the provisions on circumstantial applicability of the underlying law in Schs 2.1 to 2.4, elsewhere Sch 2 pursues goals of consistency in and certainty of judicial decisions, doing so through the doctrine of judicial precedent. Under Sch 2.9, decisions of the Supreme Court bind all other courts including the National Court, decisions of the National Court bind all lower courts, and decisions of courts other than the Supreme Court or the National Court bind other courts lower in the hierarchy. On the face of it these provisions apply to judicial decisions on the underlying law. If so, decisions on custom and common law, as well as judge-made rules under Sch 2.3, would always bind lower courts. That this outcome was one intention of Sch 2.9 is supported by the provision on "Conflict of Precedents" in Sch 2.10, which includes provision for resolving any conflict or inconsistency between a decision of law that binds a court by virtue of Sch 2.9, and any custom that is part of the underlying law and is applicable in relation to the matter.

In *Madaha Resena v State of Papua New Guinea* [1991] PNGLR 174, referred to in our above discussion of "adoption" of common law principles, there was also mention of rules of custom being "adopted". This language is consistent with the application of the doctrine of judicial precedent. Although this is not spelt out, the implication seems to be that once adopted, an underlying law rule will subsequently be binding.

It is difficult to see, however, how the doctrine of judicial precedent could be applied consistently in relation to any of the three elements of the underlying law (custom, common law, and judge-made rules under Sch 2.3). In general, despite the binding hierarchy of decisions envisaged by Sch 2.9, courts cannot simply apply previous decisions on the underlying law. Rather, in each case where a court needs to resort to unwritten law to resolve an issue, the wording of Sch 2 requires that the court begin afresh with the search for possibly applicable rules of custom and common law.

As for custom, if a rule is applied by a court, it will normally only apply to the group of people whose custom is involved. With a matter of national importance (Kapi J in *Somare*), a "universal" custom may be applied only because the same custom applies to all or most groups. Change in circumstances at a later date could then result in a previously universal custom ceasing to be of universal application, and becoming thereby inapplicable in a later case.

As we have already discussed, decisions applying common law rules are not easily generalisable: first, because it will always be possible in a particular case that custom may apply and, secondly, because the rules about circumstantial applicability seem to require that the court always examine whether or not a rule is applicable and enforceable in the particular case. While it might be argued that where there is no relevant custom there would not often be changes in circumstances so great as to render a common law rule non-applicable, if the circumstances to be taken into account under Sch 2.2(4) when determining appropriateness and applicability of common law rules can mean "physical, social, economic, legal and political" matters,[296] then the scope for changing applicability of common law rules on a case-to-case basis may not be insignificant.[297] As to

[295] We emphasise that we are referring here only to the doctrine of precedent as a fundamental common law doctrine, as reflected in Sch 2.9 of the *Constitution*. The extent to which that doctrine is applied or manipulated in the process of judicial decision-making involves a quite separate set of issues.

[296] Lynch, above n 1, p 51.

[297] For discussion of how varying socio-economic circumstances might determine the unwritten law of a community, see PNG Law Reform

judge-made rules under Sch 2.3, these also cannot be applied automatically in later cases, because courts will always first be required to consider the possible application of custom and the common law. If circumstantial applicability of the common law is potentially as far-reaching as we have indicated, then even previous decisions to the effect that there is no applicable or appropriate rule of the common law could be re-visited. In short, while judge-made rules under Sch 2.3 are not thereby made completely nugatory, their continued applicability depends in each case upon the prior sources of law in Sch 2.2 having first been considered and rejected.

It is, of course, possible to reconcile aspects of the requirements of circumstantial applicability of each of the elements of the underlying law with the doctrine of precedent. In particular, it is precisely because custom is particular to each group that the adoption, application and enforcement of a rule of custom could not bind in subsequent cases involving groups with different customs, and so the requirements of Sch 2.9 could be read down in relation to custom. We do not see, however, any obvious way of reconciling all aspects of the test of circumstantial applicability with the doctrine of precedent, and so it remains a key aspect of the incoherence of the underlying law provisions.

CONCLUSION

The lack of progress since independence in the development of the underlying law has been attributed over the years to a number of different causes. Suggested failings include: the lack of sympathy towards custom shown by expatriate lawyers and judges;[298] the uncritical willingness of lawyers and courts to assume the appropriateness and suitability of the common law;[299] the technical problems of proving the existence of custom;[300] and the methods of education and training given to Papua New Guinean lawyers.[301] In addition, reference has also been made to the lack of a consistent judicial methodology when elements of custom are raised,[302] and the need for the Parliament to pass the legislation concerning custom contemplated in Sch 2.1(3) of the *Constitution*.[303]

Even if these various problems could be attended to, however, it would not follow that the underlying law would develop and flourish in the way envisaged by the constitutional founders. As we have tried to show, the very concept of the underlying law reflected in the wording of Sch 2 is essentially incoherent, and these fundamental defects of drafting have been augmented and magnified at times by unhelpful judicial analysis and interpretation on specific points. The various deficiencies (whether of drafting or interpretation) to which we have referred include the problems of cut-off dates for adoption of the common law; the idea of "universality" of custom; the practical difficulties involved in the applicability and appropriateness provisions concerning the common law; the precedent value of decisions on custom, common law and judge-made rules

---

Commission, *The Role of Customary Law in the Legal System* (Port Moresby: Government Printer, 1977), p 19.

[298] D Weisbrot, "The Impact of the Papua New Guinea Constitution on the Recognition and Application of Customary Law", in P Sack (ed), *Pacific Constitutions* (Canberra: ANU, 1982), p 278.

[299] Ibid, p 280; B Sakora, "Judicial Law-making under the Papua New Guinea Constitution" in P Sack (ed), *Pacific Constitutions* (Canberra: ANU, 1982), pp 265-66.

[300] J Zorn, "Common Law Jurisprudence and Customary Law" in R James and I Fraser (eds), *Legal Issues in a Developing Society* (Port Moresby: UPNG, 1992), pp 109-110; D Weisbrot, "Integration of Laws in Papua New Guinea: Custom and the Criminal Law in Conflict", in D Weisbrot, A Paliwala, and A Sawyer (eds), *Law and Social Change in Papua New Guinea* (Sydney: Butterworths, 1982), p 94.

[301] See, for example, J Nonggorr "Development of Customary Law: Replacing the Customs Recognition Act" (1993) 21 *Melanesian Law Journal* 49 at 51; T Deklin, "The Future of Papua New Guinea Customary Law: Rot Wei?" in J Aleck and J Rannells (eds), *Custom at the Crossroads* (Port Moresby: UPNG, 1995), p 34.

[302] A Amet, "Severing the Umbilical Cord from the Common Law" in J Aleck and J Rannells (eds), *Custom at the Crossroads* (Port Moresby: UPNG, 1995), pp 63-64.

[303] B Sakora, above n 80, p 268.

of the underlying law; the question of choice of remedies; tests for inconsistency; and the restrictive wording of the *Customs Recognition Act* (Ch 19).

Certainly, it is time for a closer look at these issues by the legislature, since the defects outlined in our discussion cannot be cured by judicial activity alone, even given the sort of time frame identified by some commentators as a necessary prerequisite.[304] In reconsidering Sch 2, the matter of the precedent value of decisions (whether concerning custom or common law) must be a central concern requiring a decision as to the appropriate balance to be struck between the competing legal goals of certainty and predictability, on the one hand, and flexibility and adaptability to changing circumstances, on the other.

As recommended by some observers,[305] an obvious place to begin the search for new models might be the Papua New Guinea Law Reform Commission's Underlying Law Bill 1977. Even were this to be adopted in full, however (a course which we do not recommend), the major issues would still remain for treatment. As it would make custom the primary source of the underlying law, it seems that the universality problem would be dealt with (although that issue is not addressed explicitly by the Bill). The common law and judge-made law would continue to be "supplementary sources" of the underlying law, with common law principles able to be "adopted" into the underlying law if there is no "developed principle or rule of the underlying law" or "no applicable rule of custom" (cl 5).[306] However, the same problems concerning cut-off date would apply, as would the problems with the appropriateness and applicability tests. In addition, the Bill does not deal with the question of the extent to which underlying law rules can be precedents in subsequent cases. While the emphasis on the primacy of custom is helpful, the difficulties presented by the remaining problems suggest that it may be time to consider again the whole question of an appropriate and workable underlying law for Papua New Guinea.

---

[304] See D Roebuck, "Custom, Common Law and Constructive Judicial Lawmaking" in R De Vere, D Colquhoun-Kerr and J Kaburise (eds), *Essays on the Constitution of Papua New* Guinea (Port Moresby, 1985), p 129; Nonggorr, above n 82, p 50.

[305] See, for example, Weisbrot, above n 79, pp 287-89; Nonggorr, above n 82.

[306] PNG Law Reform Commission, above n 78, p 20.

DECENTRALISATION

Chapter 11

DECENTRALISATION: 1976-1995

YASH GHAI AND ANTHONY J REGAN

INTRODUCTION

In 1976, one year after Papua New Guinea achieved independence, amendments to the *Constitution* were passed providing the basis for a radical redistribution of powers and resources away from the state to a new system of elected provincial governments. The new governments were to be established under a subsequent *Organic Law on Provincial Government*, which was authorised by the constitutional amendments and passed by Parliament early in 1977. The decentralisation arrangements involved operated with little change until July 1995 when they were replaced by constitutional amendments and a new Organic Law,[307] providing for a new system of non-elected provincial government with much reduced autonomy and a dominant role for members of the Parliament.

This chapter examines Papua New Guinea's experience of decentralisation from 1976 to 1995,[308] and explores the role of law in that experience. It seeks to explain the operation of the system of decentralisation both within the terms of the legislation governing it and factors external to the system. The chapter examines the status and structure of the law, including the disposition of powers and responsibilities as mandatory or discretionary, and the methods of adjudication and enforcement, and relates these to the implementation of decentralisation. The operation of the law on decentralisation in Papua New Guinea has to be understood within the broader context of the state: the constellation and contradictions of social forces that find their reflection and expression in the apparatus of government.

In order to undertake such an examination, it is necessary first to:

(a) consider the renewal of interest in the international development community about the importance of law (an interest inherent in much of the discourse about governance);

(b) review, in summary form, previous research on the role of law in developing countries; and

(c) provide a brief analysis of the establishment and implementation of decentralisation.

---

[307] *Organic Law on Provincial Governments and Local-level Governments.*

[308] The cut-off date for this study is July 1995, because at the time of writing (March 1996) it is too early to comment on the operation of the complex constitutional changes that have introduced the new system of provincial government, especially as the new provincial governments will only be operating under transitional provisions until the next general elections, scheduled for mid-1997. Only after those elections will the long-term arrangements come into operation.

LAW IN DEVELOPING COUNTRIES

The rehabilitation of law

Until recently the international development community has paid little attention to the role of law. This neglect of law may have arisen either from taking law for granted or from a consideration that law had little relevance to development. Those observers who sought to raise resources to promote the study of law in development were convinced early on that the latter issue was central. Due to the lack of resources (and the general notion among educational planners that legal education and legal research can be had on the cheap), there has been little systematic research on the role of law in social, political and economic change in the Third World. In recent years, however, there has been the beginning of a reversal of attitudes towards law. Indeed some writers and institutions now ascribe the widespread failure of development to inadequacies in the legal system. As an example, we may look to the analysis of the World Bank. It identifies the following key symptoms of poor governance:

(a) failure to make a clear separation between what is public and what is private, and hence a tendency to direct public resources for private gain;

(b) failure to establish a predictable framework of law and government conducive to development, or arbitrariness in the application of rules and laws;

(c) the existence of excessive rules, regulations, licensing requirements and so on, which impede the functioning of markets and encourage rent-seeking;

(d) priorities inconsistent with development; and

(e) excessively narrowly-based or non-transparent decision-making.

These factors are regarded as creating an environment that is hostile to development:

> "In such circumstances, the authority of governments over their peoples tends to be progressively eroded. This reduces compliance with decisions and regulations. Governments then tend to respond through populist measures or, as in some authoritarian regimes, they resort to coercion. Either way, the economic cost can be high, including a diversion of resources to internal security, and escalating corruption. Poor development performance can in turn contribute to poor governance by further eroding the confidence of citizens in their governments, and causing governments to behave insecurely."[309]

Hopes are high currently that the reform of the law and its institutions can pave the way for fair and rapid development.

There would appear to be two principal reasons for this concern with law. The first springs from the new preoccupation with democracy and human rights: the law and its processes are widely perceived to be linked to the re-establishment and maintenance of democratic orders. The other is the push towards the strengthening of the market as the organiser of the economy. The two are

[309] The clearest and most authoritative statement of this position is World Bank, *Managing Development: The Governance Dimension* (Washington: World Bank, 29 August 1991), from which this quotation is taken.

not unconnected; at least, various people see a close link between democracy and the market. Recent papers of the World Bank illustrate its new conceptualisation of the role of law.[310]

The current concern with law goes under the designation of governance. The World Bank has defined governance as "the manner in which power is exercised in the management of a country's economic and social resources for development". Aspects of governance include accountability, open and transparent decision-making processes (with strictly limited administrative discretionary powers), and a fair and predictable framework for investment and other decisions. Central to these objects are "rules and institutions which create a predictable and transparent framework for the conduct of public and private business, and also to accountability for economic and financial performance".[311] The World Bank has identified the Rule of Law as a key element of predictability and stability where business risks may be rationally assessed, transaction costs lowered, and government arbitrariness reduced. It notes, for its purposes, five constitutive aspects of the Rule of Law:

(1) There must be a set of rules known in advance.

(2) These rules must actually be in force.

(3) There must be mechanisms to ensure application of the rules.

(4) Conflicts must be resolved through binding decisions of an independent judicial body or through arbitration.

(5) There are known procedures for amending the rules when they no longer serve their purpose.[312]

These points cover most features of a modern legal system (although this would also include a well-trained and independent legal profession). More specifically, one would emphasise clear and enforceable rules of property and contract.

The World Bank's primary concern is with economic policies and management (and market processes), and consequently its view of governance is somewhat narrower than that of other institutions. For example, the Ford Foundation emphasises the political dimensions of governance. Linked to its program of rights and social justice, its governance policies support activities that stimulate pluralism and participation in the governing process, improve the quality and responsiveness of government institutions, and encourage independent research and action on major public policy issues. It attaches a particular importance to the re-establishing and strengthening of democracy. Like some other agencies it is concerned to see the promulgation and observance of fair electoral systems. Stemming from its support of pluralism, it encourages the decentralisation of government powers and the strengthening of capacity at the local levels.[313] This broader view of governance is more relevant to this chapter, which looks at the role of law in decentralisation.

---

[310] Ibid, and see also World Bank, *Governance: The World Bank's Experience* (Washington: World Bank, 29 November 1993).

[311] World Bank, above n 3.

[312] Ibid, and see also World Bank, above n 4.

[313] This summary of the Ford Foundation's concept of governance is based on a reading of internal Foundation papers. There is a growing literature on the broader aspects of governance: see, for example, G Hyden and M Bratton (eds), *Government and Politics in Africa* (Boulder: L Rienner, 1992), and the references therein.

The role of law

In either view of governance a central role is assigned to the law. How well founded is this faith in law? In the early 1960s too there was much confidence in the ability of the law to cure the ills of underdevelopment. As a response to these official efforts, legal scholars attempted to understand the relationship between law and social change. Confident that they would be quickly able to uncover the underlying dynamics of the relations between law and society and so aid government in their development plans, these scholars soon found themselves in something of a blind alley. The research began with a paradigm that was seriously flawed. It was based on the notion of a "modern legal system" and inspired by an instrumental view of law. Operating with ideological assumptions (of impartial and autonomous law), rather than the practical realities of western legal systems, they were unable to explain the actual operation of the law in the developing countries.[314]

The reality is, however, that much of the time legislation fails to achieve its objectives. At other times its provisions are manipulated for totally different purposes.[315] Those to whom the law is directed discover various modes of evasion. More frequently than is realised, those who promulgate a particular law[316] have little intention of implementing it,[317] and sometimes deliberately build into it obstacles to implementation.[318] At other times a law is made largely for symbolic purposes, to buy off domestic or international pressures, or to project a particular image of the regime.[319] Even if the promulgation of the law is not cynical, it may be inefficacious because not enough attention has been given to the process of implementation, the lack of access of the target group to the machinery of the law, or the effectiveness of sanctions.[320]

The failure of the initial research on law and development to better illuminate the relationship of law and society arose in large part because the scholars had failed to appreciate the complexity of law or its interconnections with political and economic power. The relationship between law and social change is complex and our understanding of it is limited. There are certain broad theoretical paradigms (for example, the law and capitalism, the legal framework of a planned economy, or the communism of subsistence and small-scale societies), which claim to explain the links between law and society[321] and there are some well-known ideological positions about the

---

[314] There is now considerable literature on these efforts at "law and development". Early attempts at the conceptualisation of the subject include: M Galanter, "The Modernisation of Law" in M Weiner (ed), *Modernisation: The Dynamics of Growth* (New York: Basic Books, 1966); R Seidman, "Law and Development: A General Model" (1972) 6 *Law and Society Review* 311; and D Trubek, "Toward a Social Theory of Law: An Essay on the Study of Law and Development" (1972) 82 *Yale Law Journal* 1. In 1972 an international committee of scholars reported on the objectives and methodology of law and development: *International Legal Centre, Law and Development: The Future of Law and Development Research* (Uppsala: International Legal Centre, 1974). This report criticised some western assumptions behind law and development, which led to something of a crisis in the movement, reflected in D Trubek and M Galanter, "Scholars in Self-estrangement: Some Reflections on the Crisis in Law and Development Studies in the United States" (1974) *Wisconsin Law Review* 1062. For an unrepentant view of the virtues of law and development, see R Seidman, *The State, Law and Development* (New York: St Martins Press, 1978). For surveys of writing within this movement, see Y Ghai, "Law, Development and African Scholarship" (1987) 50 *Modern Law Review* 750; and also F Snyder, "Law and Development in the Light of Dependency Theory" (1980) 14 *Law and Society Review* 723.

[315] A good early study of this (the use of discretionary bureaucratic powers) is G Myrdal, "Operational Controls over the Private Sector" in his book *Asian Drama: An Inquiry into the Poverty of Nations* (New York: Twentieth Century Fund, 1968).

[316] For an example of how this was done in relation to the indigenisation decree in Nigeria, see T Biersteker, "The Illusion of State Power: Transnational Corporations and the Neutralisation of Legislation" (1980) 17 *Journal of Peace Research* 3.

[317] A good example is the land reform legislation under Emperor Haile Selassie in Ethiopia: see P Brietzke, *Law, Development and the Ethiopian Revolution* (Lewisburg: Bucknell University Press, 1982).

[318] For a classic study of this phenomenon, see E Feder, "Counter-reform" in R Stavenhagen (ed), *Agrarian Problems and Peasant Movements in Latin America* (New York: Doubleday, 1970).

[319] T Arnold, *The Symbols of Government* (New Haven: Yale University Press, 1938); and V Aubert, "The Housemaid: An Occupational Role in Crisis" (1955) 1 *Acta Sociologica* 149.

[320] For various examples, see Seidman 1978, above n 8.

[321] A modern example is the World Bank's position, which sees a clear connection between the development of the market and a particular, western-type legal system. This connection is often attributed to Max Weber, though not entirely correctly. See also the World Bank publications, above n 3 and n 4.

role of law.[322] The paradigms operate essentially at the macro-level and have limited utility in uncovering the precise links between a specific law and social reality,[323] while the ideological representations are frequently more mystifying than illuminating. One reason for the lack of understanding is that different societies differ in their attitudes to the law and the tasks they assign to it (some relying much more on communal traditions and ethics than the formal law).[324] Such variations make the discovery (indeed the existence) of universal rules about the role of law problematic. They also raise the danger that legal theories elaborated for the developed countries may be used to try to explain the social reality of, and prescribe policies for, Third World countries. While the World Bank analysis tends to show awareness of cultural complexity and diversity, its prescriptions tend to disregard such phenomena.

Another reason for the lack of understanding is the enormous variety of phenomena that passes under the name of law. Some rules are addressed to the government, while many are addressed to private actors. Some rules prohibit certain activities, while others facilitate other activities. Some laws are precise and detailed, while others are broad and vague. Some laws are self-operating, their policing being left to private groups; others require implementation by state agencies. Some laws are the result of deliberate decisions of a legislature; some the whim of an autocrat. Some are merely the codification of the customs of a community; while others have grown slowly over long periods through judicial development. The dynamics of statutory law are frequently very different from the dynamics of communal or judicial law. Some laws are easier to enforce than others (compare a law confiscating foreign property with a law seeking to abolish polygamy in a rural area, say in the Highlands of Papua New Guinea, or even with a law aiming to introduce greater efficiency in the management of nationalised or state-owned enterprises). Above all, the causes or consequences of law are not the outcome of any autonomous workings of the law: they acquire significance from - and in turn influence - social contexts and forces. (For example, the consequences of the law of corporations depend less on the precise terms of the legislation than the economic markets and social energies that are harnessed to corporate enterprise.)[325]

These elementary remarks[326] suggest that our knowledge of law and social change is limited and unreliable. This proposition sets the stage for the purpose of this chapter, which is to examine the role of law in decentralisation in Papua New Guinea with a view to developing some basic propositions about law in development.

---

[322] Sociology of law studies have been divided mainly between those who adhere to the Marxist view of the marginal (and oppressive) nature of law, and those who follow Weber in attributing a more central (and facilitative) role to it.

[323] I have, for example, argued that, contrary to official and popular ideology, the role of the formal legal system in the development and maintenance of capitalism in Hong Kong has been marginal (at least insofar as Chinese capitalism is concerned). In doing so, I have drawn upon a large body of sociological and management literature; for example, G Redding, *The Spirit of Chinese Capitalism* (Berlin: Walter de Gruyter, 1990), and other works referred to in my paper, "The Rule of Law and Capitalism: Reflections on the Basic Law", which appears in R Wacks, *Legal Theory: China, Hong Kong and 1997* (Hong Kong: University of Hong Kong Press, 1993).

[324] The best known example of this is of course contrasting Confucianist attitudes towards law and morality (concurred with in large measure by the Chinese Marxists). A useful account is provided in B Schwartz, *The World of Thought in Ancient China* (Cambridge, Mass: Harvard University Press, 1985). For more extended accounts, see S van der Sprenkel, *Legal Institutions in Manchu China* (London: Athlone Press, 1962); A Tay, "Law in Communist China" (1969) 6 *Sydney Law Review* 153 and 335; and V Li, "The Evolution and Development of the Chinese Legal System" in J Lindbeck, *China: Management of a Revolutionary Society* (Seattle: University of Washington Press, 1971). There has been some change in Chinese attitudes towards law and in legal practices with the shift to a market economy: see, for example, E Epstein, "China's Legal Reforms" in Kuan Hsin-chi and M Brosseau (eds), *China Review* (Hong Kong: Chinese University Press, 1991).

[325] See, for example, Hurst's discussion of the role of law in creating and deepening market relations in the United States: *Law and Markets in the United States* (Madison: University of Wisconsin Press, 1982).

[326] Unfortunately, space constraints do not permit a fuller discussion here.

Two preliminary points must first be made. The first involves distinguishing the law on decentralisation from much of the law aiming to promote development, which is addressed to or for the benefit of private actors (for example, tax incentives, land tenure reforms, family law). By contrast, the law on decentralisation is primarily addressed to officials and the institutions it sets up are public (although some objectives of the law, like participation and accountability, do depend on the enthusiasm or activity of private actors). The point of the distinction is that many factors that may hinder the implementation of the law promoting development, like the ignorance and stubbornness of private parties or their difficulties of access to legal institutions or the inadequacies of sanctions, would not, at least theoretically, apply to the law on decentralisation. On the other hand, decentralisation involves contest over power; some politicians and officials lose while others gain. Also, unlike most law promoting development, decentralisation is often forced on a government as a result of political pressures from within a country, and government may seek to evade or neutralise its provisions. These propositions are examined in this chapter.

The second point is that there are many varieties of decentralisation. The most familiar distinction is between, on the one hand, de-concentration, which applies to the delegation of administrative responsibilities to the field officers of central ministries and, on the other hand, devolution, which provides for the sharing of political, legislative, administrative and financial powers. Even within the latter, there may be different modalities for the transfer of the powers and the institutions to sustain them. The role of law in this process has varied greatly. Experience in Tanzania, where legislation of four pages or so underpinned its experiment of decentralisation (leaving matters largely to ministerial directives), can be contrasted with that of Papua New Guinea, where the *Constitution* had to be amended to accommodate an Organic Law over 50 pages long. In these circumstances, generalisations about the law in relation to decentralisation are difficult.

DECENTRALISATION IN PAPUA NEW GUINEA[327]

Establishing decentralisation

As an Australian colony, Papua New Guinea was highly centralised and bureaucratised.[328] The proposal for decentralisation of significant powers to the provinces (hitherto purely administrative units) was made by the Constitutional Planning Committee (CPC) set up by the legislature to advise on the independence constitution.[329] After some resistance by the central government, the proposals (in a modified form) were accepted in 1976.[330] This required amendments to the *Constitution*,[331] which had already been adopted, and the promulgation of a lengthy *Organic Law on Provincial Government* (OLPG), itself enjoying a constitutional status.[332] It became possible to take these measures because one of the richest provinces (Bougainville) had attempted to secede, and decentralisation was the price it demanded for ending the secession. Apart from an ethnic factor, the impulses towards decentralisation included concerns related to the need to overhaul the colonial apparatus of rule, to promote greater participation of people in government, to increase governmental accountability, and to render decisions on policy and administration speedier and more responsive to local needs/wishes. These aims were articulated in some detail in the CPC's Report.[333] Although the final form of decentralisation differed in some respects from the CPC's recommendations, its views of what decentralisation would achieve remained a yardstick of its success.

The OLPG was an attempt at a major transformation of political and bureaucratic powers. The following are some features of the constitutional and legal arrangements for decentralisation.

(1) The principal provisions for it were entrenched in the *Constitution*, and because the process of constitutional amendment is complex[334] this was an important safeguard against its easy removal.[335]

(2) Decentralisation involved the transfer of significant political, legislative, executive and financial powers.[336] The provinces were guaranteed a specified share of the national revenue as unconditional grants, especially through a minimum unconditional grant calculated by reference to levels of expenditure by the central government just before decentralisation on the activities transferred to provincial control, and (considerable) additional money was intended to be made available by the National Government in

---

[327] This part of the chapter draws upon a study of decentralisation in Papua New Guinea, which I conducted with A J Regan, the principal findings of which were published as *The Law, Politics and Administration of Decentralisation in Papua New Guinea* (Boroko: National Research Institute, 1992). Detailed accounts of many of the points made concerning Papua New Guinea in this chapter are to be found in that book.

[328] See W Tordoff and R Watts, *Report on Central-Provincial Government Relations* (Port Moresby: unpublished, 1974); and D Conyers, *The Provincial Government Debate: Central Control versus Local Participation in Papua New Guinea* (Waigani: IASER, 1976). Professors Tordoff and Watts, with their considerable knowledge and experience of developing countries, found Papua New Guinea to have the most centralised administration of any colony or state.

[329] CPC, *Final Report of the Constitutional Planning Committee: Part 1* (Port Moresby: Government Printer, 1974). See also Part 2 of the same report.

[330] One of the best accounts of the politics and process leading to the decision to decentralise is J Ballard, "Policy making as trauma" in J Ballard (ed), *Policy Making in a New State: Papua New Guinea 1972-77* (St Lucia: University of Queensland Press, 1981).

[331] *Constitutional Amendment Act No 1* 1976.

[332] *Organic Law on Provincial Government* 1977.

[333] CPC, above n 23, Part 1, particularly Ch 10.

[334] See ss 13-17.

[335] Ultimately, of course, it was not a sufficient safeguard, and the discussion of the political economy of decentralisation, below, illuminates the reasons for this.

[336] See Ghai and Regan, above n 21, Chs 5-7.

accordance with recommendations of an independent National Fiscal Commission. In addition, provinces enjoyed limited revenue-raising powers, including taxation powers reserved to them. The provinces had the right to employ a small core of key staff outside the public service (the provincial policy secretariat) but otherwise the national public service was intended to be a shared resource between the centre and the provinces, with public servants seconded to the provinces and required to take instructions from the provincial government through the head of the policy secretariat.

(3) Provinces had their own representative institutions: they were free, within broad parameters prescribed in the national *Constitution* and the OLPG, to adopt their own constitutions.[337]

(4) There was an attempt to build in considerable flexibility, particularly with regard to the gradual establishment of provincial government[338] and the further transfer of powers to provinces. Although there was a small list of exclusively provincial legislative subjects (most of purely local concern), most subjects fell within a concurrent legislative list (for example, agriculture, secondary education, transport, and so on). In the case of conflict of laws on concurrent subjects, national laws prevailed, but the expectation, stated as a requirement in the OLPG,[339] was that the central government would gradually vacate these areas for policy and legislation by the provinces.[340]

(5) An attempt was made to avoid "over-legalism" in the relations between the centre and the provinces. The provision for the gradual transfer of powers (in the concurrent list) through political agreement is an example. Another is the restriction on the jurisdiction of courts in inter-governmental disputes. The law established a number of political institutions for dealing with inter-governmental relations, most importantly the Premiers' Council, which brought together all the heads of provincial governments and the national Prime Minister with his key Ministers. The Council was also expected to take decisions on the further transfer of powers to provinces, and to resolve disputes between the central government and a province (or provinces) and between two provincial governments, through mediation or arbitration. The National Government had powers in certain circumstances to suspend a provincial government, but the procedure that had to be followed emphasised political processes of negotiation and consultation. It was also expected that the national Parliament would both act as a referee between national and provincial governments, and protect the latter against abuse of power by the former.[341]

Implementation of decentralisation

Given the initial official resistance to the notion of decentralisation in Papua New Guinea, and the size and complexity of the tasks involved in establishing new governments and their institutions, and developing their complex relationships with the National Government, the OLPG was remarkably successful. Provincial governments were established in all of the 19 provinces by the end of 1978, and all were fully elected by the end of 1980 (some operating on a transitional non-elected basis for a period prior to the first elections).[342] A special office for implementation of the

[337] Ibid, Ch 4.
[338] Ibid, Ch 3.
[339] Section 114(3).
[340] See Ghai and Regan, above n 21, pp 178-182.
[341] Ibid, Chs 8-10.
[342] Ibid, Ch 3.

OLPG was set up in the central government under a Minister sympathetic to decentralisation.[343] Largely through their own endeavours, provincial governments established democratic political orders. There was much political activity at the provincial level, with fiercely contested elections and endless motions of no-confidence. Provincial consciousness and identity were sharpened (a key goal of the CPC, which envisaged provincial identities mediating between small-scale local societies and the nation).[344] For some politicians, provinces provided a base for power or influence at the national level, including a base for launching careers in national politics. Provincial governments were increasingly becoming integrated into national politics.[345]

Significant powers were transferred to the provinces. Some powers were shared with the National Government, or implemented in accordance with its policies. The provinces had power to make policies and determine priorities over a wide range of matters. Autonomy in policy-making was not uniform. Informal control devices developed by the National Government had the effect of reducing autonomy in many provinces. "Full financial responsibility" was the most notable of such devices, being administrative arrangements under which provincial governments that were classified as having inadequate financial control and budgetary systems did not achieve full financial responsibility, and as a consequence did not receive funds for most activities through the minimum unconditional grant, but rather through normal public service departmental allocations which were controlled largely from the centre. (The full financial responsibility arrangements were not found in the law and were probably unconstitutional.)[346] Likewise, the capacity to analyse problems and formulate solutions was not uniform. Some provinces were content anyway to exercise their powers within the broad framework of national legislation; others made interesting innovations (but were sometimes frustrated by the lack of co-operation from the centre). There was often considerable confusion about the precise scope of provincial powers; this aggravated the incapacity of provinces to plan for provincial development.

Provinces had the resources, both of finance and personnel, to buttress their powers and functions. Their funds consisted of moneys from the National Government, some compulsorily transferred and some as conditional grants paid at the option of the National Government, as well as self-raised revenue. Only a few provinces had a significant surplus available to fund new development after they had met the costs of existing services and the maintenance of assets. In general, provinces had less money at their disposal than was originally expected; but in many cases provinces did not have the capacity to spend effectively all the money to which they were entitled. The bureaucracy in the provinces was for most purposes under provincial direction, and while there was limited capacity in the bureaucracy in some provinces, relations between politicians and bureaucrats were reasonable.[347] In fact, by the early 1980s most provincial governments found it unnecessary to have their own independent advisers (the provincial policy secretariats). Public servants tended to work in their home provinces and remain there, and to identify more closely with the government they worked for than had been the case before. Despite the weakness of bureaucratic capacity, there was also severe weakness in policy-making capacity in most provincial executive bodies, and as a result the bureaucracy exercised overwhelming influence on administration and policy.

---

[343] John Momis, who had been de facto chairperson of the CPC, was the Minister for Decentralisation for most of the period from 1977 to 1982.

[344] Ghai and Regan, above n 21, pp 33 and 50-53.

[345] See A J Regan, "The Politics of Provincial Government" in R J May and A J Regan (eds), *Political Decentralisation in a New State: The Experience of Provincial Government in Papua New Guinea* (Bathurst: Crawford House Press, 1997), pp 72-73.

[346] Ghai and Regan, above n 21, pp 265-72.

[347] However, the position was far from uniform: see Regan, above n 39, pp 74-75.

The institutions for intergovernmental relations worked - after a fashion. The premiers got together on an annual basis with senior Ministers of the National Government for wide-ranging discussions. The National Fiscal Commission (and the responsibilities it was to carry out) had atrophied by the mid-1980s. The Parliament did not protect provincial interests as intended by the CPC, but the courts in several instances protected the powers or autonomy of provinces. Provinces organised forms of co-operation among themselves, principally on a regional basis, and in this unity enhanced their powers to bargain with the National Government.[348]

It is possible, therefore, to say that provincial government significantly modified the old colonial state by redistributing resources and establishing a more diverse and pluralistic system. This description does not, however, convey the complete picture, for beneath the forms of decentralised power lurked considerable central control. Just as the implementation of decentralisation got under way, the national bureaucracy laid the basis for increasing central control through not only full financial responsibility arrangements, but also the National Planning and Expenditure Plan. Under the National Planning and Expenditure Plan funds remaining after meeting recurrent costs and the constitutionally guaranteed grants to the provinces were dispersed for "development" purposes to new projects. Launched about the same time as the OLPG, not only was the National Planning and Expenditure Plan tightly administered from the centre in accordance with national priorities, but it also soaked up the funds that had been expected to be disbursed to provinces as unconditional grants. Central control was facilitated by the relative meagreness of provincial finances, the result of declining value of the minimum unconditional grant,[349] absence of other unconditional grants, and the small provincial share of National Planning and Expenditure Plan funds. The consequential loss of an effective role for the National Fiscal Commission (which, but for the National Planning and Expenditure Plan, had been expected to have responsibility for recommending allocation of significant conditional grant funding to the provinces) enhanced the latitude in financial policy and allocations of the National Government.

Methods for the transfer of powers to provinces and their exercise by provinces made inroads into provincial autonomy. The vast majority of the transfers were through delegations from the National Government.[350] There was little consultation with provinces on the powers to be transferred, and the method employed denied provinces safeguards against their unilateral recall by the National Government. The simultaneous transfer to all the provinces of powers over a wide range of matters also, paradoxically, did little to reduce the salience of the National Government, since the new functions exceeded the capacity of many provinces, compelling reliance on national departments. The method used to provide for provincial administration, involving separate public service departments for each province operating under the national public service legislation, rather than as autonomous organisations as envisaged by the OLPG, tied most provinces closely to national administration.[351] The national bureaucracy maintained its hold on the machinery of the state, and its influence both at the national and provincial level continued to be pervasive.

Provincial governments, even when they were active, did little to modify or question the framework or principles of national policies. Provinces asserted and, in some instances, made good their claims to a share in national resources and the administration of these principles and

[348] Ibid, pp 73-74; and see Ghai and Regan, above n 21, pp 306-310.
[349] Ibid, pp 241-43.
[350] Ibid, pp 196-208.
[351] Ibid, pp 208-217.

policies. Neither ideologically nor materially did they challenge the premises or practices of the National Government. Nevertheless, the harmony over fundamentals belied considerable tensions between the national and provincial governments, stemming primarily from the hostility of the National Government towards provinces.

That hostility was rooted in fact in the opposition to the very concept of provincial government, although it took specific forms when national Ministers or members fell out with particular provincial governments. Opposition to provincial government was expressed not only by the national executive, but also, and even more vigorously, by the Parliament. Several attempts (and threats) were made to reduce the status and powers of the provinces, and even to abolish them.[352] The *Constitution* and the OPLG were altered to the disadvantage of provincial governments, notably in relation to the powers of the centre to suspend provincial governments.[353] A number of provincial governments were suspended, not perhaps without justification but with questionable motives. Intergovernmental institutions were largely ignored by the National Government, and even the conferences and resolutions of the Premiers' Council were reduced to mere rituals.

As against that record, the objectives of the CPC were only partially met. The central state was somewhat weakened, but not the policies that it wished to pursue. There was a greater degree of political pluralism and stronger safeguards against the authoritarianism of the National Government, but most provincial governments failed to establish higher standards of participatory democracy and public accountability. While new centres of decision-making, with important allocations of financial and staff resources, were established at provincial level, they were largely captured by local elites and so often provided, at best, a basis for inter-elite negotiations and bargaining. Nor did most provincial governments provide alternative development strategies to those pursued by the centre.

Discussion so far has focused on relations between governments. A word needs to be said about popular participation and public accountability, since the dominant theme in the CPC goals for decentralisation was the empowerment of the people. In one sense the OLPG brought democracy to lower levels of government. However, little space was created for provincial assembly members to participate in policy or administration. Further, there was little devolution from the province to local or community authorities. People were not enabled to participate in local policy-making or to exact more accountability from provincial government (the only instance being periodic elections, which in Papua New Guinea are not really instruments of accountability). On the other hand, provincial government did involve more people directly in the business of government, compelled some consideration of policy at local levels, and was useful in educating people in problems of public choice, scarcity and administration.

---

[352] Regan, above n 39, pp 68-72.

[353] Ghai and Regan, above n 21, Ch 10.

THE ROLE OF LAW IN DECENTRALISATION

It is not easy to define precisely the role played by law in these developments. It is clear that some parts of the OLPG were more successfully implemented than others, but that may be less due to the law itself than to surrounding circumstances. Nor, in one sense, does it make much sense to talk of the success of the OLPG. To do so, for example, assumes a clear consensus on its objectives. The expectations of the CPC undoubtedly provided a clear rationale for its recommendations of decentralisation. However, not only was the entire CPC not of one mind, but the OLPG was the result of competing notions of how public power should be organised. Even then, not all those who acceded to it were committed to the values that justified it. Many at the centre saw it merely as a means to bring to an end a dangerous situation caused by certain secessionist tendencies, without losing control of policy or administration. Others may have seen it as providing a local base for the exercise of influence in, if not power through, national politics. Yet others may have perceived it as a staging post for secession.

The 1976 amendment to the *Constitution* and the enactment of the OLPG, although representing a victory for the proponents of decentralisation, did not bring the controversies on provincial government to an end. Although the law changed the battle lines, it did not terminate the struggle between the different views. The open-endedness of the OLPG on some matters, and the room it provided for further negotiations, ensured that competing views would seek to capture the process of implementation and operation of provincial government.

Notwithstanding that it is not easy either to make generalisations uniformly applicable to all provinces, or to ascribe any one intention to the OLPG, it may be useful to summarise those aspects where there are grounds to believe that it has been effective either in its own terms or in the purposes underlying it (as deduced from the historical background). The OLPG was effective in:

(a) re-allocating financial and human resources away from the centre to a number of provincial governments;

(b) establishing legislative and executive bodies in the provinces through constitutions prepared by local constituent assemblies and by a series of provincial elections;

(c) ensuring the transfer of certain minimum functions previously exercised from the centre to provinces;

(d) creating, at least in some provinces, some capacity to plan, co-ordinate and carry out various executive functions;

(e) promoting discussions between the National Government and provinces on national priorities and the allocation of powers and functions between the two levels of government;

(f) establishing a degree of political pluralism and broadening the democratic base for policy and executive functions; and

(g) providing a more secure basis for national unity.

On the negative side, the OLPG failed to:

(a) bring about a fundamental change in the political system or economic and social policies;

(b) create greater political consciousness and mobilisation at the grass roots level to act as a pressure for progressive policies and against inefficient and corrupt administration and practices in the manner envisaged by the CPC;

(c) establish democratic institutions below the provincial level or involve voluntary and community organisations in policy-making or administration;

(d) bring about efficient administration uniformly across all provinces;

(e) establish "co-operative federalism" in which there could be extensive consultations between the two levels of government on national policies leading to agreed policies and action and the sharing of responsibilities; and

(f) bring about a significant transfer or delegation of functions to provinces on concurrent matters.

The manner in which the OLPG operated can be explained in two main ways. The first concerns reasons within its own terms, and involves examining its status and structure, and then the external environment that influenced its operation, particularly in those areas where the law provided a measure of discretion. The OLPG was enacted after the *Constitution* was amended to accord an entrenched status to the legal provisions for decentralisation. This strategy represented a repudiation of that advocated by the National Government before independence, that decentralisation should be provided for through ordinary legislation. The entrenchment was important in two respects. First, the amendment of the *Constitution* signified a new political and constitutional settlement, underlying the centrality of decentralisation to the constitutional system of Papua New Guinea, and gave a measure of legitimacy to it. Secondly, it proved an important element in the continuance of provincial government in warding off the repeated attacks on it by the National Government or national parliamentarians. It is most probable that attempts to repeal legislation for provincial government would have succeeded long before 1995 if they had not had to run the gauntlet of the constitutional amendment process.

Turning to the structure of the OLPG, there are a number of features that influenced the direction of developments. These principally concern the binding nature of provisions and the mechanisms for the resolution of conflicts and the enforcement of the law. A series of provisions was mandatory, while others were discretionary or facilitative. The balance between the two represented a judgment on what was minimally essential to establish provincial government, and what was best left to decisions in the future as to the respective functions of, and co-operation between, the national and provincial governments. In general, where the provisions were mandatory, the law was more successful in its aims than when they were discretionary or facilitative. Examples of mandatory provisions were:

(a) those concerning the minimum unconditional grant, requiring the transfer of prescribed funds to provinces;

(b) other provisions for compulsory transfer of funds;

(c) the establishment of legislative and executive bodies and the holding of elections;

(d) the structure of provincial administration, including the appointment of the administrative secretary;

(e) the machinery for intergovernmental relations, including meetings of the Premiers' Council;

(f) the vesting of primarily provincial matters in the provinces; and

(g) the procedure for the notification of proposed laws.

Not all of these provisions were fully implemented. For example:

(1) The doctrine of full financial responsibility meant the incomplete application of the rules for minimum unconditional grant for a number of provinces.

(2) The arrangements for the department of the province were incompatible with the law (as the Supreme Court ultimately declared).[354]

(3) The notification of law provisions were not always satisfactorily observed.[355]

None of these deviations (with the possible exception of that relating to the department of the province), however, undermined the basic premises of the law, and some of them arose because of a miscomprehension of the legal provisions. There are a number of factors that account for the relatively good record of the implementation of the mandatory provisions. One of them is the persistence of the colonial tradition of the Rule of Law. Such a tradition is different in many ways from the metropolitan model of the Rule of Law, particularly in the values it seeks to protect, but it does nevertheless emphasise that the law also binds the government. The public service in Papua New Guinea was trained to respect and implement the law. Unlike many developing countries, there is still considerable respect attached to the law; the judiciary is generally competent as well as independent, and enjoys considerable prestige. Once it was clear that a particular provision of the OLPG required a specific action on the part of a department or official, it was normally carried out. The mandatory nature of many provisions enabled the Department of Provincial Affairs, sometimes armed with an opinion from the relevant law department, to put pressure on other, more recalcitrant, departments to carry out the mandates of the law.

Discretionary powers and facilitative provisions were essential to the concept of decentralisation: flexible, gradual, diverse and co-operative. Discretion was vested in various bodies:

(a) the people of a province originally (through a constituent assembly), and then the provincial assembly designed a provisional constitution (subject only to a few constitutional limits);

(b) the provincial government, in determining the structure and powers of local authorities;

(c) the National Parliament, in holding the balance between the national and provincial governments, and in protecting the provinces against the abuse by the National Government of powers of disallowance of taxes and the suspension of provincial governments;

(d) the National Government most of all, in deciding on the pace of transfers and delegations of powers, especially on the concurrent subjects, initiating the suspension of a provincial government, the allocation of revenues to provinces additional to the minimum unconditional grant, and the primary decisions on the implementation of the resolutions of the Premiers' Council.

---

[354] *SCR No 1 of 1984; Re Morobe Provincial Government v PNG* [1984] PNGLR 212.

[355] See Ghai and Regan, above n 21, pp 152-55.

Sometimes, but not always, the OLPG provided guidance for the exercise of the discretion (examples being the presumption that most of the concurrent powers would be exercised by the provinces, the specification of grounds for the discretion of the National Government to suspend a provincial government, and the guidance to the National Fiscal Commission in determining the validity of provincial taxes and deciding the allocations of additional funds to provinces). As the law was drafted against the background of the CPC Report, the assumption was that it would be exercised to promote its goals.

In practice, discretionary powers were seldom exercised for the purposes that might be considered inherent in the OLPG. Nor was the worst offender always the National Government; provincial governments did little to promote grass roots democracy, accept accountability or maintain high standards of probity.

Most of the discretionary powers, however, were vested in the National Government, which in exercising the powers paid little regard to the overall aims of decentralisation. By negating the role of the National Fiscal Commission and establishing the National Planning and Expenditure Plan, it disposed of larger sums directly than was assumed, and by the practice of full financial responsibility it retained considerable control over what should have been the unconditional grant funds (minimum unconditional grant) of several provinces: far greater control than the law permitted. It facilitated much smaller exercise by provinces of concurrent powers than the OLPG suggested. It used the powers of the suspension of provincial governments somewhat selectively, for ulterior political motives rather than for the cure of inefficiencies and corruption that undoubtedly existed. It failed to consult, or consult adequately, the provinces on the various matters that it was required to consult about. The Parliament did not fulfil its role of holding the balance between the National Government and the provincial governments, especially with regard to the suspension of provincial governments.

A central reason why in these instances discretionary powers were exercised in ways contrary to the underlying assumptions of the OLPG, and sometimes in violation of its provisions, lies in part in the complexity of the OPLG. Paradoxically, the attempt to provide for a flexible and co-operative system of decentralisation resulted sometimes in complex procedure (as in the regime for the sharing and transferring of powers, and the scheme of concurrent powers). Complexity was compounded by the style of drafting, occasionally prolix and sometimes convoluted, which characterises constitutional instruments in Papua New Guinea. There was also a significant degree of ignorance or misunderstanding of the law on decentralisation. Complexity combined with ignorance enabled the central government to shift the balance in its favour in the implementation of the OLPG, since it enjoyed a predominance of legal and bureaucratic resources. The control mechanisms outside the framework of the OLPG are a case in point. The grievances of the provinces at the incomplete implementation of the law were not dealt with satisfactorily, since the OLPG placed such a premium on political process: consultation, negotiation and mediation. Such an approach depends greatly on good faith and assumes a certain equality of bargaining power among the participants. The latter was patently not the case, and the former did not materialise. The regime of interpretation and dispute resolution tended, therefore, to favour the initially powerful party, the National Government.

The unsatisfactory outcome of the regime led the provinces to bring the courts into the equation, as was permitted by the law. Some judicial decisions were legalistic – as the CPC had feared – but the clarification (or more accurately, the authoritative statement) of the law sometimes served to restore something of the balance of the OLPG. However, this in turn may have contributed to increasing resentment of devolution on the part of the National Government. Thus, while court intervention may have resolved some legislative ambiguities, it did little to mitigate the tensions between the centre and provinces. It is not unlikely that, in a paradoxical way, the greater adherence to the law may have put in jeopardy the entire scheme for devolution. The CPC had foreseen the tension between legal regulation and politics. Unfortunately, the political system failed to provide the flexibilities, compromises and accommodations originally expected of it. The key to understanding the operation of the OLPG lies essentially in politics.

This analysis of factors inherent in the law is not unimportant. Nevertheless these matters were themselves largely dependent on the broader political context, which influenced decisions on the implementation of the OLPG. It is the political economy that constitutes the primary explanation of the fortunes of decentralisation.

THE POLITICAL ECONOMY OF DECENTRALISATION

The central explanation offered by political economy lies in the nature of the state, in both its colonial and post-colonial variations. The mission of the colonial state was to subordinate the peoples of Papua New Guinea to imperial authority, to provide the conditions, as well as the infrastructure, for the economic exploitation of the colony for the benefits of metropolitan commercial interests, and to promote the strategic and defence needs of Australia. To achieve these purposes, a complex set of laws and practices were necessary. A prerequisite was a relatively strong state, which could subdue indigenous communities to its will, and penetrate existing modes of economic organisation to lay the basis of new, largely capitalist relations of production. However, the penetration of both the state and the market was partial and limited.

The market was the handmaiden of the state. The goal of the colonial state is to establish forms of capitalist economy, although the precise form depends on the scale and nature of colonial economic interests (for example, plantation or peasant-based agriculture, the extraction of mineral or other raw materials. or marketing of metropolitan products). Because colonialism seeks to promote metropolitan interests, it seldom institutes a general, unfettered market; rather, the market is administered, aided by discretionary laws that permit discrimination and control the spread of monetary or market relations.

The mediation of the market through the state makes the state an object of desire; and many colonial struggles have been for the control of it. But as the market and market relations expand, they acquire a dynamism of their own, tending towards some autonomy from the state, if not control over it. Often the corrosive effect of the market on traditional systems is more powerful than the subordination of those systems by the state. By the time of independence in Papua New Guinea, the market had not achieved a position where it could expand without the assistance of the state; both the state and the market needed the symbiotic relationship characterised by the colonial period. The CPC (and such nationalist movement as there was) overestimated the potential of the state, and underestimated the dynamics of market relations.

Underlying the recommendations of the CPC, especially on provincial government, was a great faith in the good sense, judgment and ethics of the people. Its suspicions of the colonial structure of authority ran sufficiently deep that it wanted to transform it at the national level, and prescribe in detail the provisions for its replacement. However, it was content to leave questions of the organisation and control of power at the provincial level to the "people". It regarded the people as the custodians of traditional as well as democratic values. It was blind to the fact that belief in this form of populism ran counter to the underlying contours of state and economic power.

The explanation of the attitudes towards and, the fortunes of, decentralisation lies in the peculiar conjuncture of political and economic power that resulted from the adoption of the Westminster system at the national level. It was clear that the apparatus of the state would be instrumental in any basic change in the economy, whether it was to be moved to accommodate the economic aspirations of the emerging indigenous elite, or a more fundamental transformation in economic relations in the direction of egalitarian development favoured by the CPC. In fact, the importance of the state would be emphasised as it became the conduit for foreign aid and began to mediate between the local elite and international capital. There was little in the political history of Papua New Guinea to suggest that the state would be pressed into the service of socialist re-orientation of society and economy. Colonial development had ensured that few Papua New Guineans had a hold in the economy and the rhetoric of nationalism was directed mainly towards a redistribution of resources on a racial basis; towards opening up of opportunities for indigenous people within a broadly market-oriented economy. In these circumstances it was more than likely that this process would be parasitic upon the state and that those who acquired access to its apparatus would use it for forms of primitive accumulation through a plunder of public and private resources.

The access to the apparatus of the state was to be mediated through a Westminster parliamentary system and public service. The operation of that system has become important to the process of accumulation and explains why it is that some of the CPC's expectations for the *Constitution* - and more especially decentralisation - did not materialise. The search for the spoils of the system meant that no fundamental change was made to it, other than modifications needed to incorporate sections of the indigenous elite. The same considerations motivated provincial politicians, so that there was no prospect that they would develop an alternative paradigm of development. The importance of a political position, particularly membership of the national legislature and the National Executive Council, as a means of gaining access to state resources, has given a sharpness and primacy to the politics of numbers. Political parties have been unable to organise and discipline either their supporters or candidates. No party has ever secured a majority, so that the politics of coalition dominate the legislature and the executive.

There are few differences of policy among political parties in Papua New Guinea, so that coalition-forming is largely a matter of negotiating for ministries. For that same reason coalitions are unstable; offers of more prestigious ministries in a coalition headed by the leader of the Opposition have sometimes been enough to break a ruling coalition. The instability of the executive is aggravated by the constitutional rule that encourages votes of no confidence in the government, as a successful vote does not lead, as in many parliamentary systems, to the dissolution of the legislature and fresh elections, but in the fall of the government and the installation of another. Consequently no government feels safe in this environment of plots and intrigues. Since the Cabinet, and particularly the Prime Minister, must always cover their back, coalition management takes precedence over policy-making, reinforcing the conservatism of the system.

The whole parliamentary system is now lubricated by cash. Candidates for election to the Parliament cannot rely upon party organisation or loyalty to win elections, and so are under pressure to win votes by various forms of bribing. Forms of clientage emerge, reinforced by ethnic politics. Governments cannot maintain their cohesion by common purpose, but must instead rely upon patronage and trade-offs. Some of the cash to maintain this system may come from private resources, but the vast bulk of it comes from the state. To 1995, this was as true for most of the provinces as for the National Government. Politicians were therefore involved in a constant struggle for state resources. With the establishment of elected provincial governments from 1976, national parliamentarians and the executive saw some of the resources and forms of patronage previously available to them slip away to provincial politicians and governments. Perhaps even more importantly, it was in the 20 years after independence that the imperatives towards extraction of resources from the state escalated in intensity, and the lack of access to the resources of provincial governments combined with political competition from provincial governments, and provincial politicians, became increasingly irksome for politicians at the national level. The question of access to provincial resources constituted the nub of, and united most national politicians in, their attack on provincial government, since there was little in the policies of provinces that they objected to.

These were not the circumstances in which co-operation could flourish. Instead, an atmosphere of escalating tension and hostility developed. Nor were these circumstances, which placed such high premium on access to and use of state resources, conducive to efficiency or public accountability, which, as discussed, suffered at both levels of government.

The lack of policies to change the inherited colonial structures and economy, indeed the lack of any firm policies, left the power of the bureaucracy largely intact.[356] The traditions of the colonial bureaucracy favoured hierarchy, opposed power-sharing, and suspected politicians. These traditions combined to make the bureaucracy oppose provincial government, and while it has shifted from its initial basic opposition, it has seldom supported any moves towards decentralisation with any degree of enthusiasm.

It was the factors just outlined which led to the repeal and replacement of the constitutional arrangements for decentralisation in July 1995. Under the new arrangements, elected provincial governments were abolished and replaced by new provincial bodies in which the provincial assembly comprises the members of Parliament from a province, the heads of local-level governments and a few other appointed members. The members of Parliament dominate the new bodies, thereby getting the access to the resources of the provincial governments they had long sought.

[356] But see the discussion by Ghai in Chapter 4, "Establishing a liberal political order through a constitution: The Papua New Guinea experience", concerning the politicisation of the bureaucracy.

CONCLUSIONS: THE CONTINGENCY AND AUTONOMY OF LAW

It is clear from this case study that the law played an important role in decentralisation in Papua New Guinea. Law was able to establish a broad and, in some cases, detailed framework for implementation and operation of decentralisation. The law enjoyed a constitutional status. Those opposed to decentralisation were still finding their feet in the national political and administrative system (but subsequently, having found their feet, did much to deflect the main thrust of the legislation). Many of the provisions of the law were mandatory, leaving limited options for the central government. Papua New Guinea operated under a form of the Rule of Law. Its judiciary is independent and competent, and on the whole its decisions are respected. Although the proponents of decentralisation were concerned to keep courts out of inter-governmental relations, the courts came to play an important role in protecting it.

Several of these circumstances are specific to Papua New Guinea, and as a result its experience does not provide a reliable base for generalisations on the role of law in relation to decentralisation in other developing countries. But it does show that it is worthwhile to pay particular attention to the content and structure of the law.

However, in another way, the Papua New Guinea experience does suggest a basis for generalisation. This study shows that the law does not operate autonomously of social and economic forces. The formulation and adoption of the constitutional laws on decentralisation were themselves intensely political. The law became a battleground for opposing views on how state power should be organised. The compromises eventually struck were by no means to the liking of the dominant interests at the time. The outcome shows that political action to change the law can sometimes be a worthwhile exercise. The periphery and communal organisations were able to exploit the weakness and fragility of the colonial state, which had lacked legitimacy in the eyes of the people. The national leaders were insecure in their newly acquired positions and uncertain how to wield the levers of power. It was this contingency which enabled the proponents of decentralisation to win their victory in 1976. A similar challenge a few years later would have stood less prospects of success (as the present challenges from Bougainville demonstrate).

Our study also shows that the law can sometimes be used to consolidate political gains. In this case the law enjoyed constitutional status and thus helped to entrench the gains in a form not susceptible to easy removal. As far as the *Constitution* is concerned, the courts maintained the principles of legality, and provincial government received some protection from the judiciary. It is true of course that provincial government posed no real threat to dominant economic interests. Had provincial governments tried to change the nature of economic relations, the system may well have become vulnerable to more sustained attacks, and its survival would then have been questionable. This point is underlined by the fact that ultimately it was the need for expansion of access to state resources by the national elite that led to the demise of the elected provincial government system in 1995.

This study also shows that the operation of the OLPG was shaped by the wider political and economic circumstances. The provisions of the law were manipulated, evaded, ignored, re-interpreted, observed, and used as a resource to suit the various parties concerned. Where there was discretion, it was frequently exercised in ways that were inconsistent with the basic purposes of the legislation. In various ways the forms of provincial government were observed, but the expectations of its founders were largely negated. The experience points to the limits of law in shaping values. It can set up institutions and give them resources and competencies, but it can seldom infuse them with particular values. However, as the study of the operation of the *Constitution* as a whole elsewhere in this volume shows,[357] the law can rarely operate against the tide of social and economic forces.

[357] Ibid.

ACCOUNTABILITY AND DISTRIBUTION OF POWER

Chapter 12

SEPARATION OF POWERS

MICHAEL A NTUMY

INTRODUCTION

Several provisions in the *Constitution* invoke the theory of separation of powers. These include: s 100, which vests the legislative power of the people in the Parliament; s 138, which vests the executive power of the people in the Head of State; and s 158, which vests the judicial authority of the people in the National Judicial System. However, the most explicit reference to the theory is contained in s 99 of the *Constitution*, which provides as follows:

> "Structure of Government.
>
> (1) Subject to and in accordance with this Constitution, the power, authority and jurisdiction of the People shall be exercised by the National Government.
>
> (2) The National Government consists of three principal arms, namely:-
>
> (a) the National Parliament, which is an elective legislature with, subject to the Constitutional laws, unlimited powers of law-making; and
>
> (b) the National Executive; and
>
> (c) the National Judicial System, consisting of a Supreme Court of Justice and a National Court of Justice, of unlimited jurisdiction, and other courts.
>
> (3) In principle, the respective powers and functions of the three arms shall be kept separate from each other.
>
> (1) Sub-section (2) is descriptive only and is non-justiciable."

What were the original aims of inserting these provisions in the *Constitution*? Does the judicial interpretation of the provisions correspond to the original aims? If so, what factors have made this possible? If not, which factors militate against the realisation of the original aims? This chapter attempts to answer these and related questions in order to illustrate how the theory of separation of powers operates in Papua New Guinea. To do this, the chapter reviews the decided cases that have discussed the relevant constitutional provisions and other literature that shed light on the questions against the background of the theory.

THE THEORY OF SEPARATION OF POWERS

The theory of separation of powers is the doctrinal basis for the traditional tripartite division of governmental powers into legislative, executive and judiciary in western democratic systems. Popularly regarded as a constitutional or legal safeguard against tyranny and the arbitrary use of power, the function of the theory is to control the exercise of power by the three arms of government.

Although the theory of separation of powers has been traced to the feudal era when the concepts of governmental functions and theories of mixed and balanced government were evolved, it was not until the 17th century that it emerged for the first time as a coherent theory of government. In England, following the civil war and the disapproval of a system of government based upon a "mixture" of kings, lords and commons, the theory emerged as a response to the need for a new constitutional theory.

As a result of the socio-political developments of the 19th and early 20th centuries, the theory came under several attacks. This led to a sharp re-appraisal of the theory as formulated by Montesquieu. First, as the middle class gained a place in the political organisation of the state in the 19th century, the need for the theory as essentially a challenge to the power of an aristocracy diminished. However, the lessened enthusiasm for the theory did not result in its outright rejection. Rather, it took the form of a re-examination and re-formulation, retaining particularly the idea of a balance.

The second attack upon the theory came with the realisation that the functional concepts of the theory were inadequate to describe and explain the operations of government. This realisation was heightened by, inter alia, the emergence of administrative agencies and an awareness of the nature of the modern bureaucracy. This led to a complete reassessment of the "executive" function and a demand for the establishment of "harmony" between the legislature and government, which characterised the theory of parliamentary government in Britain and France. In the United States, a new notion of "separation of powers" – that between the "political" branches of government and the administration (bureaucracy) – emerged, which distinguished between "politics" and "administration" (developed in the Weberian theory of bureaucracy) and opened a new chapter in the establishment of semi-autonomous branches of government (that is, the administration) with great emphasis on unity and cohesion, and checks and balances.

Changing ideas about the role of the state and the structure of government were accompanied by a changing emphasis on the nature of sovereignty. Whereas in the earlier centuries the theorists of absolutism stressed the necessity of a single, omnipotent source of power, liberal constitutionalists who regarded themselves as defenders of liberty against arbitrary government, appealing to Montesquieu, stressed the division of power, and the limitations imposed upon the exercise of power by the constitution or a higher law. A new notion of sovereignty (limited/popular sovereignty) emerged, spearheaded by Rousseau, which linked unlimited sovereignty not with the monarch but the people. This new notion was used by Bentham and Austin to denounce arbitrary rule and to demand political reforms that would increase the freedom of the individual. Ironically, even though all these liberal writers were most concerned to establish laissez-faire capitalism, their ideas became the instrument for the working class, which was used to destroy laissez-faire capitalism.

Other equally important intellectual challenges to the theory specifically rejected Montesquieu's formulation of the triad of government powers and the 18th century view of the functions of government, and stressed the role of discretion and prerogative in government as a prerequisite for a unified system of government.

Notwithstanding these attacks, it is instructive to note that even in countries such as England and the United States, which are regarded as models for the modern application of the theory, no alternative coherent formulation of the structure of government and the articulation of its parts has risen up to take the place of the earlier theory. As a result, both the theory and its vocabulary continue to be in usage. The persistence of the theory and its terminology also reflects the fact that western societies have not since the advent of capitalism undergone any radical transformation of their socio-economic systems and, hence, the political and legal theories continue to reflect feudalist ideas with modifications.

Today, though not the original source of the doctrine, Montesquieu is regarded as the chief exponent of, and authority on, the doctrine of separation of powers. His formulation of the theory, which is widely accepted as the model theoretical basis for the structure of government and the exercise of state power in all western democracies and countries that adopt the western democratic system of government, may be summed up as follows:

(1) If the executive and the legislative powers are vested in the same person or body of persons, there is bound to be the danger of the legislature enacting oppressive laws, which the executive will administer to attain its own ends. This type of situation is particularly likely to occur where there is a personal executive not responsible in law to the courts or politically to a representative assembly. For when laws are enforced by the same body that enacts them, the end result is bound to be arbitrary rule, and the judges would then be more legislators than interpreters of the law.

(2) In the same way, if one person or body of persons is allowed to exercise both executive and judicial powers in the same matter or cause, it is bound to result in arbitrary rule, which would be tantamount to tyranny if that same body is vested with legislative power.[358]

In practice, the theory has been reduced to the following assertions:

(1) The agencies of government have been divided into three categories; namely, the legislative, the executive and the judiciary.

(2) There are three specific "functions" of government and each of these functions should be entrusted solely to the appropriate, or "proper", branch of the government.

(3) The three branches of government should be composed of quite separate and distinct groups of people, with no overlapping membership; that is "separation of persons".

(4) If the recommendations are followed with regard to agencies, functions and persons, then each branch of the government will act as a check on the exercise of arbitrary power by the others and each branch, because it is restricted to the exercise of its own function, will be unable to exercise undue control or influence over the others.

[358] Montesquieu, L'Esprit des Lois (Paris: Editions Sociales, 1969).

It should be emphasised, however, that, while this paradigm provides a universal standard of the theory, there is no uniform application of the theory. In practice, the operation of the theory varies considerably from country to country.

APPLICATION OF THE THEORY IN PAPUA NEW GUINEA

The practical application of the theory of separation of powers varies from country to country. In Papua New Guinea, the *Constitution* makes provision for the theory. In order to gain a thorough understanding of how the theory operates in Papua New Guinea, it is important to examine how the courts have interpreted the various constitutional provisions that invoke the theory.

The first major case that discussed the theory was *Peter v South Pacific Brewery Ltd* [1976] PNGLR 345. This was a reference under s 18 of the *Constitution* by the District Court at Port Moresby requesting the interpretation and application of s 37(5) of the *Constitution.* This constitutional provision guarantees that "the trial [of any person] shall not take place in his absence". However, this right is subject to certain exceptions, including situations where the person consents, and, in respect of offences for which imprisonment is not a penalty, where it is established that the person has been served with a summons. Section 131 of the *District Courts Act* (Ch 40) allowed for the summary trial of "simple offences", but defined these to include offences punishable by imprisonment. The issue before the court, therefore, was whether s 131 of the *District Courts Act* was authorised by s 37(5) of the *Constitution.*

The majority of the Supreme Court (Frost CJ and Kearney J) found that s 10 of the *Constitution* permitted the court to "read down" s 131 of the *District Courts Act* so that it applied only to offences not punishable by imprisonment. Prentice DCJ was prepared to go further and add a phrase to s 131 of the *District Courts Act* to allow it to apply to imprisonment offences if the accused consented to trial in his absence.

For the purposes of this chapter, the important point was the reliance of the court on the theory of separation of powers to interpret s 10 of the *Constitution* and the differences in approach between the judges. Adopting Australian cases without qualification, Frost CJ and Kearney J held that, while s 10 of the *Constitution* permitted the court to give to a general phrase in an Act a limited operation, so that, "read down", it conformed to the *Constitution,* it could not add words to the Act. Frost CJ pointed to the similarity between s 10 and s 15A of the Australian *Acts Interpretation Act* 1973, and concluded that the view expressed in the Australian cases that a court could not legislate when applying this section was relevant in Papua New Guinea. In his view:

> "The restriction that in no case can the court be required to legislate cannot be excluded under s 10, for this court has no function in relation to the legislative power which is vested in the National Parliament (*Constitution*, ss 99, 100)."[359]

In a similar vein, Kearney J also agreed that s 10 of the *Constitution* must be applied in the light of s 99(3) of the *Constitution* which, as he said:

---

[359] [1976] PNGLR 345 at 546.

> "does not warrant an incursion by the court upon the law-making power of Parliament, so as to create, by reading down, an Act which differs in its substance from that passed by Parliament. The court's function remains one of construction . . . not one of legislation."[360]

Prentice DCJ, on the other hand, concluded that s 10 of the *Constitution* allowed the court to add words to an Act to bring it within the *Constitution* and proceeded to interpret the section without reference to any Australian cases. The judge referred to the National Goals and Directive Principles and also to s 32 of the *Constitution* (the right to freedom) to arrive at the conclusion that the policy behind the legislative provision in question was desirable, and was clearly influenced by this policy to find that the provisions could be wholly saved under s 10 of the *Constitution.* Without considering the constitutional provisions relating to the theory of separation of powers, he was prepared to override whatever obstacle the theory might pose:

> "I consider that *any* solution which saved the operation of s 131 of the *District Courts Act* [which included the view of the majority] in regard to offences not carrying penalty of imprisonment, would involve in fact the deletion or insertion of words either in the definition of 'simple offence' or in s 131 itself - and may frankly be recognised as 'judicial legislating' of a permissible kind."[361]

In essence, the Supreme Court was unanimous in this case that the celebrated tripartite division of the government into the legislature, executive and judiciary with their corresponding functions applied in Papua New Guinea and, more specifically, each of the three specific functions of government should be entrusted solely to the appropriate or proper branch of the government. The court, however, appeared not to be dogmatic about the theory, preferring instead to modify it to suit the particular circumstances of Papua New Guinea.

The next major case that discussed the application of the theory of separation of powers in Papua New Guinea was *Constitutional Reference No 1 of 1978* [1978] PNGLR 345. The main legal issue in this case was whether the Public Solicitor was within the category of "other governmental body" as stipulated in s 219(1)(a)(ii) of the *Constitution,* and thus, within the complaints jurisdiction of the Ombudsman Commission. Schedule 1.2(1) defines "governmental body" to include "an arm . . . of the National Government", and s 99(2) describes the "three principal arms" of the National Government as: the National Parliament, the National Executive, and the National Judicial System.

The Ombudsman Commission claimed jurisdiction on the ground that the Public Solicitor was an "arm" of the National Government outside the three "principal arms" described by s 99(2). Prentice CJ rejected this argument for reasons that stressed desirable policy as much as proper interpretation, but the Chief Justice appeared to proceed on the basis that the National Government is limited to its three arms. To him, it was clear that the Public Solicitor is not within these three arms.

Wilson J also accepted the notion that the National Government comprised the three principal arms, but added that there are "many and varied lesser arms of government within the three principal arms",[362] such as the Judicial and Legal Services Commission. However, the judge

[360] Ibid at 560.
[361] Ibid at 558.
[362] Ibid at 361.

excluded the Law Officers (the Public Prosecutor and the Public Solicitor), on the ground that the National Judicial System excludes the Law Officers. However, it may be pointed out that the Judicial and Legal Services Commission is also not listed as part of the National Judicial System.

At any rate, the important point for the purposes of this chapter is that Wilson J's argument about lesser arms of government that are within the principal arms indicates the difficulty of adapting the paradigm notion of the theory of separation of powers to the particular circumstances of Papua New Guinea.

Pritchard J, who dissented on the issue, found that the Public Solicitor was within the definition of "governmental body". Justice Pritchard found that the Public Solicitor was "a separate arm of the National Government not an instrumentality responsible or subservient to any one of the three principal arms".[363] This conclusion was based on a detailed analysis of the structure of Part VI of the *Constitution* (which is titled "The National Government"), supported by a rejection of the view that the traditional separation of powers approach was reflected in the *Constitution.* As he categorically stated:

> "I say here and now, there is no such tradition [that is, 'three traditional functions of government'] in Papua New Guinea. Except to the extent that the principles and rules of common law and equity in England are adopted under Sch 2.2 of our *Constitution,* in Papua New Guinea we do not call on traditions of government from anywhere in the world at all; we look to our constitutional laws and them alone. The *Constitution* and the Organic Laws are the Supreme Law of Papua New Guinea and their provisions are self-executing to the fullest extent their respective natures and subject matters permit (*Constitution* s 11)."[364]

Pritchard J backed his position by arguing that the constitution-makers did not envisage the traditional English concept of the three arms of government only, otherwise "the word 'principal' need never have appeared in s 99" of the *Constitution.*[365]

This argument may be countered by the fact that if the constitution-makers had envisaged the so-called "lesser arms" of government, since the mention of "principal arms" of government, according to Pritchard J, suggests a ranking in terms of importance, then after mentioning the "first in rank" (that is, the "principal arms"), it would have been logically necessary, for the sake of clarity, to mention what comes next (that is, the so-called "lesser arms"). The fact that there is no such reference to any other category of arms of government in the *Constitution* is, in my view, significant.

It is instructive to observe that Pritchard J's argument is reminiscent of the criticism of the theory in Britain, France and the United States that was occasioned by the realisation in the 19th century that the functional concepts of the theory were inadequate to describe and explain the operations of government. Hence, if the argument is valid, then it calls for a complete reassessment of the underlying concepts and theoretical basis of the structure of government in Papua New Guinea. At any rate, the argument is significant for its candid admission of the incongruence between the theory of separation of powers and the governmental framework adopted in the *Constitution.* For it is not unreasonable to surmise that the other judges in this case (as in the case of *Peter v South Pacific Brewery Ltd*) were also aware of this fact, but apparently opted to live with it. In this

---

[363] Ibid at 383.
[364] Ibid at 377.
[365] Ibid at 384.

respect, Pritchard J's dissenting judgment breaks new ground from the past judicial attitude towards the theory of separation of powers.

In *SCR No 1A of 1981; Re Motor Traffic Act* [1982] PNGLR 122, the Supreme Court again relied on the theory of separation of powers as an aid to the interpretation of the *Constitution.* This was a reference by the Public Solicitor pursuant to s 19 of the *Constitution* to determine the legal validity of certain amendments to s 19AB(2)(e)(iii) of the *Motor Traffic Act* (Ch 243), s 138A(1)(b) of the *District Courts Act* (Ch 40) and s 138A(1)(c) of the *Local Courts Act* (Ch 41). The amendments sought to enable police officers to issue summonses for traffic infringements, which contained the information that, if the fine imposed in the summons was paid within 14 days, that would be the end of the matter. However, if the fine was not paid within this time period, the charge would come before the court designated in the summons, and should the defendant fail to appear by counsel or in person, the court if "satisfied that the Traffic Infringement Summons has been served . . . shall record a plea of guilty and shall consider the sentence which shall be pronounced in open Court".[366]

The Supreme Court unanimously held that the amendments were unconstitutional. In handing down their judgments, Kidu CJ and Kearney DCJ found it relevant to refer to the theory of separation of powers as one of their reasons for invalidating the amendments. Kidu CJ was brief and to the point. As he put it, the amendments were unconstitutional because they purport "to exercise the judicial authority of the People in respect of criminal offences, an authority vested exclusively in the National Judicial System by the *Constitution*".[367] Kearney DCJ's remarks were more elaborate. He asserted:

> "any Act which requires a court to record a plea of guilty to an offence in circumstances in which the court is not first required to be satisfied, in its independent judgment, that the person charged wishes freely and with full understanding to admit his guilt, amounts to a usurpation by the legislative arm of government of a function reserved by the *Constitution* to the judicial arm of government; and is accordingly unconstitutional and a nullity, of no legal effect. I respectfully agree with the Chief Justice that the procedure set out in the provisions referred to do not amount to the summary hearing required by the proviso to the *Constitution,* s 37(5), and are unconstitutional for that reason. But more fundamentally, I think, they are unconstitutional because they amount to an exercise by the legislature of the judicial authority of the people in respect of criminal offences, which by the *Constitution,* s 158(1), is vested exclusively in the National Judicial System. It is of course true that judicial authority may be conferred on other tribunals under the *Constitution,* s 159, but that is irrelevant for present purposes, since s 159(3) prevents any such tribunal from imposing any penalty for a criminal offence."[368]

It is clear from its structure that the *Constitution* contemplates a general separation of powers between the three principal arms of government: the legislature, executive and judiciary (see the *Constitution*, s 99). As a parliamentary system with an executive responsible to Parliament, the separation of powers between the arms cannot be rigid. But the separation principle remains of basic importance in the *Constitution* and prohibits incursions by one arm of government upon basic functions of another. The legislation presently in question, I think, is an example of the

[366] Section 138A(1)(b) Motor Traffic Act (Ch 243).
[367] [1982] PNGLR 122 at 129.
[368] Ibid at 134.

legislature having gone too far in prescribing rules that control judicial decisions in certain cases, thus invading the realm of judicial power. It is of the essence of the judicial function that the court, when considering whether a plea of guilty should be recorded, brings to bear its own independent judgment as to whether materials put before it are probative of guilt, whether they bear that character; and also as to whether a defendant fully and freely is waiving her or his right to a trial, in which he or she cannot be convicted unless the elements of the offence are proved against her or him to the required standard of proof, and is unequivocally admitting every element of the offence. The fact that the evisceration of the essential judicial function in considering whether a plea of guilty should be recorded is achieved by the surgical knife of procedure, does not affect the character of what was done; what cannot be done directly, cannot be done indirectly. Here there are, in truth, no judicial functions for the court to perform; the legislation has wholly absorbed the judicial process.

In view of the controversy generated by Pritchard J's dissenting view on the theory of separation of powers in *Constitutional Reference No 1 of 1978,* this case presented a golden opportunity for the Supreme Court to address the question of the apparent dichotomy between the theory of separation of powers and the structure of government identified by the controversy and, if possible, attempt to resolve it.

Unfortunately, the court let the opportunity slip by without even as much as acknowledging the existence of the controversy. Certainly, even if the problem identified by Pritchard J was so fundamental that it was not susceptible to a judicial solution, the legal profession stood to benefit by a mere acknowledgment and discussion of the problem.

To date, all other cases that have invoked the constitutional provisions relating to the theory of separation of powers and discussed its application in some detail have consistently adopted what Pritchard J referred to as the "traditional view" of the theory and proclaimed its inviolability without coming to grips with the controversy. Thus, in *SCR No 1 of 1984; Re Minimum Penalties Legislation* [1984] PNGLR 314, Kapi DCJ reasoned that:

> "Under s 37(2) [of the *Constitution*] only the Parliament can define a criminal offence and prescribe the penalty for that offence. As to what is the proper punishment for these offences is a power given only to the Parliament. The power of prescribing punishment for an offence is only limited to the extent that punishments which are prescribed are not of a kind that affect the inherent dignity of the human person in the way I have interpreted s 36. It has nothing to do with the proportionality of the punishment imposed for a particular criminal act. To read the principle of proportionality into s 36 is to allow the courts to exercise a power which is given to the Parliament to determine in relation to punishment of criminal offences. Such an interpretation, in my view, violates the principle of separation of powers of the legislature and the judiciary: s 99(3) of the *Constitution*."[369]

Sheehan J followed the same trend in *Haiveta v Wingti* [1994] PNGLR 160, by subscribing to the view that the National Government comprises three branches; namely, the legislature, the executive and the judiciary, which according to him are in principle required by s 99(3) of the

[369] [1984] PNGLR 314 at 328.

Constitution to function separately.[370] Finally, in *Re Internal Security Act* [1994] PNGLR 341, Kapi DCJ reiterated the view that:

> "In principle, therefore, the exercise of each power [that is, executive, legislative and judicial power] must be kept separate from the exercise of other powers vested in different arms of the government: *Constitution* s 99(3). If one of the arms attempts to perform any of the power assigned to another, then that authority is acting contrary to the *Constitution,* because it is usurping the power of another arm."[371]

The controversy surrounding separation of powers in Papua New Guinea

Given the silence of the courts about the controversy surrounding the application of the theory of separation of powers in Papua New Guinea, the attempt by Deklin to keep the debate alive deserves special mention. The theory of the separation of powers adopted by the *Constitution,* according to Deklin,[372] is not a "strict separation in the traditional sense", thus recalling Pritchard J's dissenting opinion in *Constitutional Reference No 1 of 1978.* He supported this argument by referring to the Final Report of the Constitutional Planning Committee (CPC), which, according to him, reveals two underlying concepts about the organisation and use of governmental power.

The first concept states that if the National Goals and Directive Principles were to be achieved, it would be necessary to have maximum co-operation between all the agents of governmental power. This concept, according to Deklin, was derived from the CPC's view that:

> "If government is to be truly responsive to the people, it is vital that those whom the people elect to represent them should be able to contribute actively and effectively to the government of the nation. The legislature should not be seen as a rival to the executive arm, *but rather as a full and constructive partner.*
>
> . . . [C]ourts do not . . . exist in a vacuum. Like other institutions of the government of a country they are caught up in political realities, and often their decisions have important political consequences. In carrying out their judicial role, judges and magistrates must take full account of the goals of the society in which they live; they must be attuned to the wishes of that society and to that extent must be politically conscious (although not party politically conscious) . . . At the same time, the judiciary has a duty to protect the rights of the individual and minority groups: its job is not simply to reflect the will of the government of the day . . . These two principles may well be contradictory in a given situation and the courts are therefore faced with the need to make a satisfactory compromise between them" (emphasis added).[373]

The second concept expresses the need to avoid concentrating one particular type of governmental power in one single institution. To illustrate this concept, Deklin points to other constitutional powers which, in his view, do not fit into any of the categories of power labelled as

---

[370] [1994] PNGLR 160 at 176.
[371] [1994] PNGLR 341 at 345.
[372] A P W Deklin, "The Legal Control of the Executive in Papua New Guinea" in P Sack (ed), Pacific Constitutions (Canberra: ANU, 1982), pp 173-87.
[373] CPC, Constitutional Planning Committee Final Report: Part 1 (Port Moresby: Government Printer, 1974), pp 6/1 and 8/1.

legislative, executive and judicial by the *Constitution.* For example, the legislative power, according to him, was to be exercised by agents, such as the Electoral Commissioner, and not the Parliament alone. Similarly, there were few very specific executive functions that the CPC proposed should be exercised by bodies other than the National Executive and to be performed strictly in accordance with the *Constitution.* This includes the functions of constitutional office-holders,[374] which, in functional terms, are not strictly executive since some of their activities fall into the semi-legislative field. Finally, the *Constitution* permits the exercise of the judicial power by bodies other than the courts.

The effect of incorporating these two concepts into the *Constitution,* in Deklin's view, is to qualify the separation of powers that is formally adopted by the *Constitution.* He therefore concludes that what obtains in Papua New Guinea is better viewed as a modified form of the separation of powers. Significantly, while relying on the concepts derived from the CPC recommendations, Deklin omitted another very important one; namely, popular sovereignty. The relevance of this concept will be explained later.

On the basis of his view of the modified form of the separation of powers, Deklin proceeded to critique the decision of the Supreme Court in *Constitutional Reference No 1 of 1978*, which, according to him, misconceived the separation of powers embodied in the *Constitution.* Adopting the position of Pritchard J in that case with total approval, he demonstrated how, in his view, the problem in that case could have been resolved if full consideration had been given to the relevant constitutional provisions that govern both the separation of powers and the judicial power.

Illustrating this approach, Deklin suggested that, if the court had construed the phrase "in principle" in s 99(3) to mean "notwithstanding any other provisions in the *Constitution*", that would have reconciled the inconsistency between s 99(3) and the other constitutional provisions and resolved the problem in *Constitutional Reference No 1 of 1978*. However, this construction of the phrase "in principle" is difficult to appreciate as the two phrases have little, if anything, in common.

[374] For example, the office of the Public Prosecutor, the office of the Public Solicitor, the Public Service Commission, the Electoral Commission, the Auditor-General, the Clerk of Parliament and the Ombudsman Commission.

CONCLUSION

The construction of the theory of separation of powers "in the traditional sense" as a tripartite division of governmental powers and functions is well known. There is no doubt that, although the theory is still highly regarded as an important - perhaps the most important - safeguard for the protection of individual liberties against arbitrary government in the Anglo-European countries, even those countries, which, by the way, never complied with the tripartite division of powers and functions, have lost any claim to the purity of how the theory is to be applied. The subtle combination, fusion and liaison of the legislative, executive and judicial powers in all the functions of governmental bodies in these countries which are necessitated by the operation of administrative bodies endowed with discretionary powers makes the idea of the triad of governmental powers seem an anachronism.

The modification of the theory to embrace "principal and lesser arms of government" may therefore be defended as a variant of the theory. If so, then Deklin's modified form has merely broadened the application of the theory, but has not otherwise altered it. Viewed against the traditional concept of the theory, however, the modified form described by Deklin, with its multi-layered system of co-operative power-sharing constitutional bodies, appears to be an amorphous monstrosity. If indeed this monstrosity is the "basic scheme of the *Constitution*", as Deklin argues, then in my view, the CPC ought to have spelt it out more clearly. Otherwise, the courts, especially the superior courts, may be excused for what Deklin labelled an "ambivalent attitude" towards this modified form of the theory of separation of powers.

The multitude of problems involved in interpreting the constitutional provisions that govern the separation of powers in Papua New Guinea cannot be discussed in detail here. However, if one takes the approach adopted by Deklin, which relies essentially on the rules and techniques of statutory interpretation, it is doubtful if it could lead to the evolution of any general rules that may be relevant for future application. The courts could engage in semantics, as Deklin did, in order to attempt to reconcile other constitutional provisions that may be inconsistent with the constitutional provisions on separation of powers. That, however, in my view, cannot resolve the controversy surrounding the theory of separation of powers. At best, it would simply institutionalise what Prentice DCJ referred to as "judicial legislating of a permissible kind".[375]

The goal of the theory of separation of powers - and on this point Deklin is right - is not to enforce a rigid tripartite division of governmental powers and functions. Its major premise is that, in order to guard against tyranny and arbitrary use of power, there should not be a concentration of power in one person or body of persons. The task of implementation is to achieve a structural organisation that creates a balance between the legislative, executive and judicial powers. Putting this task into practice is only partly a legal problem. The legal aspect of the problem is a juridical problem of defining the legally permitted spheres of power between the various bodies of government and delineating their boundaries. But there is also a political aspect of the problem; namely, the problem of the power relations among the various classes in the particular society on the one hand, and the combination/fusion and liaison of these classes necessary to maintain a balance in the control of the powers of government. It is therefore not possible to resolve the controversy without taking into account this political factor.

---

[375] 1976] PNGLR 345 at 558.

Seen in context, this perspective of the theory of separation of powers requires an understanding of the social forces and the power relations in Papua New Guinea that uncover the real political struggle between those who actually control the economic and political power of the state (that is, foreign investors, national businessmen, politicians and senior bureaucrats) and those (that is, the "grassroots") who, notwithstanding constitutional guarantees of equality, have no real power. The stark revelation from such an understanding is that, even though the source of all constitutional powers is said to be "the people", the interests of the latter group have been marginalised to a point where it can hardly be said that they have any realistic power base in any of the bodies among which governmental power is divided. This fact shows that the squabbles about who is usurping whose power or encroaching on whose power is an intra-class conflict among the ruling classes which is considered necessary in order to maintain the balance of power among the dominant political and economic interests. This conflict goes on daily in hotel rooms and the dark alleys of power and is an acceptable mode of power-brokering. The only time it surfaces publicly in the courts is when the conflict threatens to destabilise the balance of power. On such rare occasions, the political in-fighting is translated into legal terms and expressed in theoretical disputes and settled by reference to legal theories such as the theory of separation of powers. The fundamental conflict between the ruling classes and the grassroots who are actually the victims of the usurpation of power is, however, resolved either by silence or violence. It is this conflict that is carefully hidden by the myth of the theory of separation of powers. Once the myth is broken, it becomes clear that the theory serves not only to legalise the exclusion of the grassroots from sharing power but also to maintain the balance of power among those that share state power in order to preserve the alliance necessary as a counterweight to the grassroots.

Support for this interpretation of the theory may be found in the critical works of Eisenmann[376] and Althusser.[377] Indeed, the line of argument adopted by these writers is also reflected in the CPC's view of "the basis of the *Constitution*". This view, which is reminiscent of Rousseau's notion of popular sovereignty, was expressed in the following terms:

> "Power belongs to the people
>
> 1. The Committee proposes that the first part of our *Constitution* should include an article which states:
>
> 'Power belongs to the people and it shall be exercised in accordance with the *Constitution*'."

We believe it is important to make clear in this way that the power exercised under the *Constitution* is derived from the people. In the great majority of the societies that make up our nation, colonial rulers took power from the people rather than from kings or chiefs. It is therefore appropriate that it be the people to whom that power should now be returned. The principle that power derives from the people provides the basis of the *Constitution*.[378]

Although Pritchard J admitted that this view found its way into s 99(1) of the *Constitution*,[379] he glossed over it because, in his view, since "the overall framework of the *Constitution* concerning

---

[376] Eisenmann, L'Esprit des Lois et la Separation des Pouvoirs (Paris: Melanges Carre de Malberg, 1933).
[377] L Althusser, Montesquieu: la politique et l'histoire (Paris: Presses Universitaires de France, 1959).
[378] Above n 16, p 7/1.
[379] This section states: "Subject to and in accordance with this Constitution, the power, authority and jurisdiction of the People shall be exercised by the National Government."

the National Government is quite different to the layout recommended in the [CPC] Report",[380] it was not helpful in relation to the concept of the Structure of Government described in s 99 of the *Constitution.* As indicated above, it is precisely the absence of the "people's power" that underlies the controversy surrounding the application of the theory of separation of powers in Papua New Guinea.

In my opinion, therefore, if this controversy is to be resolved in the future, it will be necessary to understand that s 99(3) of the *Constitution* merely requires a separation of the powers and functions of the three arms of government *as a matter of principle.* This does not mean a rigid separation *in practice* as it has to take into account that the CPC's view of the "the basis of the *Constitution*" envisages a unity of power whose ultimate source is the people. The fact that this power is currently divided among determinate persons and bodies and used to protect and further sectional political and economic interests lies at the root of the controversy surrounding the application of the theory of separation of powers. The resolution of the controversy, therefore, lies in giving overriding importance to this concept of popular sovereignty in the interpretation of the constitutional provisions relating to the theory of separation of powers.

[380] 1976] PNGLR 345 at 377.

Chapter 13

THE OMBUDSMAN COMMISSION OF PAPUA NEW GUINEA: JURISDICTION, FUNCTIONS AND PERFORMANCE

DAVID CANNINGS

INTRODUCTION

The Ombudsman Commission is one of the more complex institutions established by the *Constitution*. It is often perceived as having just two functions; namely, to perform the role of a "traditional" Ombudsman (under its general jurisdiction), and to administer the Leadership Code (the specific jurisdiction). But that is an over-simplification. To put the Commission in its proper constitutional context, it is necessary to consider the full ambit of its powers and functions. In fact, the Commission has three primary functions, and a number of subsidiary functions.

FUNCTIONS

Primary functions

The primary functions are summarised in the table below.

Primary Functions of the Ombudsman Commission	
Function	**Source of power**
1. Investigation of alleged wrong conduct and defective administration by governmental bodies.	*Constitution*, s 219(1)(a) and (b); *Organic Law on the Ombudsman Commission.*
2. Investigation of alleged discriminatory practices, by any person or body.	*Constitution*, s 219(1)(c); *Organic Law on the Ombudsman Commission.*
3. Investigation of alleged misconduct in office under the Leadership Code.	*Constitution*, s 219(1)(d); *Organic Law on the Duties and Responsibilities of Leadership.*

The first function allows the Commission to perform the role of a "traditional" Ombudsman by investigating, either on complaint or on its own initiative, administrative practices and decisions of governmental bodies which may be unreasonable, unjust, oppressive, and the like.

Under the second function, the Commission performs the role of what in other jurisdictions are called anti-discrimination or equal opportunity commissions. In this context, its jurisdiction is not restricted to the investigation of governmental bodies. Section 219(1)(c) speaks simply of investigation of discriminatory practices "within the meaning of a law prohibiting such practices". There is only one relevant law in this area; namely, the *Discriminatory Practices Act* (Ch 269), which applies to all bodies and persons. Though the Commission was established primarily as a means of imposing accountability and control on the public sector, this peculiar area of jurisdiction gives it an extra dimension in terms of its relationship with the private sector.

Under its Leadership Code jurisdiction, the Commission performs the role of conflicts-of-interest commissions in other countries. But even that does not give a full picture of its responsibilities. In the absence of an independent, adequately resourced anti-corruption body, it has also become a de facto anti-corruption agency. It has been able to combine its extensive powers under the Leadership Code, together with the exercise of powers as a traditional Ombudsman institution, in the overall fight against corruption in Papua New Guinea.

Subsidiary functions

In addition to its primary functions, the Commission has a number of subsidiary functions.

Subsidiary Functions of the Ombudsman Commission

Function	Source of power
1. Power to make special references to the Supreme Court on questions of constitutional interpretation.	*Constitution*, s 19.
2. Power (implied) to enforce the Basic Rights.	*Constitution*, s 57.
3. Power to advise (jointly with the National Executive Council) the Queen and Head of State, to consent to the Governor-General holding another office or position or engaging in another calling.	*Constitution*, s 87(3) and (4).
4. Power (potential) to administer the (envisaged) Organic Laws regulating political parties, political donations and the protection of elections from outside or hidden influences.	*Constitution*, ss 129 and 130.
5. Power given to Chief Ombudsman to participate in judicial appointments etc, by virtue of membership of the Judicial and Legal Services Commission.	*Constitution*, s 183; *Organic Law on the Judicial and Legal Services Commission.*

The Commission is one of a limited range of public bodies authorised by the *Constitution* to make special references to the Supreme Court, to seek the court's binding opinion on questions relating to the interpretation or application of the constitutional laws. In this respect, the Ombudsman Commission has been authorised to maintain a watching brief over the nation's constitutional development. By dint of this "hotline" to the Supreme Court, the Commission has become, to some extent, a guardian of the *Constitution*. Since independence, it has been a fairly regular referrer of constitutional questions to the Supreme Court.

In recent years, for example, it has:

(a) tested the constitutionality of the increase in the nomination fee for candidates to the National Elections from K100 to K1,000 (*Supreme Court Reference No 1 of 1992* [1992] PNGLR 73);

(b) tested the jurisdiction of leadership tribunals in the situation where leaders resign from office (*Supreme Court Reference No 2 of 1992* [1992] PNGLR 336); and

(b) tested the constitutional validity of the *Internal Security Act* 1993 (*Supreme Court Reference No 3 of 1993* [1994] PNGLR 341).

A second subsidiary function is given under s 57 of the *Constitution*: the Commission appears to have been given the power to enforce the Basic Rights. Section 57(2) suggests that any persons "with an interest . . . in the maintenance of the principles commonly known as the Rule of Law" ought to be given standing to make applications on behalf of others in the Supreme Court or the National Court for enforcement of the Basic Rights. The Ombudsman Commission would appear to fall squarely within this category of persons.

However, the Commission has never exercised this power. When it has investigated alleged abuses of the Basic Rights, it has confined its role to preparing reports and recommendations. It has never actively pursued the results of its investigations through the courts. The rationale for this approach lies in the Commission's perception of its role when it undertakes a human rights investigation. It performs the role of an independent investigator. Although it acts on a complaint, it is not acting for the complainant. The complainant is not its client. The Commission therefore has no paramount duty to the complainant. It would be inconsistent with the Commission's impartiality for it to assume the adversarial role required of it if such matters were pursued through the courts.

The other reason for reluctance to engage in human rights litigation is that there is another institution that is far better equipped constitutionally (if not in terms of resources) to deal with this task: the office of the Public Solicitor.

As a third subsidiary function, the Commission has an important role to play concerning the office of Governor-General, the only senior office established by the *Constitution* not subject to the Leadership Code. The Governor-General is prohibited by s 87 of the *Constitution* from holding any other office or position or engaging in any other calling, except with the consent of the Queen as Head of State, acting with and in accordance with the joint advice of the National Executive Council (NEC) and the Ombudsman Commission. In this way, the Commission is included in the system of checks and balances that regulates the official conduct of the Governor-General.

The Commission's fourth subsidiary function - that is, the (potential) power to regulate political donations and ensure that elections are protected from outside or hidden influences - has not come fully to fruition. The Organic Laws envisaged by the *Constitution* have not been enacted. This has forced the Ombudsman Commission to partially implement the intention of Part VI Division 2.H of the *Constitution* by means of directions issued under s 27(4) of the *Constitution*.

Finally, membership of the Judicial and Legal Services Commission gives the Chief Ombudsman (and the Commission) an influential role in the appointment process for all the judges of the

National and Supreme Courts, members of the Magisterial Service and key constitutional office-holders such as the Public Prosecutor and the Public Solicitor.

CONSTITUTIONAL INDEPENDENCE OF THE COMMISSION

Besides its multiplicity of functions, the feature of the Ombudsman Commission that sets it apart from equivalent institutions in other countries is that the institution itself and the laws it administers are established directly under the *Constitution*. One of the hallmarks of an effective Ombudsman institution is its independence, and in Papua New Guinea this has been conscientiously guaranteed by the *Constitution* through an array of legislative techniques.

Freedom from direction and control

Section 217(5) of the *Constitution* states:

> "In the performance of its functions . . . the Commission is not subject to direction or control by any person or authority."

This does not, of course, mean that the Commission is free to apply the constitutional laws as it sees fit. Schedule 1.19 of the *Constitution* ensures that the Commission's independence does not affect its control or direction by a court or regulation of its powers by or under statute. Nor does it affect the jurisdiction of the Auditor-General or the Public Accounts Committee.

Section 217(5) was relied on by the Commission in *Ombudsman Commission v Ellis* [1992] PNGLR 437. This case arose after the Chief Ombudsman declined to comply with a summons served on him under the *Commissions of Inquiry Act* (Ch 31). An inquiry had been established to inquire into the awarding of contracts for the Poreporena Freeway project. Before the inquiry was established, the Ombudsman Commission had initiated its own investigation into the same matter and had acquired a large range of documents, some very confidential. The Commission took the view that it ought not to disclose some documents that had been acquired on the understanding that they would not be used for any purpose other than the Commission's investigation.

Ultimately, the Supreme Court held that the Chief Ombudsman's actions were justified. The effect of the Commission's freedom from direction and control was to give it a constitutional right to withhold documents from the Commission of Inquiry. *Ellis'* case is a peculiar example of the assertion of the Commission's independence. However, the importance of such independence cannot be overstated. In a practical day-to-day sense, it is an imposing barrier to any form of interference (especially undue political influence) in the work of the Commission.

Other supporting provisions

Section 217(6) of the *Constitution* states:

> "The proceedings of the Commission are not subject to review in any way, except by the Supreme Court or the National Court on the ground that it has exceeded its jurisdiction."

There is also a degree of constitutional entrenchment of the Commission. A proposed law to alter the *Constitution* and abolish the Ombudsman Commission would need to be supported by a three-quarters absolute majority vote of all members of the Parliament eligible to vote (see *Constitution*, ss 14 and 17(3)). In the first 20 years of independence, there has only been one formal proposal to abolish the Commission. In 1991, the then member for Tewai-Siassi, Mr Peter Garong, introduced a private member's Bill (which was actually gazetted). His Bill sought to alter the *Constitution* by abolishing the Ombudsman Commission and the Leadership Code. (Twelve months later, Mr Garong was dismissed under the Leadership Code for misconduct in office.)

Section 223(5) of the *Constitution* further provides that the office of a constitutional office-holder cannot be abolished while there is a substantive holder of that office. Schedule 1.17 of the *Constitution* also states that the repeal of any part of the *Constitution* or an Organic Law does not affect the previous operation of the repealed provisions or anything done under them. Schedule 1.17 also specifically refers to the Ombudsman Commission and the Leadership Code. Thus, repeal of a constitutional law does not affect any liability under the Leadership Code. Nor does it prevent the Ombudsman Commission or a leadership tribunal from investigating any act to which the repealed provisions were relevant.

Appointment and removal of members

All three members of the Commission are appointed by a special body established under the *Constitution* called the Ombudsman Appointments Committee. It consists of the Prime Minister as chairman, the Chief Justice, the leader of the Opposition, the Chairman of the Permanent Parliamentary Committee on Appointments, and the Chairman of the Public Services Commission.

Security of tenure is a critical feature of any office that purports to be independent. This is achieved in the case of members of the Commission by the length of their appointments (six years in the case of citizens; three years for non-citizens) and the provisions of the *Organic Law on the Guarantee of the Rights and Independence of Constitutional Office-holders.*

In summary, s 7 of that Organic Law states that a member of the Commission can only be removed from office on four grounds:

(1) inability to perform the functions and duties of the office; or

(2) misbehaviour; or

(3) misconduct in office in accordance with the provisions of the Leadership Code; or

(4) breach of any condition of employment (for example, a member of the Commission must not actively engage in politics or engage either directly or indirectly in the management or control of a corporation or other body of persons carrying on business for profit).

In addition, the manner in which a member of the Commission may be removed from office is tightly controlled. It can only be done in two ways: first, by prosecution for misconduct in office under the Leadership Code; and secondly, by the procedure prescribed by Part III of the *Organic Law on the Guarantee of the Rights and Independence of Constitutional Office-holders.*

The Ombudsman Appointments Committee, if satisfied that the question of removal from office should be investigated, must request the Chief Justice to appoint a "Constitutional Office-holders

Rights Tribunal", consisting of three judges of the National Court. The Committee is required to give a statement of reasons for its opinion to the tribunal. The tribunal is then required to make "due inquiry" into the matter. If the tribunal reports that a member of the Commission should be removed from office, the Ombudsman Appointments Committee is obliged to effect the removal.

It will be observed that irrespective of whether a prosecution takes place under the Leadership Code or an inquiry is conducted by a Constitutional Office-holders Rights Tribunal, a member of the Commission can only be removed from office upon the recommendation of an independent and impartial tribunal, in accordance with s 223(2)(a) of the *Constitution*.

Funding and resources

The salary and conditions of service of members of the Commission are guaranteed by ss 217(3), 217(4), 223(2)(b) and 223(4) of the *Constitution*. Further, one of the most effective guarantees of independence is that provided by s 225 of the *Constitution*, which deals with provision of resources and facilities. This provides that:

> "[I]t is the duty of the National Government and of all other governmental bodies and all public office-holders and institutions, that all arrangements are made, staff and facilities provided and steps taken to enable and facilitate, as far as may reasonably be, the proper and convenient performance of the functions of all constitutional institutions and of the offices of all constitutional office-holders."

Ombudsman Commission and the "fourth arm" of government

The diverse range of functions given to the Ombudsman Commission, combined with its constitutional independence, gives it a special place in the constitutional framework of Papua New Guinea. In many respects, the Ombudsman Commission (together with some of the other constitutional institutions and office-holders) forms a fourth arm of government.

The Ombudsman Commission is not a legislative body. It has no general judicial powers (though it is arguable some of its powers under the Leadership Code may tend to fall into this category). The Commission is certainly not part of the National Executive. Under s 148 of the *Constitution*, there is a Minister designated with political responsibility for the Commission. But the Minister has no power of direction or control over the Commission. The Commission therefore stands well apart from the three principal arms of the National Government recognised by s 99 of the *Constitution*.

The unique position of the Ombudsman Commission and the other constitutional institutions was in fact recognised quite soon after independence by the Supreme Court. In *Constitutional Reference No 1 of 1978* [1978] PNGLR 345, the court drew a distinction between those bodies created directly by the people, through the *Constitution*, and those created by the Parliament, through other legislation. Prentice CJ stated:

> "Insofar as such bodies are created independent of direction and control, they would seem to be exercising the power of the people given to them as a direct grant by the *Constitution* and Organic Laws and their exercise of powers could not I think be said to be an exercise of power 'by the National Government' in such a sense as would by itself

> constitute any of them 'an arm' of the National Government, or department or agency or instrumentality thereof."[381]

Whatever label or description is applied to the Commission, it is indisputably a complex and unique constitutional institution with wide powers and a high degree of independence.

THE CONSTITUTIONAL PLANNING COMMITTEE'S VISION OF THE OMBUDSMAN COMMISSION

The Constitutional Planning Committee (CPC) gave a number of reasons for establishing an Ombudsman institution:

(1) Traditional customs and beliefs (which imposed restrictions on land use, human relations and personal obligations) were no longer adequate to cope with the increasingly interdependent nature of Papua New Guinea's societies and the widespread activities of government.

(2) The "modern control system" had therefore become too complex.

(3) Those exercising public powers could not be adequately supervised.

(4) Careful superintendence of a lot of government decisions had become difficult.

(5) Negligence or wilful abuse of administrative power had resulted in hardship and injustice.

(6) The court system was restricted in the remedies it could provide, and was still operating on the adversarial model.[382]

The Ombudsman Commission was envisaged as the institution that would provide a quick, flexible means of redress for aggrieved citizens suffering from administrative injustice. But the CPC stressed that the Commission was not intended to take the place of the courts:

> "We believe that our Ombudsman Commission should have more the supervisory and investigatory role in relation to those vested with the administrative power to make decisions, rather than for the Commission to be seen as a substitute for the courts."[383]

This "supervisory" role of the Commission did not receive an elaborate treatment in the Final Report of the CPC. But some indication of what was really intended is provided by s 218 of the *Constitution*. This section provides an extra dimension to what was expressed by the CPC, by stating that the purposes of establishing the Commission are:

(a) to ensure that all governmental bodies are responsive to the needs and aspirations of the People;

(b) to help in the improvement of the work of governmental bodies and the elimination of unfairness and discrimination by them;

---

[381] [1978] PNGLR 345 at 350.
[382] CPC, *Final Report of the Constitutional Planning Committee: Part 1* (Port Moresby: Government Printer, 1974), pp 11/1-11/2.
[383] Ibid, p 11/1, para 8.

(c) to help in the elimination of unfair or otherwise defective legislation and practices affecting or administered by governmental bodies; and

(d) to supervise the enforcement of Division III.2 (Leadership Code).

Whereas the CPC focused on the need for the Commission to assist individual citizens in achieving administrative justice, the *Constitution* went one step further. It envisages a much broader role for the Commission. The Commission is to actively "help" in the work of governmental bodies. It is to ensure that they are "responsive"; that is, that they are efficient and that they carry out their statutory functions. The Ombudsman Commission is enjoined to lift the overall standard of public administration in Papua New Guinea. It does not simply exist to assist individual citizens. It has a much broader constitutional mandate.

This was a profound vision. It is all too easy to portray an Ombudsman as a fearless protector of *individual* rights. But such an image can be dangerous. Ombudsmen can lose their impartiality and independence, and hence the respect they command, if they see themselves as simply representing the interests of their complainants. Section 218 of the *Constitution* discourages the Ombudsman Commission from falling into this trap. It constantly reminds the Commission of the purposes of its existence and it provides a good benchmark against which the performance of the Commission in its traditional role can be judged over the first 20 years.

LEGAL FRAMEWORK FOR THE COMMISSION'S "TRADITIONAL" ROLE

The legal framework for the discharge of the Commission's "traditional" functions is provided by Part VIII Division 2 of the *Constitution*, and the *Organic Law on the Ombudsman Commission.*

Scope of jurisdiction

The Commission is authorised by s 219(1)(a) of the *Constitution* to investigate conduct which "is or may be wrong" on the part of a specified range of bodies and persons. In summary, these are:

(a) any state service or provincial service, or a member of any such service;

(b) any other governmental body, or an officer or employee of a governmental body;

(c) any local government body, or an officer or employee of that body;

(d) any body set up by statute that is wholly or mainly supported out of public moneys of Papua New Guinea, or the members of whose controlling authority (or a majority of them) are appointed by the NEC, or any officer or employee of any such body;

(e) any member of the personal staff of the Governor-General, a Minister or the leader or deputy leader of the Opposition; or

(f) any other body or person prescribed for the purpose by an Act of the Parliament.

The term "governmental body" is defined by Sch 1.2(1) of the *Constitution* to mean:

"(a) the National Government, or

(b) a provincial government, or

(c) an arm, department, agency or instrumentality of the National Government or a provincial government; or

(d) a body set up by statute or administrative act for governmental or official purposes."

This rather general definition has given rise to jurisdictional problems over the last few years. A number of statutory authorities have seized upon its looseness to challenge the Commission's jurisdiction.

These problems began in 1989, when the Commission was conducting a fairly routine investigation into the dismissal of some officers from the Investment Corporation. When the Commission summoned the Managing Director of the Corporation to appear before it, he refused. As a result, the Commission instituted criminal proceedings against him under s 30 of the *Organic Law on the Ombudsman Commission*. His defence was that the Commission had no power to issue the summons because the Investment Corporation was not a governmental body. Surprisingly, this argument was successful. Brown J held in the National Court that because the Corporation was constituted by an Act of Parliament, it could not be regarded as a governmental body (*Eliakim ToBolton v The State* (1990) N907). An attempt was made to have the National Court decision reviewed under s 155(2)(b) of the *Constitution*. Because of procedural difficulties, however, the Supreme Court held in July 1991 that the National Court decision could not be challenged (*Supreme Court Review No 9 of 1990* [1991] PNGLR 239).

Around the same time that the Investment Corporation case was before the Supreme Court, the Commission faced another challenge to its jurisdiction, this time from the National Provident Fund Board of Trustees (NPF). This challenge arose after the Commission commenced an investigation into the NPF's decision to award the contract for management of its superannuation fund to an overseas company, without following the public tender procedures of the *Public Finances (Management) Act.* When the Commission summoned the NPF's Acting Managing Director, he challenged the decision to issue the summons on the ground that the NPF was not a governmental body. This case was argued before the National Court in October 1991. However, the company that had been appointed by the NPF completed its work, and the NPF paid the company, before the court's decision could be handed down. As a result, some uncertainty still remains as to the precise extent of the Commission's traditional jurisdiction, especially in relation to statutory corporations.

There are some provisions of the *Constitution* that exclude the Commission's jurisdiction. These are set out in s 219. To begin with, by s 219(3), the Commission may not inquire into the justifiability of a policy of the National Government, a Minister, a provincial government, or a member of a provincial government or a provincial executive. There is, however, an exception. If the policy is contrary to law or to the National Goals and Directive Principles, the Basic Rights or the Basic Social Obligations or any Act of the Parliament, that policy *can* be investigated and reported upon by the Commission.

Further, by s 219(4), the Commission may not inquire into the exercise of a rule-making power by a local government body. Finally, according to s 219(5), the Commission cannot inquire into a decision by a court. However, there is also an exception here. If the court decision shows an apparent defect in law or in an administrative practice by a governmental body, the decision can be inquired into. It should also be noted that there appears to be nothing in s 219(5) to prevent the

Commission inquiring into the administrative conduct of a court; for example, a delay in giving judgment (see *Constitutional Reference No 1 of 1978* [1978] PNGLR 345 at 387 per Pritchard J).

Conduct of an investigation

Commencing an investigation

The Ombudsman Commission is authorised by s 219 of the *Constitution* to investigate the conduct of governmental bodies and the like in two general situations: either "on its own initiative", or "on complaint by a person affected".

Any person can make a complaint to the Commission. Once it receives the complaint, the Commission is then obliged by s 16(3) of the *Organic Law on the Ombudsman Commission* to investigate it unless, in its "deliberate judgment", it decides not to do so for any of the following reasons:

(1) The complaint is trivial, frivolous, vexatious or not made in good faith.

(2) The complainant has another remedy or channel of complaint available that could reasonably be expected to be used.

(3) The complainant does not have a sufficient interest in the subject of the investigation.

(4) The Commission has before it other matters more worthy of its attention.

(5) The Commission's resources are insufficient for adequate investigation.

Section 17(1) of the *Organic Law on the Ombudsman Commission* then states that before investigating any matter, the Commission must inform the "responsible person" of its intention to make the investigation. The purpose of a "traditional" Ombudsman Commission investigation is:

(a) to determine whether any of the "conduct" under investigation was "wrong"; or

(b) to determine whether there were "defects" in any "law or administrative practice".[384]

Section 219(2) of the *Constitution* indicates that conduct is "wrong" if, for example, it is:

(a) contrary to law; or

(b) unreasonable, unjust, oppressive or improperly discriminatory, whether or not it is in accordance with law or practice; or

(c) based wholly or partly on improper motives, irrelevant grounds or irrelevant considerations; or

(d) based wholly or partly on a mistake of law or fact; or

(e) conduct for which reasons should be given but were not.

However, s 219(2) of the *Constitution* also states that the Commission is not constrained, in its determination that conduct is "wrong", by the examples listed above. Most importantly, the Commission can conclude that conduct is wrong irrespective of its legality. The Commission is required to make a host of value judgments when it determines whether conduct is "wrong". For

[384] See s 219(1)(a) and (b) of the *Constitution*, and s 22(1)(a) and (b) of the *Organic Law on the Ombudsman Commission*.

instance, by virtue of s 25(4) of the *Constitution*, it is specifically obliged to take the National Goals and Directive Principles fully into account in all cases as appropriate.

Privacy and secrecy

Unlike a court or a commission of inquiry, when it performs its fact-finding role, the Ombudsman Commission is subject to a number of constraints which are intended to maintain the privacy and confidentiality of the proceedings. According to s 17(2) of the *Organic Law on the Ombudsman Commission*, every investigation conducted under that Law must be conducted in "private". Public hearings are not permissible. There is also a duty of secrecy imposed on officers and members of the Commission by s 20 of the *Organic Law on the Ombudsman Commission*. There are, however, qualifications to that duty. For example, under s 20(3), the Commission may disclose matters that would otherwise be subject to the secrecy provisions if this is necessary in order to properly investigate the matter before it.

Investigative powers

The Ombudsman Commission has extensive powers of investigation. They are aimed at enabling it to obtain information, documents and evidence in an orderly and efficient fashion. The powers available to the Commission under the *Organic Law on the Ombudsman Commission* are summarised in the table below.

Powers Available for a "Traditional" Ombudsman Commission Investigation	
Power	**Source of power (*Organic Law on the Ombudsman Commission*)**
The Commission may hear or obtain information from any person it considers can assist and make whatever inquiries it thinks fit.	s 17(3)
The Commission may require any person who in its opinion is able to give any information relating to a matter being investigated to: (a) furnish information (b) produce any documents, papers or things that may be in the possession or control of that person.	s 18(1)
The Commission may summon any person to attend the Commission for examination on oath or affirmation.	s 18(3)
A member of the Commission may, at any time, enter the premises of a State Service, provincial government body, local government body or statutory body and inspect the premises and carry out an investigation within the premises.	s 36(1)

Natural justice and procedural fairness

Any person who the Commission proposes to make an adverse comment on, in a report prepared under the *Organic Law on the Ombudsman Commission,* is entitled to a right to be heard, before the Commission finalises its opinions. The Commission must also ensure that the person's point of view is set out in the report. These rights are conferred by s 17(4)(b) of the *Organic Law on the Ombudsman Commission*, which states:

> "The Commission shall not make any comment in its report that is adverse to or derogatory of any person without –
>
> (i) providing him with reasonable opportunity of being heard; and
>
> (ii) fairly setting out his defence in its report."

Since the decision of the Supreme Court in *Ombudsman Commission v Donohoe* [1985] PNGLR 348, it has been accepted that the Commission has a strict obligation to comply with s 17(4). This incorporates the rules of natural justice and procedural fairness into the proceedings of the Commission. (In *Donohoe,* the Commission had argued unsuccessfully that its proceedings were immune from judicial review on the ground of breach of natural justice.)

In most situations it is necessary to consult or seek comments from the permanent head of a governmental body. Section 17(4)(a) of the *Organic Law on the Ombudsman Commission* provides that where a report of the Commission "may affect" a state service, provincial government body or statutory body, the Commission must give that body's permanent head a reasonable opportunity of commenting on the subject of the investigation. This requirement exists, irrespective of whether the body is the subject of adverse findings. Likewise, in any case where an investigation relates to a recommendation made to a Minister, s 17(6) provides that the Minister must be consulted.

Reports and recommendations

Section 22(2) of the *Organic Law on the Ombudsman Commission* provides that the Commission must prepare a report of its findings upon forming a positive opinion in relation to two matters. The first matter is whether the Commission, after making an investigation, is of the opinion that:

(a) the conduct, the subject of the investigation, was wrong; or

(b) a law or administrative practice is defective; or

(c) a practice, the subject of the investigation, is discriminatory.

If so, the second matter to be addressed is whether any "service, body, person or other appropriate authority" should:

(a) consider the matter further; or

(b) take certain specific action; or

(c) modify or cancel any administrative act; or

(d) alter any regulation or ruling; or

(e) explain more fully any administrative act; or

(f) do any other thing.

As mentioned earlier, the Commission has a wide discretion when forming its opinions under s 22. It cannot be over-emphasised that the Commission is not a court of law. It is not restricted in drawing its conclusions about the conduct under investigation by the lawfulness of that conduct.

The Commission's recommendations

Though the Commission has no direct power to enforce its recommendations, it is suggested that any person to whom a recommendation is directed has a positive duty to treat the recommendation with respect and to carefully consider whether or not to implement it. In *Niggints v Tokam* [1993] PNGLR 66, Amet J stated such a principle in relation to the recommendations of the Public Services Commission. The National Court was determining an application for judicial review of a decision of the Commissioner of Corrective Institutions. The Commissioner had disregarded a recommendation of the Public Services Commission to reinstate a dismissed officer. The court stated:

> "The departmental head is, in my view, required by commonsense and the need for public administrative accountability to give *serious consideration* to the Commission's recommendation and the reasons for it. Having considered the recommendation, if it is decided not to accept it, then *reasons* for not so accepting the recommendation should be provided to the aggrieved officer, because the officer has a right to seek judicial review as the applicant has done in this case . . .
>
> The statement of principle I enunciate is that the departmental head who decides in his discretion, on proper consideration of the Public Services Commission's recommendation, not to accept it should state the reasons for not so accepting the recommendation . . .
>
> Public officials discharging public duties are required for public accountability to provide reasons for their actions and decisions. If their decisions affect substantial interests and welfare of other officers and their families good management and commonsense principles of fairness require that reasons be given" (emphasis added).[385]

Niggints v Tokam is, from the Ombudsman Commission's point of view, one of the most significant cases ever to be decided about its powers. This is so, even though the Commission itself had no involvement in the case. It clearly suggests that it is not permissible for a person to whom an Ombudsman Commission recommendation is directed, simply to ignore the recommendation or to disagree with it without giving reasons.

HAS THE VISION OF THE CPC BEEN FULFILLED?

The "traditional" function of the Ombudsman Commission is among its most important tasks. It has an extensive array of investigative powers at its disposal. It does a tremendous amount of good work - in individual cases - in this area of its jurisdiction. The Commission has deservedly acquired a reputation for fearless independence in the discharge of its constitutional duties.

---

[385] [1993] PNGLR 66 at 71-72.

Nevertheless, an objective assessment of the Commission's performance over its first 20 years could only draw the conclusion that the CPC's vision of the Commission as an efficient and effective traditional Ombudsman institution has not yet been fulfilled. The benchmarks provided by s 218 of the *Constitution* have not been satisfied. There are far too many governmental bodies that are not responsive to the needs and aspirations of the "people". Some bodies are notorious for their administrative delays. They have had this reputation for years. Unfairness and discrimination by governmental bodies have not been eliminated as required by the *Constitution*. Defective legislation and administrative practices have not been stamped out. The Ombudsman Commission must bear some responsibility for this. There are a number of reasons why the CPC's vision has not been entirely fulfilled.

Diverse jurisdiction

As well as investigating alleged wrong conduct on the part of governmental bodies, the other area of jurisdiction that attracts the bulk of the Commission's time and resources is the Leadership Code. Breaches of the Leadership Code are so extensive and frequent, the Commission is often forced by necessity to divert its scarce resources to leadership investigations. The Commission gains much more publicity from leadership matters than it does from maladministration investigations. The sanctions provided by a leadership investigation are more immediate and more personal. They actually result in individuals being prosecuted and (often) dismissed from office. They generate far more attention from the media and the public. This is beneficial from the point of view of enforcing the Leadership Code. But it has had the effect of drawing attention away from the Commission's traditional role.

A related phenomenon is that, because of its diverse functions, the Commission has a "split personality" problem. On the one hand, in exercising its leadership jurisdiction, it has to be a fearless, sometimes aggressive, law enforcement agency. It has by necessity assumed the mantle of the nation's de facto anti-corruption agency. But on the other hand, it is still required to be an impartial and independent investigator of the grievances of citizens. It is supposed to assist government departments and statutory authorities in improving the efficiency of their operations.

These objectives are not necessarily inconsistent. But in practical terms, it can create problems. For instance, a Minister, departmental head or another leader being investigated under the Leadership Code, may at the same time be the person from whom the Commission is trying to enlist co-operation for the purposes of a maladministration investigation. The maladministration investigation may have nothing at all to do with the personal conduct of the leader concerned. Nevertheless, confusion surrounding the different roles of the Commission can lead to a breakdown in communication and a lack of co-operation.

Regrettably, there are not enough senior public officers who realise that an Ombudsman Commission investigation can actually assist them in their work. They fail to appreciate that the Ombudsman Commission has a positive role to play in assisting (in the words of s 218 of the *Constitution*) in the improvement of the work of governmental bodies. Departmental heads do not see Ombudsman Commission investigations as a tool of management. They do not realise, for example, that a maladministration investigation can help them in streamlining administrative procedures, or in identifying particular officers in their organisation who are not performing, or who may be corrupt and against whom disciplinary action should be taken. Rather than welcoming an investigation with open arms, some departmental heads pull down the shutters.

Too many refuse to co-operate, or at least only reluctantly hand over documents and information (under summons).

Of course, there needs to be more give and take on the part of the Commission. It can reasonably be argued that the Commission has historically not promoted itself very well. Its pre-occupation with leadership matters has meant it has not devoted enough time to public education in general, and education of public officers in particular. Too many are simply ignorant of the Commission's traditional role.

Government departments and statutory authorities have also failed to appreciate that under s 225 of the *Constitution* they have a positive obligation to assist the Ombudsman Commission in its investigations. They are obliged to ensure that all arrangements are made and staff and facilities provided to facilitate the Commission's work. Most governmental bodies are ignorant of this obligation.

The office of the Auditor-General is one constitutional institution that seems to have been successful in getting this type of message across to governmental bodies. Perhaps in this respect there is something for the Ombudsman Commission to learn from the Auditor-General.

Overlapping jurisdiction

The Ombudsman Commission can investigate a broad range of matters under its traditional jurisdiction. In fact, its jurisdiction tends to overlap with that of other constitutional institutions. For example, if the Commission receives a complaint about a police raid on a village, the matter might just as efficiently (and usually more effectively) be handled by the Public Solicitor, who is well placed to take action under s 57 of the *Constitution*. (In the future, perhaps, such complaints will be handled by the proposed Human Rights Commission.)

Another example is where the Commission receives a complaint from an aggrieved public servant on a personnel matter. Such a complaint can be adequately dealt with by the Public Services Commission. Yet the Ombudsman Commission still receives many complaints of this nature and in some cases proceeds to investigate. Likewise, when allegations of misappropriation of public money arise, the Commission's jurisdiction overlaps to a large extent with that of the Auditor-General.

In light of these alternative methods of dispute resolution, a valid criticism that can be made of the Ombudsman Commission is that it tends to investigate too many complaints. It has failed to make sufficient use of the discretion available to it under s 16 of the *Organic Law on the Ombudsman Commission* not to investigate certain matters. Because it has been too accommodating of complainants, it has also failed to put pressure on other constitutional institutions to perform their own jobs properly.

Insufficient presence in the regions

The Ombudsman Commission has only three regional offices (presently at Kavieng, Lae and Mt Hagen). They were established soon after independence. Since then, the decentralisation program that was envisaged by the CPC, for both the Ombudsman Commission and the Public Solicitor, has not been implemented. The CPC envisaged that a single officer would act as the "agent" for both the Commission and the Public Solicitor in each of the provinces.

The failure to fulfil the vision of the CPC in this respect means that there are still vast tracts of the country left without ready access to the Ombudsman Commission or the Public Solicitor. Even in major provincial centres such as Alotau, Daru, Kerema, Kimbe, Kokopo, Lorengau, Popondetta, Vanimo, Wabag and Wewak, access to the Ombudsman Commission is very difficult. As a result, the Commission has been limited in the amount of investigative work it has done in relation to the operations of provincial and local government bodies.

Implementation of recommendations

Compared to the relatively high success rate enjoyed by Ombudsman institutions in some other countries, the level of acceptance of recommendations prepared by the Ombudsman Commission is quite low. History has shown that too many recommendations are not implemented. Some are completely ignored.

This problem is being addressed by the Commission. For example, the Commission is at the moment considering whether to proceed with a test case in the National Court, where it appears that its recommendations have been disregarded (or ignored) by a departmental head, in breach of the requirements to be implied from the National Court's decision in *Niggints v Tokam* (discussed above).

There are many reasons for the relatively low level of acceptance of recommendations. In some cases, the Commission has been guilty of the same sorts of administrative delays that it should be eradicating. Some departmental heads have, not unreasonably, taken the view that the Ombudsman Commission has been so slow in resolving complaints that it is really a case of "the pot calling the kettle black". In this environment, the respect that the Commission clearly commands under its leadership jurisdiction has not been reflected in the responses to its recommendations under the traditional jurisdiction.

The Commission has generally taken on too many investigations. Rather than investigating a smaller number of complaints thoroughly, it has investigated too many matters in a cursory fashion. It has not been selective enough. There has also been a tendency for the Commission to regard its job as done once a report is finalised and recommendations are made. The better approach, managerially, is to regard the publication of recommendations as the performance of only half the job. The remaining half is the following-up of recommendations, by pursuing the matter through the courts if necessary, along the lines of a *Niggints v Tokam* proceeding (bolstered perhaps by an action for enforcement of constitutional duties under s 23 of the *Constitution*).

Another reason for the Commission's low success rate perhaps lies in the very close relationship that exists in Papua New Guinea between the Ministers and the departments and agencies for which they are politically responsible. In other jurisdictions, the distinction between the role of the Minister and the role of the department is sharply drawn. There is little overlap. This is supposed to be the case in Papua New Guinea. The constitutional limitations on the powers of Ministers were clearly explained by the Supreme Court in *Supreme Court Reference No 1 of*

1982; Re Bouraga [1982] PNGLR 178. But the reality is vastly different from the principles affirmed in that case.

Ministers have far too much control over the running of their departments. They get involved on a day-to-day basis in matters that should administratively be left to their departmental heads. In this environment, it can be difficult for Ministers to divorce themselves from criticism of their departments in an Ombudsman Commission report. Ministers sometimes perceive the report as a criticism of them, rather than of their departments. Consequently the process of independent, objective assessment of the Commission's reports and its recommendations is lacking.

CONCLUSION

There are very few, if any, Ombudsman institutions in the world with such a vast array of functions to perform as the Ombudsman Commission of Papua New Guinea. This diversity of functions and the degree of independence given to it by the *Constitution* gives the Commission considerable influence in the constitutional framework of the nation. Indeed, the Commission can properly be regarded as part of the "fourth arm" of government.

The *Constitution* envisages a far-reaching role for the Commission under its traditional jurisdiction. It does not exist only to redress the grievances of citizens. It is also to actively assist in ensuring that all governmental bodies do their jobs efficiently. It has been given an extensive array of investigative powers to achieve these aims. But after 20 years, it is fair to say that the Commission has struggled to achieve the goals laid down by the *Constitution.* Its diversity of functions has led to difficulty in coming to grips with its traditional function. Responsibility for administering the Leadership Code has meant that its resources are often diverted away from its traditional functions.

These problems are being actively addressed by the Commission. They are essentially managerial problems, rather than flaws in the constitutional mandate. Public education should be given a higher priority by the Ombudsman Commission. But equally importantly, the Commission needs to target senior public officers and Ministers and educate them about the positive assistance that can be provided by the Commission.

On a more general level, the role of the Commission in its traditional jurisdiction can be expressed in economic and social terms. The Ombudsman Commission is required to ensure that governmental bodies are responsive to the needs and aspirations of the "people". It therefore has, in the language that is current, a key role to play in improving the delivery of goods and services to the people. The Commission also has a role in the overall system of justice. By promoting good governance throughout the public sector, the Commission can actively assist other law enforcement agencies in promoting the rule of law.

Chapter 14

THE LEADERSHIP CODE: THE OMBUDSMAN COMMISSION AND OFFICIAL CORRUPTION

GREGORY TOOP

INTRODUCTION

Twenty years after independence, official corruption is a major problem for Papua New Guinea. Virtually unknown in the period immediately after independence, official corruption today threatens to stifle national development and undermine the *Constitution.* Whilst official corruption manifests itself in all of its usual forms, it has, in recent years, been concentrated in the rich resources sector, especially forestry and fisheries, where the profits to be earned from participating in official corruption can be staggering.

For example, in 1991, a serving Deputy Prime Minister who had previously been Minister for Forests was found guilty by a leadership tribunal[386] of numerous counts of misconduct in office, after it was found that while Minister for Forests in 1985 he had compromised his office by, among other things, awarding a lucrative timber permit to a foreign company in which he secretly held shares. Further, the company did not meet the national forestry guidelines, and had neither the finance nor the experience to conduct logging operations. He also accepted numerous undisclosed benefits from the logging company, including a luxury motor vehicle, cash payments and trips overseas.[387]

To a large extent, official corruption has its roots in the political system, where becoming a politician is often seen as the first step on the road to riches. Without a strong political party system, individual members of Parliament are forced to buy votes in order to become elected. When elected, the government of the day is forced to buy political support in order to remain in power. Buying support often involves handing out huge amounts of public funds to individual members of Parliament under the guise of funding projects in their electorates.

Furthermore, each year, members of Parliament demand and receive huge amounts of public funds (amounting to K500,000 per member in 1996) under a government-sponsored program known as the Electoral Development Program, better known as the "slush" fund. Under this program, members are deliberately given the freedom to spend the funds in their electorates almost as they please. Whilst the funds are nominally intended to be spent on projects in their electorates, there are virtually no guidelines controlling expenditure, and those guidelines that do exist are hopelessly inadequate and ineffectual. Needless to say a large proportion of these funds ends up in the pockets of the members.

[386] A leadership tribunal is established to deal with any charge of misconduct in office laid against a leader under the Leadership Code. The composition and role of the tribunal are discussed later in this chapter.

[387] *Reference by the Public Prosecutor: Re Diro* (unreported, decision of the Leadership Tribunal, September 1991).

The present situation is a far cry from the heady optimism of the nation's founding fathers at the time of independence. Then, there was an almost naive belief that the newly independent nation could create a constitutional system capable of controlling and, if possible, eliminating corruption from public life.

The daunting tasks of not only deciding that this was to be an issue dealt with by the independence constitution, but also of recommending how to deal with official corruption, were taken up to a multi-disciplinary Constitutional Planning Committee (CPC), which in the short space of only two years was able to publish a comprehensive report of its final recommendations and strategies. The CPC's recommended solution was surprisingly simple. It was to entrench a stringent code of conduct for leaders in the *Constitution* - the Leadership Code[388] - directed towards regulating the public and personal conduct of the new nation's leaders; that is, those in positions of power and authority, elected or otherwise.[389]

The CPC believed that rather than constituting "mere directives", the Code needed to be firmly enforced, with appropriate sanctions, against leaders who breached it. It was proposed that the Code should be implemented and enforced by an independent constitutional institution outside the three main arms of government (the Parliament, the National Executive and the National Judicial System). Of necessity, those involved in implementing the Code needed to be persons of the highest integrity.[390]

The CPC recommended that the Ombudsman Commission, which it had also proposed should be vested with the traditional maladministration role exercised by Ombudsman institutions in many other countries,[391] was also the best body to be given the task of supervising the Leadership Code. The reasons were convincingly stated as follows:

> "It is our firm view that the Ombudsman Commission is particularly well suited to carrying out this role as its members should be people who themselves have complete integrity, and its procedures and powers can readily be adapted to this purpose. Experience in other countries has shown that Ombudsmen quite frequently come upon instances of corruption in the course of their investigations into administrative malpractices, so that we would anticipate that this additional role will mesh in quite well with its general jurisdiction."[392]

Although not all of the CPC's recommendations about the Leadership Code were included in the independence *Constitution*, key elements were. Consistent with the CPC's views, the *Constitution* regards the Code to be of such fundamental importance that it is enshrined as the second of the five "Basic Principles of Government".[393] The reasons for the significance accorded to the Code in the *Constitution* are clearly stated in the following extract from the CPC's Final Report:

---

388 CPC, *Final Report of the Constitutional Planning Committee: Part 1* (Port Moresby: Government Printer, 1974), Ch 3.

389 The CPC recommendations about the definition of a "leader" (ibid, p 3/13/2) have largely been incorporated into s 26 of the *Constitution*, which is discussed below.

390 Ibid, p 3/4/35.

391 Ibid, Ch 11. For a discussion of the Ombudsman Commission and its jurisdiction in relation to maladministration, see Chapter 13, "The Ombudsman Commission of Papua New Guinea: Jurisdiction, Functions and Performance", by David Cannings.

392 CPC, above n 3, p 3/4/35.

393 *Constitution*, Part III, Division 2, ss 26-31.

> "No-one can do more to set the tone and style of the nation than the leaders. Contrariwise, no-one in the nation can do more to lower the standards than the leaders . . . Both by inaction and improper action the leaders can betray the people's confidence in them. What the leaders do and how they are seen to do it; these are things that can legitimate them in the eyes of the people and set the standard for the nation."

We believe that perhaps the single most important factor in determining the direction of national development is the quality of leadership. If Papua New Guinea is to have any chance of implementing its National Goals and Directive Principles, it must ensure that its leadership has a genuine commitment to these goals.[394]

THE LEADERSHIP CODE: AN OVERVIEW

The legal basis for the Code

The basic principles of the Leadership Code are set out in ss 26-31 of the *Constitution*. Section 28 of the *Constitution*[395] prescribes that an Organic Law shall be enacted for the purposes of the Code. Organic Laws flesh out the details of some of the key provisions of the *Constitution*. They have a higher status in the hierarchy of law of Papua New Guinea than ordinary Acts of Parliament.[396]

The Organic Law-making provision for the Leadership Code is the *Organic Law on the Duties and Responsibilities of Leadership*. It was enacted by the Constituent Assembly prior to independence, just after the enactment of the *Constitution*. At about the same time another equally important Organic Law was passed; namely, the *Organic Law on the Ombudsman Commission*, which provides for the establishment and composition of the Ombudsman Commission and for its powers, procedures and immunities in the exercise of the traditional maladministration jurisdiction of the Commission.

The Leadership Code is therefore made up of Part III Division 2 (ss 26-31) of the *Constitution* and the *Organic Law on the Duties and Responsibilities of Leadership*. In addition, the *Leadership Code (Alternative Penalties) Act* (Ch 1A) makes provision for penalties short of dismissal from office for persons found guilty of misconduct in office.

---

[394] CPC, above n 3, p 3/2/11-13.
[395] See also ss 26 and 27 of the *Constitution*, which also authorise provision concerning aspects of the Code by way of an Organic Law.
[396] *Constitution*, ss 9-12.

Who is subject to the Leadership Code?

The CPC's notion that the Code should have as wide an application as possible, covering all persons placed - by election or otherwise - in positions of power and authority, is reflected in s 26 of the *Constitution*, which lists the holders of public office treated as leaders for the purposes of the Code. They are:

(a) the Prime Minister, the Deputy Prime Minister and all the other Ministers of the National Government;

(b) the leader and deputy leader of the Opposition;

(c) all other members of the Parliament;

(d) all members of provincial assemblies and local-level governments;[397]

(e) all constitutional office-holders, a category that includes the Chief Justice and Deputy Chief Justice; all the other judges of the superior courts (the National Court and the Supreme Court); the Public Prosecutor; the Public Solicitor; the Chief Magistrate; the Electoral Commissioner; the Clerk of the Parliament; members of the Public Services Commission; the Auditor-General; and members of the Ombudsman Commission;

(f) all heads of departments of the national public service;

(g) all heads of, or members of the boards or other controlling bodies of, statutory authorities;

(h) the Commissioner of Police;

(i) the Commander of the Defence Force;

(j) all of Papua New Guinea's ambassadors, and other prescribed senior diplomatic and consular officials;

(k) the Public Trustee;

(l) the personal staff of the Governor-General, the Ministers and the leader and deputy leader of the Opposition;

(m) executive officers of registered political parties; and

(n) the holders of any other public offices declared by statute to be subject to the Leadership Code.

Standards of conduct for leaders

Misconduct in office – generally

The standards of conduct leaders need to comply with are set out in s 27 of the *Constitution*. A leader who breaches any of its provisions is liable to be prosecuted for misconduct in office.

[397] Provision for extension of the Code to members of provincial assemblies was added to the *Constitution* by amendment in 1976, and that in respect of local-level government members by amendment in 1995.

Section 27 aims to be an all-embracing code of personal conduct, consistent with the CPC's notion that the Leadership Code should impose stringent standards of conduct for leaders. It achieves this result by ingenious drafting, which casts the Code in such broad terms as to catch virtually all wrong or improper conduct by leaders. Leaders are also potentially liable for the actions of their spouses, children and associates,[398] even though they may not have been personally involved in the alleged misconduct. Section 27 states:

> "(1) A person to whom this Division applies [that is, a leader] has a duty to conduct himself in such a way, both in his public and private life, and in his associations with other persons, as not -
>
> (a) to place himself in a position in which he has or could have a conflict of interests or might be compromised when discharging his public or official duties; or
>
> (b) to demean his office or position; or
>
> (c) to allow his public or official integrity, or his personal integrity, to be called into question; or
>
> (d) to endanger or diminish respect for and confidence in the integrity of government in Papua New Guinea.
>
> (2) In particular, a person to whom this Division applies shall not use his office for personal gain or enter into any transaction or engage in any enterprise or activity that might be expected to give rise to doubt in the public mind as to whether he is carrying out or has carried out the duty imposed by Subsection (1).
>
> (3) It is the further duty of a person to whom this Division applies -
>
> (a) to ensure, as far as is within his lawful power, that his spouse and children and any other persons for whom he is responsible (whether morally, legally, or by usage) do not conduct themselves in such a way that might be expected to give rise to doubt in the public mind as to his complying with his duties under this section; and
>
> (b) if necessary, to publicly disassociate himself from any activity or enterprise of his associates, or of a person referred to in paragraph (a), that might be expected to give rise to such a doubt."

Specific types of misconduct in office

The *Organic Law on the Duties and Responsibilities of Leadership* develops the notion of misconduct in office contained in the general statement in s 27 of the *Constitution*. It does this by prohibiting leaders from engaging in particular kinds of conduct. Like the *Constitution*, the Organic Law uses wide-ranging definitions of key terms. For example, the term "benefit" (used mainly in relation to "benefits" which a leader is prohibited from receiving) is defined in s 1 to include "any gift, loan or service, whether or not it has a monetary value, and all other personal advantages and favours given beyond the normal standards of hospitality".

[398] The term "associate" is so widely defined that it could be taken to mean just about any person that a leader is likely to come into contact with, except possibly casual acquaintances.

The specific types of conduct that constitute misconduct in office include:

(a) intentional misapplying of government funds (Organic Law, s 13);

(b) using office for personal benefit (s 5);

(c) failing to reveal to the Ombudsman Commission the nature and extent of an interest in a matter dealt with in any official capacity (s 6);

(d) holding shares or any other investments in any company or unincorporated profit-seeking association that could reasonably be expected to give rise to a situation where the leader could have a conflict of interests or might be compromised when discharging public or official duties (s 8);

(e) engaging in any paid employment other than a leadership office without the consent first obtained from the Commission (s 9);

(f) seeking, holding, or accepting any gift from any person or a foreign enterprise (s 12); or

(g) disclosing official information except in the course of duty, or obtaining personal gain through disclosure of such information (s 14).

Finally, leaders who are members of a legislative or executive body, and who have a direct or indirect beneficial interest in a matter before the body, must first disclose the nature of their interest before taking part in any debate or vote on the matter (s 15). Their disclosure must be recorded in the minutes of proceedings of the body. After the disclosure, the leader is prohibited from taking any part in any deliberations or decisions of the body unless the body otherwise resolves.

The Organic Law imposes additional limitations on how Ministers of state should conduct themselves. For example, they must give priority to official business over personal business and cannot involve themselves in any activities that could conflict with their ministerial responsibilities. Furthermore, neither leaders nor their spouses or children can hold directorships in any company except with the approval of the Ombudsman Commission (s 7).

Annual statements of income, assets and liabilities

The Organic Law also obliges a leader to submit a statement of income, assets and liabilities to the Ombudsman Commission within three months after assuming office, and annually thereafter while holding leadership office. The statement must provide specified information in relation to both leaders and their spouses and children under voting age (18 years). The information relates to total assets, including money, personal property, real property, business connections, shareholdings, total income received, all sources of income, directorships or other offices held in profit-making organisations, business transactions, gifts received, assets acquired and liabilities incurred or discharged during the relevant period (s 4).

This system of detailed annual statements provides an effective means of monitoring a leader's affairs in order to determine whether he or she is living up to the responsibilities of her or his office. The provisions are given more teeth by virtue of the fact that a leader who either knowingly or negligently gives a statement or explanation or detail in any way false, misleading or incomplete in a material particular, is guilty of misconduct in office (s 4(b)). Despite this, it is not uncommon for leaders to try and get around their s 4 obligations by filing statements that are false in order to cover up their activities. Usually, this is easily detectable, as upon receipt they are thoroughly audited by officers of the Commission. Leaders who do not file their statements on time are given an appropriate warning, and are then prosecuted if the default continues.

Annual statements are received in confidence and are not available to public scrutiny. In 1992, the issue of confidentiality of the statements was tested by a former judge of the Supreme Court conducting an official Commission of Inquiry under the *Commissions of Inquiry Act* (Ch 31). A summons was issued compelling the Ombudsman Commission to make available to the Commission of Inquiry certain documents, including a number of annual statements of leaders. The Commission refused to comply with the summons on the ground that all the documents, including the statements, were privileged. The matter was referred to the National Court for interpretation.

While the court held that the Commission had a right to refuse to hand over annual statements, this did not extend to the other documentation being sought under the summons. The Commission still refused to hand over the other documentation, and appealed to the Supreme Court. In upholding the appeal, the Supreme Court said:

> "In our view, the National Court was in error in applying common law principles and in failing to give full effect to the constitutional privilege afforded to the Ombudsman Commission. The matters which were the concern of this dispute involved the unique nature of immunity and privilege specifically given to the Ombudsman Commission by the *Constitution* and can only be determined by application of the *Constitution* . . . The combined effect [of the *Constitution* and the Organic Law] means that the Ombudsman Commission has the constitutional right to withhold documents from a Commission of Inquiry."[399]

THE OMBUDSMAN COMMISSION AND THE LEADERSHIP CODE

The *Constitution* and the Organic Law give the Ombudsman Commission extensive powers to supervise the Leadership Code. However, other bodies have primary responsibility for both prosecutions of leaders alleged by the Commission to have breached the Code and for determining guilt or innocence in relation to such allegations.

General supervisory functions of the Commission

Issuing guidelines

The Ombudsman Commission has power to make rules and publish guidelines concerning the conduct, and the financial and business affairs, of leaders, their spouses and children (Organic Law, s 12(3)-(4)). The Commission also has power to make provision in those rules and guidelines for certain permissions and exemptions from the provisions of the Code.

[399] *Ombudsman Commission v Ellis* [1992] PNGLR 437 at 446.

Giving directions on disposal of assets or interests

The Commission can give a direction to any leader to dispose of particular assets or interests which, in the opinion of the Commission, are held contrary to the Code (Organic Law, s 26).

Declaring prohibited interests

The Commission has the power to declare as prohibited interests, in relation to a particular leader or any class of leader (or any "associate" of a leader) any interests, benefits or property of the leader or associate (s 24). A leader who, or whose spouse or child under 18 years, seeks, accepts, obtains or holds any prohibited interest, benefit or property is guilty of misconduct in office (s 25).

Ordering forfeiture of prohibited interests

If the Commission is of the opinion that a leader (or spouse or child) holds any prohibited interest, the Commission may, as an alternative to dealing with the matter as misconduct in office, and after giving the leader concerned adequate opportunity of stating her or his case, order the leader (or spouse etc) to dispose of the interest on such terms and conditions as it considers fit (s 26).

This is a significant power, for it gives the Commission quasi-judicial powers, blurring the traditional notion of separation of powers which otherwise appears to underpin the *Constitution*. An example of the invoking of the power occurred in November 1995, when the Commission ordered Mr Albert Karo MP to forfeit to the state his interests in the controversial former residence of the Premier of Central Province at Touaguba Hill, Port Moresby.

Investigative role of the Ombudsman Commission

Power to investigate

The Commission is authorised to commence an investigation under the Code, either on its own initiative or on complaint from any person, about the conduct of a leader (Organic Law, ss 17(c) and 18). The investigation must be conducted in private. There is no obligation to inform the leader of the investigation. The absence of a requirement to notify the leader of the investigation is quite different from the position with investigations of allegations of wrong conduct under the *Organic Law on the Ombudsman Commission.*

Curiously, in 1995 the Supreme Court came to the opposite conclusion in *Karo v Ombudsman Commission* [1995] PNGLR 547. It was held that the Commission was obliged to notify leaders of its intention to conduct an investigation into their conduct. However, that decision involved a fundamental error of interpretation, resulting from the court's reliance on a provision of the *Organic Law on the Ombudsman Commission* (s 17) that has no application to the Leadership Code. The error was recognised by Sheehan J (who was one of the members of the court in *Karo*) in his decision a few months later in *Nilkare v Ombudsman Commission* (OS 216/95, unreported), and eventually overruled by the Supreme Court decision in *Nilkare v Ombudsman Commission* (unreported, 3 May 1996).

The decision in *Karo* suggests that the courts have some difficulty in fully comprehending the differences in the two main distinct roles of the Ombudsman Commission: on the one hand, its role in relation to the Leadership Code, and on the other its "traditional" Ombudsman role in relation to maladministration. As a result, the courts are not always clear on the interaction between the two Organic Laws administered by the Ombudsman Commission, and the different procedures that are laid down for the two main types of investigations carried out by the Commission.

The Commission's investigative powers under the Code are extensive. It is authorised to make whatever inquiries it thinks fit. The Commission may summons any person who in its opinion is able to give any information relating to any matter being investigated. A person summonsed must attend before the Commission, and may be required to produce documents, papers or things, and other information in their possession or control. Failure to comply with a summons, refusing to be sworn in or give evidence, giving false evidence or being in contempt of the Commission are all acts that constitute serious criminal offences punishable by a fine or imprisonment (Organic Law, ss 20, 21, 31, 33).

There is an important exception to these wide powers. The Commission cannot require production of information, documents or things certified as classified on various grounds by the Prime Minister (for example, national security, public interest). Nevertheless, before exercising this power the Prime Minister must first consult with the Chief Ombudsman (Organic Law, s 22).

Otherwise, any leader who obstructs, or fails to co-operate to the best of her or his ability with the Ombudsman Commission in any investigation under or in relation to the Leadership Code, whether in relation to the leader or to any other person, is guilty of misconduct in office (s 23).

Experience has shown that the courts invariably take a tough stand against leaders who commit offences related to the Commission's investigative powers. For example, in 1992 the National Court jailed a former Fisheries Minister for one month, over his failure to answer a summons issued by the Commission. At the time he was being investigated over allegations of accepting bribes for issuing fisheries licences to foreign fishing companies.

Object of investigations

The object of an investigation by the Ombudsman Commission is to determine whether there is a prima facie case that the leader is guilty of misconduct in office. Prior to reaching this point, the Commission is obliged to grant the leader a right to be heard. In other words, the Ombudsman Commission must comply with the principles of natural justice enshrined in the *Constitution*, ss 59 and 60. If, after considering the leader's explanation, the Ombudsman Commission decides that there is a prima facie case against that leader, it is obliged to refer the matter to the Public Prosecutor for prosecution before an independent leadership tribunal (*Constitution*, s 29; Organic Law, ss 17, 20).

Relationship of the Leadership Code to the Criminal Code Act

One of the underlying assumptions of the Leadership Code is that breaches of it are disciplinary offences rather than criminal offences. However, it was clearly intended that a leader should be subject to both the provisions of the Leadership Code and other relevant laws, such as the

Criminal Code Act (Ch 262). Section 30(1) of the *Organic Law on the Duties and Responsibilities of Leadership* especially provides that:

> "The result of any proceedings in respect of a charge of misconduct in office is not a bar to proceedings in respect of the same act under any other provision of the *Constitution* or any other law."

This means that leaders involved in serious cases of misconduct in office, such as misappropriation of public funds and bribery, are also liable to be charged with these offences under the *Criminal Code Act.*

The Commission is currently reviewing the procedures that should apply when it uncovers evidence of criminal conduct during the course of its investigations under the Leadership Code, with a view to streamlining the procedures to allow an early transfer of matters to the Public Prosecutor or the Fraud Squad. This will obviate the delays that are experienced under the current system, where a leader is usually not dealt with under the *Criminal Code Act* until some considerable time after the case has been heard by a leadership tribunal. These procedural changes are necessary if the Commission is to adapt to the changing circumstances in the country, and be in a position to respond to endemic corruption.

PROSECUTION FOR MISCONDUCT IN OFFICE

Relationship between the Public Prosecutor and the Ombudsman Commission

It is at this point in the constitutional process that the role of the Ombudsman Commission begins to diminish and that other constitutional office-holders and institutions take active roles.

It is the Public Prosecutor (another constitutional office-holder, free from direction or control) that normally decides whether to prosecute the case. However, if the Public Prosecutor fails to prosecute within a reasonable period, the Ombudsman Commission may prosecute instead (*Constitution*, s 29(2)). In recent years, the Public Prosecutor and the Ombudsman Commission have developed a close working relationship, and it is now many years since the Ombudsman Commission has used its "reserve" powers of prosecution.

The leadership tribunal

Under the Organic Law, determining the guilt or innocence of a leader charged with misconduct in office is a matter for a special tribunal called a leadership tribunal. The composition of such a tribunal depends on the nature of the public office occupied by the leader being prosecuted (s 27(7)). Most prosecutions for misconduct in office have been against Ministers and other members of the Parliament and, in such a case, the tribunal is appointed by the Chief Justice and consists of a judge as the chairman, together with two senior magistrates. By contrast, if the Ombudsman Commission were to find a prima facie case of misconduct against the Prime Minister, or the Chief Justice, or any other judge of the Supreme or National Courts, the tribunal would consist entirely of judges; either judges of Papua New Guinea courts, or judges co-opted from any country with a legal system similar to that of Papua Guinea (s 27).

Leadership tribunal hearings

A leadership tribunal is obliged by the Organic Law to make "due inquiry" into all matters referred to it "without regard to legal formalities or the rules of evidence, and may inform itself in such manner as it thinks proper, subject to compliance with the principles of natural justice" (s 27(4)). Other than these requirements, the tribunals have a very broad discretion as to the procedures to be adopted. The leader against whom the allegations of misconduct have been made is invariably given the right to legal representation and the right to cross-examine prosecution witnesses and produce any evidence in defence of her or his actions.

In my view, the Code envisages the tribunal acting as an inquisitorial body. The duty of a tribunal is to inquire into allegations of misconduct in office before it. Two constitutional provisions impose that duty:

(1) s 28(1)(g)(i) of the *Constitution,* which requires that an Organic Law "shall establish independent tribunals that . . . shall *investigate* and determine any cases of alleged or suspected misconduct in office referred to them in accordance with the Organic Law" (emphasis added); and

(2) s 27 of the *Organic Law on the Duties and Responsibilities of Leadership*, which requires that a tribunal "shall make due inquiry into the matter referred to it, without regard to legal formalities or the rules of evidence".

These requirements were unfortunately not recognised or complied with by a leadership tribunal in a significant decision, reported as *Re Sir Julius Chan* [1988] PNGLR 200. As a result, that tribunal failed to recognise its constitutional function as an inquisitorial body.

Chan's case involved a reference to a tribunal of allegations of misconduct concerning the purchase of shares in a mining company, Placer Pacific Ltd. Sir Julius Chan, then Minister for Finance, was the Minister responsible for decision-making and policy implementation generally relating to the allocation of shares by companies in Papua New Guinea. It was alleged that he breached s 6 of the *Organic Law on the Duties and Responsibilities of Leadership* by dealing with the matter (the allocation of shares) in his official capacity, without revealing the interest of himself and his associates (his family companies had purchased shares in the company).

In my view, the tribunal in *Re Sir Julius Chan* was incorrect in taking the approach that it was not incumbent on the tribunal to adduce evidence, which may have established that the leader had an interest in the matter at the same time as he was acting in his official capacity.[400] That is, the tribunal failed to appreciate that, under the *Constitution*, it was required to adopt an inquisitorial stance, rather than act like a court under the adversarial system.

As the Leadership Code is not a criminal code, the standard of proof before a leadership tribunal is less than the standard required in a criminal trial (beyond reasonable doubt), but is a little higher than the standard required in a civil trial (the balance of probabilities).[401]

The essential task of the tribunal is to determine whether the leader is guilty of misconduct in office. In the case of a finding of guilt, the *Constitution* requires a penalty of dismissal from

[400] [1988] PNGLR 200 at 263.
[401] *Re James Eki Mopio* [1981] PNGLR 416.

office, unless there is a finding that there was "no serious culpability" on the part of the leader and that "public policy and the public good do not require dismissal" (*Constitution*, s 28(1A)). In such cases, the tribunal may recommend alternative penalties such as fines, suspensions (with or without pay) or reprimands.[402] Dismissal from office carries with it an automatic three-year disqualification from the holding of elective public office.[403]

Review of decisions of a leadership tribunal

There is no appeal against the decision of a leadership tribunal. However, the National Court does have an inherent right under the *Constitution* to review the legality of the procedures and deliberations of any court or tribunal. A leadership tribunal is regarded as a normal administrative tribunal susceptible to judicial review according to established common law principles of administrative law.[404]

Assessing the role of the Ombudsman Commission

It can be seen from the above that the Ombudsman Commission is the linchpin in enforcement of the Leadership Code. It is the Ombudsman Commission that decides which leaders to investigate, which leaders may be prosecuted, and when those prosecutions will commence. Because the Ombudsman Commission does not determine the question of a leader's guilt or innocence, any potential for abuse of power by it is minimised.

CONSTITUTIONAL SAFEGUARDS FOR THE COMMISSION

Because of the extreme sensitivity of the roles of the Commission, especially in relation to the Leadership Code, the *Constitution* contains a number of safeguards intended to maintain the integrity and independence of the Commission. The aim is to enable the Commission to exercise its functions in a totally independent manner, free of any outside influence or control. In practice, the Commission has a well-deserved reputation of being scrupulously fair and honest in its dealings with leaders and the bureaucracy in general, a reputation assisted by the constitutional safeguards. The most important safeguards relate to the composition of the Ombudsman Commission, the processes for making appointments to the Commission, and guarantees of security of tenure for those persons appointed as members of the Ombudsman Commission. The Commission's independence is also enhanced by interesting provisions enabling it to stand aside from particular matters and give responsibilities under the Code to alternative authorities, as well as by the entrenchment of detailed provisions about the Commission's powers and functions.

Appointment to the Ombudsman Commission

Instead of a lone Ombudsman (as is the case with Ombudsman institutions in many jurisdictions), the Ombudsman Commission of Papua New Guinea consists of three members: the Chief Ombudsman plus two other Ombudsmen (*Constitution*, s 217). This feature sets the Commission apart from many other institutions and prevents its powers being monopolised by a single person.

---

[402] *Leadership Code (Alternative Penalties) Act* (Ch 1A).
[403] *Constitution*, ss 28 and 31.
[404] *Constitution*, s 155(3).

The members of the Commission are appointed by the Head of State, acting in accordance with the advice of a body established under the *Constitution* called the "Ombudsman Appointments Committee" (s 217(2)). It consists of the Prime Minister, the Chief Justice, the leader of the Opposition, the Chairman of the Permanent Parliamentary Committee on Appointments and the Chairman of the Public Services Commission. By establishing such a broadly based Committee, the *Constitution* aims to ensure that only persons of the highest integrity are appointed Ombudsmen, and further that they will have the full confidence of the three main arms of government when discharging their important constitutional duties. Another advantage of the appointment process is that it reduces the likelihood of political appointments being made.

This system has so far worked very well, in that every appointment to the Commission since independence has been based on merit without even a hint of politics being involved. Moreover, there is no reason to suggest that this will not remain the case in the future.

Security of tenure

The *Organic Law on the Guarantee of the Rights and Independence of Constitutional Office-holders* guarantees security of tenure for members of the Ombudsman Commission. It provides that a member of the Commission can only be removed from office on prescribed grounds such as "inability to perform the functions and duties of his office" and "misbehaviour" (s 7). In addition, the *Constitution* ensures that a member of the Commission can only be removed from office upon the recommendation of an independent and impartial tribunal (s 223(2)(a)).

Other constitutional safeguards for the Ombudsman Commission include:

(a) an express prohibition against the abolition of the offices of all constitutional office-holders (s 223(5));

(b) the automatic continuation of prosecutions under the Leadership Code in the event of its repeal by the Parliament (Sch 1.17);

(c) guaranteed funding of staff and facilities (s 225);

(d) the express guarantee that the Ombudsman Commission is not subject to direction or control by any person or authority in the exercise of its functions (s 217(5)); and

(e) a provision that the proceedings of the Commission cannot be judicially reviewed, except by the National or Supreme Court on the ground of excess of jurisdiction (s 217(6)).

Alternative authorities

Another important constitutional safeguard is provided by s 19 of the *Organic Law on the Duties and Responsibilities of Leadership*. It empowers the appointment of an investigating authority (consisting of one or more constitutional office-holders) where the Ombudsman Commission "is itself unable for any reasons to conduct an examination or investigation". This provision has only been invoked once, in relation to an inquiry into the purchase of shares in Placer Pacific Ltd.

In the mid-1980s, an investigating authority consisting of Supreme Court Judge Mr Justice Los and Auditor-General Mr Makena Geno was appointed to inquire into the purchase of shares by various leaders in Placer Pacific Ltd. The reason the Commission appointed the authority was that members of the Commission had purchased shares in the company. The Placer Pacific saga was a good example of how the Leadership Code and the Ombudsman Commission coped well with what had loomed as a crisis.

Entrenchment

Perhaps the single most important safeguard for the Ombudsman Commission is that as a constitutional office-holder deriving its powers directly from the *Constitution*, the only way that it can be abolished, or any of its jurisdiction removed, is through an amendment to the *Constitution*. Needless to say, this is a rather complex procedure. A proposed law to alter the *Constitution* and abolish the Ombudsman Commission would need to be supported by a three-quarters absolute majority vote of all members of the Parliament eligible to vote (that is, not only those present and voting), expressed on at least two occasions during different meetings of the Parliament separated in time by at least two months (*Constitution*, ss 14 and 17). If the Commission was not a constitutional institution and had been established under an ordinary Act of Parliament, it could be abolished by a mere majority of the members present and voting.

COMPLEMENTARITY OF JURISDICTIONS: THE COMMISSION AND CORRUPTION

There is a degree of complementarity between the explicit anti-corruption jurisdiction of the Ombudsman Commission in relation to the Leadership Code, and its "traditional" Ombudsman jurisdiction in relation to investigation of wrong conduct. In the exercise of the latter jurisdiction, the Commission often comes upon instances of serious official corruption. If there is a finding of "wrong conduct" as defined under the *Organic Law on the Ombudsman Commission*, then in addition to its general powers in the exercise of its "traditional" jurisdiction to make recommendations for change, the Commission is specifically empowered to refer such matters direct to the Public Prosecutor, "if action by him is warranted and [the Commission] may make such recommendations as it thinks fit" (*Organic Law on the Ombudsman Commission*, s 22(2)).

Simply by referring persons involved in criminal offences direct to the Public Prosecutor with an appropriate recommendation, the Commission can function as a de facto anti-corruption commission. There are two reasons why the Commission cannot, however, compel the Public Prosecutor to act on its recommendations. First, the Public Prosecutor is also an independent constitutional office-holder, and so is not subject to direction or control by any other authority. Secondly, and more importantly, when exercising its "traditional" Ombudsman jurisdiction under the *Organic Law on the Ombudsman Commission*, the Commission has no power to enforce any of its recommendations.

Although the Commission cannot unilaterally enforce the recommendations made by it in the course of its investigations of wrong conduct (however urgent or proper the recommendations may be), it can publish reports of its investigations, recommendations and findings. Investigations under the *Organic Law on the Ombudsman Commission* often uncover not only serious instances of official corruption within the public sector, but also practices which although they may not be corrupt may nevertheless create the conditions in which corruption can easily take root. The publication of reports by the Commission can be a very effective means of exposing actual corruption. Equally, the publication of its reports can be a very effective means of controlling and preventing corruption.

For example, in 1992, the Commission published a report of an investigation, conducted under the *Organic Law on the Ombudsman Commission,* into the awarding of contracts for the construction of a major freeway project in Port Moresby (known as the "Poreporena

Freeway").[405] During the investigation, the Commission found that the relevant departments had not followed correct public tendering and other administrative procedures. This resulted in the contract being awarded to a foreign consortium without proper tendering procedures being followed. It was alleged that this would lead to the state having to pay amounts far in excess of the actual worth of the contracts.

The Commission also uncovered the fact that the then Minister for Transport had consistently misused his ministerial powers by not following the proper tendering procedures, and by arbitrarily excluding Papua New Guinea-based companies from the project in favour of a number of foreign consortiums from whom he had accepted benefits, such as fully paid overseas trips to discuss the project with them. As well, it was discovered that the Minister had illegally executed a contract for the construction of the freeway, without the advice or knowledge of the Department of Transport and without authorisation from the Cabinet. After completing its investigations, the Commission concluded that senior officers from the departments involved in the project (including senior lawyers in the Department of Justice who drew up the legal documentation to allow the project to proceed) were derelict in their duties by allowing, if not encouraging, the Minister to engage in conduct which they must have known was in excess of his lawful powers and in breach of the *Constitution*.

In its report, the Commission vigorously attacked the incompetence of the departments and officers concerned, recommending the immediate implementation of steps to avoid a repetition of such practices. These included:

(a) the revision of public tendering procedures to make them more corruption proof;

(b) the issuing of a public statement by the Prime Minister to all Ministers reminding them of the need constantly to observe the requirements of the conflict of interests provisions of the *Organic Law on the Duties and Responsibilities of Leadership*;

(c) the maintenance of a register by the Secretary to Cabinet recording all declarations of conflict of interests made by Ministers during Cabinet deliberations;

(d) the updating of financial management manuals used in the public service; and

(e) a recommendation that the Minister for Trade and Industry produce a handbook for foreign investors describing and explaining acceptable methods of doing business in Papua New Guinea, for distribution as widely as possible overseas (especially to the country's High Commissions, Embassies and Consulates).

Finally, the Commission refused to rule out the possibility that the Minister had awarded the contract to a company of his choosing for corrupt motives. At the very least, his actions, and those of the government departments and senior officials, had created an environment conducive to corruption. In the Commission's opinion:

> "One of the central themes to this report is that the decision-making process must be above suspicion. Decisions as to who is going to be awarded a multi-million kina contract to build a freeway and how much it is going to cost should be made fairly and in accordance with the law and the nation's constitutional requirements.
>
> When decisions are made in this way, people become suspicious, allegations of corruption inevitably arise and reputations suffer. That is the price paid by all those

[405] Ombudsman Commission of Papua New Guinea, *Report of an Investigation into the Spring Garden Road/Poreporena Freeway Project* (Port Moresby: Ombudsman Commission, 1992).

> involved in the making of these decisions, and also by those who benefit from them.
>
> Procedures are provided by law and they must be followed for the benefit and interests of all concerned.
>
> In the opinion of the Commission, the environment for corruption was created by the way in which normal and established procedures were disregarded . . . in particular by the way the Minister for Transport . . . took control of the decision-making process . . . This is the sort of situation in which corruption can flourish."[406]

The combined effect of the diverse jurisdictions and powers of the Commission make it an effective anti-corruption body. Arguably it has available to it more powers than most conventional anti-corruption commissions elsewhere in the world.

EVALUATING THE ANTI-CORRUPTION ROLE OF THE OMBUDSMAN COMMISSION

Co-ordination of the functions of the Commission

The Ombudsman Commission of Papua New Guinea can be regarded as a traditional Ombudsman commission and a de facto anti-corruption commission rolled into one. As one of the most important constitutional institutions in Papua New Guinea, it has a potentially extensive capacity to fight official corruption in all of its forms. It has not only an impressive array of powers, but also a high degree of independence guaranteed by the *Constitution* and the Organic Laws. Co-ordination of its dual functions is, however, the key to its effectiveness as an anti-corruption body.

Despite the Commission's potential, official corruption continues to be a major problem in Papua New Guinea today. There are, of course, many reasons for this, most of which are outside the Commission's control. For example, some of the blame can be attributed to a political system that allows, and almost encourages, corruption to take root and thrive.

Official corruption in Papua New Guinea is big business. Millions of dollars can be made simply by the stroke of a pen. The rich resources sector is particularly vulnerable to high-level corruption. Corruption has its impact everywhere in the country, against the background of chronic unemployment, an economy in the hands of the World Bank, and a widening gulf between the rich and poor. Papua New Guinea, with its abundant resources, is a striking paradox: the poorest richest country in the world!

There is little doubt that if the recommendations of the CPC concerning the Ombudsman Commission were to surface for the first time in the mid-1990s, they would be thrown out as being too idealistic or too impractical or too tough. Simply put, the Leadership Code was a product of its times.

Continuing relevance of the Leadership Code

It is certainly arguable that there are no measures available, however well intended, that could have prevented the evil of corruption from taking root in Papua New Guinea. Nevertheless, I do not believe that the underlying assumptions of the Leadership Code are in any way less valid today than they were 20 years ago. Papua New Guinea's survival as a nation heavily depends

[406] Ibid, pp 287-89.

upon how effectively the Commission enforces it. The Code is the vehicle for the attainment of the National Goals espoused by the *Constitution*.

The Leadership Code was not only ahead of its time, but it is perhaps unrivalled in any other major democracy. After 20 years, Papua New Guinea is still one of the great democracies in the Pacific region. Both the *Constitution* and those institutions created under it have weathered the test of time and proven their worth despite the turbulence of recent years. The attainment of the National Goals and Directive Principles is not an impossible dream. The problem of corruption will not go away, but this does not mean that it is not controllable, or that it will continue indefinitely to stifle national development. The mechanisms for controlling it remain intact, and firmly entrenched under the *Constitution*.

The Ombudsman Commission's enforcement of the Code has been exemplary. It has consistently demonstrated that there is not one law for the leaders and another law for the rest. In the 20 years since independence, it has referred more than 40 leaders to the Public Prosecutor for prosecution before leadership tribunals. The list of leaders referred includes numerous Ministers of state, a former Prime Minister and a former Deputy Prime Minister, leaders of major political parties, and numerous high-ranking public servants.

Behind the scenes, the Commission endeavours to promote good government, to raise the standards of the public service, and to devise ways and means of minimising corruption in the workplace. The Poreporena Freeway Report[407] is a good example of this. The Commission also endeavours to raise the standards of leadership by counselling leaders on a daily basis and explaining to them their duties and responsibilities under the Leadership Code. The old adage "prevention is better than cure" is central to its approach, with referral being the last resort.

Whilst the first few years of the Commission's existence were learning years, the last five or six years, in particular, have been years of high achievement. In this period alone, 18 leaders have been referred to the Public Prosecutor for prosecution before appropriate tribunals, on multiple counts of alleged high-level corruption. All were either found guilty on the counts for which they were referred, or resigned from office in order to take advantage of a loophole created in 1980 by the Supreme Court, in the case of *Re Joseph Auna* [1980] PNGLR 500.

The major loophole in the Code

In *Auna's* case, the Supreme Court held that a leader may only be dealt with, by a leadership tribunal, for misconduct in office whilst remaining the holder of an office to which the Code applies. The key reasons for this finding were stated as follows:

> "The entire thrust of the legislation is directed towards removing a person who is considered, after due inquiry, to be unworthy of continuing in office . . . Once the primary purpose is clear, it is not anomalous that a person, having ceased to hold leadership office becomes immune from proceedings under the Leadership Code in respect of any alleged misconduct in office, during the time he held office."[408]

[407] Above, n 19.
[408] [1980] PNGLR 500 at 504.

Thus, a leader who is referred to a leadership tribunal can avoid accountability for her or his actions simply by resigning her or his office, either before or during the hearing of the case. This loophole was not further exploited until nine years after *Auna's* case, when a former Minister for Communications resigned his office after being referred by the Ombudsman Commission to a leadership tribunal on multiple counts of misappropriation and abuse of office. Unfortunately, this established a precedent for other leaders to follow, with resignations becoming the preferred option to facing a leadership tribunal (since 1989, of the 18 leaders referred, 10 have resigned rather than face the findings of a tribunal). This development has led to a public outcry and a belief in some sections of the community that the Leadership Code has become an ineffective means of preserving the people from their corrupt leaders. There have even been calls for the Code to be abolished, in favour of dealing with corrupt leaders in accordance with normal criminal procedures in open court.

In an effort to redress the situation, the Commission took the unusual step, in 1992, of asking the Supreme Court to overrule *Auna*'s case. The Commission argued that *Auna* was no longer applicable to the changing circumstances of Papua New Guinea (*Supreme Court Reference No 2 of 1992* [1992] PNGLR 336). In relation to the above-quoted passage in *Auna*'s case (concerning the "thrust" of the Code) the Commission argued that the purpose of the Code, today, should be to protect the people of Papua New Guinea from misconduct by its leaders, and that this goal could only be achieved by ensuring that leaders are held accountable for their misconduct in office; that is, by plugging the loophole.

Whilst agreeing that the thrust of the Leadership Code was to preserve the people from the misconduct of its leaders, the court nevertheless refused to overrule its earlier decision, even though under the *Constitution* it had the power to do so. The court's reasons for so finding, in my opinion, were confused, illogical and arguably an abandonment of its constitutional responsibilities. If, as the court agreed, the thrust of the Code had changed by virtue of the spate of resignations since 1989, then it was duty bound to plug the loophole. Needless to say, the court's unconvincing judgment has done little to quell the concerns of the people over the future of the Leadership Code.

There is no doubt that the deterrent effect of the Code has been significantly reduced by the 1992 Supreme Court decision. If a leader can effectively choose to ignore the law by resigning from office either before or during the hearing of a case, then the Supreme Court may have inadvertently created one law for the leaders and another law for the rest of the population. It is hard to believe that this was the intended result of the CPC's recommendations or of the provisions in the *Constitution*.

Future of the Leadership Code

Although arguments are sometimes advanced in favour of the abolition of the Code it seems clear that this would in fact be a regressive step. In fact, the arguments in favour of its abolition are founded on false premises. One argument concerns the use of the criminal law as being preferable to the Code. But, of course, there is nothing to prevent breaches of the Leadership Code that also constitute criminal offences from being dealt with under the *Criminal Code Act* (Ch 262). This is actually one of the underlying assumptions of the Leadership Code. Indeed, if there is misconduct that constitutes an offence under the *Criminal Code Act*, it is preferable to deal with the leader under the *Criminal Code Act* than under the Leadership Code.

On the other hand, there is no reason to believe that the enforcers of the *Criminal Code Act* - the Police Force - will be as diligent in the enforcement of the *Criminal Code Act* in relation to official corruption as the Ombudsman Commission has been in the enforcement of the Leadership Code. History has shown that the Police Force has not been effective in enforcing the *Criminal Code Act* against leaders. One reason for this may be that, unlike the Ombudsman Commission, the Police Force is part of the executive arm of government and is therefore more susceptible to political pressure.

There are, of course, a number of factors that detract from the effectiveness of the Leadership Code in its present form. One concerns the loophole originally created by the Supreme Court by its decision in *Auna*'s case. Another factor is the fact that the penalties available in cases of misconduct in office are hopelessly inadequate. The maximum sanctions provided for (that is, dismissal and ineligibility to stand for elective office for a period of three years from the date of dismissal) are unrealistic. Further, the sanctions fail to differentiate between different degrees of culpability, and do not have a cumulative effect. There is only one maximum penalty available, irrespective of the seriousness of the leader's misconduct in office, or the number of counts in respect of which the leader is found guilty. This problem has become more apparent in recent years, with leaders almost routinely being referred on multiple counts of misconduct in office involving extremely serious breaches of the Leadership Code.

The inadequacies of the Code are compounded by the fact that it does not provide for the forfeiture of ill-gotten gains by a leader found guilty of misconduct in office. Although, as noted above, the Commission can order forfeiture of "prohibited interests", this is only intended as an alternative to referral of a charge of misconduct in office, and therefore can only be used in situations where a leader's conduct, although improper, is not corrupt. The reality, therefore, is that a leader found guilty of misconduct in office is allowed to retain the profits of the misconduct. While forfeiture of ill-gotten gains can be ordered by a criminal court, the likelihood in practice of the leader being charged with a criminal offence is remote.

Another issue concerns the need for the Commission to have available to it the resources necessary to engage in the various forms of international co-operation needed to deal with the fact that official corruption in Papua New Guinea is fast becoming internationalised. It is now not unusual for leaders to be approached by foreign business representatives, who offer huge cash inducements and a percentage of profits in return for favourable treatment, especially in relation to the rich resources sector. It is extremely difficult for the Commission effectively to counter this type of activity, because the profits are usually being secreted offshore. To make matters worse, unlike many other anti-corruption bodies throughout the world, the Commission does not have at its disposal an international police network such as Interpol to facilitate the making of inquiries overseas. More international co-operation by the Ombudsman Commission is needed, particularly in relation to information sharing, if the international dimensions of corruption are to begin to be controlled.

Although the ultimate solutions to most of the problems just identified are in the hands of the legislators, they have shown little interest to date in either plugging the loophole created by the decision in *Auna*, or in introducing more effective deterrent measures into the *Code*. It may be that some legislators have a vested interest in ensuring that the Leadership Code is ineffective, in case they one day become the target of an investigation!

CONCLUSION

Whilst the Leadership Code has certainly been weakened by the Supreme Court's decision in *Auna* and its subsequent refusal to overrule the decision, the evidence shows that the Code remains the most viable means for the control and combat of official corruption in Papua New Guinea. The Ombudsman Commission has consistently demonstrated that it is able to confront the problem head on, by seeking to deny corrupt leaders the thing they treasure most: the perks and illicit benefits of their high offices.

Although it is an impossible task to create a corruption-free society in Papua New Guinea (or anywhere else for that matter), the Commission has both the capacity and commitment to restrict the problem. In summary, while official corruption is a major problem, without the Ombudsman Commission and the Leadership Code the extent of the problem would have been far worse.

Chapter 15

PROTECTION OF THE INDEPENDENCE OF CONSTITUTIONAL OFFICE-HOLDERS*

ANTHONY J REGAN

INTRODUCTION

Protection of the independence of constitutional office-holders has been a matter of growing importance in constitution-making since World War II. Previously there had been an assumption that political processes could be relied on to achieve accountability of public office-holders: control of the executive by the legislature in the parliamentary executive system, or the checks on the executive involved in presidential executive systems. Much of the focus was on the separation of powers doctrine.

Among the factors contributing to increased questioning of reliance on political processes to achieve accountability was the development of strong political parties that from the 20th century tended to make transparent the weaknesses in checks on the executive arm of government built on various conceptions of the separation of powers doctrine. The control of both legislature and executive by the same political party (or group of parties) in the Westminster system and its variants results in the leadership of the dominant party controlling both legislature and executive. While party politics does not necessarily have quite the same stifling effect on the possible supervisory role of the legislature in countries with a presidential executive system (especially where different parties control the executive and the legislature), it nevertheless reduces the effectiveness of legislative checks.

Of course, there has seldom been a complete reliance on political process to achieve accountability. For example, bodies such as the Auditor-General have been set up with a view to achieving financial accountability. However, experience in many countries has showed that there were many ways of interfering with institutions intended to enhance accountability of the executive. Appointments to such institutions as well as others that carry out politically sensitive roles (such as bodies responsible for electoral administration) could be made on a political basis. Such institutions could be given political directions and, where they were not responsive, incumbents could be removed from office or the institutions starved of resources.

*This chapter is an edited and revised version of a 1996 paper for the Fiji Constitution Review Commission and published as "Accountability of government as a Constitutional Imperative: protection of the independence of constitutional office-holders" in B V Lal and T R Vakatora (eds), *Fiji and the World - Research Papers of the Fiji Constitution Review Commission*, Vol 2 (Suva: School of Social and Economic Development, USP, 1997).

Writing in 1964, the eminent constitutional lawyer S A de Smith discussed how the constitutions of many newly independent former British colonies created "politically neutral zones". The aim was "insulation of sensitive areas of public activity from direct political influences".[409] Protection was focused on appointment and removal processes for the judiciary, judicial service commissions, Attorneys-General and public prosecutors, public service commissions, the police and bodies responsible for electoral administration. In most cases, only the principles were stated in the constitutions, with detailed provision in normal statutes.

Since the 1970s, in part responding to concerns that the first wave of post-colonial constitutions had not done enough either to guarantee independence of special institutions or to increase accountability of government, some new constitutions have gone still further. New constitutional institutions have been established with major roles directed towards increased accountability, especially of the executive. These include Ombudsmen and human rights commissions. Secondly, constitutions have specified more detail concerning the measures needed to guarantee the independence of both the older institutions with politically sensitive roles and the newer "accountability" bodies.

Accountability of government is an important focus of the Papua New Guinea *Constitution*: it contains a greater range of provisions on the subject with considerably more detail than most other constitutions. The origins of most such provisions can be found in the 1974 Final Report of the Constitutional Planning Committee (CPC). There were several main factors involved in the CPC's concern that the *Constitution* should ensure a high degree of accountability in government. First, there was reaction to experience of often arbitrary colonial rule in Papua and New Guinea, where government had been largely unaccountable for what it did. Secondly, the CPC gradually found itself in conflict with the pre-independence Papua New Guinea Government under Chief Minister Somare, in power from 1972 to 1975, and was at times deeply concerned at the pragmatism of the government. Thirdly, distrust of government was reinforced by the CPC's study of post-colonial experience in Africa, Asia and the Caribbean, where by the early 1970s arbitrary and corrupt government had become a common pattern, something the CPC aimed to prevent in Papua New Guinea. Fourthly, there was already some evidence of corruption in government in Papua New Guinea.[410]

The CPC envisaged accountability being pursued through numerous overlapping aspects of its recommendations. For example, provision for independence of constitutional office-holders was to operate in conjunction with that in relation to the Ombudsman Commission and a Leadership Code and restrictions on the powers of the executive; for example, human rights provisions. In general, the establishment of independent constitutional office-holders was intended to ensure the spread of power horizontally, at the National Government level, far beyond the limits of the separation of powers doctrine. In addition to the three "traditional" arms of government – legislature, executive and judiciary - numerous constitutional institutions would all accept limits on their powers and encourage the accountability of the others. In particular, constitutional office-holders would be able to carry out their sensitive responsibilities without excessive political and other pressures.

---

[409] S A de Smith, *The New Commonwealth and its Constitutions* (London: Stevens, 1964), p 136.
[410] CPC, *Final Report of the Constitutional Planning Committee: Part 1* (Port Moresby: Government Printer, 1974), p 3/2/15-17.

OVERVIEW OF PROTECTION OF CONSTITUTIONAL OFFICE-HOLDERS

The systematic nature of the constitutional scheme for protection of the independence of constitutional office-holders in the Papua New Guinea *Constitution* is unusual. First, it goes to unprecedented lengths to establish the constitutional office-holders as independent and "politically neutral zones". It aims to prevent use of as many means as possible by which government might seek to apply political pressures to the main institutions with roles in providing for accountability.

Secondly, most constitutions that deal with the independence of constitutional office-holders do so through specific provisions pertinent to each officer-holder. By contrast, on the basis of the CPC's recommendations,[411] the Papua New Guinea *Constitution* defines the positions to which a common scheme applies.[412] There are, however, variations in some of the arrangements made for particular offices.[413]

There are important advantages in a common scheme applicable to all constitutional office-holders. First, it ensures focus of attention on the importance of the group of offices covered by the scheme. Secondly, it reduces the repetition of detail that would be required if separate provision had to be made in respect of each office.[414]

The Papua New Guinea scheme contains a number of distinct elements.

(1) The protections are extended to specific offices.

(2) Independence of office-holders is a goal of criteria applicable to appointment to and disqualification from office, and technical qualifications are set to ensure that appointments are of the highest possible quality.

(3) Appointments to the offices in question are insulated from political interference, to varying degrees, by special appointment procedures.

(4) The offices are further insulated from political interference by provisions on suspension and removal from office that not only require just cause but also establish elaborate procedures to be followed in such cases.

(5) Office-holder's emoluments while in office are protected from reduction except in restricted circumstances.

(6) None of the offices in question can be abolished while there is a substantive holder of the office.

(7) The provision by government of the resources needed to carry out the functions of the offices is the subject of a limited guarantee.

---

[411] CPC, above n 2, p 14/6-9.

[412] *Constitution*, s 221 defines the offices while ss 222-225 provide for the common scheme.

[413] Provisions specific to each office are provided for in the sections of the *Constitution* creating the offices in question, and in the Organic Laws discussed below.

[414] By contrast, the 1995 Ugandan *Constitution*, which provides special protection for numerous constitutional office-holders, re-states most of the basic detail concerning protection of their independence for each of the offices, thereby adding to its length and also resulting in some anomalies.

(8) While the *Constitution* assumes that most aspects of the scheme for protection of office-holders will be provided for by Organic Laws and other statutes, where necessary provision has not been made, the office-holders have power to fill the deficiency.

(9) All holders of any of the offices are free from direction and control from any person or authority while carrying out their constitutional functions.

(10) Constitutional office-holders are required to act in a way that ensures they are not subject to party political and commercial pressures.

(11) The holders of the constitutional offices are made accountable for the exercise of their functions.

(12) The limited tenure of office-holders is balanced by the guarantee of either further employment by government or a suitable pension at the end of her or his period in office.

The major elements of the scheme are provided for in broad outline in ss 223-225 of the *Constitution*, provisions that envisage that the details will be provided for elsewhere in the *Constitution* and in Organic Laws. The following discussion identifies the main aims of each aspect of the scheme, in most cases by reference to the views of the CPC, and examines the operation of the statutory provisions implementing the recommendations. Some weaknesses in certain aspects of the constitutional provisions are identified. The analysis shows that the scheme does not offer equal protection to the independence of all of the constitutional office-holders.

THE OFFICES PROTECTED

At the outset, a distinction must be made between "constitutional office-holders", on the one hand, and "constitutional institutions" on the other hand. The complete scheme of protection outlined above applies to the former while a much more limited level of protection applies to the latter (as discussed later in this chapter).

The term "constitutional office-holder" applies to nine categories of office listed in s 221, namely: all judges; the Chief Magistrate (but not other magistrates); the Public Prosecutor; the Public Solicitor; members of the Ombudsman Commission; members of the Electoral Commission; the Clerk of the Parliament; members of the Public Services Commission; and the Auditor-General.[415]

The term "constitutional institution" extends to every office or institution established or provided for by the *Constitution*, with the exception of the Head of State, a Minister and the National Executive Council. Constitutional office-holders are at the same time constitutional institutions, and enjoy the two areas of protection extended to constitutional institutions (see below); the higher degree of protection afforded to constitutional office-holders is not extended to constitutional institutions.

Constitutional office-holders are presumably singled out for a higher degree of protection because they carry out accountability or other politically sensitive responsibilities where restriction of political interference is important. The judiciary has many relevant roles, including its judicial review functions, and roles in enforcement of the criminal law and the Leadership Code. The

[415] In addition, s 221 permits an Organic Law or an Act of the Parliament to declare other offices to be constitutional offices for the purpose of the section. No such declaration has ever been made.

Public Prosecutor is responsible for all criminal prosecutions, including offences intended to prevent corrupt practices, and is also the main authority for prosecutions of persons alleged to have committed breaches of the Leadership Code. The Public Solicitor may have a role in relation to accountability to the extent that it provides representation to persons wishing to take legal actions of various kinds against politicians and bureaucrats.[416]

The Ombudsman Commission administers the Leadership Code and deals with complaints about maladministrations. The Auditor-General has the crucially important constitutional responsibility for ensuring accountability of government for its use of public funds and property of the state. The Electoral Commission, the Public Services Commission, and the Clerk of the Parliament are all offices that carry out politically sensitive functions. Protecting their independence from political interference is important if accountability is to be maintained; otherwise those in control of government would have considerably increased scope for manipulating the political system and the resources of government to their advantage. Elections would be more open to manipulation; procedures of the Parliament could be more readily organised to suit those in power.

QUALIFICATIONS FOR APPOINTMENT TO OFFICE

Two sets of qualifications apply to appointments to constitutional offices. One involves criteria largely directed towards establishing that a person is not subject to various commercial and political pressures that might compromise her or his independence. Failure to meet those criteria constitutes both a bar to appointment and grounds from disqualification from office after appointment (the latter issue being discussed further below). The second set of qualifications relates to various professional and other standards that may have to be met for appointment to particular offices.

Criteria establishing independence as qualifications for appointment to and grounds for disqualification from office

The CPC emphasised its concern in relation to constitutional office-holders that because "the responsibilities and trust placed in them are so great . . . it is necessary to place . . . restrictions upon their personal and professional conduct".[417] Accordingly, it recommended basic criteria that would have to be met if a person was to become or remain an office-holder: criteria relevant to the person's independence from overt political and commercial influences. The constitutional arrangements reflect the CPC's concerns. In general, a person is not qualified either to become or remain a constitutional office-holder if he or she is: a member of the Parliament, or of a provincial government or a local-level government; an office-holder in a registered political party; an undischarged bankrupt; of unsound mind; or under a sentence of death or imprisonment.[418]

[416] In fact, since 1978, the Public Solicitor has been so lacking in resources that it has largely restricted itself to providing representation to persons charged with criminal offences in respect of which the potential penalty exceeds two years' imprisonment, the core function of the Public Solicitor's role as provided in s 177(2) of the *Constitution*.

[417] CPC, above n 2, p 14/3/26.

[418] See *Organic Law on Certain Constitutional Office-holders*, s 14; *Organic law on National Elections*, s 11; *Organic Law on the Ombudsman Commission*, s 7; and *Organic Law on the Terms and Conditions of Employment of Judges*, s 4.

Technical, professional and other qualifications

The technical, professional and other similar qualifications for appointment vary considerably from office to office. For the most part, they are laid down either in the provisions of the *Constitution* creating the office in question, or in Organic Laws or statutes. Depending on the nature of the office, they may either involve technical requirements or general requirements as to broad experience in a relevant field of work and/or high moral standing. For example, an Act of Parliament provides that the basic qualifications for a citizen of Papua New Guinea to be appointed a judge involve being a graduate in law of at least six years' standing, and legal practice experience of at least four years.[419] The *Organic Law on the Ombudsman Commission*, s 4, provides that an appointee as Chief Ombudsman must be "in the opinion of the committee,[420] a person of integrity, independence of mind, resolution and high standing in the community", with no technical or professional qualifications being required. The *Organic Law on Certain Constitutional Office-holders*, s 10, requires that an appointee to the office of Auditor-General must "possess such professional accountancy qualifications" as the appointing authority (the National Executive Council) decides, after receipt of a report from the Public Services Commission, to be appropriate.

APPOINTMENT PROCEDURES

Overview

The procedures for appointments of constitutional office-holders vary. In the case of the procedures applicable to judges (other than the Chief Justice), the Chief Magistrate, the Public Prosecutor, the Public Solicitor and members of the Ombudsman Commission, the arrangements seek to shield the appointment process from political interference, but without entirely excluding it. In these cases, provision is made for an independent body to make the appointment, with the government having minority membership in each appointing body. The rationale for including government in the process is that the positions are so important that ideally appointees should have the confidence of all major interested parties, and hence government should have input into the process.[421]

Appointments to most of the other constitutional offices - those of the Chief Justice, the Auditor-General, members of the Public Services Commission and the Clerk of Parliament - can be made by government subject to consultation with relevant authorities. The position is similar with appointments of the Electoral Commissioner, for while a three-person appointing authority makes them, the government may well dominate the membership. The relevant arrangements require elaboration.

[419] *National Court Act* (Ch 38), s 1.

[420] That is, the Ombudsman Appointments Committee, which is the appointing authority for the members of the Ombudsman Commission established under the *Constitution*, s 217.

[421] See the discussion by the CPC, above n 2, p 11/3/23, concerning its reasons for wanting the Prime Minister to chair the committee to appoint members of the Ombudsman Commission.

Appointment procedures for particular offices

Judges, Chief Magistrate, Public Prosecutor and Public Solicitor

The Judicial and Legal Services Commission appoints all judges - other than the Chief Justice - as well as the Chief Magistrate, the Public Prosecutor and the Public Solicitor.[422] The Commission comprises the Minister responsible for justice administration, the Chief Justice, the Deputy Chief Justice, the Chief Ombudsman and a member of the Parliament appointed by the Parliament.[423] Its independence from direction and control is guaranteed.[424] (Some aspects of the constitutional provisions concerning the Judicial and Legal Services Commission are discussed later in this chapter.)

The Ombudsman Commission

An Ombudsman Appointments Committee appoints the members of the Ombudsman Commission.[425] It comprises five members: the Prime Minister; the Chief Justice; the leader of the Opposition; the chairman of the "appropriate Permanent Parliamentary Committee"[426] (provided that should the chairman of that committee not be committed to supporting the government, the deputy chairman should substitute for the chairman); and the Chairman of the Public Services Commission. Hence there are two members who could be expected to support government views (the Prime Minister and the chairman or deputy chairman of the parliamentary committee) and three who could be expected to be independent of government.

The Electoral Commission

The sole member of the Electoral Commission is appointed by the Electoral Commission Appointments Committee, comprising three members: the Prime Minister or a Minister nominated by her or him; the chairman or deputy chairman of "the appropriate Permanent Parliamentary Committee", and the Chairman of the Public Services Commission.[427] By contrast with what seems intended by the provisions in respect of the Ombudsman Appointments Committee (above), there is no requirement that the representative of the Parliamentary Committee be a person supporting the government. As a result, it will depend on the leanings of the leadership of the relevant parliamentary committee in question as to whether the government has support from a majority of the three members of the Electoral Commission Appointments Committee.

The Auditor-General, Public Services Commission and Clerk to the Parliament

Quite different provisions apply to appointments of the Auditor-General, the three members of

[422] See *Constitution*, s 170 (in respect of judges), s 175 (Chief Magistrate) and s 176 (Public Prosecutor and Public Solicitor).
[423] *Constitution*, s 183(2).
[424] *Constitution*, s 183(4).
[425] *Constitution*, s 217(2).
[426] Schedule 1.11 of the *Constitution* provides that where the *Constitution* or an Organic Law refers to "the appropriate Permanent Parliamentary Committee", then it is for the Parliament to determine the appropriate committee, and in the absence of such a determination, the Speaker is to decide.
[427] *Organic Law on National Elections*, s 5.

the Public Services Commission and the Clerk to the Parliament. They are all appointed "by the Head of State, acting with, and in accordance with, the advice of the National Executive Council". That formulation in fact means the appointment is made by the National Executive Council (the national Cabinet).[428] Before any of those appointments can be made, the National Executive Council is required to receive reports from, or consult with, specified authorities with an interest in the appointment or with expertise that may be expected to guide the appointing authority.

In the case of an appointment of Auditor-General or the Clerk of the Parliament, two reports are required. For the former office, they must come from the Speaker of the Parliament and the "appropriate Permanent Parliamentary Committee",[429] while in the latter case they must come from the Public Services Commission and the Public Accounts Committee.[430] In the case of appointments of members of the Public Services Commission, consultation is required "with any appropriate Permanent Parliamentary Committee".[431]

The Chief Justice

It is perhaps curious that the least level of protection from political considerations affecting the appointment procedure applies to the position of Chief Justice; a curious contrast, especially in the light of the degree of protection applicable to appointments of other judges. In fact, there are significant weaknesses in the constitutional provisions on the mode of appointment and security of tenure of the Chief Justice. In contrast to all other judges, the Chief Justice's position is a political appointment. Section 169(2) provides for the appointment to be made "by the Head of State, acting with and in accordance with, the advice of the National Executive Council given after consultation with the Minister responsible for the National Justice Administration". The reason for this provision can be found in the views of the CPC that the Chief Justice's position was one that had to be filled by a person who had "broad political support".[432]

Further, the *Constitution* does not offer long-term security of tenure to either the Chief Justice or other judges or constitutional office-holders. A judge of the National Court - including the Chief Justice - who is a citizen holds office for a term of 10 years, and is eligible for reappointment (save that in the first 10 years after independence, the first term for a citizen judge was three years).[433] A weakness in the combination of a political appointment and limited tenure is that political pressures on a Chief Justice could be created. For example, an incumbent Chief Justice could feel pressure - or be subject to actual pressure - to "co-operate" with government in order to secure a re-appointment. Alternatively, a person aspiring to become Chief Justice might be tempted to offer to "co-operate" with the appointing government. In any event, the arrangements are such as to lead to open questioning about the independence of the position.

The problems inherent in the provisions were highlighted by the circumstances of the replacement of the Chief Justice in 1993. Sir Buri Kidu had been Chief Justice for one term of

[428] Under s 86 of the *Constitution*, the Head of State has no reserve powers, and is required always to act with and in accordance with the advice of the National Executive Council or another authority specified by law.
[429] Above, n 18.
[430] In respect of the Clerk of the Parliament, see *Organic Law on Certain Constitutional Office-Holders*, s 7, and in relation to the Auditor-General, see *Constitution*, s 213(2).
[431] *Constitution*, s 190(2) (as amended in 1986 by *Constitutional Amendment No 8 - Public Services Commission*). As to the meaning of "appropriate Permanent Parliamentary Committee", see n 18 above.
[432] CPC, above n 2, p 8/4/41.
[433] See *Organic Law on the Terms and Conditions of Judges*, s 2.

three years beginning in 1980, and a further term of 10 years expiring in 1993. It was widely believed that he had sought re-appointment from the Wingti Government in 1993. If so, it was a request that was rejected. To the great surprise of many observers, both he and his long-serving and respected Deputy Chief Justice were by-passed in favour of one of the senior puisne judges, the then Justice Amet.

There was widespread concern in the legal profession and among other observers that government had rejected Sir Buri Kidu because of the record of the Supreme Court in finding against successive governments in various constitutional cases. This concern fuelled speculation that the court might not exhibit the same independence in the future. In fact, the new Chief Justice had a solid record of ruling against the government in constitutional and other cases prior to his appointment to the highest judicial position.

More importantly, the controversy over Sir Buri's replacement led to public questioning of the judiciary, and certainly weakened its public standing. There is therefore a need to amend the *Constitution* to provide for at least security of tenure for the Chief Justice and ideally an independent appointment process for the position, similar to that applicable to all other judges.

Assessment

There is a considerable range in the extent to which the appointment process is shielded from political interference. The highest degree of protection is provided in respect of the judges (other than the Chief Justice), the Chief Magistrate, the Public Prosecutor, the Public Solicitor and the Ombudsman Commission. A much lesser degree of protection applies to the appointment of the Electoral Commission, where the government of the day may enjoy, but is not guaranteed, a majority of members. Very little insulation from political considerations applies to appointments of the Auditor-General, the Clerk of the Parliament and the members of the Public Service Commission: they are the responsibility of the government, subject only to a requirement for reports from or consultation with interested authorities. The least possible degree of insulation applies to the Chief Justice, where the only requirement for consultation involves a Minister in the government.

With the exception of the Chief Justice, it would seem the range of protection reflects the degree of importance attached to the independence of the office, with judges, the Chief Magistrate, Public Prosecutor, Public Solicitor and members of the Ombudsman Commission requiring the highest degree of independence. It is suggested that in view of the significance of all the offices, it would be preferable if the same high degree of protection applied to all of them. In particular, the appointment procedures applying to the Chief Justice require change. The varying degrees of protection also add to the complexity of the arrangements in respect of constitutional office-holders. A common set of appointment procedures applying to all the offices would simplify the situation.

GROUNDS AND PROCEDURES FOR SUSPENSION AND REMOVAL FROM OFFICE

The CPC recognised that constitutional office-holders could not be independent unless they could "not be easily dismissed".[434] Hence it recommended that they should only be removed from office for limited causes stated by law, and following a three-stage procedure.[435]

[434] CPC, above n 2, p 14/4/31.

[435] The CPC made distinct recommendations about the grounds for and procedures applying to suspension and dismissal of judges, on the one

CPC recommendations

As to the basic grounds for removal from office, in addition to the grounds for disqualification from office already discussed ("Qualifications for Appointment to Office", above), the CPC suggested chronic infirmity of mind or body, breach of the Leadership Code, misconduct in office and gross negligence.

As to the removal procedure, the first stage would involve the appointing body referring to a special tribunal of three judges any allegations that the body believed were serious enough to warrant investigation. The second stage would involve the tribunal investigating the allegations. The appointing body would have power to suspend the constitutional office-holder while the investigation proceeded. The third stage would involve the tribunal recommending whether or not the office-holder should be removed from office, and the appointing body would then be required to act on the tribunal's recommendation.[436]

Grounds for suspension or removal

In general, the CPC recommendations have been implemented. As for the grounds for removal from office, they are a little more limited than the CPC envisaged. The *Constitution* (s 223(3)) states the basic principle that no constitutional office-holder can be "suspended, dismissed or removed from office during his term of office except in accordance with a Constitutional law". Separate provisions are made elsewhere in the *Constitution* as to the mode of suspension or dismissal of the judges, the Public Prosecutor, the Public Solicitor and the Chief Magistrate, on the one hand, and the other constitutional office-holders on the other hand.

As to the former group, under the *Constitution*, s 178, the only grounds for removal are: physical or mental inability to perform the functions and duties of the office in question; misbehaviour; and misconduct in office constituting a breach of the Leadership Code. For all other constitutional office-holders, the same grounds apply with the addition of a ground as to breach of a condition of employment laid down in a relevant Organic Law.[437]

Procedures for suspension or removal

As for the three-stage procedure envisaged by the CPC in relation to removal and suspension from office, it has been implemented in most respects. Sections 179-182 of the *Constitution* contain the relevant provisions in relation to judges, Public Prosecutor, Public Solicitor and Chief Magistrate. Except for the Chief Justice, the Judicial and Legal Services Commission is the appointing authority with power to refer matters to an independent tribunal. The appointing authority for the Chief Justice is of course the National Executive Council. The tribunal investigating the allegations made by the appointing authority can consist of past or present judges of the National Court, or judges of superior courts of countries with legal systems similar to that of Papua New Guinea.[438]

---

hand, and other constitutional office-holders, on the other. In relation to the judges, see ibid, Ch 8, and in relation to other constitutional office-holders see ibid, Ch 14. The nature of the two sets of recommendations is very similar.

436 Ibid, p 14/4/31 and p 14/8/13-15.

437 *Organic Law on the Guarantee of the Rights and Independence of Constitutional Office-holders*, s 7.

438 *Constitution*, s 181.

As for the other constitutional office-holders - the members of the Ombudsman Commission and the Public Services Commission, the Electoral Commission, the Auditor-General and the Clerk of the Parliament - the procedures recommended by the CPC apply, as specified in ss 4-8 of the *Organic Law on the Guarantee of the Rights and Independence of Constitutional Office-holders*.

GUARANTEEING REASONABLE LEVELS OF EMOLUMENTS AND ENSURING PAYMENT

Protecting the level of emoluments payable to a constitutional office-holder involves three distinct issues. They are: first, the extent to which adequate or reasonable levels of emoluments are specified in constitutional laws; secondly, the extent of government influence permitted in the setting of salaries and other emoluments; and thirdly, the capacity of government to reduce levels of emoluments. A further matter, of course, is to ensure that the appropriate levels are actually paid.

Constitutional guarantees of levels of emoluments?

The CPC envisaged that constitutional office-holders would be paid benefits "appropriate to the circumstances of Papua New Guinea", which should be "sufficient to live on the income attached to their respective offices".[439] With the exception of the Ombudsman Commission, it did not recommend constitutional provision directed to guaranteeing a reasonable level of emoluments. For the Ombudsman Commission, however, the CPC recommended, and the *Constitution* provides (s 217(3) and (4)), that the Chief Ombudsman be paid emoluments "at least the equivalent to those of a judge", and the other members of the Ombudsman Commission be paid at levels equivalent to the Public Prosecutor and Public Solicitor.[440]

Limiting government influence on determinations of levels

The CPC was not concerned about this issue, arguing that "the salary and conditions of all people in public employment in Papua New Guinea, including constitutional office-holders, should be set by the government".[441] This is perhaps a surprising omission, in that setting low levels of emoluments would be one obvious way of making life very difficult for constitutional office-holders that were a problem for the government. Reflecting the views of the CPC, when originally enacted the *Constitution* provided for the National Executive Council to determine the "salary and other conditions of employment" for all constitutional office-holders, subject to prior receipt of a report from the Judicial and Legal Services Commission (in the case of the Public Prosecutor, Public Solicitor, and Chief Magistrate) or from the Public Services Commission (in all other cases except the Public Services Commission itself, where no report was required).[442]

These arrangements were changed in 1988 when the *Constitution* was amended to establish a

[439] CPC, above n 2, pp 14/3/24 and 14/4/29.
[440] Ibid, p 11/4/33.
[441] Ibid, p 11/3/24.
[442] In relation to the Public Prosecutor, Public Solicitor, Chief Magistrate, Clerk of the National Parliament, and Auditor-General, see the *Organic Law on Certain Constitutional Office-holders*, ss 4, 6, 9 and 11; in relation to the Electoral Commission, see s 9 of the *Organic Law on National Elections*; in relation to the Ombudsman, see *Organic Law on the Ombudsman Commission*, s 6; in relation to the judges, see *Organic Law on the Terms and Conditions of Judges*, s 3; and in relation to members of the Public Services Commission, see the *Organic Law on the Public Services Commission*, s 4 (a law repealed following the passing of *Constitutional Amendment No 8 - Public Service Commission*, in 1986).

Salaries and Remuneration Commission, with responsibility for determining the salaries and other emoluments of all members of the Parliament, members of provincial government legislatures, and constitutional office-holders.[443] The amendment abolished an independent constitutional institution – the Parliamentary Salaries Tribunal – which previously had responsibility to determine the emoluments of members of the Parliament and members of provincial legislatures.[444] That tribunal had consisted of a judicial officer appointed by the Judicial and Legal Services Commission and two appointees of the Public Services Commission. The main aim of the amendment was to give members of the Parliament more control over the determination of their own emoluments. Hence, the composition of the new Commission involved three members of the Parliament (Speaker, Prime Minister – or a Minister nominated by the Prime Minister – and the leader of the Opposition), the Chief Justice and the heads of the Department of Personnel Management and the Department of Labour and Employment.[445]

It seems likely that the main reason for including the constitutional office-holders in the purview of the new Salaries and Remuneration Commission was to add to the legitimacy of the amendment by making it appear more as a general rationalisation of arrangements than a self-interested action by members of the Parliament. Whatever its aim, the amendment did in fact result in the process of determining emoluments of constitutional office-holders being removed from the hands of the National Executive Council and placed in the hands of a body that may be more independent.[446]

Restrictions on reductions of emoluments

The CPC recognised that reducing - or threatening to reduce - the emoluments of a constitutional office-holder would be an effective method of applying pressure to office-holders or forcing them out of office. On the other hand, it recognised that there might be times of "trouble" when the government would need power to reduce salaries and other emoluments of all public officials.[447] Hence it recommended that the emoluments "attached to a constitutional office shall not be reduced during an individual incumbent's tenure of office except as part of a general reduction throughout all constitutional offices".[448] That recommendation has been implemented by s 223(4) of the *Constitution*, which only permits reductions which are "part of a general reduction applicable equally or proportionately to all constitutional office-holders", or "as a result of taxation that does not discriminate against [a person] as a constitutional office-holder, or against constitutional office-holders generally".

Ensuring applicable emolument levels are paid

The CPC sought to ensure that political pressures were not applied to constitutional office-holders by the withholding of salary and other emoluments. Hence, it recommended that all "salaries, allowances and other benefits attached to their offices be paid directly from a consolidated fund".

---

[443] *Constitutional Amendment No 9 - Salaries and Remuneration Commission* (1988).

[444] See *Constitution*, s 131.

[445] *Constitution*, s 216A(2).

[446] The fact that four of the six members of the Salaries and Remuneration Commission are government politicians or appointees (Speaker, Prime Minister and two departmental heads) means government views are likely to dominate. On the other hand, setting reasonable levels of emoluments for constitutional office-holders also tends to legitimise the grant of high levels of benefits to politicians. To date there has been no evidence of any government attempts to influence the Commission to the detriment of constitutional office-holders.

[447] CPC, above n 2, p 14/3/24. The CPC also suggested that there could be times when the Parliament "believes that salaries and conditions generally should be held down or even reduced as a matter of principle": ibid.

[448] Ibid, p 14/7/10(2).

The reason given was: "In that way, the professional activities of constitutional office-holders are less likely to be influenced by pressures brought to bear upon their personal lives."[449] This recommendation was not given effect to in either the *Constitution* or the Organic Laws.

NO ABOLITION OF OFFICES WITH SUBSTANTIVE OCCUPANTS

The CPC recommended that the offices of the three members of the Ombudsman Commission should not be abolished while any such office "has a substantive holder".[450] That recommendation has been provided for in the *Constitution*, but applied to all constitutional office-holders.[451] To the extent that this provision might be regarded as a fetter on the power of the Parliament to abolish offices by means of amendment to the *Constitution*, it is likely to be invalid.

GUARANTEE OF RESOURCES

CPC recommendations

While the CPC did not make recommendations in respect of guaranteeing resources to constitutional office-holders generally, it did recommend that there should be "constitutional provision to safeguard the [Ombudsman] Commission's requirements" in respect of staffing and other "facilities",[452] and similar recommendations were made in respect of the Public Solicitor.[453] The main concern stated in relation to the Ombudsman Commission was that there was a great shortage of skilled personnel available in the public sector, and so the CPC was concerned that the Commission should be guaranteed access to such resources. It is also possible, however, that reductions in resources made available by government to constitutional office-holders could be used by government as a device to reduce the effectiveness of such offices whose activities are found to be unduly worrying by government. Hence, a constitutional guarantee of resources may be an important protection if the effectiveness and independence of constitutional office-holders are to be preserved.

---

[449] Ibid, p 14/3/24.

[450] Ibid, p 11/18/9.

[451] See *Constitution*, s 223(5). That provision does not apply to any additional constitutional office created by Act of Parliament as permitted by s 221(i), but apparently does apply to additional offices created by Organic Laws.

[452] CPC, above n 2, p 11/11/34.

[453] Ibid, p 8/29/71.

Terms of the guarantee

Section 225 of the *Constitution* goes further than the CPC had recommended. It provides, so far as relevant, that:

> "it is the 'duty of the National Government and all other governmental bodies, and of all public office-holders, and institutions, to ensure, as far as is within their respective legal powers, that all arrangements are made, staff and facilities provided and steps taken to facilitate, as far as may reasonably be, the proper and convenient performance of the functions of all constitutional institutions and of the offices of all constitutional office-holders."

When government provides members of the public service as staff for any constitutional office-holder, they are not subject to direction or control by any person other than the office-holder when acting on instructions of the office-holder in the performance of the office-holder's constitutional functions.[454]

Section 225 has been the subject of judicial consideration in a number of cases, both as an answer to claims by constitutional office-holders that they have been unable to fulfil their duties due to lack of adequate resources,[455] and as the basis for orders directed to government authorities requiring provision of resources to constitutional office-holders necessary for the effective performance of their functions.[456]

Extent of the guarantee

The judicial decisions on s 225 have not considered the terms of this section in detail. On close examination, it is arguable that the extent of the guarantee of resources is limited. First, it applies to all "constitutional institutions". As already discussed, under s 221 that term involves all offices and institutions created or provided for by the *Constitution* other than the Head of State, a Minister or the National Executive Council. The requirement to facilitate "as far as may reasonably be" necessary for the proper performance of functions of such institutions presumably involves balancing the claims of all such institutions. In practice, it might amount to little more than a requirement not to unfairly prejudice any particular institution in the process of distribution of resources.

If the section is interpreted as imposing a heavier burden than that, then to the extent the provision is resorted to in court actions seeking orders that resources be provided, the court could be placed in a difficult position. It would often be involved in making policy decisions, potentially with wide political implications. Nevertheless, the existence of at least a limited guarantee of resources will tend to be a major protection for constitutional office-holders, though ideally more as something to use to pressure government behind the scenes, rather than through court actions.

---

[454] *Organic Law on the Guarantee of the Rights and Independence of Constitutional Office-holders*, s 13.

[455] *Electoral Commissioner of Papua New Guinea v Maniho* [1987] PNGLR 449 at 456, and *Pogu v State* [1986] PNGLR 203 at 205.

[456] See *Re Conduct of the National Court Circuit, Southern Highlands Province* [1988-89] PNGLR 435, and *Re Criminal Circuit in Eastern Highlands and Simbu Provinces* [1990] PNGLR 82.

FILLING STATUTORY DEFICIENCIES WITH REGARD TO PROCEDURES AND POWERS

It is again constitutional institutions that are the subject of s 224 of the *Constitution.* Section 224(1) requires that Organic Laws and Acts of Parliament make the necessary provision for the powers and functions of such institutions necessary to facilitate the performance of their functions. Presumably anticipating that there could be delays in passing such laws, or that there might be gaps in the laws when passed, s 224(2) provides that where no such provision has been made, any constitutional institution may provide for its own procedures to the extent of any deficiency in the law, and "has all reasonable powers necessary or convenient for the exercise and performance of its powers, functions duties and responsibilities".

As far as I am aware, there has been just one instance that could be regarded as a purported exercise of the enabling powers under s 224(2). Prior to the 1987 elections for the Parliament, the Ombudsman Commission published a document entitled *Guidelines for Giving and Acceptance of Election Campaign Contributions and Other Related Matters.*[457] To a large extent, the guidelines made provision in respect of matters intended to be covered by the proposed Organic Laws on Integrity of Candidates and Integrity of Political Parties provided for by ss 129 and 130 of the *Constitution* but never passed. The relevant constitutional provisions envisaged either "the Ombudsman Commission or some other authority prescribed by law" administering the reporting and other requirements which the proposed Organic Laws were to impose on all political parties and candidates for election. The 1987 guidelines sought to impose strict limits on giving and acceptance of election campaign contributions, including imposing a prohibition on acceptance of donations and benefits from non-citizens and "foreign enterprises". They also required all political parties to make annual returns to the Commission of all assets, loans and income.

The Guidelines were expressed to be issued in part under the authority of s 224, and in part under s 27(4) (Leadership Code) of the *Constitution.* To the extent they were issued under s 224, the Guidelines were expressed to be voluntary.[458] By contrast, to the extent they were issued under s 27(4), they were expressed to be directions made under the Leadership Code, as s 27(4) empowers the Ombudsman Commission to issue such guidelines to ensure the attainment of the objects of the Code. In seeking to rely on s 224, the Guidelines were expressed to be voluntary, presumably because they went beyond what is empowered by s 224(2). They sought to provide the Ombudsman Commission with the substantive powers which ss 129 and 130 only indicate might be vested in the Commission: the powers could be vested in some other authority instead. Section 224(2) only enables the Commission to make good deficiencies in relation to its own procedures, and provides it with powers necessary to exercise "powers, functions, duties and responsibilities" that it has been vested with elsewhere. As there is no clear vesting of the powers, functions and so on envisaged by ss 129 and 130, it is hard to see how s 224(2) could come into operation to support such guidelines.

---

[457] Ombudsman Commission, *Papua New Guinea National Gazette*, No G12, 26 February 1987, pp 239-46.

[458] Ibid, p 240.

FREEDOM FROM DIRECTION AND CONTROL

The CPC made recommendations in relation to the independence of several of the constitutional office-holders, to the effect that in the exercise of their constitutional functions they were not to be the subject of direction or control of any other person or authority.[459] With the exception of the Clerk of the Parliament and the Public Services Commission, the *Constitution* extends the recommended protection to all of the constitutional office-holders, with some qualifications, as follows:

(1) In respect of judges, s 157 provides that in the exercise of judicial powers or functions, no court is subject to direction, except by the Parliament through legislation, a protection that extends to the Chief Magistrate, as well as other magistrates.

(2) In respect of the Public Prosecutor, s 176(3) protects the office from direction and control, except that the National Executive Council can give directions on matters that might prejudice the security, defence or international relations of Papua New Guinea.

(3) In respect of the Public Solicitor, s 176(5) protects the office, except that the Supreme Court or the National Court can give her or him directions to provide legal aid, advice or assistance to particular persons.

(4) In respect of the Ombudsman Commission, the protection under s 217(5) from direction and control in the exercise of its constitutional functions is not qualified in any way and, indeed, that body enjoys further immunities (see below).

(5) In respect of the Electoral Commission, the protection under s 126(6) is unqualified.

(6) In respect of the Auditor-General, the protection under s 213(3) is unqualified in respect of the performance of functions under the *Constitution*.

As for the Clerk of the Parliament, no protection is offered. He or she heads the Parliamentary Service, which is separate from the public service. It is a body that serves the Parliament, and is subject to the direction and control of the Speaker of the Parliament.[460] By contrast, the Public Services Commission originally enjoyed freedom from direction and control, subject to complying with general directions on policy from the National Executive Council. That protection was withdrawn by a 1986 constitutional amendment. From then, the Commission was free from direction and control solely in carrying out its function of conducting reviews of personnel matters connected with the public service. That is a limited protection given that the recommendations it makes in the course of such review are not binding on the public service authorities whose decisions it reviews.[461]

Because of its unique role, and to ensure that it is free from "harassment by legal action" in the same way as judges and magistrates,[462] the Ombudsman Commission enjoys other immunities. Under the *Constitution*, s 217(6), its proceedings are "not subject to review in any way", save on

[459] See, for example, CPC, above n 2, p 8/26/53 and p 8/28/64, in respect of the Public Prosecutor and the Public Solicitor.
[460] *Constitution*, s 132.
[461] See *Constitution*, s 192, as amended by *Constitutional Amendment No 8 - Public Services Commission* (1986).
[462] CPC, above n 2, p 11/11/75.

grounds of excess of jurisdiction, and it enjoys much the same privileges as a court by virtue of s 35 of the *Organic Law on the Ombudsman Commission.*[463]

INDEPENDENCE FROM POLITICAL AND COMMERCIAL PRESSURES

The CPC recommended that not only should constitutional office-holders be free from political direction and control, but they also should have "a reciprocal obligation of political neutrality". Further, they should be adequately remunerated to enable them to live a reasonable life, but reciprocally, they "should not be allowed to compromise their independence . . . through involvement in other economic activities".[464] Such recommendations were presumably directed in part towards achieving the independence of the offices concerned in that they were intended to shield office-holders from suspicions or attacks concerning political or commercial activities.

The scheme for protecting the independence of constitutional office-holders implements those recommendations in several main ways. Several Organic Laws provide that a person is not qualified to become or remain a constitutional office-holder if he or she holds office in a political party (an issue discussed already). Provision is also made that such a person is not to:

(a) "actively engage in politics";

(b) "engage either directly or indirectly in the management or control of a corporation or other body of persons carrying on business for profit";

(c) "acquire by way of gift or otherwise, or use or hold in any other manner any interest in, any property . . . or solicit, accept or receive any other benefit in addition to his terms and conditions or employment".[465]

In addition, a special condition applies to the Auditor-General, who, in accordance with a recommendation of the CPC,[466] is not permitted to "directly or indirectly accept or receive any benefit from, or participate in, any enterprise, institution, fund or other body" which might conceivably be subject to the jurisdiction of the Auditor-General.[467]

ACCOUNTABILITY OF CONSTITUTIONAL OFFICE-HOLDERS

While the primary emphases of the CPC recommendations about constitutional office-holders concerned their important functions and the protection of their independence, the CPC was also concerned to ensure that the office-holders were accountable. A number of recommendations were directed towards achieving such accountability, or limiting the likelihood of conflicts of interests or insulating the office-holders from political or commercial pressures that might lead to

---

[463] A range of issues concerning the immunities of the Commission was considered by the Supreme Court in *Ombudsman Commission v Ellis* [1992] PNGLR 437.

[464] CPC, above n 2, p 14/4/27-29.

[465] See *Organic law on Certain Constitutional Office-holders*, s 15; *Organic Law on National Elections*, s 12; *Organic Law on the Ombudsman Commission*, s 8; and *Organic Law on the Terms and Conditions of Employment of Judges*, s 5. Exceptions of very limited scope apply to the limits as to involvement in businesses and receipt of income etc from alternative sources.

[466] CPC, above n 2, p 14/8/12(e), a recommendation discussed at p 14/4/27-29.

[467] See *Organic Law on Certain Constitutional Office-holders*, s 10(2).

office-holders compromising their positions. First, the limits on party political and commercial activity already discussed were intended to insulate the office-holders from pressures. Secondly, the office-holders were all made subject to the Leadership Code, as well as to normal legal restraints, inclusive of the criminal law and administrative law (save that the Ombudsman enjoys the special immunities already mentioned). Thirdly, all constitutional office-holders were required to submit annual reports to the Parliament. The concern of the CPC in recommending this requirement was to ensure that "the people of Papua New Guinea be kept informed, through their representatives, of the work that the constitutional office-holders are doing" and of "their achievements and problems".[468]

The recommendation concerning annual reports was implemented through various provisions in the *Constitution* and Organic Laws that require submission of such reports to the Speaker for tabling in the Parliament.[469] In practice, however, only some of the constitutional office-holders keep up to date with their reports, and there is little or no discussion of the reports in the Parliament.

LIMITED TENURE BALANCED BY GUARANTEE OF FURTHER EMPLOYMENT OR PENSION

The CPC was convinced that constitutional office-holders should have limited tenure. They were not to hold their offices indefinitely, but were to "have their work periodically evaluated by the body that originally chose them".[470] There was a need to review "suitability for office in a rapidly changing society".[471] Hence, the basic term of appointment for all constitutional office-holders was six years, the main exception being judges, whose term should be 10 years. On the other hand, the need to "to ensure that constitutional office-holders are able to perform their functions independently of outside pressures" was also recognised.[472] Accordingly, the CPC made recommendations designed to ensure constitutional office-holders had a secure future if they decided not to seek renewal of appointment, or if the appointing authority passed them over for re-appointment. Hence it was recommended that such office-holders be offered appointment to another public office at a salary and on conditions equivalent or better than those enjoyed as a constitutional office-holder.[473]

The *Organic Law on the Guarantee of the Rights and Independence of Constitutional Office-holders* has taken the matter further. For persons who were officers in the Public Service prior to holding a position as constitutional office-holder, on ceasing to hold constitutional office they are to be offered an appointment as suggested by the CPC, provided that if the Public Services Commission decides there is no such position available, they are to be entitled to a pension equivalent in value to 70 per cent of the salary payable from time to time in respect of the vacated

[468] CPC, above n 2, p 14/5/35.
[469] See *Constitution*, s 187, in relation to the annual report of the National Judicial System (inclusive of judges and Chief Magistrate); *Organic Law on Certain Constitutional Office-holders*, s 19, in respect of the Public Prosecutor, Public Solicitor, Chief Magistrate, Clerk of the national Parliament and the Auditor-General; *Constitution*, s 220, in respect of the Ombudsman Commission; and *Constitution*, s 191(4), in respect of the Public Services Commission. There seems to be no requirement in respect of the Electoral Commission.
[470] CPC, above n 2, p 14/1/7.
[471] Ibid, p 14/2/8.
[472] Ibid, p 14/2/11.
[473] Ibid, p 14/75.

office. For persons who were not public servants prior to appointment, they are to be offered the choice of a public service appointment at equivalent remuneration level, or a 70 per cent pension.

"CONSTITUTIONAL INSTITUTIONS": LIMITED PROTECTION

Constitutional institutions - all offices and institutions created or provided for by the *Constitution* other than the Head of State, a Minister and the National Executive Council - involve not only the constitutional office-holders but also: the Citizenship Advisory Committee (s 65(6)); the Interim Constitutional Commission and the General Constitutional Commission (ss 260-262); the Advisory Committee on the Power of Mercy (s 152); the Salaries and Remuneration Commission (s 216A); the Law Reform Commission (s 19(3)(d) and Sch 2.13-2.14); the Public Trustee (ss 26(1)(k), 28(1)(c), 28(3) and Sch 1.2(1)); the Boundaries Commission; and the Judicial and Legal Services Commission.

The limited form of protection of independence extended to "constitutional institutions" involves a partial guarantee of resources and a power to fill statutory deficiencies in procedures and powers. As these are, in effect, also part of the full range of protection extended to constitutional office-holders (discussed below). The limited degree of protection offered to most constitutional institutions is presumably because they are bodies that either exercise purely technical functions (as in the case of the Public Trustee) or advisory functions (as with the other bodies mentioned).

However, two of the constitutional institutions receive a higher degree of protection - beyond the two areas just mentioned - but not as complete as that extended to the constitutional office-holders. They are the Boundaries Commission and the Judicial and Legal Services Commission.[474]

The Boundaries Commission (which has responsibility for recommending electoral boundaries to the Parliament) is independent to the extent that the *Constitution*[475] provides that it is not subject to direction and control. Members of the Commission are subject to much the same requirements with regard to qualifications for and disqualification from office, and to a prohibition on involvement in political and commercial activity, as those that apply to the constitutional office-holders.[476] The members of the Commission do not, however, enjoy the other protections applicable to the constitutional office-holders, such as protection from reduction of emoluments, a guarantee of resources, and so on. In part this may be because the majority of members of the Commission are senior public officers who hold their offices ex officio (meaning emoluments are not a major issue), and because the chairman of the Commission is the Electoral Commissioner (meaning that necessary resources should be provided by the Electoral Commission).

The protection of the independence of the Judicial and Legal Services Commission is similar to that applying to the Boundaries Commission. It is guaranteed freedom from direction and control,[477] and is subject to some conditions as to qualifications for and disqualification from office. Because a majority of its members are constitutional office-holders (the Chief Justice,

[474] The Police Force also enjoys protection from direction and control in the exercise of its prosecution function: *Constitution*, s 197(2).
[475] See *Constitution*, s 125(4).
[476] See *Organic Law on National Elections*, ss 26-28.
[477] *Constitution*, s 183(4).

Deputy Chief Justice and the Chief Ombudsman), it may be that it was not thought necessary to apply the full range of protections of independence to this body.

Nevertheless, given the importance of the functions carried out by these two bodies, there would seem good reason to insulate them from the possibility of political interference to the same degree as the constitutional office-holders.

CONCLUSIONS

The provisions protecting the independence of the constitutional office-holders served their intended aims well in the first 20 years of Papua New Guinea's independence. In a situation where there is ample evidence of increasing tendencies towards corruption and other forms of abuse of power, the high degree of protection of independence of the constitutional office-holders has enabled them to carry out their respective functions with much greater freedom from threat or interference than would have been possible otherwise. In particular, the Ombudsman Commission and the judiciary have shown a remarkable degree of independence and willingness to challenge dubious action by government as well as by individual politicians and bureaucrats.

Some undoubted weaknesses in the arrangements have been identified, notably:

(1) The Judicial and Legal Services Commission and the Boundaries Commission were not classified as constitutional office-holders.

(2) The wide variation in the degree to which appointment procedures are insulated from political influence offers too little protection to a majority of constitutional offices, and unduly adds to the complexity of the scheme to protect the independence of constitutional offices.

(3) In particular, the combination of the political appointment of the Chief Justice and the limited tenure of the position open the possibility of political pressures being applied to incumbents and those aspiring to the position.

In general, the arrangements are complex, a characteristic reinforced by not only the numerous appointing authorities (bodies that continue to have authority over office-holders beyond appointment, as they can initiate complaints against the office-holders leading to suspension or removal from office), but also by the way elements of the scheme are scattered through various parts of the *Constitution* and the Organic Laws.

The position could be improved by having a single appointment authority, or at most two: the Judicial and Legal Services Commission in respect of those involved in the administration of justice (judges, Chief Magistrate, Public Prosecutor and Public Solicitor), and a new and independent constitutional offices appointments committee in respect of all other bodies. In addition, the inclusion of most provisions on the protection of independence of constitutional offices in a single Organic Law would greatly simplify the tasks involved in understanding and administering the scheme.

CONSTITUTIONAL FRAMEWORK — OTHER ASPECTS

Chapter 16

CITIZENSHIP

GRAHAM HASSALL

INTRODUCTION

The *Constitution* was drafted against a background of Australian colonial rule under which discrimination on the grounds of race had pervaded all aspects of the colony's social and economic life and had been given form and substance in the colony's legal regime.[478] The issue of citizenship was, then, as Ghai has pointed out in relation to a number of states in the region, "at once a deeply emotional subject and a highly complex and technical one".[479] Inhabitants of the Territory of Papua and New Guinea did not have status as citizens as such: Papuans had the international status of Australian citizens (but without the right to residence in Australia), and New Guineans had the status of Australian protected persons (without the right to residence in Australia). The *Papua New Guinea Act* 1949 set out the terms of Australian trusteeship and administration in Papua and New Guinea, but did not set out the rights of the people of the Territory (apart from s 71, which prohibited slave trade and forced labour). As Wolfers explains:

> "Under Australian rule, Papuans, just like New Guineans, required an entry permit to go to Australia; they were paid at local rates of pay (while whites, wherever born, were paid at overseas rates); and after World War II, New Guineans were made subject to the same forms of domestic discrimination and government paternalism as Papuans. Post-war Acts of the Australian Parliament did not distinguish between Papuans and New Guineans so much as between "natives" or (after the *Papua and New Guinea Act* was amended in 1963) "indigenes", and "non-natives" or "non-indigenes". Under Australian law, colonial society was effectively cut in two with small mixed-race and Asian minorities located uncertainly between the white and indigenous population."[480]

Because status in the colonial era was defined by race and ethnicity, the articulation of laws of citizenship for the Independent State of Papua New Guinea was inevitably viewed by many as an opportunity to redress past imbalances. There was another, contrasting, view of the law, which established a "society of equals", irrespective of race. For the subsequent two decades the tension between these two viewpoints has informed discussion on the subject of citizenship.

PRE-INDEPENDENCE CONSTITUTIONAL DEBATES

With independence came the opportunity to assert the primacy of national interests over expatriate interests. Whereas the majority of residents of Papua New Guinea were easily nominated as "automatic" recipients of citizenship on the basis of descent, contention surrounded

---

[478] See E P Wolfers, *Race Relations and Colonial Rule in Papua New Guinea* (Sydney: ANZ Book Company, 1975); I Downs, *The Australian Trusteeship, Papua New Guinea 1945-75*, (Canberra: AGPS, 1980).

[479] Y P Ghai, "Systems of Government: II", in Y P Ghai (ed), *Law, Politics and Government in the South Pacific Island States* (Suva: Institute of Pacific Studies, University of the South Pacific, 1988), p 35.

[480] E P Wolfers, "Defining a Nation: The Citizenship Debates in the Papua New Guinea Parliament" in F S Stevens and E P Wolfers (eds), *Racism, the Australian Experience, Vol 3: Colonialism and After: A Study of Race Prejudice in Australia* (Sydney: ANZ Book Company, 1977), pp 303-304.

the conditions under which members of non-indigenous minority groups could become "naturalised" citizens. While not great in total number, many of them held advantageous positions in the economy and bureaucracy, especially Europeans and Chinese. Europeans generally already possessed citizenship elsewhere, and the suggestion that they be allowed dual citizenship status following independence was rejected outright. Residents of Chinese and mixed-race descent had access to Australian citizenship at the discretion of Australia's Minister for External Territories, and as independence approached each had to decide to which state it would give its primary allegiance.

Also, the new state's borders cut across traditional connections, based on kinship, trade, and migration, into neighbouring states, and threatened to deny citizenship to people with genuine claims to be Papua New Guineans who, for reasons of history and culture, lived beyond those borders.[481] The *Constitution* needed to establish a membership boundary that excluded residents in Papua New Guinea whose forebears were not principally Papua New Guinean, yet included some residents of neighbouring states whose forebears were principally Papua New Guinean. Furthermore, it had to distinguish the grounds, if any, on which non-Papua New Guineans could become citizens, and what distinctions, if any, should be made between "inherent" and "acquired" citizenship.

The first articulation of solutions to this problem was contained in the Final Report of the Constitutional Planning Committee (CPC).[482] The CPC's view was that Papua New Guinea's citizenship laws should first and foremost protect the interests of indigenous Papua New Guineans, while bearing in mind the new country's historical relationships with its nearest neighbours: Australia, the Torres Strait, Indonesia (Irian Jaya) and the Solomon Islands. Against a backdrop of Australian laws that discriminated on grounds of race, the CPC urged that the *Constitution* define "Papua New Guinean" in terms of locality rather than race.[483] However, educational and other literature produced by and for the CPC suggests that the proposals for citizenship laws for (black) Papua New Guinea were made in conscious contrast to the influence of (white) Australia.[484]

Dual citizenship was opposed, as were distinctions between citizens on the basis of racial descent. Provided a person had two "indigenous grandparents" (persons whose own grandparents were born in Papua New Guinea or an adjacent area (Irian Jaya, the Solomon Islands or the Torres Strait Islands)), they would be entitled to "automatic citizenship".[485] The issue of the number of "indigenous" grandparents required was vital to some prominent figures at the time of independence, who were themselves of mixed racial descent. Ironically, the desire for stringent requirements in this regard was resisted because it would have disenfranchised these leaders. The debate on this subject pointed to the futility of identifying automatic citizenship with a notion of racial or ethnic purity.

Concerning citizenship by naturalisation, the CPC recommended that foreigners could acquire Papua New Guinea citizenship only after eight years residency (and then providing they met

---

[481] The Australian *Migration Act* 1958 (s 13) recognised the right of Papua New Guineans to enter the islands of the Torres Strait for the purposes of "traditional activities" as "lawful non-citizens".

[482] CPC, *Final Report of the Constitutional Planning Committee: Part 1* (Port Moresby: Government Printer, 1974); Government Paper, *Proposals on Constitutional Principles and Explanatory Notes* (Port Moresby: unpublished, August 1974).

[483] For detailed discussion see Wolfers, above n 3.

[484] See, for instance, Government Liaison Branch, *Citizenship. Information Paper Prepared for the Constitutional Planning Committee* (Port Moresby: unpublished, no date).

[485] CPC, above n 5, p 4/3.

various criteria, including good character, respect for and knowledge of the cultures of Papua New Guinea and knowledge of at least one of its languages other than English).[486]

Other submissions on the subject of citizenship also reached the House of Assembly; notably a government "White Paper". The major differences between the CPC and the government concerned the definition of "automatic" citizens, and the requirements for naturalisation (the government's proposals involving fewer barriers to entry).

Following debate in the House of Assembly, draft constitutional provisions were debated, amended and approved by the House of Assembly, sitting as the National Constituent Assembly. Wolfers notes that the Assembly debated the citizenship provisions for "substantial portions" of six of its 27 sitting days.[487] The overwhelming concern expressed during debate on the citizenship provisions was the prevention of both the entry of negative outside influences and the acquisition of citizenship for individual gain rather than for the benefit of the nation. Fears were also expressed that unrest similar to that between traditional and immigrant communities in former African and Asian colonies might also occur in Papua New Guinea.[488]

Citizenship in the Constitution

Provision on citizenship is found primarily in Part IV (ss 64-81) of the *Constitution*. In overview, it prohibits dual citizenship, provides for the methods of acquisition and loss of citizenship, specifies the privileges of citizenship, and provides for administration of the citizenship provisions.

Dual citizenship

The prohibition on dual citizenship (s 64) is subject to one very important exception. This exception involves persons under the age of 19 who, as a result of their parents being citizens of different countries - one being a Papua New Guinean citizen, and one a citizen of another country - are not forced to choose citizenship while still children. Rather, they are entitled to dual citizenship until they turn 19. At that point they must make a choice. At the point of choice, a person with dual citizenship can renounce Papua New Guinean citizenship (s 72).

Methods of acquiring citizenship

Citizenship is acquired either automatically, or by descent, or by naturalisation.

Automatic citizenship

Automatic citizenship was granted on Independence Day to persons who were born in Papua New Guinea prior to that day and who had "two grand-parents born in the country or an adjacent area" (s 65(1)). An "adjacent area" is defined as the Solomon Islands, Irian Jaya, or Australia's Torres Straits islands (s 65(3)). In addition, to take account of persons who were born outside of the country but who had indigenous roots in Papua New Guinea, persons born elsewhere who had

[486] The deliberations of the CPC concerning citizenship are discussed in Wolfers, above n 3, pp 313-22.
[487] Ibid, p 342.
[488] See generally National Constituent Assembly, *Debates*, Third Meeting of the Third Session, 22 July to 31 July 1975, Vol 1, No 3.

two grandparents born in Papua New Guinea could apply for registration as a citizen within one year after independence, provided any other citizenship was renounced and a Declaration of Loyalty to Papua New Guinea made (s 65(2)).

It has been suggested that at the time of independence there were 100 "automatic" citizens in the country who were not ethnically Melanesian.[489] Wolfers records that 224 people applied for automatic citizenship in the first two months of independence, a figure that Sir Maori Kiki (Deputy Prime Minister and Minister for Defence, Foreign Affairs and Trade, and hence the Minister with responsibility for citizenship) felt to be low, although no exact figures were available concerning the numbers of residents eligible to make such an application.[490]

Citizenship by descent

Persons who were born in the country on or after Independence Day and who had one citizen parent were regarded as citizens (s 66(1)), while persons who were born outside the country on or after Independence Day who had one citizen parent could register as citizens (s 66(2)).

Citizenship by naturalisation

To be eligible to become a naturalised citizen, a person must have "resided continuously" in the country for at least eight years (s 67(1)) and meet the requirements of s 67(2), which are as follows:

(a) be of good character;

(b) intend to reside permanently in the country;

(c) unless prevented by physical or mental disability, speak and understand Pisin or Hiri Motu, or a vernacular of the country, sufficiently for normal conversation purposes;

(d) have a respect for the customs and cultures of the country;

(e) be unlikely to be or become a charge on public funds;

(f) have a reasonable knowledge and understanding of the rights, privileges, responsibilities and duties of citizenship; and

(g) renounce, in such a manner as is prescribed by or under an Act of the Parliament, any other citizenship and make the Declaration of Loyalty.

Applications for citizenship by naturalisation by persons who had "resided continuously in the country for eight years or more before Independence Day" were to be made within two months of independence (s 69(1)). For the purposes of determining whether the requirement of eight years of continuous residence has been met, periods of temporary absence do not necessarily constitute a break in the eight-year residence period.[491]

---

489 *PNG Post Courier*, 8 October 1987, p 4.
490 Wolfers, above n 3, pp 380-81.
491 *Constitution* Sch1.15 and *Organic Law on Residence*.

The *Constitution* (s 68(2)) also provided transitional provisions, relevant to applicants for naturalisation. In the first eight years after independence, if an applicant met each of the requirements of s 67(2) (see above), a number of additional criteria were to be taken into account in considering the application:

(a) whether the applicant had voluntarily applied for permanent residency or citizenship in Australia despite being eligible to apply for automatic citizenship in the two months following independence;

(b) whether the applicant had accepted employment and pay on conditions generally applicable to indigenes before independence and to citizens thereafter;

(c) whether the majority of the applicant's investments and business interests were in Papua New Guinea;

(d) whether the applicant was married to a citizen of Papua New Guinea;

(e) the length and nature of the residency;

(f) performance of services beneficial to the country and its people;

(g) sacrifices made in the interests of the country and its people;

(h) knowledge of a vernacular language;

(i) whether or not the application included the applicant's minor children;

(j) references given as to the applicant's good character; and

(k) place of birth and parentage of the applicant.[492]

Laws in effect prior to independence that conferred privileges on Papua New Guineans continued to have effect for 10 years after independence, unless repealed by an Act of the national Parliament. In the first 10 years of independence, the majority of the members of all corporate bodies established under the *Constitution* (other than the two highest courts) were to be citizens.[493]

In the first five years after independence property held by persons other than automatic citizens could be acquired for the benefit of citizens, particularly traditional owners of such property (s 68(4)). That provision follows the suggestions of the 1973 Committee of Inquiry into Land Matters, and other schemes consistent with the National Goals and Directive Principles for the redistribution of property that had been alienated from traditional owners.[494]

Reflecting the concerns of the CPC about possible motives of foreigners seeking citizenship, the naturalisation requirements are stringent in a number of ways. They require a resident to remain in the country for a long period prior to becoming eligible to apply for citizenship. An application for citizenship soon after becoming resident was generally thought to derive from ulterior motives, particularly a desire to benefit from business ventures, or to participate in politics and to exercise political authority. Renunciation of all other citizenships was emphasised because retention of former loyalties was viewed as evidence of an intention subsequently to leave Papua New Guinea, or at the least to give the country only partial loyalty.

---

[492] *Constitution*, s 68(2).
[493] *Constitution*, s 274.
[494] J Goldring, *The Constitution of Papua New Guinea* (Sydney: Law Book Company, 1978), p 211.

In the light of events in public life in the 1990s (discussed below), these concerns appear to have had some validity. However, concerns at the motives of naturalised citizens should be considered in the light of an equally compelling twofold argument put forward in 1985 by Colquhoun-Kerr in comments made on proposals for amendment of the citizenship provisions. First, he suggested that that to continue to regard "naturalised citizens" as foreigners following acquisition of citizenship is to repudiate their adopted status (since all citizens are equal before the law). Secondly, he argued that to label naturalised citizens as (generally) self-seeking is unfairly to seek a scapegoat:

> "Doubtless there have been naturalised citizens who have placed their own self-interest before that of the nation. It would be surprising, however, if that sin was restricted to such citizens. Yet individual self-seeking, individual wrong-doing by foreigners can be controlled. Structural economic forces are by contrast both less easy to control and more significant. The forces that lock Papua New Guinea into the 'developing' sector of the capitalist world are not generated by a handful of naturalized citizens."[495]

Privileges of citizenship

The privileges of citizenship specified in the constitutional laws[496] include a number of rights and freedoms the enjoyment of which the *Constitution* guarantees only to citizens ("special rights of citizens"), namely:[497]

(a) freedom of movement and residence within the country, freedom to enter and leave the country (s 52(1)), and freedom from deportation, save in respect of court orders pertaining to extradition arrangements (s 52(2));

(b) equality, meaning that citizens enjoy "the same rights, privileges, obligations and duties irrespective of race, tribe, place of origin, political opinion, colour, creed, religion or sex" (s 55(1));

(c) the right to vote in elections, and to hold elective public offices (s 50(d));

(d) the right to "take part in the conduct of public affairs, either directly or through freely chosen representatives" (s 50(c));

(e) the right to hold public office and to exercise public functions (s 50(e));

(f) the right to freedom of information (s 51); and

(g) the right to acquire freehold land (s 56(1)).

Writing in 1978, Goldring suggested that the last of these was of the most importance, especially because of the special rights of automatic citizens in the first five years after independence.[498]

---

[495] D J Colquhoun-Kerr, "Sources of Political Legitimacy in Conflict and Naturalised Foreigners: Some Comments on the General Constitutional Commission's Final Report, 1983", in R de Vere, D Colquhoun-Kerr and J Kaburise (eds), *Essays on the Constitution of Papua New Guinea* (Port Moresby: Tenth Independence Anniversary Advisory Committee, 1985), pp 121-22.

[496] Constitutions of some provincial governments explored notions of "provincial citizenship" through terms which grant people of a province preferential access to certain public offices: see Y P Ghai and A J Regan, *The Law, Politics and Administration of Decentralisation in Papua New Guinea* (Boroko: National Research Institute, 1992), p 306.

[497] By contrast, there are a number of rights that are enjoyed by all persons in the country, irrespective of citizenship, namely: the right to freedom itself (s 32); the right to life (s 35); freedom from inhuman treatment (s 36); the right to protection of the law (s 37); liberty of the person (s 42); freedom from forced labour (s 43); freedom from arbitrary search and arrest (s 44); freedom of conscience, thought and religion (s 45); freedom of expression (s 46); freedom of assembly and association (s 47); freedom of employment (s 48); and the right to privacy (s 49).

[498] Above n 17, p 211.

However, other rights have been taken seriously by the courts. For example, in *SCR No 2 of 1982; Re Organic Law* [1982] PNGLR 214, the Ombudsman Commission brought a reference querying the constitutionality of a provision of the *Organic Law on National Elections* requiring candidates for election to the National Parliament to deposit K1,000 when nominating. The Supreme Court held the provision unconstitutional, finding that this amount was so great as to effectively deny the majority of the citizen population a reasonable chance of standing, and this transgressed their constitutional right in s 50(c) of the *Constitution* to "take part in the conduct of public affairs, either directly or through freely chosen representatives".

Certain public offices are reserved for citizens, namely:

(a) the Governor-General (s 87(1));

(b) all members of the Public Services Commission (s 190(3));

(c) all members of the General Constitutional Commission (s 260(3));

(d) all members of the Law Reform Commission (Sch 2.13(2));

(e) the Clerk of the Parliament;[499] and

(f) the five members of the Citizenship Advisory Committee, who must be citizens other than naturalised citizens (s 75(1)).

The Chief Justice need not be a citizen but, if this is not the case, the Chief Justice may not act as Governor-General (s 95(3)).

In addition, no non-citizen can give financial or other assistance to candidates for elections to the Parliament (s 130(1)(b)). In respect of constitutional offices where non-citizens can be appointed, their term of appointment is for three years only, in contrast to the term for citizens of six years.[500]

Loss of citizenship

Under s 70 of the *Constitution,* a Papua New Guinea citizen who is at least 18 years of age loses citizenship if he or she:

(a) obtains the nationality or citizenship of another country by a voluntary act (other than marriage); or

(b) exercises a right that is exclusive to nationals or citizens of another country, unless the Minister responsible for citizenship matters is satisfied that the right was exercised inadvertently; or

(c) takes an oath or makes a declaration or affirmation of allegiance to another country or to the Sovereign or Head of State of another country; or

(d) does, agrees to or adopts any act (other than marriage) by which he becomes a national or citizen of another country; or

---

[499] *Organic Law on Certain Constitutional Office-holders*, s 8(2).
[500] *Organic Law on Certain Constitutional Office-holders*, s 13(c).

(e) enters or serves in the armed forces of another country, except with the express approval of the Head of State, acting with, and in accordance with, the advice of the National Executive Council; or

(f) except as permitted by an Act of the Parliament, votes in a national, provincial, state or local election, or accepts elective office, of another country; or

(g) (with certain exceptions shortly after independence) travels under the protection of a passport or purposed passport of another country in which he is described as a citizen or national of that country.

There are other ways that citizenship can be lost. First, where a court finds that a person has obtained citizenship by fraud or false representation, citizenship is lost unless the Minister is satisfied the offence involved was minor (s 70(2)). Secondly, as already discussed, a person with dual citizenship who has reached voting age may renounce Papua New Guinea citizenship (s 72). Finally, where the parent of a child loses Papua New Guinea citizenship, the Minister may, by order, also deprive the child of Papua New Guinea citizenship, if the Minister "is satisfied on application on behalf of the child that it is for the welfare of the child to do so" (s 74).

Administration: the Citizenship Advisory Committee

The *Constitution* establishes the Citizenship Advisory Committee (ss 75-76) to administer key provisions on citizenship. The Committee is an important part of the most constitutionally entrenched citizenship procedures of any of the Pacific Island nations. The committee comprises only citizens (other than naturalised citizens: see s 75(1)). It consists of four permanent members, including two backbench members of the Parliament (s 75(2)(a)) and one ad hoc member "to represent the community in which the person to whom a matter before the Committee relates resides" (s 75(2)(b)). Under s 10(4) of the *Citizenship Act* (Ch 12), the ad hoc member is a "person recommended to the Minister by the provincial government" of the place where the applicant resides. A provincial government can only recommend a person for appointment as an ad hoc member following consultation with the local government council or, where there is no local government council, with "leaders of the local community".[501] The permanent members are appointed by the Head of State acting on advice given after consultation with the Permanent Parliamentary Committee with special functions in relation to citizenship matters (*Citizenship Act* (Ch 12), s 10(3)). The term of appointment for permanent members is six years,[502] but members of Parliament sit on the Committee until the first meeting of the Parliament after the next election.[503] By contrast, ad hoc members are appointed by the Minister and their appointments end immediately the Committee concludes deliberations on the matter in relation to which the member has been appointed (s 10(9)(c)).

The Committee deals with issues referred to it from the Minister responsible for citizenship, and provides advice on such matters (s 76(1)).[504] When the Minister refers a matter to the Committee "members of the Committee shall have the same powers as Commissioners in respect of a matter referred to them under the *Commissions of Inquiry Act*".[505] If the Minister refuses the

[501] *Citizenship Act* (Ch 12), s 10(5).
[502] *Citizenship Act* (Ch 12), s 10(10)(b).
[503] *Citizenship Act* (Ch 12), s 10(10)(a).
[504] The advisory function of the Committee was the subject of constitutional amendment in 1977, as discussed below.
[505] *Citizenship Act* (Ch 12), s 10(12).

Committee's advice on a matter and a person affected by the decision or the Committee so requests, the Minister is required to inform the Parliament of the reasons for her or his decision (s 76(2)).

The *Citizenship Regulation* (Ch 12) provides the procedures for making applications for citizenship and for the work of the Citizenship Advisory Committee. The Committee is required to meet at least every three months (s 13(1)). When given a reference under s 76 of the *Constitution*, the Committee is empowered to "make such enquiries as to it seem necessary so as to enable it to advise the Minister in relation to the matter" (s 14).

ASPECTS OF OPERATION OF CITIZENSHIP PROVISIONS

There is limited material available on the public record of the number of applications for naturalised citizenship that have been made to the Citizenship Advisory Committee, or the number of applications approved, especially in the first 10 years after independence. In fact, a recommendation made by the General Constitutional Commission in its 1983 review of the *Constitution* was for a report to be commissioned studying those issues.[506] Although more information is available for the second 10 years after independence, it is also far from complete.

In that second decade, the Citizenship Advisory Committee struggled to cope with a demanding workload, and with problems caused by breaks in continuity consequent to having two members of the Parliament as permanent members of the Committee. Under the *Citizenship Act* (Ch 12), the Prime Minister was responsible for citizenship matters, and the Committee was administered by the Director General of Citizenship and Immigration Division within the Department of Foreign Affairs and Trade.

The Committee did not meet through most of 1987-88, and by 31 November 1988 there were 300 outstanding applications awaiting consideration.[507] In 1989, under Citizenship Advisory Committee chairman Joel Paua, the committee held sessions in six regions.[508] In 1990-91 the Committee met just twice,[509] and although 200 applications had accrued since 1991,[510] it was initially not reconstituted after the 1992 national elections.[511] By the time Prime Minister Sir Julius Chan eventually reconstituted the Committee in 1994 under Kabwum MP Ginson Saunu in 1994, there were 300 applications awaiting decision.[512] Hearings scheduled for March 1995 were delayed,[513] prompting criticism of the secretariat by chairman Saunu. The hearings eventually took place in October 1995.

---

506 General Constitutional Commission, *Final Report* (Port Moresby: 1983), p 64.

507 Papua New Guinea National Parliament, *Debates*, 3rd Day, 23 February 1989. It its interesting to note that, despite the requirement established in the *Citizenship Regulation* (Ch 12) that the Committee meet at three-monthly intervals, no applicant for citizenship appears to have applied for its enforcement judicially.

508 National Capital District, Milne Bay and Oro, Islands, Highlands and Momase: *PNG Post Courier*, 14 February 1989, p 5.

509 In Islands, and in Port Moresby: Papua New Guinea National Parliament, *Debates*, 21 May 1991.

510 *PNG Post Courier*, 16 December 1994.

511 In April 1992, more than 150 citizenship applications were considered by the Citizenship Advisory Committee for the southern region. The national elections then intervened, as MPs on the Citizenship Advisory Committee had electoral matters to deal with (Joel Paua, Jacob Lemeki, Gabrial Dusava, Pomat Paliau): *PNG Post Courier*, 25 July 1994.

512 Mr Paul Mambei had accepted appointment to the Committee in July 1994, but had then become Police Minister. Other members were MP Mathias Karani, Foreign Affairs Secretary Gabriel Dusava, and Attorney-General's secretary Sao Gabo. There were also 20 ad hoc members representing the provinces: *PNG Post Courier*, 10 November 1994.

513 *PNG Post Courier*, 2 March 1995.

Available figures in respect of naturalisation are confusing. According to one source, 960 applications for citizenship by naturalisation were made between 1975 and 1995, and in the same time 435 people had been granted automatic citizenship status. Of these 85, or 6.09 per cent, had renounced Papua New Guinean citizenship.[514] According to another source, by 1988 there were some 2,000 naturalised citizens in Papua New Guinea[515] (although no certificates of citizenship were awarded between 1980 and 1988).[516]

Concerning renunciation of citizenship, Papua New Guinea citizenship has been renounced by both automatic citizens and by naturalised citizens. By 1987 there were some 1,000 Papua New Guineans in Australia as permanent residents,[517] and some 10,000 Papua New Guineans had become Australian citizens, including a number of former public figures, some of whom had been naturalised citizens. In 1990-91 an estimated 330 Papua New Guineans migrated to Australia and became Australian citizens.[518]

REFORM PROPOSALS

Citizenship being a controversial issue well before independence, it should be no surprise that there has been considerable debate on proposals for change to the law. But in fact the debate has generated no substantive change to the law, there having been just one relatively minor change to the citizenship provisions of the *Constitution*.

Constitutional amendment

The only change to the constitutional provisions was a relatively minor change to s 76(1), made in 1977 in relation to the advice of the Citizenship Advisory Committee. *Constitutional Amendment No 5 - Citizenship* made it clear that the Minister could exercise constitutional powers in relation to citizenship only after receiving the advice of the Committee, and not merely after making a reference of an issue to the Committee.

Proposals of the Constitutional Review Commission (1983)

Major reform proposals were made by the General Constitutional Commission (GCC), which was established by the *Constitutional Commission Act* (Ch 21A) and published its Final Report in 1983.[519] Prior to the appearance of the Report, Camillus Narokobi, who was then legal adviser to the Citizenship Advisory Committee, presented an important paper on the working of Papua New Guinea's citizenship laws since 1975.[520] Narokobi pointed out that as the date of independence receded, constitutional provisions concerning automatic citizenship would become less important, and provisions concerning citizenship by naturalisation would become correspondingly more important. Narokobi described the existing ss 67, 68, and 69 as "inadequate to deal with the

[514] Papua New Guinea National Parliament, *Debates*, Fifteenth Meeting of the Fifth Session, 28 March to 29 March 1995.
[515] *PNG Post Courier*, 8 October 1987, p 4.
[516] *PNG Post Courier*, 30 April 1990, p 3.
[517] Information put forward by E Donpos of Rabaul in response to Kerowagi MP Jim Yer Waim's press statement about naturalised citizens: *PNG Post Courier*, 8 October 1987, p 4.
[518] *PNG Post Courier*, 1 October 1991.
[519] Above n 29.
[520] C S Narokobi, *Citizenship Matters in PNG* (Port Moresby: unpublished, 1981).

magnitude of the whole naturalisation question",[521] and made a number of recommendations, most of which were reflected in the Commission's recommendations in its Final Report.[522]

Concerning the issue of dual citizenship (prohibited by s 64 of the *Constitution* except in relation to persons under the age of 19 who as a result of parents holding different citizenship need not make a final choice of citizenship until they are 19), the GCC recommended that the age at which a person holding dual citizenship is required to make a declaration of loyalty be reduced from 19 to 16 years.

In relation to citizenship by naturalisation, the GCC recommended that:

(a) non-citizen children and spouses of citizens be prevented from "abuses of the system which are to the detriment of Papua New Guinea";[523]

(b) naturalised citizens be prevented from reassuming their previous citizenship;

(c) spouses and children (over 16 years) apply for citizenship at the same time as an applicant;

(d) applicants be "accepted and adopted" by a Papua New Guinean community and "identify" with that community as a requisite for citizenship;

(e) all of an applicant's business interests must be in Papua New Guinea and that all majority shareholders of such business be automatic citizens or citizens by descent.[524]

On the subject of resumption of citizenship by naturalised citizens who lose Papua New Guinea citizenship, the GCC recommended that they be prevented from regaining it.

In relation to automatic loss of citizenship, the GCC took the view that a naturalised citizen should lose citizenship in cases of "abuses or misuses" of Papua New Guinea citizenship, or where a citizen "divorces himself from the customary obligations of the community into which he has been adopted or identified with", or "abuses or breaches known customs" of his adopted community.[525]

Concerning the Citizenship Advisory Committee, the GCC recommended that the members of the Committee be the Premier of the province of a particular applicant, "four Papua New Guinean automatic citizens", and an ad hoc member from the "surrounding village communities within which the applicant lives".[526] It also recommended that there should be Provincial Citizenship Advisory Committees, distinct from the National Committee, and that they be enabled to advise their respective Provincial Executive Councils on "all questions relating to citizenship in their provinces".[527]

The GCC also recommended a moratorium on naturalisation applications for 15 years, during which time there should be a general review of citizenship laws. At the same time, it wanted a report to be commissioned to identify the number of applicants for citizenship since independence, together with the figures regarding rates of acceptance and rejection, and an

---

[521] Ibid, p 6.
[522] Above n 29, pp 60-74.
[523] Ibid, p 61. These "abuses" are referred to on p 66, but their nature is not discussed.
[524] Ibid, p 62.
[525] Ibid.
[526] Ibid, p 63.
[527] Ibid.

assessment of "any problems associated with the administration of citizenship laws in the country encountered since independence".[528]

In making these recommendations, the GCC acknowledged that it was seeking to address problems that lay as much with the administration of the law as with the provisions of the laws. It felt that the Citizenship Advisory Committee had not given sufficiently close scrutiny to citizenship applications, and that this was partly due to the Committee's lack of administrative support:

> "We have been made aware from submissions that some of the information the Citizenship Advisory Committee relies on are either biased or have been improperly influenced. We have been told too that the committee does not have a full-time Secretariat from which professional and full-time services may be obtained or through which a constant surveillance of the citizenship laws and procedures may be monitored and policed. We also note that the apparent lack of reviews and publicity of the citizenship administration, laws and procedures does deprive the public [of] the right to be informed."[529]

The strong expression of national interests that informed the recommendations by Narokobi and the GCC are understandable, given that Papua New Guinea was at the time the GCC completed its Final Report an independent nation of less than 10 years standing. On the other hand, converting the concerns and hopes underlying the recommendations into workable laws was something different, and as a result the ideas have not found practical expression.[530]

In addition, there were obvious difficulties involved in some of the key recommendations. While it is understandable that Papua New Guineans do not embrace the idea of "renouncing" Papua New Guinea citizenship in an absolute sense, legal means for such loss are very real (*Constitution*, ss 70-74). The removal of citizenship from naturalised citizens who reside elsewhere "without proper justification for a certain period of time", as was proposed to the GCC by its legal adviser (Mr C Narokobi),[531] is possible, but would be very arbitrary. Preventing naturalised citizens from regaining citizenship after having lost it, as was recommended by the GCC, is also possible, but denies the reality of international mobility in contemporary times. It presumes, furthermore, the very worst intentions on the part of the naturalised citizen: a presumption to which should be joined the possibility that the very best intentions may also be present. Insisting that spouses and children of applicants apply for citizenship simultaneously with the applicant for naturalisation would also place significant restrictions on the rights, for instance, of children from inter-racial marriages. They would be forced to choose between the nationality of father and mother. It would not be possible either to prevent a naturalised citizen from reassuming a previous citizenship elsewhere, or to require a citizenship applicant to have business interests in Papua New Guinea only, with automatic citizens or citizens by descent as majority shareholders, as proposed by the GCC.

More relevant were the GCC recommendations that the members of the Citizenship Advisory Committee report fully on the numbers of applicants for citizenship since independence, together with rates of acceptance and rejection (since such reports to the Parliament are required by law

[528] Ibid, p 65.
[529] Ibid, p 69.
[530] See the criticisms of the Final Report by Colquhoun-Kerr, above n 18.
[531] Above n 43, p 7.

anyway); and that a thorough study be conducted into the administration of citizenship, and into the actual effect of the country's citizenship regime in economic, moral, cultural, and political terms. However, no such study has ever been carried out, and as a result data on citizenship continues to be poor, and debate on the sensitive and closely connected issues of naturalisation and the continuing economic importance of non-citizens continues unabated.

NATURALISATION AND ECONOMIC IMPORTANCE OF NON-CITIZENS

Economic importance of non-citizens

Sensitivity about access to citizenship for people other than those clearly indigenous to Papua New Guinea has always been connected to concerns about possible economic exploitation of Papua New Guinea by outsiders. Twenty years after independence, the continued domination of the economy by foreign interests, and the large number of foreigners resident in Papua New Guinea, continue to contribute to concern about naturalisation.

Under the *Migration Act* (Ch 16), aliens can only enter Papua New Guinea under strict visa requirements, and there is mandatory reporting to the Parliament by the Minister for Foreign Affairs on matters relating to illegal entry and illegal presence. A regular Ministerial Statement to Parliament reads:

> "The migration laws were designed to protect the people of Papua New Guinea to ensure employment opportunities for Papua New Guineans are not taken up by foreign nationals and to protect our communities from unwelcome, illegal or offensive practices by foreigners. It is an important function and responsibility of my Department to require foreigners to leave Papua New Guinea if they are found to be involved in activities which are illegal or in breach of Papua New Guinea immigration laws and other laws of the country in general."[532]

In 1981, the Department of Foreign Affairs and Trade (Migration and Citizenship Division) reported the presence of 39,000 foreigners on contracts, and a further 3,000 having status as permanent residents. The Department expressed special concern at the presence of nationals of other countries, particularly those from South East Asia, "whose standard of living is less than offered in this country".[533] In 1994, 119 foreigners had their entry permits cancelled for such offences as living in Papua New Guinea on expired visas, or working illegally.[534]

The economic impact of both naturalised citizens and other foreigners residing in the country has been a long-standing concern. In November 1977 Tony Bais, member for Wewak, introduced into Parliament a motion calling for a select committee to investigate the business activities of "non-nationals and some naturalised citizens . . . in areas such as partnerships, public companies, corporations and business activities under the names of their wives, who are nationals". In particular, the committee was to investigate the involvement of nationals in the purchasing of shareholding, control and management, benefits, and plans for complete take-over by "true

[532] Papua New Guinea National Parliament, *Debates*, 9th day, 17 March 1986, p 17.
[533] Papua New Guinea National Parliament, *Final Report of the Select Committee on Expatriate Involvement in Business* (Port Moresby: 1981), p 33.
[534] *PNG Post Courier*, 29 March 1995.

nationals" in businesses.[535] This motion reflected a widespread desire to control the capacity of non-citizens to profit at the expense of citizens.

The *Employment of Non-Citizens Act* (Ch 374) was intended to determine the conditions under which foreigners entered the country for employment. The Act prohibits the employment of non-citizens who do not possess work permits, and sets out the procedure for acquisition of work permits.

In 1981 Jacob Lemeki, Minister for Labour and Employment, presented the first progress report on the employment of non-citizens in Papua New Guinea under the 1978 Act, saying:

> "This report was called for in March 1981 by Glaimi Warena, chair of the Public Accounts Committee. As at 16th July there were 17,000 positions approved by the Department of labour and industry for non-citizen employment."[536]

More recent figures suggest that the Act has failed to limit the number of non-citizens entering the country to perform work that could ordinarily be performed by citizens. By the mid-1990s, the number of non-citizen workers in the country had risen to levels close to those of the colonial period. In 1994 some 5,244 registered employers engaged non-citizens, and 40,756 approved positions were held by non-citizens.[537]

Renunciation of citizenship

In most countries the act of renunciation of citizenship goes largely unremarked. In such a small country as Papua New Guinea, however, renunciation by people who had attained a level of prominence in the country, or had gained materially from it, can be viewed not merely as an act of choice by an individual who desires to exercise other options, but as a form of betrayal to a society that had opened itself to them. Thus an essentially pragmatic act (in a legal sense) becomes one that touches the core of patriotism.

In 1993, following renunciation of citizenship by a naturalised citizen who had been a member of Parliament prior to the 1992 general election, the Minister for Foreign Affairs, John Kaputin, announced that the government would not approve further citizenship applications until Cabinet reconsidered the relevant constitutional provisions and subsidiary laws. The Minister wanted to limit the number of years a foreigner could live in the country, and also announced a crackdown on foreigners working illegally in trade stores, take-away food bars, and timber and logging activities. On 30 June 1993 the *Post Courier*'s front page blazed: "Crackdown looming on citizenship laws".[538]

Rights of naturalised citizens

In 1993 Joseph Onguglo MP tabled a Bill for a proposed amendment to s 103 of the *Constitution*, intended to prevent naturalised citizens from standing as candidates for election to the Parliament.

---

535 The result was a report to the Parliament, above n 56.

536 Papua New Guinea National Parliament, *Debates*, 28 July 1981.

537 *PNG Post Courier*, 19 July 1994.

538 The campaign was joined by NCD Commission chairman David Unagi, and by Mr Laimo, South Bougainville MP, who called for revision of the *Citizenship Act*, taking the opportunity to denounce spouses holding a different passport, dual citizenship, and the granting of work permits to Asians for jobs that Papua New Guineans could do: *PNG Post Courier*, 25 August 1992, p 2.

Onguglo wanted the proposed law extended to elections for provincial assemblies, and to bar naturalised citizens from holding office as departmental heads, heads of statutory authorities, chairs of public organisations, boards, and other senior positions within the public service.[539] Tikana Tailem of Rabaul commented:

> "This proposed law should also include naturalised citizens who are departmental heads and heads of statutory bodies. These naturalised citizens are only here to exploit our resources to get maximum financial benefit."[540]

Although debated in the Parliament, the Bill was never passed.

Other proposals for change were even less workable. Simbu National Business Association President Otto Victus suggested that the only people who should be considered for citizenship were foreigners over age 55, and missionaries.[541] A 1993 letter to the editor of a national daily newspaper suggested these requirements for citizenship:

(a) an investment by the applicant of a minimum K500,000; or

(b) initiation of the applicant into a tribe - not merely marriage - and ability to speak a lingua franca that is not police motu or tok pisin; or

(c) that the applicant be a UNHCR endorsed refugee.

Discussion and conclusion

Law and policy concerning citizenship has demonstrated a curious contradiction in the first two decades of Papua New Guinea's independence. On the one hand there has been widespread concern about the danger that the interests of Papua New Guineans may become subordinate to those of foreigners,[542] a view expressed by many members of the Parliament, including Sir Pita Lus, who commented in 1992:

> "If the government is genuine, we should not allow foreigners to become citizens of our country. We must send them back to where they came from. Some of them are our good friends but we must be wary of them. Can you name some Papua New Guineans who have become citizens of countries like the United States of America, Great Britain or Australia? Shame on the lot of you.
>
> God created this country for me and my grandchildren, not foreigners. They have their own God-given country too. This law was written by you, not God, because you felt sorry for these foreigners. Why should we feel sorry for them, they have their own country and they should go back there."[543]

---

[539] The Bill received support from MP William Ekip Wii, deputy leader of People's National Congress (*PNG Post Courier*, 5 July 1993, p 12), but was also opposed by some, including Hugh Greer, a naturalised citizen who had been in Papua New Guinea for 24 years (*PNG Post Courier*, 30 August 1993).

[540] *Times of Papua New Guinea*, 9-15 January 1987, p 8.

[541] *PNG Post Courier*, 6 July 1993, p 17.

[542] Waipagi Kambe of Ialibu, for example, wrote of his concern that "the government is failing miserably by granting citizenships to foreigners . . . The present population of naturalised citizens is multiplying quickly and one could easily witness this in cities like Port Moresby, Lae and Rabaul. My prediction is that soon the population of indigenous people will be outnumbered by the naturalised citizens . . . To conclude let me remind all the leaders of PNG that the majority of our people's vision is to see pure Papua New Guineans living in this land until the end of mankind': *PNG Post Courier*, 26 September 1988, p 10.

[543] Papua New Guinea National Parliament, *Debates*, Second Meeting of the Fifth Session, 24 November to 26 November 1992.

There is, on the other hand, the view that laws of citizenship operate within a wider context of international and personal relations, and that good can come of naturalisation laws. Thus Bernard Narokobi replied to Sir Pita:

> "Papua New Guinea is a large country and we must expand our knowledge by inviting more foreigners into the country. It is going to be difficult to keep our Melanesian race unique. We are a majority and if we restrict ourselves, we will be left behind. Our country will not develop. We must broaden our horizons in order to develop and to expand our knowledge . . . It is not wrong to have money flowing into our country. We must encourage people who come in to invest. We must also educate our people to accept foreigners instead of attacking them. If we treat them with respect, they will talk highly of us in their countries."[544]

In the space between these two views was the law in operation, today still fundamentally unchanged after 20 years. What has changed in that time is the international dimension of law, and the globalisation of culture and social relations. These changes have resulted in seemingly contradictory demands, on the one hand for more openness on the part of countries such as Papua New Guinea, and on the other hand for even greater control over citizenship matters as a result of economic and other pressures within the country.

The concerns already noted in this chapter about the operation of Papua New Guinea's citizenship laws in the first 20 years of independence give rise to several observations. Concerns about the preservation of national interest and national sovereignty have led some governments to alter aspects of citizenship policy, but fundamental legal reform has not been attempted. In this same period, however, the legal provisions for citizenship have created a number of tensions. For example, while citizenship law does not recognise dual citizenship, a considerable number of Papua New Guineans have married into other cultures, both within and outside the country, and their legitimate interests in dual nationality, particularly for their children, have not been adequately addressed.

Debate has focused on issues of acquisition of Papua New Guinea citizenship by foreign nationals and their subsequent participation in the economic and political life of the country. While this is understandable given Papua New Guinea's colonial experience, it is necessary to question why concern has focused on the circumstances of the few rather than the many. The membership boundaries established by citizenship laws mark just a beginning; next comes concern for the actual benefits that citizenship brings. As discussed, in Papua New Guinea these benefits include special rights and privileges. But debate on citizenship has not dealt with such matters, except in relation to naturalised citizens.

By focusing mainly on domestic law relating to naturalised citizens, Papua New Guinea citizenship debate draws little on international perspectives and experience. The 1948 United Nations *Declaration of Human Rights* establishes a global standard of expectations for all people, irrespective of nationality. Together with the *International Covenant on Civil and Political Rights*, and the *International Covenant on Economic, Social and Cultural Rights*, the Declaration identifies comprehensive standards of relationships for states and peoples. Yet Papua New Guinea has been in no hurry to sign either of these Covenants or other significant international standards protecting the rights of its citizens.

[544] Papua New Guinea National Parliament, *Debates*, Fifteenth Meeting of the Fifth Session, 28 March to 29 March 1995.

In Europe the laws of citizenship have evolved to take into account changing circumstances. Long-term residents who are not citizens, for instance, are being granted access to education and health services, and allowed to participate in elections at the local level. By analogy, one might ask what new circumstances in the Pacific could be addressed to meet the needs of citizens. One instance might be the difficulties encountered by Papua New Guinea citizens who marry a citizen of another Pacific Island state. The offspring of such marriages have legitimate claims arising from belonging to two cultures. Yet citizenship laws oblige them to sacrifice one nationality to meet the requirements for Papua New Guinea citizenship.

The move toward a more global society, and the extent of international travel, have brought into question the notion of sovereign nations as isolated units. In a real sense the global community is much more united now than ever before. United Nations conventions and various resolutions are increasingly being adhered to by nation states. Abuses of citizens' human rights by sovereign states is no longer viewed primarily as a domestic issue. Like many developing countries Papua New Guinea is yet to update its laws and make moves to amend its laws on citizenship to take into account changes toward a more open world community.

Chapter 17

THE CONSTITUTION AND FOREIGN RELATIONS OF PAPUA NEW GUINEA

EDWARD P WOLFERS*

INTRODUCTION

Papua New Guinea's constitutional laws perform three main kinds of functions in respect of the country's foreign relations. They act as a regulator of certain aspects of official conduct, as an instrument of national interests, and as a guide to government policies and actions. For their part, government agencies involved in the conduct of Papua New Guinea's foreign relations play important roles in three key areas; namely, protecting and promoting the country's constitutional laws, implementing those laws, and (through little-remarked but potentially powerful provisions) directing the development of those laws.

The discussion that follows begins by defining key terms before going on to examine each of the six aspects referred to above. The conclusions to be reached draw attention to ways in which, in varying circumstances, Papua New Guinea's constitutional laws and foreign relations reinforce each other, conflict, or leave gaps.

*The author is grateful to Jackson Rannells, the compiler of "Papua New Guinea Constitution and Organic Laws Citator, 20 Years On: 1975–1995" in Michael Somare Library Occasional Publications 23 (1995), and to Charles Hawksley for assistance in assembling relevant materials.

DEFINITIONS OF KEY TERMS

According to Sch 1.2(1) of the *Constitution*, Papua New Guinea's constitutional laws consist of the *Constitution* itself, any law altering the *Constitution*, and the Organic Laws. But details concerning the application of many such laws are often spelt out in ordinary legislation, regulations and government notices. Government policies, including budgetary appropriations, can play a crucial role in determining the impact that constitutional and other laws have in practice.

As in other systems of government where the courts interpret constitutional laws, the precise meaning and effects of such laws may depend on what judges decide. An obvious consequence is that their full ramifications may sometimes not be known with certainty until they have been tested in court.

An unusual feature of Papua New Guinea's constitutional laws is that certain materials used in the constitution-making process can be used as aids to interpretation (see s 24 of the *Constitution*).[545] A considerable body of additional materials may therefore have to be consulted in order to clarify the meaning of particular provisions. An anomaly with the potential to complicate the process even further is that materials which can be cited as aids to interpretation under s 24 might not cast light on, and might even conflict with, later amendments or new Organic Laws. However, the courts are neither directed, nor forbidden, to refer to materials of a similar character that helped to shape the amendments.[546]

As will be discussed towards the end of this account, a variety of other materials may also be relevant to determining the precise effects of constitutional laws. They include treaties made before Papua New Guinea became independent but since adopted as part of the country's international obligations, such as the *United Nations Charter*, and agreements in which Papua New Guinea has had no say and cannot even accede to, such as the *European Convention for the Protection of Human Rights and Fundamental Freedoms*.[547] Also included are documents such as United Nations General Assembly Resolutions, whose very existence and content may owe a great deal to agencies responsible for managing Papua New Guinea's foreign relations, without being subject to the safeguards imposed on the acceptance of treaty obligations under s 117 of the *Constitution*.

Papua New Guinea's constitutional laws do not explicitly define the term "foreign relations". But they do include a number of terms related to the "international" environment (not all of which is entirely "foreign"),[548] such as "international obligations" (s 202(b)) and "international peace-keeping or relief operations" (s 205(2)(b)). While certain foreign laws were adopted as part of the laws of Papua New Guinea at independence (Sch 5), other legal standards set abroad do not necessarily form part of the law to be applied domestically, even if representatives of Papua New Guinea have helped to make or actually signed them (s 117(7) and (8)).[549] But s 39 and Sch 2.3(1)(d) state explicitly - and s 40 and Sch 2.1(2) imply - that such standards may be used to help

[1] A J Regan and E P Wolfers, "Aids to interpretation of the Constitution: some preliminary thoughts" (1986) 14 Melanesian Law Journal 153.

[2] The Organic Law on Provincial Governments and Local-Level Governments that came into force in 1996 is a case in point.

[3] While s 39(d) of the Constitution provides for the Convention to be used in determining the constitutionality of laws and Acts in Papua New Guinea, Articles 65(3) and 66(1) of the Convention itself appear to limit it to members of the Council of Europe.

[4] See the discussion below of Kapi J's remarks in SCR No 4 of 1980 (No 2); Re Petition of M T Somare [1982] PNGLR 65 at 76, concerning the way in which international law applies to Papua New Guinea.

[5] J Goldring, The Constitution of Papua New Guinea (Sydney: Law Book Co, 1978), p 45; E P Wolfers, "Provincial Governments and Foreign Affairs", (1991) Special Issue Melanesian Law Journal 145-62.

define how laws made in Papua New Guinea should be applied.

Before independence, the constitutional status of Papua New Guinea was an issue in the foreign relations of the administering authority, Australia, particularly at the United Nations.[550] It was also an issue for Papua New Guinean politicians during the 1960s and early 1970s, especially among members of the House of Assembly who resisted outside pressures for early independence.

When long-serving Australian Prime Minister, Mr R G Menzies, returned from a Commonwealth Heads of Government Meeting in 1960, his observations and experiences there led to the reform of the Legislative Council to include the first indirectly elected Papua New Guinean members. Despite denials by the Australian Government of the day, the Report of the United Nations Visiting Mission that visited the Trust Territory of New Guinea under the leadership of Sir Hugh Foot in 1962 had considerable influence on the establishment of the House of Assembly in 1964. And when Australian Opposition Leader Mr Gough Whitlam visited Papua New Guinea in 1969-70 and 1970-71, an important reason he saw for moving more rapidly towards independence was to avoid international criticism of Australia as a recalcitrant colonial power.

Then, when Papua New Guinea became independent at midnight on 15-16 September 1975, the moment when Australian law ceased to apply and the Papua New Guinea *Constitution* came into effect defined the point at which future links between Papua New Guinea and Australia became legally part of the foreign relations of both countries.[551]

A curious sidelight on the Australian Government's (dis)regard for international law had previously been provided during the constitution-making process in 1972-74, when Australia became a signatory to the *International Convention on the Reduction of Statelessness*. This was done in such a way that Australia could appear to be upholding an important principle of international law, while evading responsibility for people in Papua New Guinea whose citizenship would have been threatened by recommendations contained in the Final Report of the Constitutional Planning Committee.[552]

The treaty succession exercise that followed independence was intended to identify the international obligations that Papua New Guinea, acting through the government of the day and the National Parliament, was willing to inherit from Australia. The process adopted, of continuing all treaties for a five-year period after independence, during which they were to be reviewed and allowed to lapse unless specifically accepted, avoided uncertainty over which treaties have applied since that time. But the slow rate at which the project progressed may have resulted in Papua New Guinea not succeeding to treaties that might otherwise have been accepted. It is, moreover, not clear from the public record whether all treaties that qualified for possible succession were thoroughly reviewed, a situation which could eventually become a source of diplomatic embarrassment and difficulty if questions are asked or pressure is exercised over Papua New Guinea's failure to become a party to important international conventions (particularly in the field of human rights).

[6] W Thomasetti, "Australia and the United Nations: New Guinea Trusteeship Issues from 1946 to 1966" (1970) New Guinea Research Bulletin 36; E P Wolfers, "The Trusteeship Council, 1966" (1966-67) 1(8) New Guinea and Australia, the Pacific and South-East Asia 54.

[551] The de facto control over Papua New Guinea's foreign relations had been transferred from Australia earlier in the same year.

8Constitutional Planning Committee, Final Report of the Constitutional Planning Committee: Part 1 (Port Moresby: Government Printer, 1974), pp 4–5. For a detailed discussion of the making of the citizenship provisions in the Constitution, see E P Wolfers, "Defining a Nation: the Citizenship Debates in the Papua New Guinea Parliament" in E P Wolfers and F S Stevens (eds), "Colonialism and After", Vol 3 of Racism: the Australian Experience (Sydney: 2nd ed, ANZ Book Co, 1977), from p 301.

The realities of international relations mean that Australia is sometimes regarded - in other countries, occasionally in Australia, and even in Papua New Guinea, particularly when aid issues are discussed - as having continuing responsibility for events, including lack of development, in Papua New Guinea long after independence.

Other realities, including the shared interests of existing sovereign states, mean that the Papua New Guinea government has been able to counter efforts by supporters of an independent Bougainville/North Solomons to lobby for support abroad, including recognition at the United Nations in 1975 and again during the 1990s.

In Australia, the character of federation has required the Australian courts to try to define the term "external affairs". But judgments in major cases suggest that, while the "external affairs" power must not be used as "merely a device to procure for the Commonwealth . . . additional jurisdiction" relative to the Australian States, its scope is much broader than relations with other countries, participation in multilateral organisations, or the application of international law.[553] In fact, one critical commentator believes that "as long as the Federal Executive enters into . . . an agreement and Federal Parliament adheres to the provisions of the agreement, Federal Parliament can gain control of any kind of matter". In effect, the "external affairs" power can be used as a way of giving the Commonwealth Government powers over almost any subject it pleases, notwithstanding the constitutional division of powers between the Commonwealth and the Australian States.[554] In contrast, s 117(7) of the *Constitution* seems to preclude such a possibility without specific legislation in Papua New Guinea, though s 41(2) of the *Organic Law on Provincial Governments and Local-level Governments* makes the legislative powers of provincial governments vulnerable to overriding national legislation in "the national interest".

More importantly and more pertinently to the Papua New Guinea situation, the range of issues on which independent states co-operate, or can be held accountable for under international law, is expanding rapidly. Relevant factors include the emergence of powers with global interests, growing international economic interdependence, and the increasing irrelevance of interstate boundaries to efforts to deal with environmental and other issues. Even as the number, scale and intensity of inter- and intra-national conflicts grow, people in many parts of the world are coming to see themselves as members of a common humanity as well as part of particular nations, ethnic or other communities, and families.[555]

Not every change in state jurisdiction is in the same direction or necessarily irreversible. But the growth of worldwide communications networks has placed aspects of communications such as censorship, that were once subject to the jurisdiction of states, beyond the control of individual states. The Internet and the way in which foreign television stations beam into Papua New Guinea are only two among a growing number of examples. The overall trend towards expansion in the range of issues addressed and regulated through international co-operation seems quite clear.

Within the United Nations, as in other multilateral organisations, membership "is a consequence of the exercise of sovereignty by a state". But "the institutional aspects of . . . membership . . . qualify the exclusive jurisdiction" characteristically claimed by states. In other words, as Rajan

---

[553] R v Burgess; Ex parte Henry (1936) 55 CLR 608 at 687, cited in P Hanks, Australian Constitutional Law: Materials and Commentary (Sydney: Butterworths, 1990), pp 759–60.

[554] P H Lane, A Manual of Australian Constitutional Law (Sydney: 3rd ed, Law Book Co, 1984), p 152.

[555] Note the Constitution's references in s 40 to "the rights and dignity of mankind" and in Sch 2.1(2) to "the general principles of humanity" (see below for discussion).

has observed, "the traditional right of a sovereign state not to be bound by any new rule without its own consent has been qualified by international organisation - although a state can still pretend".[556] Moreover, consistently with what has already been said, the range of issues discussed and becoming subject to decisions by multilateral organisations is increasing rapidly. When the norms embodied in customary international law, the development of the concept of the global commons, and even more importantly the realities of international inequalities are also taken into account, then the ability of individual states to determine the body of international law that applies to them is diminishing quickly. While judges may argue, as Kapi J did in *SCR No 4 of 1980 (No 2); Re Petition of M T Somare* [1982] PNGLR 65 at 76, that the way in which international law applies to Papua New Guinea depends on how Papua New Guinea develops in the international community, I would suggest that the latter process may not be entirely subject to Papua New Guinean control.

In other words, the scope and force of international law applying to Papua New Guinea may be changing in ways that no-one in Papua New Guinea can control on their own (at least without international support). Activities that can legitimately be described as aspects of Papua New Guinea's foreign relations are becoming both more numerous and more diverse. Examples include issues over which states have long argued whether or not they are subject exclusively to national jurisdiction, such as human rights. They also include issues, such as sustainable use of national forest resources, that have been regarded as purely domestic concerns until very recently indeed. When they apply to Papua New Guinea, the changes outlined take on an additional, important dimension because of the growing likelihood that the National Government may be held accountable internationally for policies and actions for which provincial or local governments are responsible under the *Organic Law on Provincial Governments and Local-Level Governments.* If, for example, a natural resource project is held up or blocked by a provincial or local-level government, then foreign investors and other interested parties (including aid donors and banks) may criticise or put pressure on the National Government. And, if such a project is approved on terms and conditions of which environmental or human rights activists disapprove, then the National Government may attempt to do the same.

The main implication for the National Government is that it will either have to devote resources to securing co-operation from provincial and local-level governments as well as non-governmental organisations, or legislate in order to override them, thereby frustrating an essential aspect of decentralisation.

CONSTITUTIONAL LAWS AS REGULATORS OF STATE CONDUCT

Constitutional laws regulate state conduct in respect of Papua New Guinea's foreign relations in a number of different ways, including the specification of requirements for treaty-making, and sending the Papua New Guinea Defence Force (PNGDF) abroad.

[556] M Rajan, The Expanding Jurisdiction of the United Nations (Bombay: Tripathi Private Ltd, 1982), pp 1-2.

In distinguishing between rights that belong without qualification to all persons and rights that are qualified so that they apply only to citizens, constitutional laws also regulate how the state deals with foreigners present in Papua New Guinea. The citizenship provisions specify how non-citizens, including foreign citizens, can become citizens of Papua New Guinea.

Proposals that would, if accepted, have had the effect of embodying a greater role in Papua New Guinea's constitutional laws as regulator of state conduct were not eventually accepted before independence. They included a draft Foreign Investment Code and recommendations to limit foreign participation, including the provision of financial support for candidates in national elections.[557]

[557] Constitutional Planning Committee, above n 8, Part 2. A constitutional provision (s 129) requiring specifically that "[a]n Organic Law shall make provision for the integrity of political parties" has not been implemented (the Constitutional Review Commission is reported to be considering the issue).

A further form of legal regulation with potentially significant implications for Papua New Guinea's foreign relations is the *Organic Law on Provincial Boundaries.* Although the Organic Law purports to describe the country's provincial boundaries, the lines that it draws around Papua New Guinea's 14 maritime provinces and the National Capital District, based on the "picture-windows" drawn for administrative purposes during the colonial period, are, in fact, without basis in law.[558] The situation is important because of the uncertainties it perpetuates regarding the jurisdiction of maritime provincial and local-level governments (and, by implication, of the national government), as well as the distribution of revenues raised from fishing under the *Organic Law on Provincial Governments and Local-Level Governments.*

In the case of the Gulf and Western Provinces, certain maritime boundaries described in the same Organic Law are, moreover, defined in relation not to a foreign country but to an Australian State, Queensland, and in the latter case to the Indonesian Province of Irian Jaya, contrary to the *Constitution*'s general emphasis on national sovereignty and independence.

In relation to treaty-making, s 117 sets out the procedures by which Papua New Guinea can become party to international treaties. The effect intended seems quite clear: to prevent the state from being legally bound by international agreements other than those which pass through the procedures spelt out (presentation to the National Parliament for at least 10 sitting days, and failure to disapprove, as distinct from active approval, by an absolute majority of members). These procedures can be abridged in urgent situations.

Section 117 should make treaty-making transparent and ensure public accountability by making it almost impossible for the state to negotiate secret treaties. But similar provisions in other countries have, in practice, sometimes made officials reluctant to conclude formal treaties because of the difficulty of securing passage for treaty proposals through their respective legislatures. This has sometimes led them to prefer agreements of lesser status and force under international law, thereby incidentally avoiding the need for publication. Though related considerations have sometimes influenced other parties to international negotiations, including representatives of the United States,[559] they have not figured on the Papua New Guinea side. But negotiators on Papua New Guinea's behalf have sometimes cited the need for public approval of treaties as an argument for concessions sought in the course of negotiations.

In the *Somare (No 2)* case [1982] PNGLR 65, the Supreme Court seems to have turned s 117 on its head.[560] Thus, consistently with the principle that an accuser should be required to prove what is alleged, the majority of judges found that it was up to the complainant to prove that there was no obligation on Papua New Guinea, instead of insisting that the state should prove the existence of such an obligation, to send elements of the PNGDF to Vanuatu. It even seemed to accept the possibility that the state could withhold evidence of the existence of such an obligation on grounds of national security. The effect of the decision is not to ensure that governments can bind the state only with the explicit consent of the National Parliament, but to allow the state to assert the existence of an obligation about which no-one else has definitive information.

---

[558] E P Wolfers, above n 6, at 152-55. Cf Y P Ghai and A J Regan, The Law, Politics and Administration of Decentralisation in Papua New Guinea (Monograph 30) (Boroko: National Research Institute, 1992), pp 56-57.

[559] Cf L Margolis, Executive Agreements and Presidential Power in Foreign Policy (New York: Praeger, 1986), pp 45-46.

[560] The generally high regard for, and success of, of the PNGDF's intervention in Vanuatu in 1980 (the substantive action from which the case arose) means that the following remarks are made with particular regret, and limited only to the technical aspects of the Supreme Court's discussion on s 117.

Moreover, in accepting that a binding obligation could be contained in a document other than a treaty, the court seemed to blur distinctions often made in international legal texts and often raised as an issue in negotiations, thereby giving rise to questions about the basis and legal character of non-treaty agreements signed on Papua New Guinea's behalf (such as memoranda of understanding, exchanges of diplomatic notes, and other arrangements).

Already, certain agreements of less than treaty status have sometimes been regarded as confidential to government in Papua New Guinea, though publicly available abroad (the *Guidelines on the Use of Australian Defence Force Loan Personnel in Politically Sensitive Situations* appears to be an example). A more serious effect could be that documents that others explicitly do not want to have the status and force of a treaty, such as the *Joint Declaration of Principles Guiding Relations between Australia and Papua New Guinea,* might be regarded as imposing binding obligations in, by and for Papua New Guinea but not the other party (or parties).

An implication of even greater potential significance is that a government, speaking on behalf of the state, might claim to be bound by an obligation requiring the PNGDF to go abroad without anyone other than the government of the day knowing exactly what the obligation is or even being certain that it exists (one recalls President Wilson's campaign against "secret treaties" following World War I, and the Australian Government's commitment of troops to South Vietnam in the 1960s!).[561]

It might in fact allow a government to argue that, in the absence of a formal treaty, it is nonetheless bound, for example by virtue of the way in which it sees Papua New Guinea as a South Pacific island or a Melanesian state, or even as a participant in the Association of South-East Asian Nations (ASEAN) Regional Forum or the United Nations, to send troops abroad to neighbouring countries. This would be in clear defiance, it is suggested, of the true purpose and most accurate reading of s 117.

CONSTITUTIONAL LAWS AS INSTRUMENTS OF NATIONAL INTERESTS

The constitutional laws of Papua New Guinea have been repeatedly used in order to protect and promote national interests. Examples include the many occasions, particularly soon after independence, when their liberal, democratic character (and implied commitment to orderly, honest and effective government) were often invoked in order to promote Papua New Guinea abroad, particularly as a worthy recipient of aid and other support from Western countries. Others include the use of the 1995 provincial and local-level government reforms as evidence of the National Government's desire to improve the delivery of services to rural and urban communities outside Port Moresby. They also include the times when the human rights situation in Bougainville, for example, has been criticised, particularly at meetings of the United Nations Human Rights Commission in Geneva. In the latter case, the National Government has replied to allegations of official abuses by pointing to the human rights provisions in the *Constitution.*

[561] M Sexton, War for the Asking: Australia's Vietnam Secrets (Ringwood Vic: Penguin, 1981).

The efforts that the late Chief Justice, Sir Buri Kidu, made to draw the attention of and facilitate the access of citizens to legal procedures intended to safeguard human rights were, in themselves, an implicit rebuttal of the suggestion that constitutional laws on their own can guarantee a great deal.[562] A similar point appears to have been accepted by supporters of the proposal that a National Human Rights Commission is needed in order to give greater effect to existing laws and institutions.

Reference to the constitutional procedures governing Papua New Guinea's accession to treaties is often included, with varying degrees of generality, in the "machinery provisions" of drafts negotiated in preparation for presentation to the National Parliament. These references usually state that the treaties take effect in accordance with the signatory states' respective constitutional requirements.

More specific reference to the *Constitution*, contained in the body of a treaty, can be found in the *Framework Treaty Guiding Relations with Solomon Islands*. Thus, Article 3(a) requires both parties to respect "each other's . . . system of government including the National Constitution and other laws".

Article 2 of the *Treaty of Mutual Respect, Friendship and Co-operation* with Indonesia goes a step further in committing each of the parties to:

> "display and promote respect for the other country's national identity, traditions and values, including the Papua New Guinea Constitution, in which Papua New Guinea's National Goals and Directive Principles are contained, the Indonesian State Philosophy (PANCASILA) and the Indonesian Constitution."[563]

By necessary implication, Indonesia must, therefore, show and foster respect for Papua New Guinea's constitutional commitment (contained in the National Goals and Directive Principles) to integral human development, equality and participation, national sovereignty and self-reliance, natural resources and environment, and Papua New Guinean ways. The last reference, in particular, opens up some interesting possibilities, especially on the common border. (It is also, of course, encompassed by the reference to national constitutions in the previously mentioned treaty with the Solomons).

Finally, Papua New Guinea's constitutional laws can be used by outsiders as reasons or pretexts for seeking to influence official Papua New Guinean views of Papua New Guinea's national interests. A case in point is the criticism that World Bank and International Monetary Fund officials are reported to have made of the reforms embodied in the *Organic Law on Provincial Governments and Local-Level Governments*. While the government regards the reforms as consistent with, if not integral to, structural adjustment of the national economy, the thrust of the critics' argument seems to be that they are both likely to cost too much to implement and are unlikely to contribute to achieving the purposes for which structural adjustment loans were sought and provided.

[562] Niugini Nius, 12 July 1989. The issue is discussed in detail in Independent State of Papua New Guinea, Crisis in the North Solomons Province: Report of the Special Committee Appointed by the National Executive Council (Port Moresby: 1990).

[563] The text has been published in E P Wolfers (ed), Beyond the Border - Indonesia and Papua New Guinea, South-East Asia and the South Pacific: Discussion and Documentation (Waigani: UPNG, 1988), pp 177-82.

A more subtle form of external intervention in the internal affairs of Papua New Guinea comes from non-governmental organisations that seek to promote particular perspectives on the content of constitutional laws in the name of democracy, good government and human rights.

The detail and explicitness of Papua New Guinea's constitutional laws have also sometimes facilitated their use as instruments against certain perceptions of the national interest. Examples include criticism, on the alleged ground of unconstitutionality, of the National Government's record and policies in the Bougainville crisis, including the failure to seek an extension of a state of emergency.

CONSTITUTIONAL LAWS AS GUIDES TO GOVERNMENT POLICIES AND ACTIONS

It may not always be clear when a particular constitutional law is being used as an instrument of national interests, by way of providing a rationale for policies and actions based on quite different criteria, or as a guide to deliberate policy-making and implementation. The distinction may, in practice, often depend on perceptions of underlying intentions. The close resemblance that the National Goals and Directive Principles, in particular, have to important principles and developing bodies of international law (regarding respect for national sovereignty and sustainable use of the natural environment, for example) also makes it hard to be sure in some cases exactly which body of law, national or international, may be guiding state action.

However, the National Goals and Directive Principles have been repeatedly invoked in respect of various aspects of Papua New Guinea's foreign relations. The Initiative on Opportunity and Participation at the United Nations is one of many cases in point.[564] Even so, while bodies set up and persons appointed under constitutional laws are pledged to uphold them, and the courts are directed to take them into account, it is not possible to commence court action because of a claim that the National Goals and Directive Principles have not been followed (*Constitution*, s 25).

When claims are made that particular policies have been guided by Papua New Guinea's constitutional laws, critics (including outsiders) can again refer to the same laws in order to highlight areas in which the policies are alleged to fall short. Relevant instances include government policy and action in relation to human rights in Bougainville, and allegations concerning the unsustainable use of otherwise renewable resources, such as the nation's forests, fish stocks, supplies of drinking water, rivers and land.

FOREIGN RELATIONS AND THE PROTECTION AND PROMOTION OF CONSTITUTIONAL LAWS

It should come as no surprise to learn that official agencies responsible for the conduct of Papua New Guinea's foreign relations say and believe that they work to protect and promote national interests. (The only governments that do not make such claims are those whose foreign policies are determined by ideological, religious or ethnic considerations, or are acknowledged to be

[564] J Kaputin, Opportunity and Participation: A United Nations Initiative of the Government of Papua New Guinea (Port Moresby: Department of Foreign Affairs, 1993).

subject to overwhelming external pressure.) It should also not be surprising to learn that different individuals and groups may have different views of where national interests lie.[565]

The degree to which Papua New Guinea's initial foreign policy stance of "universalism" was motivated by general principle rather than national interest may be open to debate. But the *Foreign Policy White Paper* that has guided the conduct of the country's foreign relations since 1981 is quite clear in its emphasis on "Papua New Guinea's national interests" in giving effect to the basic approach recommended for foreign policy-making: active and selective engagement. National interests, it says:

> "need not be narrowly self-interested or crudely materialistic. Morally, they should not be. In practice, they cannot be. They should be defined in practical terms. They should be consistent with . . . human, financial, and other resources."

But national interests are the first consideration in foreign policy-making. While different individuals, groups and agencies have not always agreed over Papua New Guinea's national interests, it is striking how consistent successive governments have been, both in administering and in developing Papua New Guinea's foreign relations.

Foreign policy has only occasionally been an important public issue in national elections or in the Parliament in Papua New Guinea. Executive actions have rarely been subjected to serious, sustained criticism as a result of the provision allowing the Parliament to review treaties under s 117, or of the activities of the Permanent Parliamentary Committee responsible for foreign affairs.

Individuals and some non-governmental organisations have criticised government policy towards Indonesia, particularly as regards the political status of Irian Jaya and the treatment of refugees, French nuclear testing in the South Pacific, or perceived failures to prevent foreign investors from exploiting Papua New Guinea's natural resources and degrading the environment.

Officials and agencies within government have sometimes tried to propose or use international agreements in order to exert pressure on the government to enforce environmental protection standards or human rights. The risk they have taken is that their proposals may be criticised or rejected as instances of external attempts to intervene in Papua New Guinea's internal affairs. The Australian-initiated *Forestry Guidelines* approved by the South Pacific Forum in 1994 provide an example. So do efforts to have international organisations conduct first-hand investigations of the human rights situation in Bougainville.

Nevertheless, it seems to be generally accepted that the conduct of Papua New Guinea's foreign relations should be directed towards protecting and promoting national interests. Differences tend to be confined to the question of where Papua New Guinea's national interests lie, which interests come first (say, security or identification with other Melanesians), and whether and how national interests can be reconciled with other principles, such as self determination and respect for human rights. In an era when governance (often defined as implying democracy, respect for human rights, and honest, efficient, transparent and accountable public administration) is an increasingly prominent international issue, promoting Papua New Guinea's constitutional laws can be an important way of promoting vital national interests.

[565] Cf A Wolfers, Discord and Collaboration: Essays on International Relations (Baltimore: Johns Hopkins Press, 1962), pp 147-49.

The role played by the Department of Foreign Affairs in negotiating, managing and financing Papua New Guinea's participation in a wide variety of specialist, bilateral, regional and other international meetings can support exchanges involving a wide variety of institutions set up under constitutional laws. These range from the Parliament, through individual ministries, to independent offices, such as the judiciary, the Ombudsman Commission and the AuditorGeneral. As an example, legal co-operation, including judicial exchanges with Vanuatu, has helped to promote national interests as well as the reputation of Papua New Guinea's courts abroad.

Other areas in which National Government agencies have played important roles in safeguarding important national interests (including those embodied in the National Goals and Directive Principles) against outside influences and pressure are foreign aid, investment and migration, including employment. In these areas, national sovereignty is often the central issue, and the key to securing other goals and principles supported in and by constitutional laws. But, again, the degree to which government agencies actually serve or set the right priorities between competing national interests is a matter on which different segments of public opinion may disagree.

FOREIGN RELATIONS AND THE IMPLEMENTATION OF CONSTITUTIONAL LAWS

Since independence, the Department of Foreign Affairs and Trade has remained responsible for administering the citizenship provisions in the *Constitution,* even as its title and other functions have changed.

While the department and other government agencies often see themselves as implementing other elements of constitutional laws, including the National Goals and Directive Principles, their main activity has generally been to raise their images abroad, to secure the resources required to make them effective, and to protect them from unwelcome outside influences.

An area in which the Department of Foreign Affairs and Trade has played an important role in ensuring the effectiveness of other government policies and institutions is in negotiating arrangements that give decentralised units of government a role in administering the *Torres Strait Treaty* with Australia and the common border with Indonesia.[566] As with other parts of the national system of government, the Department has also provided support for provincial and local-level governmental activities abroad, including overseas visits.

FOREIGN RELATIONS AND THE DEVELOPMENT OF CONSTITUTIONAL LAWS

At a number of points, the *Constitution* seems to envisage that the agency or agencies responsible for Papua New Guinea's foreign relations, including diplomatic missions and consular posts abroad, might play an important role in shaping the development of constitutional laws, both directly and by forwarding relevant materials to the courts. In this respect, the Attorney-General's Department (and its predecessors) have often sent officials to represent Papua New Guinea in

[566] E P Wolfers, above n 6, at 149-52.

relevant committees of the United Nations General Assembly (although the practice seems to have lapsed in recent years).

Among the relevant constitutional provisions, s 39(3) invites the courts to have regard to a number of different sources of guidance in deciding what is "reasonably justifiable in a democratic society" in relation to qualified human rights. These sources include:

> "(b) the Charter of the United Nations; and
>
> (c) the Universal Declaration of Human Rights and any other declaration, recommendation or decision of the General Assembly of the United Nations concerning human rights and fundamental freedoms; and
>
> (d) the European Convention for the protection of Human Rights and Fundamental Freedoms and the Protocols thereto, and any other international conventions, agreements or declarations concerning human rights and fundamental freedoms; and
>
> (e) judgements, reports and opinions of the International Court of Justice, the European Commission of Human Rights, the European Court of Human Rights and other international courts and tribunals dealing with human rights and fundamental freedoms; and . . .
>
> (g) laws, practices and judicial decisions and opinions in other countries; and . . .
>
> (i) declarations by the International Commission of Jurists and other similar organizations."

The ambit of paragraph (c), in particular, is very broad. In effect, it gives the Department of Foreign Affairs and Trade, as well as Papua New Guinea's official representatives abroad, both the opportunity and the obligation to help shape materials that can be used as aids in interpreting the *Constitution*. At the same time, they could, of course, also participate in efforts to amend the *United Nations Charter and the Universal Declaration of Human Rights*.

Among other relevant provisions, the little-remarked references to "the rights and dignity of mankind" in s 39(1)-(2) may be of similar effect, insofar as this phrase is defined by documents which Papua New Guinean delegations can help to shape. Again, where Sch 2.1(2) refers to "the general principles of humanity" it may also give executive agencies responsible for Papua New Guinea's foreign relations a role in determining the extent to which customary law should be recognised. Who else would be better placed to help inform Papua New Guinean perceptions of such global issues (or at least to advise the government's lawyers) than the Department of Foreign Affairs and Trade, including the missions and posts abroad, particularly those accredited to the United Nations in New York and Geneva?

CONCLUSION

The preceding discussion does not exhaust the ways in which Papua New Guinea's foreign relations and constitutional laws may affect each other. Cases dealing with such diverse issues as foreign investment, migration, and the application of foreign judgments and laws show, in even greater detail, how they may in different circumstances reinforce each other, come into conflict, or simply leave gaps.

In addition to the detailed consideration given to Papua New Guinea's "international obligations" in the *Somare* case noted earlier, the courts have also referred to a number of international agreements, including some to which Papua New Guinea is not,[567] cannot be,[568] or was not at the time of judgment,[569] a party. They have also referred to international agreements of a technical kind, including the *Chicago Convention of the International Civil Aviation Organisation,* in a case where the judge referred to a policy "to maintain international standards in a setting where relatively little experienced staff of the necessary kind . . . is yet available from indigenous sources".[570]

Finally, it seems appropriate to recall that, following the constitution-making process, the Preamble to the *Constitution of the Independent State of Papua New Guinea* begins with the phrase: "We, the people of Papua New Guinea . . ." Twenty years later, with the World Bank and the International Monetary Fund pressing for structural adjustment, it seems somehow apt (if unfortunate) that the *Constitution* should still close with a list of laws adopted from other countries.[571] The main implication of the preceding analysis seems quite clear: experience both before and since independence shows that Papua New Guinea's foreign relations and constitutional laws can and do affect each other, both at home and abroad.

---

[567] See the references to the International Covenant on Civil and Political Rights in SCR No 2 of 1984 [1985] PNGLR 247 at 254.

[568] See the references to the European Convention of Human Rights in SCR No 2 of 1984 [1985] PNGLR 247 at 253, and in SC Application No 1 of 1985 [1985] PNGLR 430 at 435.

[569] See the references to the 1951 Convention Relating to the Status of Refugees, and the 1967 Protocol in SC Application No 1 of 1985 [1985] PNGLR 430 at 435, and to the United Nations Convention on the Law of the Sea in Chern Jin Fa v Naniura [1990] PNGLR 506 at 511.

[570] Costello v Controller of Civil Aviation (No 1) [1977] PNGLR 229 at 234. The Convention is cited at 244.

[571] Constitution, Sch 5.

Chapter 18

TREATY LAW-MAKING IN PAPUA NEW GUINEA: AFTER TWO DECADES YUMI STAP WE?

ERIC L KWA

INTRODUCTION

The art of treaty law-making is well settled in international law. The formulation and adoption of treaties are governed by established international rules and practices. Treaties may be global, regional or bilateral. It is one thing to accept a treaty in the international arena and it is another to apply it domestically. Different rules may regulate the application of a treaty at the domestic level. Even more so the applicability of a treaty to a member country may be unsuitable due to prevailing socio-economic and political circumstances. These existing circumstances may render a treaty inapplicable in the country.

The ability of a country to attend and participate in negotiations and the conclusion of a treaty may be enthusiastic and often indicate the country's willingness to address the issues at stake. However, this enthusiasm may be influenced by a number of factors, such as the need to attract sympathy of the other parties to the peculiar problems being confronted by the country,[572] the lack of bargaining power[573] or the need to flow with the tide.[574]

The aim of this chapter is to review the existing mechanism under the Papua New Guinea *Constitution* relating to treaty law-making and to ascertain how the mechanism has fared over the last 20 years. In the process of this review, the chapter highlights the struggle between the legislative and executive arms of government to gain control over this matter and shows that the constitutional framework on treaty law-making contains various loopholes which the executive has been able to utilise to entrench its power in this area of constitutional law.

INTERNATIONAL LAW ASPECTS OF TREATY LAW-MAKING

Any discussion on treaty law must begin with international law because it is on this plane that it derives its staturc. Treaties have been described as "an agreement between the governments of two or more states".[575] Treaties can also be concluded between the governments of states and

[572] The Lome Convention provides a good example.

[573] The arrangement between Australia and Papua New Guinea in the PACTRA agreement has been hailed as a fair agreement between these two countries. But a close examination of the agreement shows that Australia stands to benefit more than Papua New Guinea. And it is suggested that one of the main reasons why Papua New Guinea signed the agreement was because it did not have much bargaining power. See C Murphy, "Economic Duress and Unequal Treaties" (1970) 11 *Virginia Journal of International Law* 51.

[574] The events leading up to the Biodiversity Conference in Rio in 1992 illustrate this point. The smaller developing nations had to choose between joining the party, thus deriving benefits in the form of handouts from the developed nations in order to protect their environment, or miss out on these handouts by not joining the global community.

[575] R Bird, *Osborn's Concise Law Dictionary* (London: 7th ed, Sweet and Maxwell, 1983), p 328. In the Papua New Guinea context, see the definition as set out under s 117(1) of the *Constitution*. See also the definition under Article 2(2)(a) of the *Vienna Convention on the Law Of Treaties* 1969. This Convention codified the customary international law rules on treaties. The text of the Convention is set out in I Brownlie, *Basic Documents in International Law* (Oxford: 3rd ed, Clarendon Press, 1988), p 349.

international organisations. A treaty may be either multilateral or bilateral. The former involves the participation of more than two parties to the treaty while the latter is an agreement between only two parties.

A treaty can take a number of forms. It can be a single written document, or two or more related instruments, or take a particular form as designated by the parties.[576] The term is broad and does not require the precision of the philologist. This broad concept has been readily accepted by Papua New Guinea with minor variations.[577] After the conclusion of a treaty the parties to the agreement are required to indicate their consent to be bound by the treaty. This consent may be expressed by signature, exchange of instruments constituting a treaty, ratification, acceptance, approval, accession or by any means agreed to by the parties.[578] The multiplicity of methods expressing consent has introduced confusion into the law. For instance, Akehurst points out that signature, ratification and accession (adherence or adhesion) were the traditional methods of expressing consent. Today consent can also be expressed by exchange of notes, acceptance and approval.[579] The expansion of the methods of expressing consent, and their interchangeability, have deemed the prescription of form of expressing consent insignificant.

A treaty will come into force as soon as all the negotiating parties have expressed their consent to be bound by the treaty. Where it is practically difficult to obtain the consent of all negotiating parties, especially where many parties are involved, the treaty may specify the minimum number of consenting parties to enable the treaty to enter into force. A treaty once in force will apply in respect of the entire territory of the party state.[580]

On the domestic level, the implementation of a treaty depends on its status under municipal rules which may vary from one state to another. A state may become a party to the treaty either by signature, exchange of instruments constituting a treaty, ratification, acceptance, approval or accession, or by any means agreed to by the parties. As some commentators have pointed out in relation to the ratification process, "a treaty is an international agreement to which governments become parties by ratification in accordance with their own constitutional or statutory provisions".[581] By becoming a party, a state is bound by the treaty at international law. The process of domestic implementation occurs by a subsequent statutory adoption.[582]

---

[576] Article 2(1)(a) of the *Vienna Convention on the Law of Treaties* 1969.
[577] *Constitution*, s 117(1).
[578] *Vienna Convention on the Law of Treaties* 1969, Article 11. For a simplified explanation of the operation of the Convention, see M Akehurst, *A Modern Introduction to International Law* (London: 6th ed, Allen and Unwin, 1987).
[579] M Akehurst, above n 7, p 129.
[580] *Vienna Convention on the Law of Treaties* 1969, Article 29.
[581] K Burke, S Coliver, C De La Vega, and S Rosenbaum, "Application of International Human Rights Law in State and Federal Courts" (1983) 18 *Texas International Law Journal* 291 at 295. However, the practice of becoming a party by ratification is different from that of a state adopting treaties to form part of its municipal laws.
[582] As an example, see s 117(7)-(8) of the Papua New Guinea *Constitution*. This section is discussed in detail below.

THE CONSTITUTIONAL PLANNING COMMITTEE REPORT

An examination of the Papua New Guinea *Constitution* cannot be divorced from the work of the Constitutional Planning Committee (CPC), for it is in the CPC's Final Report that one finds the true meaning of the constitutional provisions which were to be a reflection of the people's aspirations.

The CPC was established by the House of Assembly on 23 June 1972. It was required "to make recommendations for a *Constitution* for full internal self-government in a united Papua New Guinea with a view to eventual independence".[583] The CPC began its task with enthusiasm. After 22 months of consultation with the people at more than 100 public meetings, and receipt of over 2,000 submissions, the CPC finally submitted its report to the Chief Minister on 13 August 1974.

In its attempt to formulate a truly autochthonous constitution,[584] the CPC did not follow any firm precedent. Instead, it borrowed a variety of ideas from the world's constitutions and transformed these ideas to "meet Papua New Guinean needs and circumstances".[585]

On the subject of treaties the CPC made the following observation:

> "[W]e believe that it is desirable also that the National Parliament should have some say as to whether or not our country should enter into proposed treaties or other international agreements, conventions or acts which give rise to rights or obligations on the part of Papua New Guineans in international law."[586]

The CPC wanted to ensure that any international agreement that gave rights or obligations to Papua New Guinea was sanctioned only by the Parliament. This proposed arrangement was intended to emphasise the power of the legislature to make laws for the peace, progress and welfare of Papua New Guinea.[587] It is suggested that this arrangement is envisaged to have a twofold effect: first, to restrain any state authority from entering into any formal agreement or agreements with another country or other countries or international institutions which may not be in the best interests of Papua New Guinea and, secondly, to strengthen the supervisory role of the legislature[588] over the executive arm of the government. It will, however, be seen below that what eventually transpired in the *Constitution* defeats the visions of the CPC.

The CPC recommended that the Parliament be given eight days to decide whether or not to allow the National Executive Council (NEC) to enter into a treaty, convention, agreement or an act after it had been tabled in Parliament. It went further by recommending that where the decision for Papua New Guinea either to enter into or not to enter into a treaty, convention or agreement was urgent, the Speaker (on behalf of Parliament) and the Prime Minister could make that decision. In

---

583 CPC, *Final Report of the Constitutional Planning Committee: Part 1* (Port Moresby: Government Printer, 1974), p iv.

584 For a discussion of the autochthony of the *Constitution*, see J Goldring, *The Constitution of Papua New Guinea* (Sydney: Law Book Company, 1978), p 27.

585 CPC, above n 12, p 1/2.

586 Ibid, p 6/7.

587 *Constitution*, s 109.

588 The supervisory role of the legislature over the executive was clearly pronounced by the Supreme Court in *Haiveta v Wingti (No 3)* [1994] PNGLR 197.

that case, the only requirement was to be a certificate jointly signed by the Speaker and the Prime Minister confirming the urgency of the matter.[589]

The second component of the CPC's recommendation was an attempt to preserve the right of the executive arm of the government to perform its executive functions. However, the performance of those functions would be limited by the involvement of the Speaker (who is the representative of the Parliament) in the determination of the issue of dispensing with the consent of Papua New Guinea to be bound by a treaty, convention or agreement.

The CPC's recommendations highlight some of the complexities in this area. The difficulty of dealing with this subject is reflected vividly by the constitutional provisions relating to treaties, to be discussed below.

THE PAPUA NEW GUINEA CONSTITUTION

Consent to treaties

The recommendations of the CPC transpired in s 117 of the *Constitution*. There are four other provisions of the *Constitution* that also deal with treaties. However, three of these provisions deal specifically with two short matters on treaties, while the fourth creates a synthesis of the treaty law-making process in Papua New Guinea. The four provisions will be examined in the next segment of this chapter. At this juncture it is appropriate to deal firstly with s 117, which primarily deals with treaties. Its eight subsections make it one of the longest provisions of the *Constitution.* The vital elements of this provision are subss (2), (3), and (5) which are set out in full below:

> "(2) Subject to Subsection (3), the consent of Papua New Guinea to be bound as a party to a treaty may be given only –
>
> (a) by the Head of State, acting with, and in accordance with, the advice of the National Executive Council; or
>
> (b) by a Minister authorised either generally or specifically for the purpose by the Head of State, acting with, and in accordance with, the advice of the National Executive Council; or
>
> (c) otherwise in accordance with international law, usage and practice,
>
> and in accordance with this section.
>
> (3) Subject to Subsection (5), the consent of Papua New Guinea to be bound as a party to a treaty shall not be given –
>
> (a) unless a treaty document relating to the treaty has been presented to Parliament for at least ten sitting days; or
>
> (b) if within ten sitting days of the Parliament after the day on which the treaty document was presented to the Parliament the Parliament, by an absolute majority vote, disapproves the giving of the consent.

[589] CPC, above n 12, p 6/25.

(5) Subsection (3) does not apply if –

(a) the Parliament has, by an absolute majority vote, waived the requirements of that subsection; or

(b) both the Speaker (acting on behalf of Parliament) and the Prime Minister are satisfied that the giving of the consent of Papua New Guinea to be bound as a party to the treaty is too urgent a matter to allow of compliance with that subsection, or that compliance would not be in the national interest."

Subsection (2) stipulates that the consent of Papua New Guinea to be bound by a treaty may be given only by the Head of State acting with and in accordance with the advice of the NEC, or by the Minister authorised for that purpose acting with and in accordance with the advice of the NEC, or otherwise in accordance with international law, usage and practice. Subsection (2) is, however, subject to subs (3). Subsection (3) expressly states that the consent of Papua New Guinea to be bound by a treaty cannot, subject to the exception in subs (3)(b), be given unless the treaty document[590] is presented to Parliament for at least 10 sitting days.

Subsection (3) is, however, subject to subs (5). Subsection (5) allows for two situations that can bypass the stringent requirements of subs (3). First, the Parliament may by an absolute majority vote waive the requirements of the provision. Secondly, if both the Speaker (on behalf of the Parliament) and the Prime Minister are satisfied that the giving of consent of Papua New Guinea to be bound as a party to the treaty is a sufficiently urgent matter, they can dispense with the requirements of subs (3).

A number of observations can be made. First, subs (3) only requires the presentation of the treaty document to Parliament. Contrary to what the CPC recommended, there is no requirement that Parliament give consent to a treaty. Instead, a treaty is assumed to have been approved by Parliament, unless by an absolute majority it disapproves the giving of consent. It would follow that Parliament can give its consent by a simple majority vote or by other lesser methods of giving consent.

Secondly, where Parliament does not give its consent within the required period, the treaty document can be presented again to Parliament at any time after the lapse of the 10 sitting days.[591]

Thirdly, it is suggested that s 117 contains two huge loopholes by which the executive has usurped power from the legislature. The first is contained in subs (3), which in a roundabout way requires that so long as the treaty document is presented to Parliament for noting within 10 sitting days, Papua New Guinea is bound by a treaty which has been signed by the Head of State acting on the advice of the NEC (or a Minister authorised for that purpose acting on such advice) or otherwise in accordance with the rules of international law, usage and practice. The second is contained in subs (5), which essentially creates an escape route for the executive to abate the requirements under subs (3).

---

590 The term "treaty document" is defined in s 117(1) to mean: "(a) the text of a treaty that it is proposed to accept or to ratify; or (b) a statement of the effect of such a treaty; or (c) a copy of the document by which it is intended that Papua New Guinea will express its consent to be bound by such a treaty."

591 *Constitution*, s 117(4).

This point is important as it sheds some light on the current practices within the administrative organs responsible for the implementation of some of the treaties and the prevailing attitude of the legislature in dealing with this subject matter.

Subsection (6) stipulates that a certificate of the Speaker as to any matter arising under the section is, before all courts and before all persons acting judicially, conclusive evidence of the facts certified to. This provision is very broad and covers all parliamentary proceedings relating to treaties under s 117. This subsection deviates from the original recommendation of the CPC. The CPC strongly pointed out that the certificate should only be used if the second option under subs (5)(b) was employed by the Speaker of Parliament and the Prime Minister. The CPC's recommendation on the issuance of a certificate was therefore limited to the process under subs (5)(b). As it is, the requirement was omitted from subs (5). It is unclear why it was left out. Subsection (6) is probably an attempt to rectify this problem. However, it falls short of clearly spelling out when a certificate from the Speaker is required. And, secondly, it creates an opportunity for abuse by the executive, especially in Papua New Guinea where the Speaker is usually from the same political grouping that forms the executive government.

Subsection (8), in unambiguous terms, stipulates that the mere fact that Parliament has dispensed with its consent for Papua New Guinea to be bound by a treaty does not give that treaty the status of a municipal law. Subsection (7) takes it further by stating that a treaty by which Papua New Guinea is bound does not become part of the domestic law unless it has been given the status of an Act of Parliament or a Constitutional Law.[592]

Visiting forces arrangements

There are four other provisions of the *Constitution* that deal with different aspects of treaty law in Papua New Guinea. These are ss 202, 205, 206 and 273. Sections 202, 205 and 206 deal with, among other things, the engagement of Papua New Guinea Defence Force soldiers in fulfilling Papua New Guinea's international obligations. Section 202 spells out the functions of the Defence Force, which include: (1) to assist in the fulfilment of Papua New Guinea's international obligations, and (2) to perform, as directed, civil functions either within or outside Papua New Guinea in accordance with the *Constitution* or an Act of the Parliament.[593] Section 205 prescribes the procedures for committing the Defence Force for active service. For our purposes, the relevant part of s 205 is subs (2)(b), which says in substance that the Defence Force may not be ordered on, or committed to, an international peacekeeping or relief operation outside the country without the prior approval of Parliament. Sections 202 and 205 must be read together.

Section 206 deals specifically with the presence in the country of a foreign force and the presence abroad of Papua New Guinea soldiers. It states that an Act of the Parliament may provide for the presence in the country, by arrangement with the National Executive, of forces of another country,[594] and the presence in another country of the Defence Force or part of the Defence Force.[595]

[592] Some of the treaties that have been converted into ordinary Acts of Parliament are contained in Appendix A.
[593] See *Defence Act* (Ch 74).
[594] The relevant Act is the *Defence (Visiting Forces) Act* (Ch 77).

[595] See *Defence (Presence Abroad) Act* 1980.

The Papua New Guinea *Constitution* was formulated at a time when there were a number of armed conflicts being experienced around the globe and the United Nations was playing a greater role as the global peacekeeper. It was against this background that ss 202, 205(2)(b) and 206 were formulated. The CPC was aware of the possibility of engaging Papua New Guinean soldiers in some peacekeeping activities of the United Nations in the future.[596] The CPC was mindful of the dangers of vesting the power to commit Papua New Guinean soldiers in international engagements in the hands of a mere handful of people, by recommending that Papua New Guinean soldiers should not participate in peacekeeping or relief operations unless these international obligations arose under a treaty considered and approved by Parliament. Section 202(a) omits the term "treaty". This omission proved fatal, as was highlighted in the case of *SCR No 4 of 1980 (No 2); Re Petition of M T Somare* [1982] PNGLR 65.

The brief facts of the case were as follows. In the middle of 1980 there was an exchange of letters between Fr Walter Lini, the Chief Minister of the then condominium of New Hebrides, and Mr Julius Chan, the Prime Minister of Papua New Guinea. By his letter, Fr Lini requested the Papua New Guinea Government to assist his government by providing military and police assistance (as from the date of Vanuatu's independence) to maintain law and order. In reply to this request, the Papua New Guinea Prime Minister gave an undertaking that Papua New Guinea would positively deal with the request.

The government then, through the Head of State, recalled Parliament to consider the request from Fr Lini. Consequently, the *Defence Force (Presence Abroad) Act* 1980 was passed by Parliament, paving the way for the deployment of part of the Papua New Guinea Defence Force to Vanuatu. The then leader of the Papua New Guinea Opposition, Mr Michael Somare, petitioned the Supreme Court to declare that the deployment of Papua New Guinean soldiers to Vanuatu was unconstitutional, as it was inconsistent with ss 202 and 205, and that the 1980 Act was unconstitutional, and so was null and void. After a lengthy court proceeding the Supreme Court refused to make the declarations as sought by Mr Somare, principally on the ground that the troops had already returned home.

For our purposes, the two relevant issues were: (1) whether or not the deployment of Papua New Guinean soldiers to Vanuatu was based on an existing international obligation as recognised by ss 202 and 205 of the *Constitution*; and (2) if there was an international obligation, what was the nature of that international obligation?

The petitioner argued that according to the facts there was no international obligation as recognised under ss 202 and 205 existing at the time the soldiers were deployed to Vanuatu. He also argued that the exchange of letters between Fr Lini and the Papua New Guinea Prime Minister did not amount to an international obligation as recognised under international law. The Principal Legal Adviser argued to the contrary. On the second issue, the Principal Legal Adviser argued that the exchange of letters between the two leaders did create an international obligation.

Of the five judges,[597] Kidu CJ concluded that the exchange of letters did not create an international obligation, and as a result no international obligation as recognised under the *Constitution* existed at the time of the deployment of the soldiers to Vanuatu. Kapi J agreed with Kidu CJ, but went further by stating that the exchange of letters was a mere request, and as there

[596] CPC, above n 12, p 13/5.
[597] Kidu CJ, Kearney Dep CJ, Greville Smith, Kapi and Miles JJ.

was no international obligation as recognised by international law and consequently the *Constitution,* an Act of Parliament under s 205 could not remedy the anomaly. Kearney Dep CJ refused to comment on these two issues. Greville Smith J took the same approach on the issues as Kearney Dep CJ, but came to the simple conclusion that as the petitioner had not proven that no international obligation existed at the time of the deployment of the soldiers to Vanuatu, he was not prepared to take the matter further. Miles J reached the same conclusion as Greville Smith J.

Kapi J and Miles J were the only members of the court to discuss these two issues in detail. Miles J gave the major judgment, which was agreed with in part by the other three judges. The discussion of these two principal issues by Kapi J and Miles J was similar, but as noted above they reached different conclusions. An analysis of the two judgments reveals a number of important points that help us to understand the operation of the three main sections discussed in this case; namely, ss 117, 202 and 205. These points are:

(1) An international obligation must be recognised by international law.

(2) An international obligation can be created by a treaty or by any other means recognised in international law.

(3) There is a connection between ss 117, 202 and 205.

(4) Any international obligation must be approved by Parliament.

(5) The Prime Minister has no power to commit Papua New Guinean soldiers in an international engagement.

(6) The functions of the Defence Force under s 202 are exhaustive.

(7) Section 205 is only procedural, and does not expand the functions of the Defence Force.

(8) The absence of an international obligation as recognised by s 202 cannot be rectified by an Act of the Parliament.

A point strongly argued by the Principal Legal Adviser was that the definition of international obligation was to be as determined by the executive. Of the five judges, only Kapi J and Kidu CJ specifically rejected this argument. Kearney Dep CJ was silent on this issue, while Greville Smith J and Miles J agreed with some reluctance with the proposition of the Principal Legal Adviser. Miles J went further by introducing a new formulation concerning the nature of an international obligation, which it is suggested will create a lot of uncertainty in the future. After considering the speeches of the Papua New Guinea Prime Minister to Parliament, Miles J stated:

> "At the least [the speeches] are statements of principles of foreign policy based on moral and political considerations; at the most they may amount to a recognition by the government of some sort of legal or quasi-legal obligation to Vanuatu. Taken as a whole they fall somewhere between the two . . .
>
> This sense of obligation derives not merely from what was seen as in Papua New Guinea's own interest: a similar obligation would have been seen by the government to rest on any nation in Papua New Guinea's position in the light of the relationship between the two countries concerned and of the understanding reached between their

> leaders. To that extent I think it would be impossible for this court to be satisfied that no international obligation existed."[598]

What Miles J has introduced is a scale for measuring the activities of the executive on the international front, but without specifying the parameters upon which these activities can be measured. It is submitted that this formulation is wrong. The very essence of the formulation defeats the spirit of the constitutional framework on treaty law-making in Papua New Guinea as envisaged by the CPC. The assessment lacks any appreciation of the concerns raised by the CPC. The CPC was very cautious about leaving open too wide a room for the executive to operate in. It tried to define the boundaries of executive power so as to limit the possible abuse of that power by the executive (as was evidenced in the above case). In the overall picture, the CPC wanted the legislature to maintain its supervisory role over the executive. This point was clearly highlighted by Kapi J, when he said that in Papua New Guinea only the Head of State can commit Papua New Guinea to international obligations with the approval of Parliament.[599] The Prime Minister (and the NEC) has no such power.

It is also submitted that the reasoning of Miles J, on this aspect of his judgment, is confusing. Having tried to explain the terms "obligation" and "international", he then concluded that an international obligation exists between Papua New Guinea and another state whereby its interaction with that state or other states is recognised in international law as creating an international obligation. He also concluded that Papua New Guinea had to develop its own system of international law on this and other matters, based on its interactions with other states in the international community. By following this analysis he finally concluded that Papua New Guinea did have an international obligation to Vanuatu based on the transactions that transpired between the two leaders. Commenting on this aspect of the court's decision, Brunton and Colquhoun-Kerr suggested:

> "[I]t is clear that an international obligation cannot be constituted by a mere request from another nation for military assistance followed by Papua New Guinea's agreement to provide that aid . . . It must be an international obligation, the nature of which is recognised by international law."[600]

As stated, Miles J's conclusion deviates from the spirit of the *Constitution* espoused by ss 117, 202 and 205, which vest the Parliament with a supervisory role over the executive arm of government.

Section 206 creates a possible confusion. On the one hand it regulates bilateral agreements concerning the presence of armed forces of another country in Papua New Guinea and vice versa. These agreements are in their very nature bilateral treaties. On the other hand these agreements are not regarded as treaties by the *Constitution*. Section 117(1), which defines the meaning of the term "treaty", excludes from its ambit visiting forces agreements under s 206. This matter has been left to the NEC. It is suggested that the exclusion by s 117(1) of agreements envisaged by s 206 exempts those agreements from the purported stringent requirements of s 117. Where then do we place visiting forces agreements? It is submitted that on the international plane these agreements will be deemed as treaties, but on the domestic plane they will not obtain that label

---

[598] [1982] PNGLR 65 at 87 and 88

[599] Ibid at 79.

[600] B Brunton and D Colquhoun-Kerr, *The Annotated Constitution of Papua New Guinea* (Port Moresby: UPNG Press, 1984), p 427.

per se. A number of issues of public international law and private international law may arise. However, it is not necessary or possible to deal with those issues in this discussion.

Since independence there have been three visiting forces agreements. The first is the *Agreement Between Papua New Guinea and Australia regarding Status of Forces of each State in the Territory of the Other State*, which was concluded in 1977. The second is the 1980 *Interim Agreement Between the Government of Papua New Guinea and the Government of Vanuatu concerning the Status of Elements of the Papua New Guinea Defence Force in Vanuatu.* The third is the *Papua New Guinea - Indonesia Agreement Regarding the Status of Forces of Each Other in the Territory of the Other State* concluded in 1992.

As noted, the deployment of troops to Vanuatu was challenged by Michael Somare in the case of *SCR No 4 of 1980 (No 2); Re Petition of M T Somare* [1982] PNGLR 65, and the Supreme Court refused to make a declaration as to the constitutionality of that deployment of soldiers. The Supreme Court, however, by majority, agreed that the functions of the Defence Force under s 202 are exhaustive. No other sections of the *Constitution* impose any other functions on the Defence Force. As to the operation of ss 202(b) and 205, Kapi J held that the existence of an international obligation is a condition precedent to the deployment of soldiers in international engagements.[601] Where no international obligation exists, this cannot be remedied by an Act of the Parliament. It is submitted that the judgment of Kapi J on this issue is correct.

Pre-independence treaties

Section 273 relates to pre-independence treaties. This section preserved Papua New Guinea's treaty obligations that immediately prior to independence applied to the Territory of Papua and New Guinea. These obligations were deemed to apply for a period not exceeding five years.[602] At independence it was estimated that over 200 bilateral, and about the same number of multilateral, treaties applied or extended to Papua New Guinea.[603]

The provision required the Head of State (after receiving advice from the NEC) to make a declaration spelling out those treaties that were binding on Papua New Guinea. To this end the Head of State made a declaration to that effect on 7 October 1975. This practice was consistent with contemporary international rules on state succession, and put to rest in Papua New Guinea the issue of the "clean slate" theory.[604]

A large number of treaties have been accepted, acceded to or ratified by Papua New Guinea. A number of them predate independence while the rest were accepted, acceded to or ratified after 16 September 1975. The questions that now face us are: How has treaty law-making fared over the last 20 years? Has Parliament or the NEC complied with the constitutional framework? Has Papua New Guinea been able to cope with its international obligations under the treaties to which it is a party? These and other issues are considered immediately below.

---

601 [1982] PNGLR 65 at 77.

602 This provision finds its roots in a declaration to the Acting Secretary-General of the United Nations in 1961 by the government of Tanzania. The declaration was to the effect that all treaties validly entered into on behalf of the territory of Tanganyika by the United Kingdom would apply to the independent state of Tanzania for a period of two years from the date of its independence: see I Brownlie, *Principles of Public International Law* (Oxford: 4th ed, Oxford University Press, 1990), p 671.

603 Papua New Guinea Department of Foreign Affairs and Trade, *Treaty List (No 2)* (Port Moresby, Department of Foreign Affairs, 1991), p 2. The author of the document mentions that most of those treaties were not relevant to Papua New Guinea.

604 The essence of the theory is that an emerging state is not bound by the treaties of its predecessor sovereign.

TWENTY YEARS OF TREATY LAW-MAKING UNDER THE CONSTITUTION

On 7 October 1975, Papua New Guinea acquired certain rights and obligations under a number of multilateral and bilateral treaties, which were entered into on its behalf by Australia.[605] By virtue of a principle of state succession, Papua New Guinea was not legally bound by those treaties.[606] The parties to those treaties were also not bound to accept a new party.[607] However, to comply with modern trends in international law, Papua New Guinea adopted the procedure under s 273. A review was conducted by the Department of Foreign Affairs to identify those treaties that were not relevant to Papua New Guinea and for which consent was to be withdrawn. Appendix D contains a list of those treaties.

The five-year grace period allowed under s 273 expired on 15 September 1980. To comply with the requirements of this provision, the Governor-General formally advised the Secretary-General of the United Nations on 24 September 1980 that Papua New Guinea would not from that date be bound by those treaties to which it had not succeeded.[608] It would follow that of the large number of treaties (about 400) that were succeeded to on 16 September 1975, only those that Papua New Guinea had specifically succeeded to by 15 September 1980 apply to Papua New Guinea. It is significant to note that s 273 became inoperative on 16 September 1980.

Ratification of treaties since 1975 has proceeded in accordance with s 117. The current and past practice has been merely to table the treaty documents in Parliament and request the Parliament to take note of them. A major cause of concern is the frequent use of the escape route under s 117(5)(b) by the executive branch of government to avoid the scrutiny of Parliament as contemplated by s 117(3).

The administration of treaties is usually the responsibility of the Department of Foreign Affairs. The day-to-day management of Papua New Guinea's treaty relationships is vested in the Treaty and Legal Branch of the Department of Foreign Affairs. Treaties that relate to credit and loans are managed by the Department of Finance. Other treaty obligations are shared between the Department of Foreign Affairs and other government agencies such as the Department of Defence.

For instance, the Defence Force in collaboration with the Department of Foreign Affairs supervises the implementation of the existing visiting forces agreements concluded pursuant to s 206 of the *Constitution*. Currently there are two. These are the agreements previously mentioned between Papua New Guinea and Australia (concluded on 26 January 1977), and between Papua New Guinea and Indonesia (concluded in 1992). The visiting forces agreement between Papua New Guinea and Vanuatu (signed on 15 August 1980) was a self-executing agreement, to expire after 180 days. The agreement therefore expired in February 1981.

Some of the treaties that have the force of municipal laws are administered by specific government instrumentalities. For instance, the policing of the *Dumping of Wastes at Sea Act* (Ch 369) and the *Prevention of Pollution of the Sea Act* (Ch 371) are the responsibility of the

[605] Appendix B contains a list of some of these treaties.
[606] These treaties do not form part of municipal law: see *Costello v Controller of Civil Aviation (No 1)* [1977] PNGLR 229 at 236.
[607] As an illustration see Appendix C, which sets out a list of some countries with which Australia had an extradition treaty prior to Papua New Guinea's independence. Following Papua New Guinea's independence, however, those countries refused to consider themselves bound by those treaties in relation to Papua New Guinea.
[608] Brownlie, above n 31, p 4.

Transport Department; the *International Trade (Fauna and Flora) Act* (Ch 391) and the *Environmental Contaminants (Amendment) Act* 1994[609] are administered by the Department of Environment and Conservation.

An outsider will easily commend Papua New Guinea on the performance of its treaty law-making program. However, a closer examination of the process in Papua New Guinea will reveal a number of disturbing factors.

First, one will find that Papua New Guinea is a strong advocate of global co-operation. Its involvement in numerous international conferences and acceptance of international obligations under many treaties is a reflection of this. The unfortunate thing is that Papua New Guinea has not been able effectively to fulfil these obligations. This failure can be attributed to a number of factors. These are:

(a) lack of political will;[610]

(b) lack of funds;[611]

(c) lack of expert personnel; and

(d) lack of co-ordination between the implementing agencies.[612] These problems are interrelated and endemic in the public sector.

Secondly, a review of the relevant treaties indicate that some of the treaties are either not in the interests of Papua New Guinea or are not relevant to Papua New Guinea.[613] Thirdly, many of these treaties require immediate to long-term policy and legislative changes at the domestic level. Papua New Guinea has not been able to comply with these conditions.[614] The issue is: what will happen to Papua New Guinea's international standing in view of this situation?

A number of other factors[615] that have contributed to the non-implementation of many of our international obligations are quite transparent and need no mention here. The treaty law-making process in Papua New Guinea over the last two decades can be described as "too much writing with less walking".

---

[609] Act No 16 of 1994. The amendment was required to enable Papua New Guinea to comply with its obligation under the *Vienna Convention for the Protection of the Ozone Layer* 1985 and the *Montreal Protocol on Substances that Deplete the Ozone Layer* 1987.

[610] Lack of political will is an entrenched problem in Papua New Guinea. Papua New Guinean politicians show a lot of enthusiasm in concluding treaties. However, after a treaty is signed and ratified that zeal is no longer there. The political pressure which was persistent before the signing and ratification of the treaty tends subsequently to fade away: personal communication with Jimmy Bokomi, an officer of the Department of Foreign Affairs.

[611] This is a two-pronged problem. First, the country lacks the necessary funds effectively to implement at home its treaty obligations. Secondly, the country lacks the funds to meet its international annual financial obligations under relevant treaties thath require financial contributions from member countries.

[612] For instance, Papua New Guinea ratified the *Convention on the Rights of the Child* 1989 on 1 March 1993. Under Article 44 of the Convention, member countries are required to submit a Country Report within two years of ratification. For this purpose, a Joint Working Committee was initiated by the Department of Foreign Affairs in 1996, with members from the Department of Foreign Affairs, Department of Education, Department of Home Affairs, Youth and Religion, Attorney-General's Department, the Child Welfare Office and the Department of Health. The initiative never in fact got off the ground. The Department of Home Affairs, Youth and Religion is planning to resurrect the Joint Working Group. This is only one example of the many initiatives involving various departments that have stalled over the years.

[613] For example, the *Antarctic Treaty* acceded to by Papua New Guinea on 16 March 1981, the *Treaty on the Principles Governing the Activities of States in the Exploration and the Use of Outer Space Including the Moon and Other Celestial Bodies* acceded to by Papua New Guinea on 16 March 1981; and the 1963 *Treaty Banning Nuclear Weapons Tests in the Atmosphere, in Outer Space and Underwater*, which was acceded to on 13 January 1982.

[614] For instance, Papua New Guinea has bilateral agreements with a number of South Pacific Island countries (for example, Fiji, Tonga, Tuvalu, Cook Islands and Kiribati), called Technical Co-operation Agreements. Under these treaties, Papua New Guinea is required to draw up programs on matters such as training and exchange of professional personnel to assist these countries where they lack the relevant expertise. To date, Papua New Guinea has not drawn up these programs to fulfil its treaty obligations.

[615] This includes bureaucratic "red tape", indifference and lack of commitment by public servants to duties associated with the implementation of the agreements, and generally poor working conditions and lack of appropriate office equipment and other technical back-up facilities.

CONCLUSION

The CPC viewed Papua New Guinea's international relations as very important and therefore recommended that Parliament should actively take on the role of treaty law-making. The CPC proposals laid the foundation for the development of a system of treaty-making in international law that was appropriate for Papua New Guinean circumstances. The proposals recognised the existing rules and the principles of international law governing treaties, and sought to modify them to suit the Papua New Guinean circumstances. The constitutional provisions pertaining to treaty law-making has to a large extent diminished this vision.

The CPC vision was abandoned by the Constituent Assembly, as is reflected in ss 117 and 206. These provisions have effectively weakened the supervisory role of the legislature over the executive. The executive over-reacted with this newly found power when it committed Papua New Guinean troops to Vanuatu in 1980 for peacekeeping duties. The Supreme Court was reluctant to make any declarations as to the constitutionality of this exercise in the *SCR No 4 of 1980 (No 2)* case ([1982] PNGLR 65). Two views have emerged from that case in relation to treaty law-making: those of Kapi J and Miles J. It is suggested that the view of Kapi J is correct, as it captures and re-establishes the vision of the CPC. The views of Miles J on this subject should be rejected.

The pressing issue that requires consideration is: how do we strengthen the traditional role of the legislature on this important matter? It is suggested that Papua New Guinea must recapture the visions of the CPC. To this end, the loopholes within the constitutional provisions as highlighted above need to be rectified.

Papua New Guinea is fortunate that it has not yet experienced another fiasco similar to the one in 1980. It is in this malleable situation that Papua New Guinea has to take stock of its constitutional framework pertaining to treaty law-making.

APPENDIX A

Some of the treaties that have the status of municipal laws in Papua New Guinea are:

Convention	Act of Parliament
1. *International Convention for the Regulation of Whaling*	*Whaling Act* (Ch 225)
2. *Convention on International Trade in Endangered Species of Wild Fauna and Flora* (CITES)	*International Trade (Fauna and Flora) Act* (CITES Act) (Ch 391)
3. *Convention on International Civil Aviation (Chicago Convention)*	*Civil Aviation Act* (Ch 239)
4. *International Convention on the Prevention of Marine Pollution by Dumping of Wastes and Other Matter*	*Dumping of Wastes at Sea Act* (Ch 369)
5. *Ozone Convention*	*Environmental Contaminants (Amendment) Act* 1994
6. *Vienna Convention on Diplomatic Relations*	*Diplomatic and Consular Privileges and Immunities Act* (Ch 83)
7. *Convention on the Continental Shelf*	*Continental Shelf (Living Natural Resources) Act* (Ch 210) [repealed in 1994 by *Fisheries Act* 1994]
8. *Agreement between Australia and Indonesia concerning Certain Boundaries between Papua New Guinea and Indonesia*	*Indonesia Border Agreement Act* (Ch 85)
9. *Articles of Agreement of the International Monetary Fund*	*International Financial Organisations Act* (Ch 86)

APPENDIX B

This appendix contains a list of some of the treaties that Australia concluded with other countries and to which Papua New Guinea acceded, or succeeded, after independence. The list is not exhaustive.

(1) *Convention between Great Britain and the Netherlands Defining Boundaries in New Guinea* (The Hague, 16 May 1895)*

(2) *Agreement Between the Government of the Commonwealth of Australia and the Government of the Republic of Indonesia Establishing Certain Seabed Boundaries* (Canberra, 18 May 1971)*

(3) *Agreement between Australia and Indonesia concerning Certain Boundaries Between Papua New Guinea and Indonesia* (Jakarta, 12 February 1973)*

(4) *International Telecommunications Convention and Additional Protocol* (Malaga–Torremollinos, 25 October 1973) (Papua New Guinea acceded to this treaty on 31 October 1973 and it became effective in Papua New Guinea on the same date.)

(5) *Convention of the World Meteorological Organisation* (Washington, 11 October 1947) (Papua New Guinea acceded to this treaty on 15 December 1975.)

(6) *Convention on International Trade in Endangered Species of Wild Fauna and Flora* (Washington, 3 March 1973) (Papua New Guinea acceded to this treaty on 12 December 1975.)

(7) *Convention on International Civil Aviation* (Chicago, 7 December 1944) (Papua New Guinea adhered to the treaty and the Protocol on 15 December 1975.)

(8) *Convention for the Unification of Certain Rules Relating to International Carriage by Air* (Warsaw, 12 October 1929) (Papua New Guinea succeeded to the treaty on 11 December 1975.)

(9) *Convention Supplementary to the Warsaw Convention for the Unification of Certain Rules Relating to International Carriage by Air Performed by Person Other than the Contracting Carrier* (Guadalajara, 18 September 1961) (Papua New Guinea succeeded to the treaty on 3 December 1975.)

(10) *Convention on Damage Caused by Foreign Aircraft to Third Parties on the Surface* (Rome, 7 October 1952) (Papua New Guinea succeeded to the treaty on 31 December 1975.)

(11) *Convention on Offences and Certain Other Acts Committed on Board Aircraft* (Tokyo, 14 September 1963) (Papua New Guinea succeeded to the treaty on 31 December 1975.)

(12) *Convention for the Suppression of Unlawful Seizure of Aircraft* (The Hague, 16 December 1970) (Papua New Guinea succeeded to the treaty on 4 December 1975.)

(13) *Convention for the Suppression of Unlawful Acts Against Safety of Civil Aviation* (Montreal, 23 September 1971) (Papua New Guinea succeeded to the treaty on 4 December 1975.)

(14) *Convention on the Privileges and Immunities of the United Nations* (London, and adopted by the General Assembly of the United Nations on 13 February 1946) (Papua New Guinea succeeded to the treaty on 4 December 1975.)

(15) *Convention on Diplomatic Relations* (Vienna, 18 April 1961) (Papua New Guinea succeeded to the treaty on 4 December 1975.)

(16) *Convention on Consular Relations* (Vienna, 24 April 1963) (Papua New Guinea succeeded to the treaty on 4 December 1975.)

(17) *Constitution of the World Health Organisation* (as amended) (New York, 22 July 1946) (Papua New Guinea accepted the treaty on 29 April 1976 and became a full member of the World Health Organisation on the same date.)

(18) *Geneva Convention for the Amelioration of the Condition of the Wounded and Sick in Armies in the Field* (Geneva, 27 July 1929) (Papua New Guinea succeeded to the treaty on 26 May 1976.)

* Papua New Guinea regards itself as bound by these bilateral treaties in its own right. Notification to this effect was served on the Republic of Indonesia on 12 September 1980.

APPENDIX C

This appendix contains as an example a list of treaties (relating to extradition) to which Papua New Guinea wanted to accede after independence on 16 September 1975. The first part indicates the countries with which Australia had concluded extradition treaties before Papua New Guinea's independence. The second part indicates the countries that refused to accept Papua New Guinea as a party to the treaties. [Note: See Sch 2 of the *Extradition Act* (Ch 49). As to the application of the Act to Commonwealth countries, see s 2 of the Act and the Regulation.]

Extradition treaty between Australia and:

(1) Albania
(2) Argentina
(3) Austria
(4) Belgium
(5) Bolivia
(6) Chile
(7) Colombia
(8) Cuba
(9) Czechoslovakia
(10) Ecuador
(11) El Salvador
(12) Finland
(13) France
(14) Greece
(15) Guatemala
(16) Haiti
(17) Hungary
(18) Iceland
(19) Iraq
(20) Italy
(21) Liberia
(22) Luxembourg
(23) Monaco
(24) Mexico
(25) Netherlands
(26) Nicaragua
(27) Norway
(28) Panama
(29) Paraguay
(30) Peru
(31) Poland
(32) Portugal
(33) Romania
(34) San Marino
(35) Spain
(36) Sweden
(37) Switzerland
(38) Thailand
(39) United States of America
(40) Uruguay
(41) Yugoslavia

Countries which refused to accept Papua New Guinea as a party to these treaties:

(1) Albania
(2) Argentina
(3) Bolivia
(4) Colombia
(5) Cuba
(6) El Salvador
(7) Finland
(8) France
(9) Haiti
(10) Italy
(11) Liberia
(12) Mexico
(13) Netherlands
(14) Norway
(15) Panama
(16) Peru
(17) Romania
(18) San Marino
(19) Spain
(20) Sweden
(21) Thailand

APPENDIX D

This appendix contains a list of treaties that were reviewed within the five-year grace period guaranteed by the *Constitution* under s 273 and regarded as of no relevance to Papua New Guinea as of 7 October 1980.

(1) *Agreement between Australia and Japan on Fisheries and Agreed Minutes* (Canberra, 27 November 1968) (Withdrawal by Papua New Guinea on 30 November 1976.)

(2) *Convention on Fishing and Conservation of the Living Resources of the High Seas* (Geneva, 29 April 1958) (Withdrawal by Papua New Guinea on 25 February 1976.)

(3) *International Sanitary Regulation* (Geneva, 25 May 1951) (Withdrawal by Papua New Guinea on 5 April 1976.)

(4) *International Health Regulation* (Geneva, 23 May 1973) (Withdrawal by Papua New Guinea on 5 April 1976.)

(5) *Convention for the Protection of Industrial Property and Final Protocol* (Paris, 20 March 1883) (Withdrawal by Papua New Guinea on 16 August 1976.)

(6) *Additional Act Modifying the Industrial Property Convention* (Brussels, 14 December 1900) (Withdrawal by Papua New Guinea on 16 August 1976.)

(7) *International Convention for the Protection of Industrial Property and Final Protocol* (Washington, 2 December 1911) (Withdrawal by Papua New Guinea on 16 August 1976.)

(8) *International Convention for the Protection of Industrial Property* (The Hague, 6 November 1925) (Withdrawal by Papua New Guinea on 16 August 1976.)

(9) *International Convention for the Protection of Industrial Property* (London, 2 June 1934) (Withdrawal by Papua New Guinea on 16 August 1976.)

(10) *Paris Convention for the Protection of Industrial Property* (Paris, 20 March 1883, as revised at Stockholm, 14 July 1967) (Withdrawal by Papua New Guinea on 16 August 1976.)

HUMAN RIGHTS

Chapter 19

HUMAN RIGHTS IN PAPUA NEW GUINEA 1996

B D BRUNTON

INTRODUCTION

We should consolidate human rights law in Papua New Guinea, rather than reform or replace it. Rapid social and economic development, and chronic mismanagement point to a need to make the existing constitutional guarantees of freedom effective, and to manage them more efficiently. The changes that are necessary touch case management, procedure, and amendments to statute law rather than the *Constitution.* Papua New Guinea's social and political development is of such complexity that altering the substantive constitutional law is unlikely to be an effective remedy. Indeed, changing the text of constitutional law can be seen as deflecting attention away from issues of its effective management and implementation. Changes in content do not necessarily produce results. Freedom comes only with hard work. This does not mean that all change must cease; rather it is the quality of change that is important.

GLOBAL PERSPECTIVES

Human rights in Papua New Guinea have a global context. Our newspapers show conflicts about nationalism all around the world: China and Taiwan, Ireland and the United Kingdom, Israel and Palestine, Yugoslavia. In the past 50 years there have been huge shifts in political attitudes towards peace and human dignity. Nationalism affects human rights by excluding international scrutiny as a violation of national sovereignty. But national sovereignty is faced with the global economy, and on the back of international trade comes international trade regulation, economic regulation, currency agreements, agreements to allow the free movement of capital and labour, and labour regulation. That is an indirect process. More directly, there are multilateral organisations such as the WHO, UNICEF, UNDID, UNHCR, and the ILO, which are all in the business of promoting human rights and human dignity. The world is beginning to come to grips with some of the hard issues. National and international agencies co-operate and reach across borders on such issues as drugs, genocide, terrorism, and tax evasion. There is a web of extradition treaties and reciprocal judgment agreements that allow national criminal and civil laws to cross borders. National sovereignty is not what it used to be. The international values and institutions are now here in Papua New Guinea as part of this process. The economy has been opened up. Chiefly as a supplier of raw materials, Papua New Guinea's hydrocarbons, minerals, timber, fish, and agricultural produce are traded for manufactured goods and services. We are part of the global community.

REGIONAL PERSPECTIVES

In order to appreciate where we in Papua New Guinea stand, we can reflect on human rights and our neighbours: East Timor, Irian Jaya, New Caledonia, Tahiti, the predicament of Aboriginal Australia, and the Maori of Aotearoa (New Zealand). An understanding of human rights in Indonesia gives us a useful contrast and helps us put our position into perspective. In referring to Indonesia, the 1995 United States State Department Report has this to say:[616]

> "The Indonesian political system, despite a surface adherence to democratic forms, remains strongly authoritarian. President Soeharto (now in his sixth five-year term), a small group of advisers, and the military dominate the political life of this heavily populated developing country, whose people come from hundreds of different cultural, linguistic, and ethnic backgrounds. The government requires allegiance to a state ideology known as 'Pancasila', which includes belief in a Supreme God, a just and civilised humanity, national unity, democracy, and social justice. It has used Pancasila as a justification for restricting the development of opposition elements."

Under a doctrine of "dual function", the military is given special civic rights and responsibilities, including unelected military seats in Parliament (DPR) and local legislatures, in addition to its defence and security roles. The 450,000-member armed forces, including 175,000 police, consider the maintenance of internal security as their primary mission. They have traditionally acted swiftly to suppress perceived threats to security, with a vigour that has often led to human rights abuses. Some military leaders have raised questions about the validity of this "security approach". There continued to be numerous, credible reports of human rights abuses by the military and police, although they exhibited some restraint in controlling crowds and demonstrations.

Indonesia is a country in rapid economic and social transformation. Amongst its most difficult political issues are the conflicts in East Timor, Irian Jaya and Aceh.

Irian Jaya is part of the New Guinea island in many senses. It has mining, river pollution and rioting. The Freeport mine, now partly owned by Rio Tinto Zinc, has attracted continual conflict over the years. There was major rioting in 1996, said to have resulted from a misunderstanding over the death of a villager after relatives had been excluded from seeing the deceased in hospital. In the same week there was rioting in Jayapura. These riots occurred at the time of the funeral of a West Papuan leader who died in a Java prison. Dr Wanggai was serving a 15 year sentence for raising the West Papuan flag. His wife, a Japanese national, was sentenced to eight years for sewing the flag; she served four years and was released in 1992. Irian Jaya (West Papua), now has experience of some 27 years of resistance to its incorporation in Indonesia. The primary legal and moral issue outstanding during this period is a people's right to freely self-determine. Frustrated, this issue produces a protracted low-intensity dirty war: rioting, flag-raising, kidnapping, hostage taking, property damage, banditry, killing, torture, imprisonment. For Papua New Guinean human rights, the ingredients and parallels of Irian Jaya are too close for comfort.

---

[616] United States Department of State, *Country Reports on Human Rights Practices for 1995* (Washington: United States Government Printing Office, 1996), section on "Indonesia".

A contrast between Indonesia and Papua New Guinea is provided by the 1995 United States State Department's Report, which says:[617]

> "[Papua New Guinea] has a federal parliamentary system, based on universal adult suffrage with periodic free and fair elections, and an independent judiciary."

The government has constitutional authority over the armed forces (PNGDF), the Royal Papua New Guinea Constabulary (RPNGC), and intelligence organisations. Government security forces committed serious human rights abuses in 1995.

Exploitation of such natural resources as minerals, hydrocarbons, and tropical timber generates significant export and tax revenues. However 85 per cent of the population resides in isolated villages and engages in subsistence and smallholder agriculture. For a majority of citizens, income and literacy rates are at a low level, and infant and maternal mortality rates are high.

A problem with this assessment is that it deals with the formality of Papua New Guinean democracy, rather than its real texture. The recent trend has been towards concentrating power in a small group of politicians, officials and businessmen. The reality is that this power is now in the hands of a very narrow group of men aged between 30 to 50; women and youth have no power. There is no power of recall of elected politicians, nor are referenda used in Papua New Guinea. Members of Parliament are effectively voted into power for full five-year terms, although they do shift allegiances across the floor of Parliament.

GENERAL DEVELOPMENT

Colonialism, decolonisation, and opening up to the global economy brought with them new institutions and values. As lawyers we administer a system of democracy and the rule of law that rests uneasily upon a host of traditional societies and cultures. The overall social process is an integration of local economies into the global economy. But there are tensions between traditional values, and wider world values.

Globalisation opens up political space, it pushes traditional values aside. The elites move into the space and take advantage of the new freedoms. In order to maintain their new privileges they transfer the blame for the tensions to others. It is the backwardness of tradition that prevents the sharing of the benefits of economic development. It is the indiscipline of youth that takes advantage of the new freedoms, and is responsible for the social unrest. As the inequalities grow, so does the need to be authoritarian. The elites use people's fear of domestic insecurity in order to protect themselves and their own deals. The overall trend with this type of political development is towards authoritarianism. The state has to get tough: it is the lawyers and the courts that are too soft, and "human rights" is a refuge for criminals and misfits. Special legislation is needed to safeguard powerful vested interests from the scrutiny of the courts and the regulation of the *Constitution*.

The impact of the global economy on Papua New Guinea has presented the government with difficulties in managing the economy. Many of the variables are beyond Papua New Guinea's control, and mistakes are made. The response of multilateral and aid agencies to correct these

[617] Ibid, p 692.

anomalies has been, in part, to reduce wages, to take money out of the social wage, and to weaken social services. These macro economic policies have a direct impact on human rights. The weakening of health services by continuous budget cuts increases the death rate of children. World Bank and International Monetary Fund amelioration programs, to cushion those affected by structural adjustment, have been badly planned and poorly implemented. Children and youth are some of those most exposed. Again, to refer to the Report of the United States State Department:[618]

> "The government did not dedicate significant resources to protect the rights and welfare of children. More than 40 per cent of the population is under 16 . . . Because of geographic isolation and remoteness of many villages, malnourishment and infant and maternal mortality rates are very high . . . [W]elfare officers believe that child abuse is increasing as village life and the extended family give way to the influences of modern society. Most programs to protect and develop youth are operated by [non-government organisation]s and religious organisations. Many government programs are severely underfunded."

Women's rights

The same United States State Department Report for 1995 states:[619]

> "Violence against women, including domestic violence and gang rape, is a serious and prevalent problem. While ostensibly protected by their families and clans, women are nonetheless often the victims of violence and force. Traditional village deterrents are breaking down, and the number of reported cases of rape in some areas is rising. Although rape is punishable by imprisonment, and sentences are handed out when assailants are found guilty, few assailants are apprehended. Domestic violence such as wife-beating is also common, but is usually viewed by police and citizenry alike as a private family matter."

The law and the court system still need to provide effective remedies for beaten and abused women. Unfortunately, the family courts are ineffective, and cannot adequately assist the victims. The Port Moresby Family Court is in particular need of attention and institutional renovation. Although National Court judges on circuit do what they can to review Village Court anomalies, most of the worst misery is hidden from the superior courts.

Because we have a Parliament in which all members are male, there is a need for the superior courts to show leadership and to address women's rights. Most women's marriages are not legally defined, and the concept of customary marriage is unclear, particularly so if parties have different customs. Sentencing patterns would suggest that the judges need to reflect on their policy on battered women syndrome, particularly with the variation we have in Papua New Guinea of deaths arising in the context of polygynous marriages.

Bougainville

The historical record elsewhere is that unless resolved peacefully, localised secessionist conflicts tend to drag on. The Defence Force Commander is on record as saying that a military solution is unlikely. The civil war may present the legal system with one of its worst crises.

---

[618] Ibid, p 696.

[619] Ibid.

First, under the *Constitution* and Acts of Parliament the use of the Defence Force inside Papua New Guinea is prescribed.[620] These laws raise questions about the constitutionality of the civil war. By what constitutional and legal authority does the state wage war on its own people? Are the budgetary appropriations which are being spent on the war justified under the *Constitution*?

Secondly, Bougainville presents itself as a human rights issue. There are a large number of properly filed human rights complaints before the National Court; some have been filed for over six years. The least that can be said about these matters is that they draw attention to the need for a review of the procedures, and management, of human rights cases.

Thirdly, to the extent that these issues are ignored, there is the matter of the legitimacy of the system. If the legal profession falls off the tackle on basic constitutional and human rights issues, as it has done with Bougainville, then the credibility of the system is put into question. If the lawyers allow the *Constitution* to be ignored, it is difficult to condemn (although they are by no means blameless) politicians who improvise outside the rule of law. A legal system has to address all sides of a dispute, even though it may appear to uphold some values more than others. To be too uneven may give rise to long-term issues of legitimacy.

SOCIAL AND ECONOMIC RIGHTS

Papua New Guinea is a country that gives no economic rights to its weakest citizens. They are left to the mercies of wider society. To be disabled or chronically sick in Papua New Guinea is a very risky business. In resource-rich Papua New Guinea, disabled people and single parents get no pension. Both depend upon the charity of their families. But if the family is unable to provide support, the disabled and the children suffer. The 1995 United States State Department Report says:[621]

> "Through the National Board for the Disabled, the government provides limited funding to more than a dozen [non-government organisation]s that provide services to the disabled. The Government does not provide direct programs or services. Services and health care for the disabled, except that provided by the traditional family and clan system, do not exist in several of the country's provinces. No legislation mandates accessibility for the disabled."

Right to education

In Papua New Guinea children have no legally enforceable right to be educated. Female children can be lawfully deprived of their right to education for no other reason than that they are females. A child can be denied an education because an official decides that there are too many children in a school, or because the parents of the child have moved from another centre. Children can also be deprived, lawfully, of an education because their parents are too poor to pay the school fees. The common law courts have traditionally protected the rights of children, although mainly through the law of equity in relation to children's property. If children are our most important

[620] *Constitution*, ss 204-205.
[621] United States State Department, above n 1, p 696.

asset, then there is a need to extend these concepts to protect Papua New Guinea's stock of human capital.

Right to health services

There is no right of access to health care in Papua New Guinea. Mismanagement for the past decade has effectively taken resources out of the health sector, to the extent that government health services in most parts of the country are severely stressed. Access to health care is increasingly based on the user pays principle. If you cannot pay, you may die. This is not an exaggeration; the fees deter those needing medical attention for a condition from seeking it at an early stage. The condition then deteriorates, and when the patient does present to the hospital the condition cannot be treated. The impact of this phenomenon across the country has seen rises in susceptibility to malaria, tuberculosis, infant and maternal deaths, and other conditions that with basic care could be avoided.

There is a need for Parliament to address the rights of citizens to access health and education services. These rights need to be given content so that they can be enforced.

Enforceability of the National Goals and Directive Principles

The National Goals and Directive Principles are non-justiciable. Legislation or government actions cannot be challenged solely on the basis that they do not conform to the National Goals and Directive Principles. The 1985 Constitutional Review Commission recommended that the National Goals and Directive Principles be made enforceable. This and other recommendations of the Commission were ignored by the Parliament. Many of the stresses we are now experiencing in society can be attributed to the distance that has developed between acts of state and the National Goals. Huge sums of taxpayers' money are often spent on projects that would seem to be at odds with the National Goals. The report of the Ombudsman Commission into the contracts to construct housing for the Defence Force is but one example.

Our legal system belongs to a tradition of gradual adaptation to changing social and economic values. In contrast, with the opening up of the economy to the world market there has been rapid social and economic transformation. The strong have prospered and the weak are exploited. Judges should not underestimate the capacity of the people to seek redress for wrongs (whether real or perceived). If redress is not available through the courts, people will look elsewhere. As the social and economic tensions increase so does the need of the people to obtain justice. We are not talking here of justice according to colonial law, or justice according to the values of the legal system, but rather real or substantive justice, the justice of social and economic equality. In the long term, these are issues that are ignored at our peril. Unless lawyers advance the system to adapt to these forces, then the forces are likely to be transformed away from the socially acceptable to the anti-social. This is what happened in Bougainville, and is happening in Irian Jaya.

HUMAN RIGHTS AND NATURAL RESOURCES

The scale of infringement of property rights associated with natural resources cases, and threats to the environment, are now very large in monetary and geographic terms. Natural resource projects affect whole river systems and hundreds of thousands of hectares of land, and thousands of people. Damage to the environment cuts across generations. Today we make decisions for our grandchildren. Human rights were never developed to protect corporations, but corporations have appropriated human rights. Under our law private companies are treated as equals to human beings and they have human rights. But large private companies have access to economic and political power, and they cannot be considered as equals of individual people before the law. In court they are formidable opponents.

During the next few years we are likely to experience a tightening of the political space available to those who oppose the monopolisation of power in the resources sector. The main arenas for struggle are likely to be freedom of speech, freedom of association, freedom of assembly, and freedom of information.

Freedom of speech

We have seen recent moves to close up the political space open to the media. It is being done under the disguise of "media accountability". This in reality means censorship, albeit that at present the tactic is to try to introduce self-censorship. The real intent of these efforts is to take the heat off incumbent politicians and cushion them from public debate.

There are now real limitations on what can be said about particular resource companies. If the words used lower the esteem of the company in the public eye, or affect its profitability, then on their face the words are likely to be defamatory. To say that a company has broken the law, bribes politicians, has damaged the environment, is oppressive to its workers, or encourages immorality, is to invite a defamation action. The burden then shifts to the defendant to show that the words can be justified under one of the standard defences. In effect, the law and the corporation's access to economic power chills or stifles debate. Effectively, there is no freedom of expression when debate of this type is frozen.

Freedom of information

The *Constitution* guarantees freedom of information. It requires that enabling legislation provide reasonable access to government files. No such law has been passed since independence, and so this freedom has not been implemented. The *Constitution* and the law of equity protect commercial secrets. There is a problem when corporations wrap their deals with the state under a cloak of commercial confidentiality. It is standard practice in resource agreements to insert a confidentiality clause. The excuse is that the investors need to be protected from unscrupulous attempts to undermine their projects. But commercial confidentiality can be used to hide corrupt deals, or deals that are inequitable, give short value to landowners, or allow resources to be taken out of the country for less than fair value, or to cover up deals that are incompetent or just plain bad. Commercial transactions with the state, or over public assets, or involving natural resources and access to customary land should not be hidden behind the cloak of confidentiality. Citizens should be able to get access to information about the details of such contracts.

Freedom of association

There are currently moves to close up the space occupied by voluntary organisations. The thrust of this is to regulate them through the Department of Home Affairs, and to make them accountable to the Ombudsman Commission. This attempt to limit freedom seems to be similar to Indonesia's *Social Organisations Law* 1985, and the draft *Presidential Decree on Social Organisations of 1994* (which is yet to be brought into effect). As most social organisations in Papua New Guinea have innocuous objectives (for example, health, education, religion), this initiative appears to be an attempt by elements within the government to restrict and contain criticism of its environmental and human rights policies.

Freedom of assembly

Peaceful demonstrations against resource exploitation can be stopped by the misapplication of the *Peace and Good Order Act*. There is beginning to be a very close relationship between resource companies and police. Vehicles and housing are provided by the companies to the police, police officers are wined and dined, and air tickets are issued. The companies get special consideration. Police badger and harass landowners who oppose resources exploitation on their land. People have been arrested for the imaginary offence of "opposing development". Youths are locked up in containers. The police and successive police Ministers maintain that they have power to regulate and license peaceful demonstrations. In fact they do not have this power. The *Peace and Good Order Act* first requires an area to be declared an area for the purposes of the Act. These declarations are subject to a sunset clause. Peaceful assembly is a right in Papua New Guinea.

Right to fair compensation for compulsory deprivation of property

The right of property owners to obtain fair compensation for deprivations of their property underlies many current resources disputes. Two trends are apparent: first, underpricing through the fixing of prices in inequitable and unfair contracts without reference to property owners and the market; and secondly, passing the costs of damage to the environment from resources companies to landowners, generally by agreement or by statute. This leads to further problems (apart from the long-term effect on the environment): the limiting by statute of civil actions, the risk of property owner frustration and consequent violence.

CONCLUSION

There is a need for judges, magistrates and lawyers to pay more attention to human rights cases. There are a very large number of human rights complaints formally before the court. There has been a polite and cautious criticism by international monitors of the lack of attention given to human rights matters. This criticism could be relieved in part by the executive establishing a Human Rights Commission, a proposal discussed last year. But there are other ways in which the courts could address human rights.

First, there is a general need to create a permanent Supreme Court to build up constitutional experience. A permanent Supreme Court could address consistently, in the judicial context, the formulation of human rights policy.

Secondly, there is a need to draft rules and practice directions to produce a quick procedure for dealing with human rights cases. We need a procedure that allows cases to be heard quickly, while at the same time giving defendants a reasonable opportunity to defend themselves.

Generally, the cumbersome nature of the *National Court Rules* and civil procedure makes it difficult for Papua New Guineans to access civil law. These rules, the same as exist in New South Wales, are inappropriate in Papua New Guinea. They suit only those who have sufficient money to buy the time of lawyers. In reality, the poor have to forego their claims. The need to re-examine civil procedure as an impediment to access to the courts is made more important now that the New South Wales rules have permeated into the District Court.

Thirdly, there is the need to manage human rights cases in the National Court. At present human rights cases are treated as a species of civil case. On circuit, there are particular problems in giving attention to them, because of the itinerant nature of some circuits, and the fact that the state as a defendant does not post lawyers out to the provinces to defend itself. In Port Moresby there must be a large number of human rights files awaiting some form of judicial attention.

Fourthly, there is a need to consider some delegation of human rights powers down to the District Court level. At present, under s 57 of the *Constitution* power to enforce the constitutional rights and freedoms is vested solely in the National and Supreme Courts. Human rights violations differ in their gravity. Some may be for claims that are well within the current jurisdictional limits of the District Court, and we need to think about the economics of insisting that these cases may only be determined by National and Supreme Court judges. Changes may be especially appropriate in relation to the enforcement of women's rights in the family context, and to deal with some allegations against the police.

While the courts have delivered some notable decisions on the protection of human rights, these positive achievements are overwhelmed by events and pressure of work. To the ordinary Papua New Guinean the human rights provisions in the *Constitution* mean little. If you are arrested in Papua New Guinea the chances are you will be assaulted while in custody. The cell you will stay in will most likely be inhuman or degrading. If you are sick, there is no guarantee of a health service. If you are disabled, the chances are you will not be assisted by the state. Children have no right to attend school. School leavers should not expect to find formal employment. If you are a woman, do not expect too much at all, except the likelihood of being bashed by your boyfriend or husband.

The negative developments of the past 20 years need to be put into perspective. Papua New Guinea has a democratic structure. It has political space. But we should not take that space for granted. It is likely we will have to defend the freedoms of speech, association, assembly and information in the near future.

Those who believe in human dignity have to learn how to use the political space constitutionally. Human rights are part of a process of development towards freedom and liberty, but it is a process that is only furthered through constitutional struggle. After 20 years we have a framework and we have a set of rules. There is a good deal of wisdom and sense in the country, and despite misgivings we can say we have the necessary ingredients to take fresh steps towards human freedom and human dignity. As I have said, freedom will come only with hard work.

Chapter 20

WOMEN AND THE CONSTITUTION: 20 YEARS OF MISSED OPPORTUNITY

TIFFANY TWIVEY

Introduction

It cannot be denied that there is incredible disparity between the legal and the factual position of women in Papua New Guinea. The *Constitution* contains provisions granting equality of the sexes and principles that make human development, equal opportunity and participation and removal of oppression and domination important goals. In practice, however, women continue to be oppressed by the threat of violence, and to have little or no representation in Parliament. Notwithstanding the sometimes favourable official government policies, the human development of women lags greatly behind that of men.

In this chapter I will examine the constitutional provisions that deal with the status of women. Secondly, I will look at the relevance to Papua New Guinea of the United Nations *Convention on the Elimination of All Forms of Discrimination Against Women.* Thirdly, I will consider how oppression of women is alive and well through domestic violence and the government's lack of commitment to necessary responses to the problem. Further, I will examine how our criminal law subordinates the position of women to that of men. Finally, I will refer to the notion of nominated members of Parliament and the effect that the use of this provision to ensure women's representation may have on the status of women.

CONSTITUTIONAL STATUS OF WOMEN

It is necessary to examine the provisions of the *Constitution* that affect the status of women specifically. These are outlined in s 55 and in the National Goals and Directive Principles.

The National Goals and Directive Principles are intended, it is submitted, to provide all those who make and implement decisions in government with a basic indication of national policy, as well as a concise statement of the political needs of the nation.[622]

Within this enunciation of national policy, the inequality and lower status of women is recognised by the explicit call for women to participate in the development of the nation. Goal 2(5) calls for "equal participation by women citizens in all political, economic, social and religious activities".

The Constitutional Planning Committee (CPC) commented in its Final Report, under the heading of "Equal status and opportunity for women", on the importance of this goal's inclusion in the *Constitution*:

> "We have also emphasised the importance of women being able to make their full contribution to the welfare of the country, on an equal footing with men. In recent years

[622] See J Goldring, *The Constitution of Papua New Guinea* (Sydney: Law Book Company, 1978), p 32.

> women have played a significantly greater part in the country's national life - in politics, in business, in social and cultural activities. But more effort should be made by government to hasten this development. Obstacles to educational and other opportunities which face women at present should be removed, and insofar as it is within the power of the government to do so, the difficulties facing women who wish to involve themselves in the affairs of the nation should be reduced."[623]

There is mention here of a desire for government to hasten the development of women as a national resource, and also to remove the difficulties and obstacles confronting women. Later in this chapter, specific obstacles to women's development will be examined.

Freedom from oppression and domination is also dealt with under National Goal No 1:

> "We declare our first goal to be for every person to be dynamically involved in the process of freeing himself or herself from every form of domination or oppression so that each man or woman will have the opportunity to develop as a whole person in relationship with others."

Unfortunately, pursuant to s 25(1) of the *Constitution*, the National Goals and Directive Principles are "non-justiciable". A duty is, however, placed on governmental bodies to give effect to them. Section 25(2) provides:

> "Nevertheless it is the duty of all governmental bodies to apply and give effect to them as far as lies within their respective powers."

The most important constitutional provision defining the status of women is s 55(1), relating to equality of citizens. This is in the following terms:

> "Subject to this Constitution, all citizens have the same rights, privileges, obligations and duties irrespective of race, tribe, place of origin, political opinion, colour, creed, religion or sex."

Notwithstanding the obvious intention of this provision, its practical application is limited. It is vague and non-specific, and even with the rights enforcement procedures referred to in ss 57 and 58, it is difficult to enforce. At present, actions to enforce gender rights can only be taken in the National Court or in the Supreme Court, which is usually an expensive and lengthy process.

There was no direct discussion of the right to freedom from discrimination in the CPC's Final Report: only a general discussion on the importance of human rights and the necessity to include them in the *Constitution*.[624]

Another problem concerning the notion of equality in s 55(1) is the nature of the ensuing subsections, especially concerning the status of women. Section 55(2) states:

---

[623] CPC, *Final Report of the Constitutional Planning Committee: Part 1* (Port Moresby: Government Printer, 1974), p 2/8, para 59.
[624] Ibid, pp 5/1-5/7.

> "Subsection (1) does not prevent the making of laws for the special benefit, welfare, protection or advancement of females, children and young persons, members of underprivileged or less advanced groups or residents of less advanced areas."

This subsection constitutionally entrenches women in a subordinate position, placing them as a whole in a provision concerned with underprivileged or less advanced groups. This undermines their status. It detracts from s 55(1), which perceives women as underprivileged rather than as holders of important human rights.[625] Gender equality is a relatively new concept and requires a change in the community's political ideology and thinking. Legally entrenched positive discrimination can lead to further inequalities as a product of resentment by those who are being discriminated against. Obviously the current imbalances need to be addressed, but this can be achieved by affirmative action within the legislative framework of equality, without having to entrench positive discrimination in the law. For example, s 102 of the *Constitution* provides for the nomination of members to Parliament, and can be used when any group in society is not properly represented. The *Constitution* does and should grant equality, rather than perpetuate inequality. By maintaining s 55(2), Parliament is able to make protective legislation that can adversely affect the position of women. For example, s 98 of the *Employment Act* (Ch 373) prohibits women from being employed to do heavy manual labour. Women should be free to choose their employment, and not be limited by paternalistic legislators.

Section 55(3) further detracts from the general concept of equality in s 55(1) by stating that the latter subsection "does not affect the operation of a pre-Independence law". This subsection operates to allow discriminatory pre-independence laws to continue in force until altered, notwithstanding the constitutional grant of equality. Although s 11(1) of the *Constitution* invalidates provisions in other legislation which are inconsistent with the *Constitution*, it cannot override the effect of other provisions in the *Constitution* itself, such as s 55(3).

What is most interesting, however, is that whilst human rights were generally discussed by the CPC[626] as being fundamentally important, and whilst the need for equal status and opportunity was seen as essential with regard to the National Goals and Directive Principles,[627] no mention was made in the Final Report of those limitations to the general grant of equality contained in s 55(2) and (3). Thus, there was no statement of a policy of positive discrimination but, rather, an emphasis on the notion of fundamental human rights being held and enjoyed by all. Again, there was no suggestion that the basic right of equality should be limited by pre-independence legislation. As a result, the wording of subs (3) appears to be in direct conflict with the CPC's support for equal status and equal opportunity.

---

[625] United Nations, *The World's Women 1995: Trends and Statistics* (United Nations: New York, 1995), p 184, n 4.
[626] CPC, above n 2, Ch 5.
[627] Ibid, p 2/8, para 59.

Gender equality is an essential element of human development. Achieving it necessitates a lengthy process in which all social, economic, political and particularly cultural norms undergo fundamental change.[628] Equality requires a wholesale political commitment. However, this dedication seems to have been lacking in the past 20 years notwithstanding the clear words of the *Constitution*. This fact was recognised by Los J in *State v Kopilyo Kipungi* (1983) N437, when he stated:

> "Although the equality of the sexes is now a constitutional principle in Papua New Guinea, at this stage it is more a matter of books, rather than practice."[629]

DOMESTIC VIOLENCE

One of the most serious barriers to equality is oppression and domination, and there is no greater barrier than the spectre of domestic violence. I will consider prevailing attitudes towards this problem, and show that despite efforts for change it still remains a major stumbling block to equality today. I will also examine how difficult it is to achieve equality when our criminal law continues to subordinate a wife's wants to those of her husband. Both of these aspects are particularly inappropriate given that on 12 January 1995 the government of Papua New Guinea acceded to the United Nations *Convention on the Elimination of all Forms of Discrimination against Women* (CEDAW). This Convention was adopted by the United Nations General Assembly in December 1979. It calls on states to eliminate discrimination against women in the enjoyment of all civil, political, economic and cultural rights. It puts obligations on states to work for equality for women both in public life (for example, in the realm of legal status and political participation), and also in private life, especially in regards to the family. The relevance of the Convention will be further considered below.

In 1982, the Minister for Justice, Mr Tony Bais, authorised a reference to the Law Reform Commission to inquire into and report on domestic violence. The Commission was also asked to recommend changes to the law that might secure the protection of women from domestic violence. It is clear from the circumstances in which the reference to the Commission was made that domestic violence was seen to be a large social problem at the time, and that the state of the law was thought to be insufficient to cope with the problem. It is also significant that the letter of reference stated that domestic violence was contrary to the principles of the *Constitution*.[630] This, I submit, is an obvious reference to the "freedom from oppression or domination" principle contained in National Goal No 1.

In 1987, the Commission released the *Interim Report on Domestic Violence*, which was then presented to Parliament.[631] The matter was duly discussed there, with several honourable members casting doubt on the necessity for such a report. Several members asserted that as long as a husband felt there was reason for it, domestic violence was quite acceptable. One Minister asserted that the fact of paying brideprice entitled husbands to feel they "owned the woman and could belt her any time they liked". It was even suggested by one member that Parliament was

[628] United Nations, above n 4.
[629] (1983) N437, p 5.
[630] See Papua New Guinea Law Reform Commission, *Final Report on Domestic Violence* (Report No 14) (PNGLRC: Port Moresby, 1992), p 1.
[631] Ibid, p 9 for discussion of the course of the Commission's reference.

wasting its time discussing domestic violence, and that instead they should be discussing the development of the country.[632]

The Law Reform Commission's *Final Report on Domestic Violence*[633] was produced in 1992. In addition to assessing the nature and extent of domestic violence in Papua New Guinea and ascertaining the potential legal remedies, the Report made many recommendations for change to the existing system and laws. It was argued[634] that under the present legislation spouses cannot be compelled to give evidence against each other in cases of assault, and that often a woman would, at the end of the day, refuse to give evidence because of pressure from relatives or threats of retaliation by the husband, which would mean that the case would not proceed. It was accordingly recommended that s 13 of the *Evidence Act* (Ch 48) (spouse of accused as witness) should be amended to read as follows:

> "(4) Notwithstanding Subsections (1) and (2), the wife or husband of a person charged with an offence of assault against the other, or against a child of either of them, is a competent and compellable witness in any legal proceedings in connection with the offence, and may be called without consent of the accused."[635]

It is submitted that this recommendation is necessary in light of the notions of equality in the *Constitution* and also, more specifically, the call for freedom from oppression in the National Goals and Directive Principles. Being able to bring an oppressor to justice is a fundamental aspect of freeing oneself from oppression.

Of the 54 recommendations made by the Law Reform Commission, very few have been implemented. According to the Commission's rural survey, over two-thirds of wives had been hit by their husbands, more than half of that group saying they had been struck with a weapon or implement.[636] It was also found that more than half of all murders of women in Papua New Guinea are committed by present or former partners. The situation would seem to be at crisis point. Fifteen years after the Minister for Justice thought the situation was so bad that a full inquiry and report needed to be done, notwithstanding the cost, the government has chosen to ignore the great majority of recommendations.

The Committee on the Elimination of Discrimination against Women affirmed in its General Recommendation No 19, adopted at its 11th session in 1992, that "violence against a woman constitutes a violation of her internationally recognised human rights regardless of whether the perpetrator is a public official or a private person". Papua New Guinea has a *Constitution* that speaks of equality and freedom of oppression for women. Papua New Guinea is now party to CEDAW. It is time the legislative arm of the government fulfilled its obligations to women.

MARITAL RAPE EXEMPTION

Another form of domestic violence is marital rape, but this issue deserves extra attention because of the blatantly discriminatory nature of the current legislation.

---

[632] Parliament of Papua New Guinea, Debates, 2 March 1987, referred to in Papua New Guinea Law Reform Commission, above n 9, p 9.
[633] Papua New Guinea Law Reform Commission, above n 9.
[634] Ibid, p 49.
[635] Ibid, Appendix 9.
[636] Ibid, p 16.

The crime of rape is defined in s 347 of the *Criminal Code Act* (Ch 262) as follows:

> "A person who has carnal knowledge of a woman or a girl, *not being his wife* –
>
> (a) without her consent; or
>
> (b) with her consent, if the consent is obtained –
>
> (i) by force; or
>
> (ii) by means of threats or intimidation; or
>
> (iii) by fear of bodily harm; or
>
> (iv) by means of false and fraudulent representations as to the nature of the act; or
>
> (v) in the case of a married woman by personating her husband,
>
> is guilty of the crime of rape" (emphasis added).

This provision ensures that there can be no conviction for rape in marriage. Section 55 of the *Constitution* grants equality to all citizens, not just unmarried ones. The provision in the *Criminal Code Act* is clearly contrary to the notion of gender equality. National Goal No 1 calls for freedom of oppression and domination for all men and women. Spouses are not allowed by law to assault each other, yet a husband is allowed to forcibly penetrate a wife's vagina whenever he feels like it. This is not only oppression, but a form of torture. Further, National Goal No 2(12) calls for:

> "recognition of the principles that a complete relationship in marriage rests on equality of rights and duties of the partners, and that responsible parenthood is based on that equality."

The fact that a husband is allowed under the *Criminal Code* to overbear the will of his wife blatantly contradicts the call for recognition of equality of rights of the partners in a marriage. This reason alone is sufficient grounds for Parliament to amend the offending legislation. After 20 years of the *Constitution*, it is only fair and just that married women finally are allowed to benefit from important rights that they are supposed to hold.

An additional ground for amending the law is the fact that Article 16 of CEDAW specifically calls for an end to discrimination against women in all matters relating to marriage. Article 16 is in the following terms:

> "1. State Parties shall take all appropriate measures to eliminate discrimination against women in all matters relating to marriage and family relations and in particular shall ensure on a basis of equality of men and women: . . .
>
> (c) The same rights and responsibilities during marriage and at its dissolution; . . .
>
> (d) The same rights to decide freely and responsibly on the number and spacing of their children and to have access to the information, education and means to enable them to exercise these rights."

The discriminatory exception in s 347 of the *Criminal Code* is obviously contrary to the terms of this Article. In order for women to participate equally, in accordance with National Goal No 2(5), in all political, social, economic and religious activities, it is necessary for women to be able to make their own life choices and to have some control over their fertility. Article 16 of CEDAW specifically calls for the same rights to decide freely on the spacing of children, but the marital rape exemption in s 347 certainly does not allow for this. To participate in the development of this country, women need control over their time. This is certainly not achieved by not being able to refuse sexual intercourse with their spouses, which may result in unplanned pregnancies.

In late June 1995, a National Court judge hearing a criminal case made some comments with regard to the law of marital rape that initiated a heated debate nationwide. The defendant was guilty of carnal knowledge of his six-year-old stepdaughter. The court heard that he had done this because his wife had refused to have sex with him. In sentencing, the judge said:

> "He abused the trust placed upon him as her stepfather. That should not have happened. If he wanted sex, then I suppose he is entitled to rape his wife to satisfy his desire for sex."[637]

Observations on the relevance of commenting on the marital rape exception in relation to sentencing a paedophile are outside the scope of this chapter, but the publicised reactions to the judge's words are most relevant. Of particular interest are the comments of two parliamentarians. The member for Kagua-Erave, Mr Daniel Tulapi stated:

> "Customary laws and not feminine rights based on Western concepts should dictate how we conduct marriages in Papua New Guinea."[638]

An interesting point to note, however, is that the judge had not been referring to custom, but rather to the marital rape exception in the *Criminal Code Act* (Ch 262), which is an adopted law. Even if it was the case that according to custom rape was excusable,[639] constitutional considerations would prevent the recognition of such a custom. As was said by Kidu CJ in *State v Wasale Nerius and Ramilang Tingas* (1982) N397:

> "If this is a custom of the Baining people then it is repugnant to the dictates of Papua New Guinea' Constitution. Women/girls are not to be raped because it is custom. They are not 'things' or 'chattels' to be dealt with by men as they wish. ... Women are equal to men in Papua New Guinea under our Constitution. They must be so treated by men."[640]

It is also important to note the view of Woods J in *Re Wagi Non* [1991] PNGLR 84 at 86:

> "Customs that denigrate women should be denied a place in the underlying law in Papua New Guinea because they conflict with the National Goals of equality and participation which have been laid down clearly in the *Constitution*."

---

[637] *PNG Post Courier*, 28 June 1995.

[638] *PNG Post Courier*, 5 July 1995.

[639] In a recent article, "When rape is not rape" (1994) 22 *Melanesian Law Journal* 59, Dr John Luluaki attempts (at 64) to explain the logic of excusable rape under custom:

"If one accepts payback killing as justifiable homicide under customary law, then using rape to express payback, aggression or revenge in this manner, although unacceptable to the victim and her kin, is excusable rape . . . In view of the foregoing, the existence of the crime of rape as understood in the Western sense and reflected in the Criminal Code needs to be questioned."

[640] (1982) N397, p 3.

The then Minister for Agriculture and Livestock, Mr Bernard Narokobi, also commented on the debate, saying that family matters should not be dragged into courts of criminal justice because they did not guarantee social harmony. He also said that Papua New Guinea should make laws that were suitable for its social and cultural conditions.[641]

The crime of rape in the *Criminal Code Act* is not merely a reflection of Western views. Its inclusion enables women to be free from oppression and domination from men in accordance with the National Goals and Directive Principles. Making rape a criminal offence is in accordance with s 36(1) of the *Constitution*, which provides that no person shall be submitted to treatment or punishment (whether physical or mental) that is cruel or otherwise inhuman, or is inconsistent with respect for the inherent dignity of the human person. These ideas are supposed to be part of the Supreme Law of Papua New Guinea. The problem with s 347 of the *Criminal Code Act* (Ch 262) is not that it reflects Western ideas about rape, but that it retains the marital exemption rule contrary to the *Constitution*, and contrary to CEDAW. After 20 years of the *Constitution*, it is time to amend the *Criminal Code* and liberate married women from potential abuse.

REPRESENTATION OF WOMEN IN PARLIAMENT

At present there are no women sitting as members in the Parliament. Their absence is not a result of legal barriers to their entrance. Equality requires a new way of thinking for both men and women. Women's enrolment rate in education lags behind that of males at all educational levels. The figures for the numbers of females enrolled at tertiary level are less than 30 per cent of the male enrolment. This may very well be part of the problem, and if so change will not come quickly enough. There is, however, affirmation action, as opposed to positive discrimination, that could be taken. Pursuant to s 102 of the *Constitution*, the Parliament may by a two-thirds majority vote appoint a person to be a nominated member of the Parliament, and s 101(1)(c) dictates that there may not be more than three nominated members holding office at any one time. When the notion of nominated members was discussed by the National Constituent Assembly,[642] the main stated purpose of the section was to protect the rights of minority groups. It was envisaged that a situation might arise that a group in a large electorate may not be adequately represented due to a variety of reasons, including customary or cultural differences, and there could be a need for a nominated member to represent them. The other reason mentioned was that there may be occasions when it would be necessary to nominate experts to fill positions, such as a lawyer to be Attorney-General. Since women, as a group, are not represented in Parliament at the present time, the problem of lack of representation could be solved by a nomination. If one or more women were nominated, this may lead to a greater acceptance of women in general leadership positions, and may encourage more women to stand for elections in future.

The United Nations Commission on the Status of Women recommended in 1990 that a critical 30 per cent female participation threshold should be regarded as the minimum for decision-making positions at the national level. Forty-four countries in the world today appoint women to their representative bodies to make sure of their presence. The concept has been successful in other countries, and there is no real reason that the same result should not occur here.

---

[641] *PNG Post Courier*, 5 July 1995.

[642] National Constituent Assembly, *Debates*, Second Meeting of the Third Session, Vol 1, No 1, p 122 (1975).

Nomination of female members can be criticised as tokenism. However, some women have used their positions in ways to advance women's agendas and plan political gains. The Preamble to the *Constitution* calls for equal participation by women in political activities. This has not occurred in these past 20 years. Therefore, if the government is seriously concerned with the development of human resources, nomination of female members is indeed a necessary step.

CONCLUSION

The *Constitution* specifically grants equality to all its citizens regardless of gender. It calls for freedom from oppression and domination, and for all citizens to be involved in the political, economic, social and religious activities of the country. It also calls for equal opportunity to participate in the development of the country.

The legal position on the status of women is therefore clear: equal status to that of men. Reality, however, reflects a different picture. Implementing gender equality has always been and remains problematic, and both governmental and political activism is needed. A first step would be to identify areas in which women are oppressed, and then attempt to break down these barriers to development. One such barrier is the incidence of domestic violence. Efforts need to be made immediately to implement the recommendations of the Law Reform Commission, particularly with respect to amendments to the relevant legislation.

Human development (see National Goal No 1) is about enlarging people's choices, and women need the ability to make their own life choices, particularly with regards to their fertility. The marital rape exception in the *Criminal Code* removes a woman's control over her life, not to mention legislatively validating oppression and abuse. This barrier to equal opportunity in development needs to be removed.

The *Constitution* calls for women to be involved in the political activities of the nation, but at present there are no women sitting in Parliament. It may therefore be necessary to take affirmative action and nominate a female representative to Parliament under s 102 of the *Constitution.* This may be seen as tokenism, but it may very well initiate further development of women as political leaders.

Real and lasting equality can only be obtained when gender equality is widely accepted as morally right. It requires fundamental change in societal norms, as well as decisive and committed government action.

LAND AND ENVIRONMENT

Chapter 21

THE CONSTITUTION AND LAND MATTERS

R W JAMES

INTRODUCTION

The relative emphasis on land matters in the *Constitution* could be explained by the fact that the Constitutional Planning Committee (CPC) and the 1973 Commission of Inquiry into Land Matters (CILM)[643] had a parallel existence and were intended to provide the blueprint for good government and an egalitarian post-independence Papua New Guinea society. They, in turn, impacted on each other in numerous ways, not the least in having a common mandate to fashion structures in order to realise the Eight Point Improvement Program that had been adopted by the Somare Government in 1972.

Specifically, some of the recommendations of the CILM Report were adopted and given constitutional status. In order to assess the impact of the *Constitution* on land matters, I will refer to three matters.

The first is the philosophical aspect contained in the commitments to policies in the Preamble of the *Constitution*. These transcend land tenure and administration, examples being the National Goals and Directive Principles on "natural resources" and the "environment" (National Goal No 4), and "Papua New Guinean Ways" (National Goal No 5). These have had some influence in shaping the underlying law, but their full realisation must be within the province of legislation, not judicial development.

Secondly, some important principles of land policy were fashioned by the CILM and articulated in the *Constitution*. These include protecting citizens from unjust deprivation of property (s 53), and "protection and control of national lands" (s 54). Some other CILM policy recommendations were adopted in part only. These included those on freehold conversion and plantation redistribution of land of "non-citizens".

Thirdly, there are statements of substantive law contained in the *Constitution*. To a large extent they take the form of legislating the sources of law, and articulating the basis for finding new equitable principles. These are contained in Schs 2.2 and 2.3 of the *Constitution*, and ss 41, 59, 60, and 155(4).

To a very large extent, the policies and principles covered in the first two of these three areas are left to later legislative Acts for their implementation. This is consistent with the form constitutional laws often take, of directives requiring legislation for their implementation. The principles discussed in relation to the third area of classification are not of the same level of

[643] CILM, *Report of the Commission of Inquiry Into Land Matters* (Port Moresby: Government Printing Office, 1973).

abstraction, but form the basis of the courts' discretion in developing the underlying law. In hindsight, the *Constitution* might have contained more details. The conclusion raises this critical perspective.

NATIONAL GOALS AND DIRECTIVE PRINCIPLES

The National Goals and Directive Principles are by their nature non-justiciable.[644] However, in developing the underlying law the judges are required to give effect to them wherever possible. Their level of abstraction has been an impediment to them having any significant impact on the non-statutory land tenure system.

The earliest case of judicial application of the National Goals and Directive Principles was *Public Curator of Papua New Guinea v Public Trustee of New Zealand* [1976] PNGLR 427. The central issue was whether a will was validly executed. As with inter vivos (between living persons) land transactions under s 2(1)(a) of the *Frauds and Limitations Act* (Ch 330), there are formality requirements where property is being left by will. To be valid s 18 of the *Wills, Probate and Administration Act* 1967 (s 13 of the current Act), [645] requires that the will should be made in writing, and properly signed and witnessed. At common law, if these formalities are not complied with, the will is completely void. In Papua New Guinea this is not so. In the case in question, the National Court (Prentice DCJ) held that attestation of the testator's signature by one witness is sufficient to save the will from invalidity. And even if the testator's signature is not witnessed at all, provided that it is proved that the document was intended by the testator to be her or his last will and testament, the will would be valid. This, the court held, was the intention of s 43 of the 1967 Act (s 35 of the current Act), which sets out to save testamentary dispositions that are defective for want of formalities.[646] In giving a liberal interpretation to that section, the court was influenced by National Goal No 2, which calls for "equality and participation", and the corresponding directive on the "equalisation of services in all parts of the country, and for every citizen to have equal access to legal processes and all services". Prentice DCJ justified his decision by reference to the conditions prevailing in Papua New Guinea:

> "The desire to make proper testamentary disposition of his property comes within the legitimate needs and aspirations of citizens. Equalisation of access to the legal processes and services necessary to achieve these needs and aspirations, including (I conceive) the drafting and making of effective wills of which probate can be granted by the court, is a declared aim. The legislators would have been fully seized of the difficulties put in the way of an intending willmaker by the geography, isolation, lack of easy, and the cost of, travel facilities, the fewness of lawyers, prevailing in Papua New Guinea. They have intended I think, to provide that the ability to make a valid will without rigid compliance with formalities, should be more widely available."[647]

Some of the National Goals and Directive Principles have informed legislative rather than judicial actions. National Goal No 4 (natural resources and environment) declares the use of natural resources for the benefit of all, with the idea of conservation and sustainability. This goal is cast

[644] *Constitution*, s 25.
[645] *Wills, Probate and Administration Act* (Ch 291).
[646] If it is proved that the testator intended the will to be his last will and that intention is clear': *Public Curator v Reinon* [1978] PNGLR 253.
[647] [1976] PNGLR 427 at 431.

in terms of "wise use" to be made of the natural resources and the environment in and on the land or seabed in the interest of development and preservation for future generations.

Pursuant to this goal, legislative steps have been taken to give adequate protection to the birds, animals, plants and trees of Papua New Guinea with the enactment of a package of environmental laws that are administered by the Department of Environment and Conservation. These include the *Environmental Planning Act* (Ch 370), the *Conservation Areas Act* (Ch 362), and the *Fauna (Protection and Control) Act* (Ch 154).

Of special significance to the student of Papua New Guinea land tenure laws is National Goal No 5. This goal calls for development through Papua New Guinean forms of social, political and economic organisations. The challenge is to reorientate the legal system so as to integrate customary concepts and institutions into the development process. This aspiration was also shared by the CILM, which was particularly concerned with the promotion of group title as the norm in the land reform process and the use of traditional mediatory and arbitration processes in resolving land disputes. One of the earliest statutes passed to implement National Goal No 5 was the *Land Groups Incorporation Act* (Ch 147). The Act was intended to recognise and facilitate the corporate nature of customary groups. However, to date no statute exists for the registration of group titles, and the corresponding land mobilisation policy is put in abeyance.

The *Land Disputes Settlement Act* (Ch 45) is intended to provide a fair, efficient and effective machinery for the settlement of disputes over customary lands. It has not satisfied expectations. The mediation and arbitration processes have broken down in some districts and for a variety of reasons. It is reported[648] that the system "is dangerously close to collapse" because of lack of funds and poor administration.

It is fair comment to observe that very little has been achieved in the implementation of the National Goals and Directive Principles relating to land matters. In 20 years, fewer than 2,000 groups have been registered as group corporations. The registration of group title has been rejected along with the land mobilisation program and the new structure of land dispute settlement is unsuccessful. Whilst the system suffers from lack of funds, there are other serious problems that hamper the efficacy of the local land courts. The security of the magistrates and mediators is a matter of concern. Fear of assaults from litigants necessitates that they hand down their judgments not in the area of the conflict, but in the court house in the city.

When the CILM recommended the new system of land disputes resolution, it was hoped that the dispute settlement process would be brought closer to the people, both in time and physically. Neither goal has been achieved, either in the initial hearing or on appeal.

LAND POLICIES

The *Constitution* is supportive of some of the recommendations of the CILM on land policies, but dysfunctional in relation to others. Examples of the former are the recommendations in Chapter 6 of the CILM Report on the need to protect and extend national lands which find form in s 54(a) of the *Constitution*, and those in Chapter 8 on land disputes settlement are reflected in ss 54(b), 159

---

[648] N Oliver, *Review of Land Dispute Settlement Organisations and Mechanisms* (Port Moresby: Department of Lands and Physical Planning, 1996).

and 172 of the *Constitution*. However, the CILM also put obstacles on the complete realisation of two fundamental principles of land policy. The first is making security of tenure dependent on land use by converting freeholds to government leases and annexing development conditions thereon (CILM Recommendations 21 and 22). The second involves limiting compensation payment on expropriation to the value of the unexhausted improvements on the land, thus excluding the free market notion of land (CILM Recommendation 91).

What is apparent is that land policy became subsumed in the political processes. Colonial history, including that of Papua New Guinea, is notorious for land alienation. The independence constitutions of past colonial states almost invariably set out guarantees of the individual's property rights for those who benefited (individuals and corporations) under the colonial administration. The CPC wanted to break with colonial history. It noted that the policy of constitutional safeguards of private property limited the ability of the nationalist government to redistribute wealth more equitably, or to carry out programs designed to achieve a fairer distribution of resources and the benefits obtained from the use of the land. It, however, found some justification for protection as a means of avoiding the unjust deprivation of people's property rights, which is the most fundamental of human rights contained in the *Constitution*. It proposed, however, limiting that protection to citizens.[649] It was no surprise, therefore, that the criteria for citizenship were unduly influenced by the subject of land rights.

The CPC was concerned to prevent the perpetuation of the status quo in land ownership and at the same time to safeguard the principle of "equality of citizens". If the land rights of the indigenous inhabitants were to be protected and the status quo altered, it saw the solution in narrow citizenship laws. In contrast, the government took a more liberal view of citizenship with the following consequences for the *Constitution*:

(1) A distinction became necessary to protect land rights of citizens based on whether they qualified as automatic or non-automatic citizens (s 68(4)).

(2) Section 68(4) also provided automatic citizens with immediate immunity from the rigours of the policies proposed by the CILM and left non-automatic citizens without protection for five years after independence.

(3) Automatic citizens were reserved certain privileges not enjoyed by the non-automatic citizens, for 10 years after independence.

A non-citizen enjoys no constitutional protection in respect of land rights. The *Land (Ownership of Freeholds) Act* (Ch 359) was passed to convert freehold to leasehold for a period of 99 years. Claims to compensation on the compulsory acquisition of a non-citizen's property is guaranteed by the rules of statute and the underlying law, and the level of compensation is no different from that of the citizen.[650]

THE UNDERLYING LAW

Any meaningful examination of judicial developments in the land laws of Papua New Guinea over the last 20 years must proceed from a constitutional base. Some of these developments have been the subject of analysis elsewhere and so only require brief comment here.[651]

[649] CPC, *Constitutional Planning Committee Final Report: Part 1* (Port Moresby: Government Printer, 1974), p 5/1/15.
[650] *Minister for Lands v Frame* [1980] PNGLR 433.
[651] R W James, *Challenges of Equity in Developing the Underlying Law* (Port Moresby: Faculty of Law, UPNG, 1996).

In *Madaha Resena v Papua New Guinea* [1991] PNGLR 174, the Supreme Court formulated the appropriate rule on the "choice of remedy" (common or customary law) from Sch 2 of the *Constitution*. Through earlier proceedings in the Land Titles Commission, the appellants had established their claim to ownership of Fisherman's Island near Port Moresby by Motuan custom. They had then taken proceedings in the National Court for damages for wrongful occupation by the government for 100 years. The central issue was whether the court was restricted to an award of a customary law remedy because the claim was founded upon and decided by custom. The trial judge thought that for the claimant to switch from custom and ask for common law remedies was incongruous.[652] He held:

> "I do not think that the plaintiffs can have it both ways, that they can choose the kind of law to give them the most advantageous claim. It seems to me that, logically, if their claim to the ownership of the island is based on custom, then their claim to compensation for the government's wrongful use of the island should also be based on custom."

On appeal to the Supreme Court, Amet J in the dissenting judgment argued for the vigorous application of customs over common law and equity, and concluded that there had not been adequate inquiry by the court to discover or ascertain if there was a relevant custom.[653] He treated the issue as one of conflict of laws and expressed support for the judge at first instance.

However, the majority view was that the *Constitution* expressly allowed the operation of a dual system and that therefore, the indigenous inhabitants were free to regulate their rights by customary law as well as common law. The *Constitution* has given them a choice of remedies. This decision could find support from s 155(4) of the *Constitution*, which gives the court power to make such order as the justice of the case requires. This provision supports a complementary approach to remedies.

In *Jivetuo v Papua New Guinea* [1984] PNGLR 174 and *Bai v Morobe Provincial Government* [1992] PNGLR 150 the squatter's equity received protection by the application of s 41 of the *Constitution*. The principle of relief against forfeiture of a lease has been justified in *Nowra No 8 Pty Ltd v Swokin* [1993] PNGLR 498 and also on the basis of the exercise of the court's power under s 41 to provide relief against "harsh or oppressive" acts.

The application of principles of natural justice in administering reserved lands is grounded in ss 59 and 60 of the *Constitution*. This development was started by Amet J in *Re Gegeyo v Minister for Lands* [1987] PNGLR 331. There he asserted a need for the appointing authority (the Minister) to observe principles of natural justice in exercising his undoubted power of removing the members of the trust board (a statutory body) responsible for land dedicated to public use. He held that a power to appoint automatically carried a power to remove, but any revocation or suspension of an appointment involved decisions affecting the status of persons.[654] Therefore there was a duty for the appropriate authority to act "judicially" in exercising those powers. To act judicially in exercising the power of revocation, dismissal or suspension of public trustees, is to act for good cause and only "after giving them ample notice and advice".

[652] *Madaha Resena v Papua New Guinea* [1990] PNGLR 22.
[653] [1991] PNGLR 174 at 191.
[654] [1987] PNGLR 331 at 338.

He extended this principle in his judgment in *Re Application of NCDIC* [1987] PNGLR 339 in order to declare as null and void the purported revocation of land dedicated as a public reserve. He expected that the minimum procedure adopted by the Minister would be to inform, advise, or consult with or give reasons to the trustees (the NCDIC) on the changes he proposed. In *NCDIC v Crusoe Pty Ltd* [1993] PNGLR 139, the principles were extended to the machinery for rezoning land from public purpose use to commercial purposes.

These are examples of the roles some constitutional provisions have played in the development of the underlying law in relation to land. Other provisions such as ss 148(2) and 155(4) have had comparable significance in tailoring the remedy to achieve justice in the circumstances of the particular case.[655]

CONCLUSION

The *Constitution* has to some extent been a positive force in shaping the land tenure laws and policies of Papua New Guinea. On the other hand, it has had some negative impact due partly to some specific provisions on land, and partly because of the openendedness of other provisions. Some judges have confused some concepts, there being notorious examples. One involves the indefeasibility principle of land registration, which in *Emas Estate v Mea* [1993] PNGLR 215 was confused with the "circumstantial applicability" limitation on the reception of the common law (Sch 2.2(1)(b)). Another involves the provisions on the hierarchy of "laws" (s 9 of the *Constitution*), which was interpreted in *Papua New Guinea v Lohia Sisia* [1987] PNGLR 102 to defeat settled principles of law including the indefeasibility principles. In this case, the learned judge had clearly gone astray in his observation that:

> "The *Constitution* is a superior law to a statute, and any statute must be read subject to the constitution - see s10 of the *Constitution*. Thus, s 155(4) of the *Constitution* overrides s 9 of the *National Land Registration Act* which provides that the Minister's declaration under s 8 shall not be subject to appeal or review nor called in question in any legal proceeding, and s 19 of the Act which states that registration is conclusive evidence of the State's title to the land."[656]

This, it is submitted, is to give s 155(4) a jurisdictional interpretation, a course of action beyond the intention of the framers of the *Constitution*. On the whole, one would agree with Brunton and Colquhoun-Kerr that, with minor exceptions, judges have refrained from construing s 155(4) as a mandate to overrule the ordinary law.[657] "Justice" in s 155(4), like the expression in s 158, must mean "justice according to law".

The property protection provisions in the *Constitution* could have some inhibiting effects on the implementation of policy. First, they frustrate the realisation of the policy of making "security of tenure dependent on land use". It is my view that the recommendation of the CILM on the need to

[655] RW James, above n 8, Chs 3-4.
[656] [1987] PNGLR 102 at 108.
[657] B Brunton and D Colquhoun-Kerr, *The Annotated Constitution of Papua New Guinea* (Port Moresby: UPNG Press, 1984), p 341.

extend the pool of national land for public purposes could be nullified by a strict interpretation of s 53(5)(e) of the *Constitution.* These issues require some further elaboration.

Recommendations 21 and 22 of the CILM on conversion of freehold titles could only be partly implemented (in relation to non-citizens), and could not be realised over citizens' holdings because of the constitutional guarantee of property rights. Conversion would amount to expropriation of the freehold reversion for which substantial compensation payments would become necessary to citizens. This limitation to freehold titles conversion has confounded the underlying policy aim of the recommendation; that is, to relate security of tenure to development.

As for waste and vacant declarations, the CILM was at one and the same time critical of the concept of such declarations, but supportive of the conversion of unoccupied lands into national lands for public purposes. So, on the one hand, it wanted such declarations to be outlawed, but then recommended that government should have the power, where "big virgin lands were idle", to declare parts of it as "national lands". Following this recommendation the phraseology of "declaration of government land" was adopted in place of "waste and vacant declaration". Section 75(1) of the *Land Act* states that:

> "The Minister may, by notice in the National Gazette, declare that any land that appears to him not to be customary land shall, unless good cause is shown to the contrary, be conclusively deemed for all purposes, at the expiration of three months from the date of publication of the notice, not to be customary land."

The CILM was of the view that all land other than alienated land was customary land and there was no ownerless land, a principle expressed by a Manus chief as "every object has a mother". It recommended what it thought were appropriate safeguards to avoid the resurgence of colonial abuses. First, the power should only be exercised when and where government had a real need for the land. Secondly, as a condition precedent, the government must engage in a thorough investigation to ascertain that the land had not been used for agricultural purposes in the past 20 years. Thirdly, hunting and gathering rights, if any, of the people should be preserved. Fourthly, all disputes arising from a declaration should be justiciable.

The issue of "waste and vacant declaration" was highly sensitive and the CPC stayed clear of it in its discussions. Although it recommended a long list of exceptions to the property protection, it only acknowledged in passing the desirability of a law that makes provisions for the acquisition of "abandoned, unoccupied, unutilised or underdeveloped land (other than customary land)".[658] This recommendation formed s 53(5)(e) of the *Constitution*, which states:

> "Nothing in the preceding provisions of this section prevents any taking of possession or acquisition of ownerless or abandoned property (other than customary land)."

Surprisingly, what appears in the parenthesis to be a clear proscription of "waste and vacant declaration" can give rise to conflicting interpretations. I have been guided by an initial assumption that all unalienated land is customary land and have taken the view that the import of the phrase is to prohibit such declarations by whatever name used. Section 75 of the *Land Act* is, therefore, on my reasoning, unconstitutional and the numerous declarations made under that section can only acquire legality from the nebulous concept of "act of state".

---

[658] CPC, above n 6, p 5/1/30.

It is obvious that a different view is taken by government, for such declarations are everyday occurrences. The 1996 Report by former Land Titles Commissioner, Norm Oliver,[659] does not clarify the issue of constitutionality. It appears to assume the legality of such declarations without arguments. It makes no comment on the subject of constitutionality, except to observe that the jurisdiction of the Land Titles Commission to hear disputes from a s 75 *Land Act* declaration was expected to be transferred to the National Lands Commission on the passage of the *Land Registration Act*. But that was not done.

Such declarations can be valid only if one takes the opposing view that some unalienated lands in Papua New Guinea are ownerless. These are not customary lands and, therefore, could be subject to a s 75 declaration. This view could lead to abuses by Ministers in the absence of safeguards of the kind recommended by the CILM. In my view there is uncertainty of the meaning of the constitutional provision and this fact begs for a special reference to the Supreme Court pursuant to s 19 of the *Constitution*.

Finally, there are areas where the *Constitution* could have been explicit, but it has unfortunately omitted some fundamentals to chance. The ownership of mines and minerals and the decentralisation of land matters are two such matters. It could be argued that clearer statements are necessary to quash speculation on these issues.

[659] Above n 5.

Chapter 22

THE CONSTITUTION AND THE ENVIRONMENT

MEG TAYLOR

INTRODUCTION

To appreciate the prescience of the Constitutional Planning Committee's (CPC) views and recommendations on the subject of the environment, it must be remembered that in the main, the environment has become a major issue internationally in the years since 1972 when the CPC began its work to frame the *Constitution* of Papua New Guinea.

Yet, as discussed later in this chapter, the CPC made the environment a constitutional issue. Undoubtedly, Papua New Guinea was one of the first countries in the world to do so. To understand the significance of the environment as a constitutional issue, it is necessary to first highlight the growing significance of the environment as a matter of major international concern.

THE ENVIRONMENT AS AN INTERNATIONAL ISSUE

The United Nations Conference on Environment and Development (UNCED) held in Rio de Janeiro, Brazil, in June 1992 generated greater expectations than any similar international conferences. The most important item on the agenda was securing a just and environmentally sustainable future for humanity. Put more dramatically, the issue was the survival of our planet Earth.

UNCED followed many years of work already done by other international gatherings, most notably the Stockholm Conference in 1972 and the Report of the World Commission on Environment and Development (popularly called the Bruntland Commission) in 1987. Over time, the focus of the international environment agenda changed from concerns about pressure on the environment caused by poverty, to one of "sustainable development". This shift in the global agenda called for a new type of development at the regional and national levels.

The spectacle of Rio left many participants with mixed feelings of euphoria, deep disappointment, doubts about the future and the stirring of new hope. Much was achieved at UNCED, as reflected in the agreements concluded there which set new directions for international action to save the planet Earth. Global environmental action would be co-ordinated through the following agreements:

- the *Framework for the Convention on Climate Change*;
- the *Convention on the Protection of Biological Diversity*;
- the *Rio Declaration on Environment and Development*;
- the action program for environmental issues known as Agenda 21; and
- the *Statement of Principles for a Global Consensus on the Management, Conservation and Sustainable Development of all Types of Forests (Forest Principles).*

The Rio Declaration contains 27 principles aimed at achieving the goals of Agenda 21. Its goal is to bring global economic and social development into harmony with the planet's resources in the decades ahead. UNCED led to the establishment of the Commission for Sustainable Development (CSD) which is tasked with the role of co-ordinating the implementation of Agenda 21. Agenda 21 is an action program for dealing with environmental issues such as soil erosion, deforestation, desertification, atmospheric change and toxic waste, and development issues such as poverty, habitation and health. On the practical side, governments agreed in principle in Rio on the outline of the institutional mechanism to oversee the implementation of Agenda 21 and began to assemble the necessary financial resources needed to carry it out.

In his speech to the international audience assembled in Rio, Papua New Guinea's Governor-General, Sir Wiwa Korowi, pointed out that:

> "We all appreciate our own responsibilities wherever we stand in the spectrum of economic development. In these crucial years ahead of us, we cannot afford to take entrenched positions, but must fully appreciate the needs and concerns of the other members of the global community, our children and their children's children.
>
> I pledge my country's commitment to global partnership stated here in Rio de Janeiro for a safer world for us and the future generation."[660]

Papua New Guinea has since ratified both the *Convention on Climate Change and the Convention on the Protection of Biological Diversity* as an indication of its willingness to be a partner in this global action. Although Papua New Guinea has shown its commitment by ratifying the conventions, the real issue is how Papua New Guinea responds to the global agenda at the domestic level.

THE ENVIRONMENT AS A CONSTITUTIONAL ISSUE

Reflecting the growing international concern about the environment, the issue is becoming not only the subject of national legislative programs, but also a matter of constitutional law in some other countries. For instance, the new *Constitution* of the Republic of Uganda, adopted in 1995, has made "a clean and healthy environment" a constitutional right (s 39). This right is enforceable in the same way as the standard civil and political rights.

Although Papua New Guinea's constitutional provisions do not go that far, it is nevertheless one of the few countries of the world which has made the environment a matter of constitutional concern. Twenty years of experience in Papua New Guinea offers lessons about the environment as a constitutional issue.

Overview of the CPC's view of the environment

The CPC's approach to the environment was to link the essential elements of the Papua New Guinea society; namely, the people, their resources and their environment. The CPC saw the need to join them for what they defined as proper development, and what we currently refer to as sustainable development.

[660] *PNG Post Courier*, 19 June 1992.

This approach meant that the CPC did not treat the environment in isolation from the people benefiting from the exploitation or use of the nation's natural resources. The CPC's reasoning recognised the nature of our natural resources. The CPC had an appreciation of the earth and nature as having its own spiritual essence. In their words, environmental degradation not only causes pollution, but "death of the earth".[661] The CPC saw the present generation as a trustee for future generations. It therefore recommended that the present generation should use the natural resources and the environment wisely so as to meet present needs while at the same time ensuring that future generations would not suffer due to the destruction of the environment and the lack of natural resources.

The CPC went further and addressed the issues arising from dominance of short-term development strategies designed only to secure short-term benefits. It warned the nation of the dangerous consequences of such strategies, and reminded us of the limits we must impose on ourselves, if the future is to be safeguarded. It talked of the need to limit the speed of exploitation of resources and the need to "replenish them".[662]

In the CPC's view, use of our resources cannot justify environmental degradation, which not only involves the destruction of land, rivers and wildlife, but also destroys the integral development of our people. The CPC strongly emphasised that we should develop a sense of respect for our natural resources and the environment. The CPC vision infers that we have definite choices for development. Unsustainable development practices, and a development agenda that neglects the human face of Papua New Guinea, would have dire consequences.

The CPC and sustainable development

The philosophy and recommendations of the CPC on the environment, and especially on sustainable development, were radical for the early 1970s. Twenty years on, they remain relevant and radical because of the accuracy of their analysis and because we remain a long way off the course set by the designers of the *Constitution*. When we compare the current definitions of sustainable development and approaches to sustainable development, we find that the thinking of the CPC was very consistent with the current concepts.

Goal No 4 of the National Goals and Directive Principles is in the following terms:

> "We declare our fourth goal to be for Papua New Guinea's natural resources and environment to be conserved and used for the collective benefit of us all, and be replenished for the benefit of future generations.
>
> We accordingly call for-
>
> (1) wise use of our natural resources and the environment in and on the land or seabed, in the sea, under the land, and in the air, in the interests of our development and in trust for future generations; and
>
> (2) the conservation and replenishment, for the benefit of ourselves and posterity, of the environment and its sacred, scenic, and historical qualities; and

[661] CPC, *Constitutional Planning Committee Final Report: Part 1* (Port Moresby: Government Printer, 1974), p 2/12.
[662] Ibid.

(3) all necessary steps to be taken to give adequate protection to our valued birds, animals, fish, insects, plants and trees."

National Goal No 4 was clearly intended to put Papua New Guinea on the pathway to sustainable development. It is illuminating to compare the *Constitution* with more recent statements of the principles. For instance, according to the Bruntland Commission:

> "Sustainable development is development that meets the needs of the present, without compromising the ability of future generations to meet their own needs."

The Bruntland Commission noted that sustainable development is not a fixed state, but:

> "a process of change in which the exploitation of resources, the direction of investments, the orientation of technological development, and institutional change are made with concern for the future as well as present needs. Painful choices have to be made. This sustainable development must rest on political will."

There is a clear connection between National Goal No 4 and the Bruntland Commission views on sustainable development. National Goal No 4 certainly laid the foundation for developing a sustainable development strategy for Papua New Guinea. It is now widely accepted that sustainable development is not sectoral in responsibility. That is, it does not separate agendas for society, economy and environment. Rather, it is the interaction of:

(a) a viable natural environment capable of supporting life, now and in the future;

(b) a sufficient economy that provides a sustainable livelihood for all; and

(c) nurturing communities that provide opportunities for meeting social, cultural or spiritual needs.[663]

As recently as the 20th Waigani Seminar in 1993 on "Environment and Development" many of us were naively looking for Papua New Guinean processes and pathways to deal with the current direction of unsustainable development in Papua New Guinea. International economic forces, modern powerful technologies, consumption patterns and new ideas have had and are having a powerful impact on our still largely "traditional" society. The consequence is that we face a major social, environmental and economic upheaval which threatens our very survival. This threat is being cultivated by the rapid changes that occur each year with new development projects, poor fiscal management, lack of good governance, lack of basic services in health and education, and the depletion of natural resources with little benefit to either local communities or to the nation as a whole. All this was predicted by the CPC.

Development through Papua New Guinea Ways

The final link in the CPC's report in linking resources, environment and development together, is the process by which sustainable development can be achieved. It was encapsulated in National Goal No 5, being Papua New Guinean Ways. In the CPC's view, development should take place primarily through the use of Papua New Guinea forms of social, political and economic organisation. From this standpoint, development must involve the full participation of the people.

[663] Ministry for the Environment, *Living for the Future: A Guide to Agenda 21* (Wellington: Ministry for the Environment, 1993).

It must be a process under which development takes place through institutions and techniques that are not only meaningful to Papua New Guinea, but which also recognise human dignity and enhance it. In promoting traditional ways, we are encouraged to recognise and use the central elements of Papua New Guinean society. Chief among these are participation, consultation and consensus.

When we looked for constructive models for sustainable development within Papua New Guinea, as we did during the 20th Waigani Seminar, we found that provinces, such as Manus, had utilised processes involving participation, consultation and consensus in drawing up development plans. As a result, priority in Manus was shifted to the development of the people, especially through education. Economic development was lower down the scale. The importance of this experience is that it provides a model where genuine Papua New Guinean ways were actually utilised, merging them with modern methods of documentation and implementation, to produce a workable plan.

IMPLEMENTING THE CPC VISION

In its wisdom the CPC recommended the inclusion of the principles of sustainable development in the *Constitution*. While there is no other mention of the environment in the Constitution, National Goal No 4 was clearly intended to be a direction to the government and the country as a whole. The question is: how far has Papua New Guinea been able to implement this constitutional policy on environment and natural resources? I will address this issue from the legal perspective.

Environmental legislation

The only legislative action taken which could be regarded as intended to give effect to the radical vision of the CPC was a package of three pieces of legislation passed by the Parliament in 1978. It comprises the *Environmental Planning Act* (Ch 370), the *Environmental Contaminants Act* (Ch 368) and the *Conservation Areas Act* (Ch 362).

The main instrument for balancing development and environmental planning is the *Environmental Planning Act,* under which ministerial guidelines are issued for the preparation and content of environmental plans. The first ministerial guidelines were issued in 1982 and later amended in 1985. The guidelines cover a wide range of matters which must be considered in preparing environmental plans for ministerial approval. The guidelines cover environmental, social, cultural, economic and commercial aspects of a proposed project. Developers are required to submit environmental plans for any project that may have "significant environmental implications", unless it is a class of development exempted by the Act.

A number of steps must be complied with before ministerial approval is given. These include:

(a) preparation of an environmental impact assessment;

(b) the circulation of the environmental plan as widely as possible;

(c) an assessment of the environmental plan by the provincial government of the province affected and by interested parties and the public; and

(d) an assessment of the environmental plan by the department.

The Act has many commendable features. It depends, however, for its full effectiveness upon a well-motivated Minister and competent department, an active and well-informed provincial government and local-level governments, and active involvement of the people affected by the proposed development projects.

The *Environmental Contaminants Act* is intended to control the release into the environment of any substance or form of energy which might adversely affect beneficial use of the environment. The term "beneficial use" means a "use" conducive to public benefit, welfare, safety or health, or the health or productivity of flora and fauna. The Act creates a range of pollution offences, including the pollution of waters, the atmosphere and land, as well as littering, breaking glass and noise pollution.

Finally, the *Conservation Areas Act* encourages the active participation of people in the conservation of their own resources. The basic approach of the statute is to enable an area of customary land to be declared a conservation area at the request of the landowners. The Minister for Environment and Conservation then makes a proclamation and encourages the landowners to form their own management committee for the area. The committee is required to prepare a management plan for the area. The Act then prohibits any development of any kind in the area, except in accordance with the management plan. Any development that complies with the management plan must be implemented in close consultation with the management committee.

The greatest disappointment for many landowners and concerned citizens is that the Act has not been implemented. And as a result no conservation areas have been declared under it.

Natural resources legislation

Whilst enlightened environmental laws were introduced in 1978, they are not entirely in harmony with the different sets of legislation which facilitate the development of natural resources in the country. Specific natural resources are regulated by their own legislation. These include the *Mining Act* 1992, the *Petroleum Act* 1976 (Ch 198), the *Forestry Act* 1991, the *Land Act* 1996 and the *Water Resources Act* 1982 (Ch 205). The basic thrust of these laws is to facilitate access to natural resources for development. Access is to be gained exclusively through the various agencies of the state responsible for these natural resources, whether the resource is regarded as state-owned, as in the case of minerals and petroleum, or capable of private ownership, as in the case of land and forests.

In the past natural resources were developed with very little input from the landowners. However, the process of developing natural resources is gradually being reformed. The reason is that landowners are making it abundantly clear that they want to be included as direct participants in negotiations for access to resources, and as direct shareholders in development projects. This approach has important implications for conservation and environmental protection. It means that landowners have the capacity to have a direct influence on the nature of the project, ensuring that their concerns about a project's impact on their physical and cultural environment can be accommodated in project planning and implementation. Whilst the aims are admirable, the reality so far, especially in relation to forestry projects, has been short-term "development" at the expense of the environment. Tragically, this choice has been pursued vigorously by landowners and their representatives with the developers in the forestry sector.

The new trend towards landowner involvement also raises three new issues which cannot be developed in any detail in this chapter. The first issue that quickly attracts attention is the environmental impact of such "development" on other stakeholders who are not direct beneficiaries or landowners in a project. An obvious example concerns communities in areas distant from a project but nevertheless subject to its impacts. They include people living along waterways and near the ocean areas which suffer impacts and environmental change caused by mining, petroleum and forestry projects. How can they be involved in the decision-making process? Are their interests covered under the various agreements concluded between the major players in a development project? Such issues need to be addressed more thoroughly in the future. Sustainable development as envisaged by the CPC would have taken such groups into consideration at the earliest possible stage of consideration of a development project.

The second issue that requires some attention is the role of the state as an independent arbiter in matters relating to the environment. The CPC's vision implies that the state should play such a role, keeping an overview of the interplay of potentially conflicting interests. Among other things, the role of the state should be to monitor environmental and social impact and to monitor the developers' performance. It is apparent, however, that when the state acquires equity in major natural resource projects, it tends to relinquish its role as the independent arbiter on matters relating to a project, especially in matters involving environmental and social impact. When the state is an equity partner, the perception is that it has a role in the management of the project and an interest in profits derived from it. It is therefore, at least in part, responsible for environmental damage caused in the pursuit of profits. In such circumstances, the state is not impartial and therefore may not be accessible to the people whose interests are adversely affected by the project.

The third issue concerns the role of landowners as direct equity partners. In that role, is it possible to maintain their independence and influence the direction of a project, and monitor environmental impacts on their environment, or will they be tempted to pursue development for short-term profits? Are they going to be concerned about those down-river, or in adjacent forests, or in ocean areas directly damaged by the development projects from which they receive direct benefit? And are they going to be concerned about the environmental problems the development projects may create for their future generations? These are issues that need to be addressed seriously if we are to ensure wise use of our environment and natural resources and the equitable distribution of wealth from the utilisation of our natural resources.

Enforcing the National Goals and Directive Principles

It is clear that the vision of the CPC as embodied in the *Constitution* is not being realised. In part, this is because the National Goals and Directive Principles are intended mainly to be a guide in judicial interpretation, and are not directly justiciable due to the limitations set by s 25(1) of the *Constitution*. In terms of National Goal No 4, there is no substantive provision in the *Constitution* giving effect to it.

Hence, a right to protect the environment cannot be enforced in the same way as the right to vote, or the right to freedom of movement. Most constitutional authorities seem to think this means that an executive act or a statute cannot be challenged before the courts on the ground that it conflicts with the National Goals and Directive Principles. Therefore, the constitutional commitment to the environment and the sustainable use of natural resources can only be treated as a statement of intent: serious and deliberate, but not ultimately enforceable.

However, there is a proposition that the National Goals and Directive Principles can be used to challenge legislative and executive actions where these actions are in conflict with the National Goals and Directive Principles. This argument is based on a careful reading of s 25(3) of the *Constitution*. It seems to say that the National Goals and Directive Principles shall be applied and given effect to unless a law or any power conferred by law explicitly excludes the application, exercise or enforcement of the National Goals and Directive Principles. This argument has not been tested in the courts as yet.

ENVIRONMENTAL RIGHTS AS CONSTITUTIONAL RIGHTS

In this section of the chapter I propose to look at the progress made in Uganda since 1994 as an example to support the proposition that environmental rights should become constitutional in Papua New Guinea. I have chosen Uganda as an example to show the global trend in making environmental rights constitutional and also because of the constitution-making process used to adopt a new constitution, which was similar to that used in Papua New Guinea.

The Uganda Constitutional Commission (UCC) was required to evolve a new constitution based on the views of the people, the government and interested individuals, and followed by accurate and critical analysis of views, and comparative study of other constitutions.

In comparing the work of the CPC and the UCC, there was clearly the desire for both constitutions to reflect the views and aspirations of its people. However, Uganda's *Constitution* gives more emphasis than ours to some similar issues that are of greater significance today than they were in 1974, the environment being one such issue.

The UCC went further in its treatment of the subject, as more is known about the importance of the environment to communities and governments today then 20 years ago. The UCC dealt with the issue of environmental impacts and actually nominated the institutions responsible to co-ordinate and implement their national environment plan of action. It also recommended that environmental awareness be incorporated through environmental education at all levels of the education system and that environmental legislation should be reviewed and updated to take into account present and future environmental and development needs of the country. These recommendations are extremely progressive. They look to the future and they look at issues both domestically and internationally.

The National Objectives and Directive Principles of State Policy of the Uganda *Constitution* are similar to our National Goals and Directive Principles. On the issue of environment they are in the following terms:

> "The Environment
>
> (i) The State shall promote sustainable development and public awareness of the need to manage land, air, water resources in a balanced and sustainable manner for the present and future generation.

(ii) The utilisation of the natural resources of Uganda shall be managed in such a way as to meet the development and environmental needs of present and future generations of Ugandans; and in particular, the State shall take all possible measures to prevent or minimise damage and destruction to land, air and water resources resulting from pollution or other causes.

(iii) The State shall promote and implement energy policies that will ensure that people's basic needs and those of environmental preservation are met.

(iv) The State, including local governments, shall:-

(a) create and develop sports, reserves and recreation areas and ensure the conservation of natural resources;

(b) promote the rational use of natural resources so as to safeguard and protect the bio-diversity of Uganda."[664]

This state policy on the environment reflects the importance that Ugandans place on their environment and natural resources. In formulating this policy, the UCC was mindful of the issues of:

(a) ozone depletion and global warming;

(b) destruction of rain forests and destruction of arable land;

(c) wasteful use of energy resources;

(d) water and air pollution;

(e) bio-diversity and bio-technology;

(f) the manufacture, testing, stockpiling and the use of nuclear and conventional weapons;

(g) dumping of industrial, nuclear and other toxic wastes; and

(h) most importantly, population pressure.[665]

To give substance to the policy, environmental protection was included as a right in the new *Constitution*, thereby giving enormous importance to the preservation and enhancement of the environment. Section 39 says every Ugandan has a right to a clean and healthy environment. The place of the environment in the *Constitution* itself, as a right, is unique. It says a lot about how the Ugandan society addresses the issue of environment. An enforceable right of this kind is a quantum shift in emphasis. The environment is now too important to be left in the category of mere guidelines for judicial interpretation.

CONCLUSION

In Papua New Guinea the question of constitutional enforceability of environmental rights needs to be considered. Do the National Goals and Directive Principles give the people sufficient rights to a safe and healthy environment? This question has not yet been resolved by the courts. If Papua

[664] Clause XXVII of the National Objectives and Directive Principles of State Policy, Preamble, *Constitution of the Republic of Uganda.*

[665] Ugandan Constitutional Commission, *The Report of the Ugandan Constitutional Commission: Analysis and Recommendations* (Kampala: Government of Uganda, 1993), p 693.

New Guinea were to adopt a constitutional provision making the right to a clean and healthy environment a constitutional right, the implications for "development" would be enormous.

This proposal is radical and would therefore create some apprehension and doubts from many sectors of our community, especially the business community. However, if we look at the behaviour of "responsible" corporations since the Rio Summit, we see a slow but significant move by corporations towards sound environmental practice. Many corporations are encompassing the principles of "environmental best practice" or "environmental excellence" standards. This trend has emerged because the public demands it.

If we entrench environmental rights in our *Constitution*, supported by enabling legislation promoting environmental best practice, corporations fearful of litigation and unable and unwilling to comply with high environmental standards would move elsewhere. In effect, such a provision would strengthen environmental performance and put greater responsibility on corporations and individuals.

APPENDIX

APPENDIX

TRANSCRIPT OF DISCUSSION BY PANEL OF CONSTITUTION-MAKERS, PORT MORESBY

28 MARCH 1996

PARTICIPANTS

- **Sir Michael Somare – Chairman of the Constitutional Planning Committee (CPC)**
- **John Momis – Deputy Chairman of the CPC**
- **Pikah Kasau – Member of the CPC**
- **Matiabe Yuwi – Member of the CPC**
- **Mackenzie Daugi – Member of the CPC**
- **Stanis Toliman – Member of the CPC**
- **Anton Parao – Member of the CPC**
- **Seaea Avosa – Executive Officer to the CPC**
- **Bernard Narokobi – Adviser to the CPC**
- **Edward Wolfers – Adviser to the CPC**
- **Sir Ebia Olewale – Minister for Justice, 1972-75**
- **Sir Barry Holloway – Speaker of the House of Assembly (1972-75) and Chairman of the National Constituent Assembly**
- **Ilinome Tarua – Adviser to the Somare Government, 1972-75**
- **Meg Taylor – Adviser to the Somare Government**
- **Nahau Rooney – Adviser to the Somare Government.**

The panel discussion was held in Port Moresby on 28 March 1996, as part of a three-day conference examining the first 20 years of operation of the Papua New Guinea *Constitution*. The discussion was in two parts. The first part, chaired by Sir Mari Kapi (Deputy Chief Justice of the Supreme Court), was a general discussion, where each panel member was invited to give her or his views on any aspect of the making of the *Constitution* that he or she wished to address. The second part, chaired by Anthony Regan (then of the Law Faculty, University of Papua New Guinea) was a more structured discussion, with the chairman introducing topics largely by reference to successive stages in the constitution-making process.

PART ONE: GENERAL DISCUSSION

Mr Pikah Kasau: When I was first elected to Parliament in 1972, I was four months short of my 25th birthday. When the House of Assembly set up the CPC in June 1972, the underlying desire was that the committee should seek the views of the people of Papua New Guinea to enable it to come up with a report to provide the basis for the House of Assembly to draw up a home-grown constitution. No member of the CPC left the shores of Papua New Guinea during our three years of work.

There were some factors that helped the work of the CPC and the House of Assembly in developing the written constitution. One involved the colonial administration, and the harsh attitude of some colonial officers towards the people and the hardship people experienced under the administration. This was a factor behind the people's support for the move for early independence. There was certainly a growing nationalism. During the third House of Assembly elections in 1972, Michael Somare campaigned for self-government and eventual independence. The feeling for national independence at that time spread beyond the corridors of the House of Assembly, particularly to the public service where a young, educated and enthusiastic workforce was waiting to take over from the colonial officers. Nationalistic support was also felt in the districts and towns and villages during the CPC's public meetings. People expressed their nationalistic views openly and at times became very emotional. A second important factor concerned the Australian Labor Party Government that was elected just after the CPC began its work. The co-operation of the colonial administration in preparing Papua New Guinea for independence was probably greater because of the election of the new government in Australia. Canberra co-operated fully.

But there were also some constraints, and they slowed the CPC's process of collecting information and created some uncertainty in the country. First, a lot of colonial officers were concerned about their employment and did not support the move to independence. These officers encouraged fear in the minds of our people by saying Papua New Guinea would become chaotic immediately after independence. Secondly, there were foreign business interests, some run by former colonial officers who had set up in plantations, transport and communication. They were not keen to see Papua New Guinea as independent, fearing they would be forced out of their businesses. Some of those people were also elected members of the House of Assembly. So when we were debating the constitution you had the feeling their business interests were a concern for them. A third factor concerned mixed race people, some of whom were caught up in the constitutional debate about citizenship status at the time of independence. Our people sympathised with many such people: ol papa i go na ol i stap. But there were also some such people who were enjoying the privileges of foreigners and they were resented. As a result, citizenship debate sometimes got out of hand and sometimes became quite personal. And fourth, the United Party in the House of Assembly did not want self-government and independence so soon. Some of them tried their best to disrupt the CPC both in the House and outside. They were not successful mainly because young United Party members like Anton Parao, and some senior people like Mackenzie Daugi, supported the CPC. The tide was turning in favour of independence, so people had to get on the canoe or else get left behind. The young members saw that and decided to participate.

Mr Matiabe Yuwi: I was a member of the House of Assembly and then of the national Parliament representing the Tari Open electorate. I agree with what Mr Pikah Kasau said. The *Constitution* was started here in Port Moresby, but then it really went into the villages of this country. The leaders of that time, Sir Michael Somare and John Momis, agreed on the rules, and they obeyed those rules. But since then many leaders have made rules as if they were fences: they have made their own fences and have then broken the fences themselves, letting in the wild dogs and wild pigs that have eaten away the gardens. I fear that the country is not united in the way we dreamt that it would be.

Mr Mackenzie Daugi: I am the former regional member of the House of Assembly for Oro province. We in the CPC were given the difficult task of coming up with a constitution, taking into account all the aspirations and needs of our people. In order to collect the views from our people, both educated and village people, the CPC members had to work together even though they came from different parties and groups. I was a member of the United Party and I thought that I would influence the bulk of the United Party to support self-government and independence. That was my motive. In fact, as a United Party representative in the CPC, I faced difficult pressure from the party and also from the governing group, which produced its own proposals.

In order to come up with an acceptable constitution, after the CPC submitted its Final Report to the House of Assembly, the CPC members formed the Nationalist Pressure Group to work in the House of Assembly and the National Constituent Assembly. We did that in order to continue to ignore party politics, to ignore the government pressure, to ignore the bureaucrats. To give you an idea of the pressure we were sometimes under, we felt that our telephones were being tapped illegally. As a result, the CPC had to change the venues it used for its work every now and again.

There are areas where perhaps the CPC overlooked possible problems or didn't have enough time to come up with what was really needed. Looking back now, I don't know why we didn't make enough provisions in our *Constitution* for the accountability of the national Parliament. The many unnecessary votes of no-confidence since independence indicate that perhaps the CPC didn't spell things out clearly enough, and as a result successive governments have had this sickness of votes of no-confidence being brought unnecessarily.

There are other areas in our *Constitution* where there are problems. For example, Mr Momis raised the issue of natural resources. In the proposals about the National Goals and Directive Principles, the CPC spelt it out, stating that anything that came out of the natural resources should be fairly distributed for the benefit of the mass of the population. Is it happening? Is it abuse of the *Constitution* for the leaders to use the products or outcome of the natural resources for their own benefit, denying the mass of the population the share of it? Do your fathers and mothers back at home have 50 toea to pay the aid post fees?

When it came up in the Parliament in 1994 about the Prime Minister resigning to escape a motion of no confidence, one wonders whether elected leaders used what the founding fathers put down on paper. I come from Oro province and my papers are in Oro province although I'm in Port Moresby. So I went to the Archives to see what was there. The only things were the CPC Report, of two volumes. I wonder whether our national leaders have the interest to go and look through these two volumes. Because when the issue came up in the Parliament and in the court, those of us who made the *Constitution* knew that it had been breached. We didn't make any noise at all but we were sitting quietly hoping that the law will take its own cause, and the law did.

Whoever advised the Prime Minister in 1994 didn't look back to see why the CPC made recommendations for provisions in the *Constitution*. I also went into the National Library to see what it holds for the younger generations. There are some things, but not enough. Where are all those documents that the CPC produced? This information should be readily available so that the coming generations can read it, so that if their leaders are stepping out of line, the people will know that they are abusing the *Constitution*.

Mr Stanis Toliman: I am from Rabaul, but it was not the people of Rabaul, the Tolai, who elected me to Parliament: it was the people of Bogia, Madang province. I was a foundation member of the People's Progress Party (PPP), and it was the PPP that nominated me to the CPC. We in the CPC collected the ideas of the people and we put them down on paper. One important thing back then was the Eight Point Plan. When that was first adopted I went back to Bogia and preached about it everywhere, and about the constitution. We took the ideas of the Eight Point Plan into the *Constitution*. But now you don't hear of those ideas anymore. That is part of the problem facing Papua New Guinea now. We don't have goals any more. Our goals have been thrown away.

We also put into the *Constitution* provision for three positions for nominated members. We expected nominated members to represent women. But there are now no women MPs, no women in Cabinet. Where is the equal participation the *Constitution* provided for?

Sir Ebia Olewale: First, I want to talk about the Head of State, the Governor-General as we call him now. The CPC recommended for the Head of State to be elected by the people. But when the Cabinet considered the CPC's report, we thought about what we were bringing together to form Papua New Guinea. Those of you who know the history will remember that before independence we were made up of two territories. One was the United Nations Trust Territory of New Guinea and the other was Australia's Territory of Papua. We were bringing both together to form one country as a Melanesian people, because we are one people. That question of unity was foremost in our minds. We were concerned about things that were happening in other developing countries, in newly independent countries in Africa, in South America and in parts of Asia. We thought that we must make a constitution that made sure that these kinds of things could not happen in our country. And we were aware that we were a young country.

The Somare Government wanted a Head of State elected by the Parliament so that both parts - Papua and New Guinea - could have one senior position. On the Papuan side at that time, in the Cabinet we had Sir Maori Kiki, Ruben Taureka, Gavera Rea, and myself. On our side we were also keen about keeping links to the Queen because Papua was then part of Australia, and although we were coming together with New Guinea we wanted to keep that. Also we believed we would have some kind of strength in unity. That's how we felt then. We thought that we should recognise the Queen as Head of State but that the Governor-General would be elected by the Parliament. Then the Parliament would advise the Queen through the Prime Minister, saying "this is our choice, you have no option, you appoint this person as our Governor-General".

Now, it was not put into the law, but there was a convention that we decided on at the time, and I want to explain it. Since Michael Somare was from the other side - New Guinea - and since he was to be the first Prime Minister, we thought that we should have a Governor-General who was going to be a Papuan. So Sir John Guise was made the first Governor-General. And those of us who made the *Constitution*, we thought that this convention was going to continue to be practised. That is why the first Governor-General was Sir John Guise, then Sir Tore Lokoloko, then Sir Kingsford Dibela. But after that Ignatius Kilage became the Governor-General.

Mr Bernard Narokobi: I was Legal Counsel with the Public Solicitor's Office in 1971. Sir John Guise was concerned that there were only white faces on the advisory team for the CPC. So I was asked to join the team also to assist the CPC.

I had first come to know Sir Michael Somare when he was my teacher in grade 6. He did a bad job on me. Anyway, he later sent me to Rabaul, to Kerevat, where I met Rabbie Namaliu, who was my Sergeant in the School Cadets. I was then sent on to Sydney, where I met that rebel Momis who had been kicked out of Madang Seminary and sent to Toongabbie in Australia to finish his studies to be a priest.

We all met here in Port Moresby to prepare for self-government and independence. At that time, I was very idealistic, like most of the CPC. We wanted the best for this country. Some of us - including me - were also very naive. We didn't know what power and politics was all about. Most of us were mostly unworldly. In those days, as long as we had a roof over our heads and we could walk and we could have food in our stomach, we were happy to serve our nation. And that, really, I think was the basis of the inspiration, the drive for self-government and for independence. That period was a great learning experience for me. It was an inspiring period. I knew before I joined the CPC that it was a sin to say "bloody". But when I went there, I learnt that it was a holy word and the use of "f's" was also necessary in politics. My best teachers were John Kaupa, John Momis and John Kaputin.

Many of the people actually didn't know what self-government was. Some referred to it as "self kambang": they thought that it was a promotion when you move from "self kambang" to "underpants", which actually was independence.

When we went to Kainantu, we were thrown out of the hotel because we didn't wear shoes. In Bereina, we almost had a big fight with Ron Slaughter: he almost slaughtered us. He wanted dual citizenship and all of us said, "no, you are either here or there. To be a citizen here you either live and die here or you don't belong here".

In Mendi, we almost had a big fight with Ron Neville. He didn't want independence. But Kaputin shouted him down, and we ended up in his hotel and had a good meal there.

That period gave me a great deal of experience in visiting way out places, like Kaintiba, Marawaka, Kasiki, Menyama. I even went to the Johnson Cargo Cult Movement country called New Hanover and we had a meeting in a tin-shed house at Taskul. We visited a few more places like Siassi, Hoskins, Rabaul, and even up to Goilala. My recent visits to the same places have made it clear to me that things have run down since the CPC days. Although we had great vision, great dreams for our country, things have run down. Even though in cities like Port Moresby at independence there would have been about maybe 10 or 20 Papua New Guineans driving their cars on dirt and dusty roads, today there are thousands of them. Today I count more than 500 as I travel from Gerehu to Boroko. Things have changed. I think our motives have changed a great deal too. Our purpose for living has changed. But the original goals are still there and I hope that as time goes on we will pick up again from where we first went off the track.

To conclude, I remember that once, during a public meeting that the CPC held, I was in the process of trying to explain what self-government and independence were. I sat there from about eight o'clock, right through. Towards the evening, at about three or four o'clock, one old man asked a basic question: "What is self-government? Will another country come and run us?" (Perhaps he was anticipating the IMF or the World Bank.) But I said: "No, no." How do you explain it? I said: "Well, it's like driving your own car. You drive it yourself." And he said: "We might go and bump." He went on: "Look, we don't have any bombs, we don't have any guns, we don't have factories to make things. How can we become independent?" I said: "Well, it's a right: it's an inherent right, a birth right." I thought: "You can't explain it, that's what we are." Anyway, in the end at about four o'clock, he pointed to the sun, and said: "Look at the sun." I looked, and he said: "I belong to that generation of the sinking sun and you belong to the new generation of the rising sun. If you think independence is good, get it but you will have to live with the decision you make." Thank you.

Dr Ted Wolfers: Twenty years ago, I sometimes wondered what would have happened in 20 years' time. Would the *Constitution* have lasted and would people like me who were associated with it still be welcomed in the country? The time of the CPC was one of great uncertainty: a time of excitement, of enthusiasm and of extraordinarily hard work for everyone involved.

When I was first asked to serve the CPC I did what academics always do. I went out and bought one of the largest, thickest books I could find on constitutions: Kenneth Roberts Wray's *Commonwealth and Colonial Law*. I never read it. The CPC made it very clear that it wasn't interested in foreign models and other people's ideas. At its very first meeting, I remember the members being insistent that we have should Papua New Guineans involved in every level of what we did. Hence the nomination of the Honourable Bernard Narokobi to join us. In some ways, the period of the CPC was the longest political science seminar in history, in that we spent months and months working through issues, because the CPC did not ask us to give them choices but rather to help them ask questions. They did not ask for recommendations but for our thoughts on what the relevant issues where. They were determined to make the decisions for themselves.

Some of those decisions were, I think, made at considerable personal cost to some of the people involved. I can remember one person at this table, who, after asking for a translation of some of what was being said in a CPC meeting on citizenship matters, turned to me and said: "But they are talking about my children."

I can remember my own knowledge of Pidgin being stretched during discussions of issues concerning a possible Administrative Review Tribunal and an Ombudsman. I still haven't worked out how to translate Administrative Review Tribunal into straightforward Pidgin. I was not at all that sure myself about what an Ombudsman was, but I explained it at length and with enormous care to several members whose English was not particularly good at that time. One of them turned to me after a while and said: "Dispela tok bilong yu em i orait tu ya, tasol long wanem yupela i laik putim busman long constitusen? Mipela i gat planti long ples ya." I learnt a great deal from people like that.

The CPC posed challenges to the existing structure of government in Papua New Guinea and to many other interests. At that time, we were working for the elected representatives of Papua New Guinea, politicians who often found themselves undermined and challenged by a variety of competing interests. I remember on one occasion we were going to Lae for a political education conference, and travelling with a number of CPC members including the late Sir Tei Abal. When we arrived at the Jacksons Airport in Port Moresby, we discovered that all of the Papua New Guinean members of the committee had been offloaded from the flight and I had been left on. I tried to explain to the Australian guy behind the counter something he couldn't understand, which was that I worked for them and that they had to get to Lae and that I was merely one of the people trying to get them there. He took a while to understand that, and so I finally said: "If you don't get these guys on the plane, you'd better get me the Chief Minister's Office on the phone." Now Sir Michael never knew this part of the story, because I never had to make that call. The guy got very worried and said: "Look, get their tickets, we'll fix it up and get them on the plane to Lae." Because I was the only English speaker in the group, I was the person having to deal with this Australian. So I got the tickets, and he said: "While we are fixing up the tickets, tell them to get on the plane." They took off while I was still sorting out the tickets in Port Moresby.

In a number of places, I think it's fair enough to say that CPC members were challenged openly - sometimes violently and deliberately - by people who were very frightened of the idea that Papua New Guineans might determine their own future. In Lavongai we watched a highly orchestrated performance of foreigners telling people what they thought about citizenship until one man - I will never forget it - stood up quivering with rage saying in very eloquent Pidgin: "Just tell them to get out and just leave us." In Kavieng, at the end of a very strange series of meetings one day, we were thrown out of a club. It was with the Honourable Sir Bernard Narokobi and Sir John Kaputin. I usually managed to be thrown out of places in very good company. In Vanimo I remember John Momis being harassed by expatriates worried about their future. In Angoram we were lectured on citizenship by Australian kiaps. But John Momis got his revenge on me in Bogia when we arrived at the airport and there were hundreds of local dignitaries to meet us. I realised that they weren't there for me, and went back to help unload the plane while John Momis and the other members of the committee shook everybody's hand. I obviously infuriated the expatriate Assistant District Commissioner who turned to Momis on our way into Bogia itself and said (referring to me): "Who is this bloke in the back seat - some kind of three-day expert?" And John Momis, ever supportive, said: "Yes."

One of my better efforts was being asked to liaise at one point between the committee and the Opposition leader concerning the very considerable political difficulties then arising in East New Britain. It was Christmas time and Sir John Kaputin had left his car with me to look after. I went out to the Opposition leader's office, which was then in town, knowing that I needed to be fairly circumspect in what I said, because the Opposition had very severe reservations regarding independence. After a very nice conversation, his executive officer walked me out to my car. I drove off, not realising that all he could see as I left was Matungan Association stickers on the back of the car.

The historical period needs to be put in context to realise the hostility sometimes experienced, as well as the challenge and the very real excitement.

I think when we look at the *Constitution* today, that it is not the document that the CPC recommended. On the other hand it is very different from what the Australians would have preferred. We can say that the CPC and the government, and in fact the commitment of all the politicians irrespective of political party, to make a Papua New Guinean constitution, has made it a very different document from what otherwise would have been.

Mr Seaea Avosa: I was executive officer to the CPC. When the committee started work, the members realised that their advisers were all white skin people, so they expressed very strong concern that they should have Papua New Guinean advisers. As a result they appointed Bernard Narokobi as legal adviser. At the same time they instructed me that I had to have another hat, and that was to be a political adviser to the committee. So I did.

To understand the CPC it is necessary to refer to the conditions in Papua New Guinea in 1972. Up to then Papua New Guinea had been administered and governed by Australia. Some people were saying that when we got our constitution we would be free to look after our affairs in our own country. But the CPC view was that it was not a matter of the colonial power granting us the freedom to decide for ourselves or to carry out our activities. Their view was that, in fact, we were picking up from the time that freedom was taken away from us by the imposition of the colonial administration. That's the feeling that the CPC members heard from the people. Many recommendations made by the committee have not been properly represented in our *Constitution* because this approach was not always understood.

Even so, looking at how the *Constitution* has worked for the last 20 years, I am happy with how it has been used by the government and by our people. One of the main concerns of the CPC was to see that change of the *Constitution* and of governments should be through peaceful means. This intention of our founding fathers has been realised, because over the last 20 years people have not resorted to violence.

Mr Ilinome Tarua: In 1972, Mr Les Johnson, the Administrator, created a special unit in the Office of the Chief Minister to assist with legal and constitutional matters. As a young graduate in 1972 I was fortunate enough to be selected to join that unit. My boss was Mr Tos Barnett. We advised and assisted the Chief Minister and Ministers on two main things. The first was the issues involved in the transfer of powers and functions from Australia to Papua New Guinea in the self-government period. The second was the preparations to achieve independence. This is where I participated, and I joined the Chief Minister and attended many CPC meetings from 1972 up to 1974.

Then, early in 1975, I was on holidays in Sydney when I was summoned by the Department's Secretary, then Philip Bouraga, to return to Port Moresby because my boss, Tos Barnett, was in hospital. So, from that time when I got back I was on my own, assisting and supporting Sir Michael and his Deputy, Mr Ebia Olewale, in the consideration of the draft *Constitution* in the National Constituent Assembly from 23 May to 26 August 1975. The meetings were, I think, held over 27 days in total. I liaised between the National Constituent Assembly and the Legislative Draftsman, Mr Joe Lynch. As he produced the drafts, I'd take them to the Chief Minister, his Ministers, and members of Parliament, and we would meet to discuss all the drafts of each section or provision. After that, of course, Sir Michael Somare would present the drafts in the Constituent Assembly for adoption.

I would also prepare statements for Sir Michael and Mr Ebia Olewale on particular legal and constitutional issues involved in the drafts, and they were able - very confidently - to put across the issues in Pidgin. I was so impressed with the way they explained the complex concepts to the members who were able to follow exactly what was put across. My role continued after the *Constitution* was adopted on 15 August, and of course after independence. In fact, after independence I helped our officers, especially people from the Department of Justice, who were assisting other officers and institutions in the country to understand their new roles and responsibilities and the effect of various sections of the *Constitution*. So my learning about the *Constitution* while it was in preparation from 1972 to 1975 stood me in good stead.

Lastly, I think that the *Constitution* has worked well for this country and I am proud of it because it was made by Papua New Guineans in this country for Papua New Guinea.

Ms Meg Taylor: Recently, I had a discussion with a young friend who wanted to provide me with all the solutions for Papua New Guinea's problems. I said: "Well, why don't you read the CPC Report? They addressed all these things. There's nothing new in what you're saying." And he said: "What's the CPC Report?"

It is perhaps presumptuous for me to say that I was a constitution-maker, but in some respects we all were. Anybody who went to a CPC meeting out in the provinces was a constitution-maker. I attended my first constitutional meeting in 1973. It was at a meeting the CPC held with a local council meeting in the Waghi Valley. Even then, there was one notable omission in the CPC composition: there were no women representatives. Nothing much has changed.

I was later a member of the Chief Minister's staff where our role was to be sounding boards for the Chief and his Ministers and to assist in the process of the briefings that Ilinome Tarua's office ran for the Ministers. At the time there was incredible pressure and tension between the CPC and the government. But it was also an extraordinary time, and very exciting, knowing that we were carving out a vision; a new way for Papua New Guinea that would mean that one day we would be a nation. The CPC members were seen as the firebrands, the visionaries for the future of Papua New Guinea. At the same time, I can't understate Michael Somare's role. He was extraordinary in the way he mediated through this process, always seeking to find compromise, a solution that would bring all the different factions together.

But perhaps the debate that meant the most to me was the one on citizenship. Here we were, a group of Papua New Guineans, many with mixed parentage, caught in this very emotional citizenship debate that really seemed to consume the CPC, the House of Assembly and the National Constituent Assembly more than a lot of the other structural issues: the issues that were very important to self-government and to independence. The arguments were heated, and emotional. The guts of the citizenship provision had to do with economic power: the structures that could stop the perpetuation of foreign control of capital and of resources. Rather than concentrating on these structural issues, the debate became subjective rather than objective. There was a lot of members of the House Assembly who were of Australian parentage. There were members like Sir Julius Chan who were of mixed descent. There were also some of us from the bureaucracy who felt not fully Papua New Guinean but we were caught up by the debate about having three grandparents born in Papua New Guinea, or two such grandparents, if we were to be automatic citizens. That was not an easy time, and the debate was - in my memory - the longest debate of my life, and I think it was for the CPC as well.

Finally, looking back on what I think was the most important, amazing and impressive part of that whole time, were the processes that were followed. I continue to be impressed by the consultative process that the CPC took and by the challenges that the CPC faced. The challenges included the minority report that was put before it by Sir John Guise and Sir Michael Somare. It was an example of a very healthy democratic system and of Melanesian consensus, things that still exist in Papua New Guinea. Thank you.

Sir Barry Holloway: I want to discuss another aspect of the constitution-making process: the National Constituent Assembly. You have all heard about the CPC travelling everywhere it could in the country and sifting through the ideas and information from the people and then producing its report. It was still necessary, once all the thoughts of the people were put together and summarised, for what the CPC proposed to be approved by a representative body. When you want to adopt the constitution of a country such a body is normally called a Constituent Assembly. It is a body that could be made up of church leaders, tribal chiefs, or even a wider selection of people. Sometimes the question of adopting a new constitution can even be put to referendum. However, it was recommended by the CPC that in our case we should use the House of Assembly, because it represented the people at that time.

The Assembly was elected on an optional preferential system and, as a result, mathematically, apart from the exhausted ballot papers, a member of the House represented an absolute majority of the people of the electorate. The people who had not voted the member as first choice would have voted for that person as second or third choice. As a result they all felt that this person was their representative. Consequently the House of Assembly was a representative group, and on that basis could rightly make itself into the Constituent Assembly.

I was Speaker of the House of Assembly from 1972, and then Speaker of the National Parliament from independence in 1975 up to the 1977 general election. In May 1975, the House of Assembly became the National Constituent Assembly, and as Speaker of the House I became the Chairman of that Constituent Assembly. Members of the House of Assembly had already debated the CPC Report from mid-1974 to early 1975. The CPC Report was not a final blueprint for a constitution. The CPC proposals had to go through democratic processes. You can see how democratic the process was, moving from the people to the CPC, through all the machinations of that group for three years, and then again back to the people's representatives for debate and approval.

Mr Anton Parao: A lot of the ideas and principles in the *Constitution* we got from the people. We worked very hard to get them and put them into this *Constitution*. Our officers also worked very hard to help us produce it. A lot of what the CPC proposed was changed and as a result the Constituent Assembly came up with a weaker *Constitution* than the CPC had wanted. If they had included a lot of the other things that we had proposed in the CPC, I think things could have been different in the years since independence. Anyway, that's my point of view.

Now some of the things are not going as we planned or as we thought of, and that's why we will contribute and discuss those things. Things like the National Government structures and the provincial government system. They have not worked well. Of course we could change them. But I think that the real problem has been in the management of the *Constitution* by the parliamentarians, and other people. I am one of those fellows who worked very hard for the *Constitution*, and I feel sad to see things are not working, that we have not followed the real *Constitution* that we proposed.

PART TWO: DISCUSSION WITH REFERENCE TO MAIN STAGES IN THE CONSTITUTION-MAKING PROCESS

Chairperson (Anthony Regan): I will set out briefly some of the main steps in the constitution-making process. We will then invite panel members to make comments on some of those steps.

The first stage of the process involved committees of the House of Assembly, which considered constitutional development for Papua and New Guinea during the 1960s and in the early 1970s. The next stage involved the establishing of the CPC by the House of Assembly, followed by its work from June 1972 until August 1974. There were a number of different stages and processes involved in the CPC's work, before finalisation of its two-volume Final Report. Among other things, they produced much awareness material as well as interim reports. After the CPC completed its work, you have heard that there was a minority report produced by two leading members of the CPC, Sir John Guise and Sir Michael Somare. That was later withdrawn and a government paper was tabled in the Parliament. It was a white paper with some explanatory notes, and responded to the CPC recommendations, especially in relation to the areas where the government had major differences with the CPC. But when you read that document now, 20 years on, it is remarkable how much agreement there was between the CPC and the government: it came down to a few key areas (such as the Head of State, and citizenship) where there were significant differences.

The House of Assembly then debated the CPC Report from August 1974 until March 1975. The debate was directed towards approving drafting instructions for the independence *Constitution* in the form of resolutions of the House that modified the recommendations of the CPC. The debates in the House of Assembly were centred on the CPC Report, the government paper, and also on a paper submitted by the Opposition, the United Party. As the House of Assembly finished debating each chapter of the CPC's Final Report, the drafting instructions went to the draftsmen. There was then a process of negotiations and debate between government officers, CPC members and the draftsmen to produce the *Fourth Draft of the Constitution (Re-numbered and Revised)*, which was tabled in the National Constituent Assembly by Sir Michael Somare in May 1975.

What was the National Constitutent Assembly? Well, the House of Assembly adjourned one morning and met again that afternoon as the National Constituent Assembly. It did so without any legal authority, other than the authority of being made up of the elected representatives of the people. The National Constituent Assembly first discussed procedural rules, and a couple of days later debated the draft *Constitution*. From May 1975 until August 1975, day after day, the House of Assembly would break and then meet again a little later as the National Constituent Assembly. It debated and agreed to the amendments to the fourth draft, eventually resulting in the independence *Constitution*, which was finally adopted by the National Constituent Assembly in August, and became law in September 1975.

At the same time that the National Constituent Assembly adopted the *Constitution*, it also adopted a number of other laws and, in particular, the Provisional Organic Laws. The *Constitution* provided that at independence they were to come into effect as the first Organic Laws. In that way all of the key Organic Laws - those on national elections, Ombudsman Commission, *Leadership Code* and so on - were adopted prior to independence, together with the *Constitution*, providing the basic legal framework at independence.

The first issues for discussion here concern the lead up to establishing the CPC. There was already a lot of pressure - from Australia in particular - for independence to come quickly, and as a result there was less focus on the contents of the proposed constitution. In fact, in the course of moving to self-government and in the constitution-making processes, the issues of independence and the timing of independence, on the one hand, became separated from the issues of the kind of constitution and the kind of government that was needed, on the other hand. How did the decision get made to put the question of the timing of independence to one side, and to focus on the making of the constitution and getting the government system right before independence was decided on?

Dr Ted Wolfers: Until 1972 the question of what shape the independent government in Papua New Guinea should take was very closely related, almost the same question, as the question of timing of independence. In part that was because once you've decided to set up a Parliament, there is a certain sense of movement in place. Once you've decided to move towards ministerial government, that creates new momentum for change. The two sets of issues (shape of government and timing of independence) had also been closely related in the work of the previous select committees. If you were moving towards self-government, you were making statements about the likely shape of ministerial government; if you were moving towards ministerial government, you were also making statements about self-government.

When the Somare Government was formed after the 1972 House of Assembly elections, part of the background to the deal was that some politicians who were then committed to early independence did not know whether or not they could form a government or hold it together. They were keen to force the question of timing of independence, but also wanted to keep working on the constitution and the institutions of an independent government. Sir Julius Chan was very influential, for example, in saying that the question of the quality of the independent government, the shape of the government, was at least as important as timing. The Opposition also felt very strongly that timing wasn't the only issue. These other views were part of the deal that made it possible to proceed as happened.

I think it is fair to say that by mid-1972 the Australians were not very interested in the independence constitution. By then it was clear that there would probably be a change of government in Australia later that year, and the form of government in Papua New Guinea was not a big issue. To illustrate that point, I can remember that in late 1971 I was called in by a person who later became very influential in the government in Australia. I was then leaving the country, and he said to me: "There's going to be a change of government in Australia, and I would like you to work for us. This place has got to be independent, and we don't care how many countries it's going to be." Now that might have been a private comment. But it rocked me. I think it is fair to say that by the time Somare came to power in 1972, the Australian Government was just not interested. They wanted to get out, and they assumed that they had things in place and that with Somare's election they had people here who were ready to draw up a constitution. In any event, people had been thinking about it and writing about it for a long time, assuming that Australian models would be followed.

Mr John Momis: I think we had an advantage in 1972, in that the people were psyched up to try something new. They had had enough of colonial rule. Even though most of us knew and felt that we were not adequately prepared for the huge task of running our own affairs, we welcomed that unique opportunity offered by political independence for the country. Most of us agreed with Australia that change must come, although I don't think we agreed on the type of change required. The CPC was less focused on the timing of independence than some others. It was more concerned with coming up with a system of government and a constitution which had relevance for the real needs and basic aspirations of the emerging Papua New Guinea society.

I don't think our Australian rulers understood this. For them the issue was simple: you must have independence and the constitution was just seen as a means to attain independence. By contrast, for us the constitution was an integral part of the process of self-determination. I think that even though we came from different backgrounds that attitude was something that moulded and united us in the CPC.

Even though we had many arguments, there were a lot of things we were really fired up about. The feeling was: Em i taim nau bilong Papua New Guinea long traim lak. So we worked very hard and had many arguments, even fights. I had broken glasses put in my face many a time as the de facto CPC Chairman. Sometimes it was from one of my best friends, John Kaupa, who was my lieutenant, not because he was against me, but because he was frustrated with the sort of things that were going on at the time. I also think that having Michael Somare as the Chief Minister at that time was a major advantage.

You must understand, we were not working in a controlled laboratory situation, where we had control factors to guide us. Rather, we were working in a real dynamic, human situation where we came under a lot of pressures from many sources, including the multinational corporations. There were also those who wanted us to remain as we were and to wait until the end of time when they thought that we might be ready for independence. Other leaders were saying: "Let's get independence, and just trust us: we will look after your interests."

At the same time we had to contend with problems in Bougainville, with the Mataungans in East New Britain, with Papua Besena, and with other groups who were demanding autonomy, demanding that they be given a clear and vested interest in the proposed new system before they would throw in their lots with the rest. There was a lot of uncertainty. People said: "Okay, we'll be part of this new national effort to become united, but on what conditions? What guarantee is there for me as part of a minority group?" So, based on the principal of subsidarity, which we believed was essential for national solidarity in a country made up of myriad diverse small groups, we insisted that we must come up with some basic constitutional guarantees under which our people could freely accept to become part of this nation.

That was necessary because we really did not know where we were going. We were like Abraham, called to a destination which he didn't know. Somare probably knew, but some of us didn't know where we were going. But we trusted him and supported him, and even in our criticisms of him in our periodic consultations with him, we believed that he too had the best interests of the country at heart. That was the culture that we operated in, and that helped us to bridge the gaps, to leave our familiar shores and move into the unknown. I considered myself to be one of the best friends of the Chief Minister at the time, but I can tell you that back then he used to say things about me which were difficult to accept.

But in spite of all that, all members of the CPC, including the Chief himself, Sir John Guise, Stanis Toliman and all the others, were very proud representatives of our people. Somehow, I don't know how, we managed to stick together and work with Somare to bring about independence on one condition: that the change had to be qualitative. We wanted guarantees that power would be distributed fairly, that people's rights and freedoms would be guaranteed in the constitution and that the interests of Papua New Guineans would also be protected through an investment code and so on. Those are some of the things that went through out minds.

Sir Barry Holloway: I want to tell another side to the story about the CPC and the problems of building a nation and the CPC's role in that process. Concerning timing of independence, I was not directly involved in such matters in the early stages. But as Chairman of the National Constituent Assembly, part of my job was getting things through to completion. Of course, well before the National Constituent Assembly was established Australia handed over a number of functions to Papua New Guinea. It was pointed out to us very clearly that with the transfer of certain key powers we were close to being independent. One of the last things, I think, was control of the Defence Force, which had basically been completed by the time the Constituent Assembly was being set up. We also had our Central Bank established, and the Papua New Guinea Banking Corporation set up and Air Nuiguini created. All these things were symbolic of a country taking on its own responsibilities and all of it moved at a fast rate from 1972. By mid-1974, Papua New Guinea was basically independent, except for the constitution. It had taken control of operational powers in the areas that you need to enable the executive and other institutions and statutory bodies to operate.

So one day at about that time, Michael Somare came to me and said that Tom Critchley, the then Australian High Commissioner, wanted to have a quiet lunch with just the two of us. Critchley said: "All these changes have taken place, and you are now effectively operational as a country, a sovereign state. But when will the constitution be through? I want you two to fix a date at this lunch, a date that we can sort of work on because the Australian Government is getting rather impatient about when the constitution will come to final fruition". So as a result of that lunch, taking into account the meetings of the National Constituent Assembly still needed, we aimed for the date of independence. This was probably some time in July or early August 1975.

Mrs Nahau Rooney: No-one has yet mentioned the formation of the National Party and the importance of that event. The National Party was really the power broker that split the Highlands, and helped create wider support for independence there. Until then the United Party was the main Highlands party. The Pangu Pati had a clear vision for Papua New Guinea as a united country. It was a vision that inspired a lot of us who were either working in the public service at that time or at the universities. So even though I was a student at the University of Papua New Guinea, I was also a Pangu Pati Councillor in the Port Moresby City Council representing the Waigani and Gerehu area. At the university I and others got together with Paul Pora, and we began to talk about a new idea: that we get the Highlands area to talk about early independence. This was to try and defuse the then very strong view from the Highlands against early independence.

I remember the first meeting where Dennis Young (then a member of the House of Assembly) and Thomas Kavali came to Paul Pora's house, and with John Noel, and we started to talk about the National Party. Thomas Kavali and Okuk eventually left the United Party, established the National Party and joined Somare. That really consolidated Somare's stand for early independence.

I think many of us who were working around him at that time knew that there was never a doubt in Somare's mind as to where Papua New Guinea must go. Nothing was going to stop it. Of course, he had a good team with him, people like Meg Taylor, Rabbie Namaliu, Tony Siaguru, Moi Avei and others. We were determined to support the Chief (Somare), so when Momis and Bele resigned from Parliament just before independence and went to the United Nations to present their case for Bougainville's secession, which could have caused many problems around the time of independence, we made sure that Ebia Olewale also went there (with Tony Siaguru and Rabbie Namaliu) before Momis arrived, and they presented the Papua New Guinea position for maintaining a united country. These were the sort of things that we were doing. Making the constitution was one part of it but at the same time we were strategising - you can call it politicking - but it was really aiming towards independence for a united Papua New Guinea.

Dr Ted Wolfers: The CPC members were very united in their position. That goes back to some initial assumptions about how the process was set up. The then Chief Minister was absolutely clear that we were talking about a home-grown constitution. We were not only talking about something that was legally home-grown in the technical sense; something that had been done in a number of places. Rather we were talking about really asking Papua New Guineans what they wanted. That meant that we were asking very fundamental questions about every existing institution. We were not asking technical questions like: "Do you want this citizenship or that citizenship?" Instead we were saying: "Who do you want in this country?" We were not saying: "Do you want to decentralise in this way or that way?" Rather we asked: "Where do you want power in the country?" Now I think that approach did a number of things. It brought the CPC members together because we were working night and day, sometimes at a very abstract level. We weren't involved in day-to-day government. We were talking about the future. The leadership of John Momis and the then Chief Minister brought people together around very fundamental questions that very rarely get asked in any political system.

At the same time, however, the Ministers had a problem. They were trying to run the country. Both Somare's Government and the Australians wanted transfer of powers to Papua New Guinea. But the CPC was saying: "We don't yet know what system of government we want." Now an example that occurs to me is the question that arose about the future of the administration field service. At the end of 1972, I think it was, the Australians wanted to give the then Chief Minister control over the kiaps. Of course, the Chief Minister, who was wanting to run the country, had every reason to want control of the kiaps. But the question that the CPC asked was: "What are we going to do with the kiaps? Do we really want this system of government?" That led to some conflict because one group wanted to get on with governing, and another group was asking these questions. As a result, very difficult compromises had to be made. In this case a group of people standing outside the Cabinet room eventually agreed that the kiaps would not become part of the Chief Minister's Department, as it then was, but instead his Department would be re-named Department of the Chief Minister and Development Administration, so that if you had to, you could later take the kiaps away again or you could re-structure the system.

The coherence of the CPC was also a very important issue. It resulted in some groups with special concerns going directly to the CPC, rather than to the government. For example, the CPC was dealing directly with the Bougainville leaders during some of the difficulties in late 1972. They came to the CPC and not to the government, because they were interested in the future, just as we were. So there was, if you like, a difference in the objectives of the Ministers at the time who legitimately wanted the powers needed to do things, the CPC that was asking questions about the appropriate system for exercising power, and the Australian Government that was mainly concerned about trying to get out. These were very different perspectives.

The Chairman: Could I ask now about political education? Part of the idea of developing a home-grown constitution was that you went out and got the people's views. But to get their views you had also to get people educated about the issues. How did you plan your political education campaign and how was it implemented? How did you decide on it as such a major issue?

Mr Pikah Kasau: The CPC was helped by the teachers, the kiaps, and almost everybody then employed by the government, as well as university and teachers' college students. They all took part in the process of educating the people. In particular we were assisted by the government liaison officers and the Information Office. They devised questionnaires and pamphlets. The dissemination of information during that period was huge. Almost every village and every person that was known to the government at that time was made aware through that kind of education. There was a lot of funding for awareness. Education was done through the radio stations, field officers and teachers. We set up discussion groups, and if teachers were interested, they were given the information material and they could sit with the people. I remember going to Telefomin where a Manus teacher had walked from a village a long way off, with the views of his committee. These committees involved the people and they gave their views. I think that this is why the coverage was very very comprehensive.

Another thing that made the Committee work well was that it was a very interesting time. (I think one reason why I was not re-elected in 1977 was that I spent three good years with the Committee, and not enough time with my electorate.) It became exciting, it became something that you had to do. During that time, there wasn't as much to do as a Member of Parliament as there is today. There were no big issues in politics or economics. What was encouraging for us in the CPC was that we felt we were going to contribute to this country, and that every citizen of Papua New Guinea at that time was activated and had to take part in it. I have never seen anything like it. If it happens again, good luck to us. I hope it happens.

One thing that kept the CPC going, that kept us together, was that there wasn't any more of the political and other differences between CPC members that there had been before the Committee was set up. Previously I used to shout across the floor against Anton Parao, for he was United Party, and I was Pangu. But when I was in the Committee, I respected Sir Tei Abal. I realised that I had to work with Anton Parao. And when I went to Tambul and Marawaka, I saw the people and the members from the Highlands differently. I had been against them because they did not want independence early. But in the CPC I could sit with the people and I could look at their side of things and their customs and their way of life. Then, when sitting in the CPC boardroom, so busy, I could visualise these people and I could hope that after 20 years, these people would have something, because I had actually seen them and met them and so could understood them a little. So I think that through the publicity and awareness the people of Papua New Guinea were prepared for independence. Nationalism was developing in the country and everybody was taking part.

Mr Mackenzie Daugi: I was in the United Party. Like other younger members, who were not the power brokers, I felt that there was an undercurrent at that time; that we must push for self-government and eventual independence. That undercurrent influenced all of us in the CPC, even though we were in different political parties. Each had to make their own decision on where they would stand. So those of us from the United Party nominated to the CPC were interested in self-government and independence, even though our party leaders wanted to defer self-government and independence. Being in the CPC group, our basic interest was for the country, not for the parties.

The Chairman: It has been said sometimes that the CPC shaped the awareness material to get the answers it wanted from the people, and that perhaps it didn't really take all that much account of the people's views. How much could the CPC really listen to the people, and how much did the people's views really influence what the CPC recommended?

Mr Mackenzie Daugi: The results of the pamphlets and discussion groups and radio programs about constitution-making were amazing. I remember in my own area - and this was probably true in most coastal areas and also in the Highlands region - that people did not stop discussing the constitution. They didn't just go to the discussion group and stop there. Sundays, after service, during the brideprice ceremony, during any gathering at all, in the sunlight and in the moonlight, people were discussing the constitution. Self-government and eventual independence were on the horizon. People were aware from 1972 that Parliament would bring this new baby, whether it was going to be a good baby or bad. So with the discussion groups people were well prepared. They were not brainwashed by the CPC. They did not just stick to those things that we raised to help them get their discussion started. They had prepared themselves over nights of discussions outside discussion groups. In each discussion group, those who were writing the views were known as writers. People put their views about the constitution in their own expression, own idioms, own phrases, own language. But the writers put their views to the CPC in a clear English form. So when the CPC was looking at the submissions coming in from throughout the country, we could see the real issues that they were raising in their own way, but usually very clearly. For example, the constitution, they used to say, has to be a post - like a kwila post for a house. It should not be getting rotten overnight. It must a post that can stand the weather.

Going back to the process of the CPC's popular consultation, a discussion paper would be prepared by the staff - by one or a number of the advisers - and would be presented to the CPC. We would discuss it, and if it was approved then it would go to Seaea Avosa and his team, and they would break it into a digestible or manageable form. They would also break the material into question form, and put it all in clear English (because some of the draft papers were initially very hard to understand). The final papers would be sent out with a list of questions. These discussion groups set up throughout the country would take this material. But of course if they wanted to use their own material, they could. But these papers were available for them. When discussion was completed and the group's submission prepared it was sent to us. We were then able to read and analyse and see who said "yes", and how many said "no" to the particular proposals; for example, to the Head of State being separate from the Head of Government. But to be honest, in the end we abandoned the idea of analysing all the submissions that came in, because there were just too many. And there was also, to a certain degree, a position taken by the CPC that we represented the people and that in some ways people had to be led and not be followed.

Sir Barry Holloway: On this question of whether the CPC influenced the public debate, I think sometimes that the CPC got carried away with their own vision, without looking at the real situation of the people. An example here is the question of decentralisation. They appeared to me to have a vision of decentralisation that did not take account of the problems of building effective local-level institutions. I was part of the colonial system before, of course, which introduced local government. That system emphasised the value of the community. Local government was a phase, and could have been the basis for what came after, for decentralisation. But the CPC moved the basic geographic unit for decentralisation away from the local level to the province. For some it suddenly went as far as taking regions - the Island region, Southern region, and Mamose and Highlands regions - as the basic unit. I always thought that was wrong, because first you had to cater for a structure of a very strong local or community government. It was there that people had to find their identity.

The decentralisation process should have begun at the lowest level. The lowest level is the family level. You must identify with the family, then friends or extended family groups, and then identify together in the form of more formalised government structures, like local government or community government. If you did that, it would not be necessary to have elections at provincial level, which involved boundaries that meant nothing to the people, with the result that those elections caused problems. Using a local base, the local government representatives could instead have been the electoral college used to elect the provincial representatives. So that is where I thought the CPC [was] a bit obsessed about its own vision: thinking of one way and not looking at the other way. That argument really could have been resolved by a middle approach.

Mr Bernard Narokobi: That's not what actually happened. The CPC was very, very aware of the way our kiaps at that time were manipulating local governments. That was resulting in collapse of the local authorities which the Australian administration had set up. By 1972, even the Australian Government was pretty well aware that they could not administer Papua New Guinea from the centre. They also found that the small local governments were ineffective. As a result they set up the area authorities, which again the kiaps effectively manipulated to achieve their objectives. And the first lot of area authorities which were set up in Mt Hagen, in Milne Bay, in Morobe, were completely rejected by the people because they did not have real power. The councillors came only to provide a forum for the kiaps to speak and act. The councillors did not have any authority and the CPC was keenly aware of concern about this in all areas. We were continuously told: "Take power away from Konedobu", and "When power comes to us from Canberra, it is not to stay in Konedobu, but to go out to the people." And that really was the basis of this whole process of decentralisation.

The question of the word "province" was brought into the discussion by Sir John Guise. He raised the possibility of a regional system of government based on the Canadian type (for example, using the word "premier" to describe the head of the provincial government, as in the provinces in Canada). It must be recorded, however, that the CPC deliberately decided that it was not wise at that point in time to go into a system of regional government (four regions). That was because they feared that large regions would be a far greater source for division and conflict than the provinces. If you were to have a Highlands regional government, with its own police force, then in no time you might have a Highlands police force fighting the Momase police force. And I think the Waterais incident in Morobe in 1994 stands as a testimony to the wisdom of the CPC. But the CPC also proposed that the constitution could enable two or more provinces to come together if they wanted to combine into a greater unit.

Sir Barry Holloway: It was not just a question of devolving power from Konedobu (where the headquarters was then). It was a question of where you started, of what the basic unit was. My argument is that we should have started at community level. If you start at the provincial level, it is too remote from the people. You may thank God that we didn't have regional government, as Bernard Narokobi explained. That's my argument. There was often an instant objection from the CPC to anything "colonial". Because they wanted an autochthonous constitution, there was a tendency to want to completely wipe out the past, to deny there was anything good in the colonial system. There is a danger in doing that.

Mr Anton Parao: A big concern of people worried about the timing of independence at that time was that there were not enough experienced Papua New Guineans to take up the position of the implementers in the public service. I was not so much scared as worried that if the Australians vacated the positions that they were occupying, without a proper handing over of duties or jobs that they were doing here, then people without effective knowledge of what they were doing would take over. Papua New Guineans would not effectively carry out the real duties of the government or the running of the government. It was all right for us to take over formal power, but how about implementation? In those days Paulus Arek was the only Papua New Guinean occupying a senior administrative post. He was in charge of a very small department (Business Development). I really thought very hard about the timing of it. I wanted to first get to a stage where 45 per cent or 50 per cent of public service posts were held by Papua New Guineans, so that they could develop the budget, and handle the implementation of it, getting the job done, feeling as if they were really doing it, with no question of mismanagement. But the Chief and his team lined up and then overrode me and my group. They achieved independence. After 20 years, when people are talking about mismanagement, no effectiveness in public service, all those same issues come back to me. These days I just sit around and think about that.

The Chairman: What the CPC recommended contained unusual elements. The shape of the constitution the CPC wanted was unique, as John Momis has said. The CPC recommendations involved a home-grown constitution in the sense of the unusual elements it brought together. It proposed [a] set of national goals, something unusual in those days. It wanted entrenched decentralisation. It recommended that there should be no formal Head of State (though in other respects it proposed a basically Westminster executive system). There was to be a strong judiciary, with advisory constitutional powers and limited tenure. In an effort to make the Parliament the central institution a strong backbench committee system was proposed to ensure the Parliament was able to act as an effective check on the executive. The proposed Ombudsman Commission with responsibility for a constitutionally entrenched leadership code was almost unique, as were constitutionally entrenched provisions for regular review of the constitution. It was a mixture that was unusual, even if most of the distinct elements could be found here and there in other constitutions. What was the government's feeling about this mixture of ideas as it emerged? The CPC came out with its ideas gradually, in discussion papers and interim reports, so obviously the Chief Minister wasn't shocked when he got the Final Report. But what was he feeling when he saw the radical agenda emerging from the CPC's work?

Sir Michael Somare: I think one of the key things that we wanted was to expedite the process, to move to make and adopt a constitution based on the CPC Report as soon as possible. For me, the main aim was to achieve independence, to set the date and go on from there. Cabinet decided, at the time, that we should have a minority report of the CPC: that was submitted by John Guise and me (although it was later withdrawn, and instead we proceeded with the government paper). Our idea was to take into account some of the basic principles that the CPC had recommended, but to simplify things, so as to make it possible to have a constitution in place before we went to independence. We thought that a lot of detailed provisions or recommendations could be left to one side, and that we could pick the main basic aims and institutions of government and make them the basis for the constitution. These were some concerns that the Cabinet at the time was raising.

One worry was that the CPC proposals were becoming thicker and thicker, as they made submission after submission. I had a lot of arguments with the CPC, and particularly with John Momis and his group, where I kept saying: "You can't have a huge constitution when you cannot implement everything that you want to." My original idea had been to have a national convention, where we would have looked at other national constitutions and then written our own constitution. But anyway, the government at that time agreed that we should have a short basic constitution that was not cumbersome, one that was easy to administer. Although there were disagreements, in the end we developed a good Melanesian consensus. The CPC agreed with some of my recommendations. I also suggested that 10 years after independence, in 1985 or 1986, we could review the constitution. Of course, with the changes of government and with all sorts of other things, this never really happened. So the government's idea was to write a short and flexible constitution, and to later go through and revise it as it works for you.

Mr Ilinome Tarua: The government was all along in touch with what the CPC were discussing. So with some of the key concepts like the Ombudsman Commission, citizenship, Head of State, the government was familiar with the issues and was able to consider the recommendations as they came, and to express a government view. I recall vividly the discussion of the proposed Ombudsman Commission with two roles: one the normal maladministration role and the other the Leadership Code role. One idea then was to split up the functions between two bodies. Back in 1982 and 1983, when I joined Sir Michael Somare as Prime Minister again, I was throwing the idea around that it might be time to talk again about that proposed split. But the Ombudsman Commission heard what I was talking about, so they came rushing to Waigani to find out what was going on. And I said: "No, it's provided in the *Constitution* that splitting up the functions might occur down the track, some years later. In order to allow the Leadership Code function to be operated independently from the other one." Other provisions such as those on the Head of State were supposed to be reviewed also. There was a review carried out by the Constitutional Review Committee, which reported in 1983, but its recommendations never got much consideration.

Mr Bernard Narokobi: The impression I had was that by 1974 things had gotten out of control. The CPC had to close down. Australia was determined to off-load Papua New Guinea, and Sir Michael was determined to take on the load. By then the CPC was actually getting in the way, and so it had to fold up. There were still quite a few things that we took up at the bureaucratic level. They included the question of drafting style, the question of common law versus customary law, the review of then existing legislation to make sure it was in line with the new vision of the *Constitution*. The CPC was very insistent that this job had to be done if the new constitutional order was to be internally consistent. But there was no time to do all of this. And so, for example, in relation to review of existing laws, all that was done was to insert a small paragraph in the *Constitution* to say that the Law Reform Commission might have to do that kind of work. I was sent off to chair the Law Reform Commission. Other CPC staff were farewelled without parties. The CPC politicians went back to their own jobs.

Mrs Nahau Rooney: I want to mention the role of the advisers, or consultants as they are now known. The two key lawyers in the work of drafting the constitution were the CPC lawyer, John Leahy, and the government's Legislative Draftsman, Joe Lynch. It was between those two people that draft provisions for the constitution went back and forth. John Leahy would comment on Lynch's drafts saying: "That's not the way the CPC wanted it to be done. This part needs fixing." John Leahy really didn't want to miss any of the issues that the CPC wanted to be included as main principles of the constitution.

Back in the government camp, there was a lot of pressure to move things along quickly, because by the time the CPC finished its Final Report, roundabout July 1974, we wanted to move quickly to independence. In fact we had this other draft constitution there. But it didn't eventuate that it was needed. I think that it was prepared by Joe Lynch in consultation with others, just to be there, in case we failed to meet Somare's deadline for independence and if everything didn't come together.

The CPC wanted a comprehensive and clear constitution, and I think that is the way the *Constitution* is written. To a lawyer's viewpoint, the *Constitution* may seem too long, including a lot of principles that perhaps should not be there. But as a layperson, not a lawyer, I can relate to it. It is a constitution that non-lawyers can read. They can understand the meaning of the guiding principles, they can understand the function and the role of the Ombudsman and the Leadership Code. It is a constitution that people can relate to, and I think that was a great achievement at the time of independence.

Sir Michael Somare: I would have to be the first one to say that, yes, I saw this other draft constitution written. It was one of those legal drafts which is just prepared in case it is needed. The government had no intention of forcing it on anyone. I had a good understanding with John Momis and his team. I could not betray the team, because I was their chairman (even if a non-working chairman). It was nothing more than a draft of what we might use if the deadline for independence was not met. It was not a matter of anyone pushing this draft in front of me and saying: "Chief Minister, agree to this, this is the *Constitution*." I had my mind fixed: I was not going to allow Canberra to write a constitution for me like Britain wrote constitutions for its African colonies.

List of References

Akehurst, M, *A Modern Introduction to International Law*, 6th ed (London: Allen and Unwin, 1987).

Allott, A, *New Essays in African Law* (London: Butterworths, 1970).

Althusser, L, *Montesquieu: la politique et l'histoire* (Paris: Presses Universitaires de France, 1959).

Amet, A, 'Severing the Umbilical Cord from the Common Law', in J Aleck and J Rannells (eds), *Custom at the Crossroads* (Port Moresby: UPNG, 1995) 62.

Arnold, T, *The Symbols of Government* (New Haven: Yale University Press, 1938).

Aubert, V, 'The Housemaid: An Occupational Role in Crisis', (1955) *Acta Sociologica* 1:149.

Ballard, J, 'Policy Making as Trauma', in J Ballard (ed), *Policy Making in a New State: Papua New Guinea 1972-77* (St Lucia: University of Queensland Press, 1981) 95.

Biersteker, T, 'The Illusion of State Power: Transnational Corporations and the Neutralisation of Legislation', (1980) *Journal of Peace Research* 17:3.

Bird, R, (ed.)*Osborn's Concise Law Dictionary*, 7th ed (London: Sweet and Maxwell, 1983).

Bogdanor, V, *The Monarchy and the Constitution* (Oxford: Clarendon Press, 1995).

Brietzke, P, *Law, Development and the Ethiopian Revolution* (Lewisburg: Bucknell University Press, 1982).

Brownlie, I, *Principles of Public International Law*, 4th ed (Oxford: Oxford University Press, 1990).

Brunton, B and D Colquhoun-Kerr, *The Annotated Constitution of Papua New Guinea* (Port Moresby: UPNG Press, 1984).

Burke, K, S Coliver, C De La Vega, and S Rosenbaum, 'Application of International Human Rights Law in State and Federal Courts', (1983) *Texas International Law Journal* 18:291.

Callick, R 'Why the Governor-General went with Diro', *Islands Business Pacific* (October 1991), 64.

Chan, J, 'Experience with Papua New Guinea's Constitution: A Prime Minister's Reflections', in Y Ghai, *Law, Politics and Government in the Pacific Island States* (Suva: Institute of Pacific Studies, University of the South Pacific, 1988) 245.

Colquhoun-Kerr, DJ, 'Sources of Political Legitimacy in Conflict and Naturalized Foreigners: Some Comments on the General Constitutional Commission's Final Report, 1983', in R de Vere, D Colquhoun-Kerr and J Kaburise (eds), *Essays on the Constitution of Papua New Guinea* (Port Moresby: Tenth Independence Anniversary Advisory Committee, 1985) 121.

Commission of Inquiry into Land Matters, *Report of the Commission of Inquiry Into Land Matters* (Port Moresby: Government Printing Office, 1973).

Constitutional Planning Committee, *Final Report of the Constitutional Planning Committee Part 1* (Port Moresby: Government Printer, 1974).

Conyers, D, The Provincial Government Debate: Central Control versus Local Participation in Papua New Guinea (Waigani: IASER, 1976).

de Smith, SA, The New Commonwealth and its Constitutions (London: Stevens, 1964).

Deklin, APW, 'The Legal Control of the Executive in Papua New Guinea', in P Sack (ed), *Pacific Constitutions* (Canberra: ANU, 1982) 173.

Deklin, T, 'The Future of Papua New Guinea Customary Law: Rot Wei?', in J Aleck and J Rannells (eds), *Custom at the Crossroads* (Port Moresby: UPNG, 1995) 34.

Dinnen, S, 'Fighting with Votes: Violence, Security and the 1992 National Election in Papua New Guinea', (1993) *Current Issues in Criminal Justice* 5(2):130.

Downs, I, The Australian Trusteeship, Papua New Guinea 1945-75 (Canberra: AGPS, 1980).

Eisenmann, C, *L'Esprit des Loix et la Separation des Pouvoirs* (Paris: Melanges Carre de Malberg, 1933).

Epstein, E, 'China's Legal Reforms', in Kuan Hsin-chi and M Brosseau (eds), *China Review* (Hong Kong: Chinese University Press, 1991).

Feder, E, 'Counter-reform', in R Stavenhagen (ed), *Agrarian Problems and Peasant Movements in Latin America* (New York: Doubleday, 1970).

Fitzpatrick, P, *Law and State in Papua New Guinea* (London: Academic Press, 1980).

Galanter, M, 'The Modernisation of Law', in M Weiner (ed), *Modernisation: The Dynamics of Growth* (New York: Basic Books, 1966).

General Constitutional Commission, *Interim Report* (Port Moresby: 1979).

General Constitutional Commission, *Final Report* (Port Moresby: Helalo Studio, 1983).

Ghai, Y, 'Constitutions and the Political Order in East Africa', (1972) *International and Comparative Law Quarterly* 21:403.

Ghai, Y, 'Human Rights and Governance: The Asia Debate', (1993) *Australian Yearbook of International Law* 15:1.

Ghai, Y, 'Law, Development and African Scholarship', (1987) *Modern Law Review* 50:750.

Ghai, Y, 'The Theory of the State in the Third World and the Problematics of Constitutionalism', in D Greenberg *et al* (eds), *Constitutionalism and Democracy: Transitions in the Contemporary World* (New York: Oxford UP, 1993).

Ghai, YP, 'Politics consequences of constitutions' in YP Ghai (ed.), *Law, Politics and Government in the South Pacific Island States* (Suva: Institute of Pacific Studies, University of the South Pacific, 1988) 350.

Ghai, YP, 'Systems of Government: II', in YP Ghai (ed), *Law, Politics and Government in the South Pacific Island States* (Suva: Institute of Pacific Studies, University of the South Pacific, 1988) 76.

Ghai, YP (ed.), *Law, Politics and Government in the South Pacific Island States* (Suva: Institute of Pacific Studies, University of the South Pacific, 1988).

Ghai, YP and AJ Regan, The Law, Politics and Administration of Decentralisation in Papua New Guinea (Boroko: National Research Institute, 1992).

Godelier, M and M Strathern (eds), *Big Men and Great Men: Personifications of Power in Melanesia* (Cambridge: Cambridge UP, 1991).

Goldring, J, *The Constitution of Papua New Guinea* (Sydney: Law Book Company, 1978).

Griffin, J, 'July - December 1975', in Moore with Kooyman (eds), *A Papua New Guinea Political Chronicle 1967-1991* (Bathurst NSW: Crawford House, 1998) 247.

Hanks, P, Australian Constitutional Law: Materials and Commentary (Sydney: Butterworths, 1990).

Held, D, *Models of Democracy* (Cambridge: Polity Press, 1987).

Hurst, JW, *Law and Markets in United States History* (Madison: University of Wisconsin Press, 1982).

Hyden, G and M Bratton (eds), *Government and Politics in Africa* (Boulder: L Rienner, 1992).

Independent State of Papua New Guinea, 'Crisis in the North Solomons Province: Report of the Special Committee Appointed by the National Executive Council' (Port Moresby 1990).

International Legal Centre, *Law and Development: The Future of Law and Development Research* (Uppsala: International Legal Centre, 1974).

James, RW, *Challenges of Equity in Developing the Underlying Law* (Port Moresby: Faculty of Law, UPNG, 1996).

Jessep O and J Luluaki, *Principles of Family Law in Papua New Guinea*, 2nd ed (Port Moresby: UPNG Press, 1994).

Kaputin, J, 'The Law: A Colonial Fraud' (1975) New Guinea and Australia, The Pacific and South East Asia 1:4.

Kaputin, J, 'Opportunity and Participation: A United Nations Initiative of the Government of Papua New Guinea' (Port Moresby: Department of Foreign Affairs, 1993).

Lal, BV and TR Vakatora (eds), *Fiji and the World - Research Papers of the Fiji Constitution Review Commission*, Vol 2 (Suva: School of Social and Economic Development, USP, 1997).

Lane, PH, *A Manual of Australian Constitutional Law,* 3rd ed (Sydney: Law Book Co, 1984).

Li, V, 'The Evolution and Development of the Chinese Legal System', in J Lindbeck, *China: Management of a Revolutionary Society* (Seattle: University of Washington Press, 1971).

Lindbeck, J, *China: Management of a Revolutionary Society* (Seattle: University of Washington Press, 1971).

Luluaki, J, 'When rape is not rape', (1994) *Melanesian Law Journal* 22:59.

Lynch, CJ, 'The Adoption of an Underlying Law by the Constitution of Papua New Guinea', (1976) *Melanesian Law Journal* 4:37.

Lynch, CJ, 'The Achievement of Independence in Papua New Guinea', (1980) *Journal of Pacific History* 11(3):175.

Lynch, CJ, 'Styles in the Drafting of Some Pacific Constitutions', in YP Ghai (ed), *Law, Politics and Government in the Pacific Island States* (Suva: University of the South Pacific, 1988) 202.

Margolis, L, Executive Agreements and Presidential Power in Foreign Policy (New York: Praeger, 1986).

McRae, H, 'Reform of Family Law in Papua New Guinea - An Analysis of the Law Reform Commission's Working Paper No 9' (unpublished draft, 1979).

McWhinney, E, *Constitution Making: Principles, Process, Practice* (Toronto: University of Toronto Press, 1981).

Montesquieu, C, *De l'Esprit des Loix* (Paris: Editions Sociales, 1969).

Murphy, C, 'Economic Duress and Unequal Treaties', (1970) *Virginia Journal of International Law* 11:51.

Myrdal, G, 'Operational Controls over the Private Sector', in Myrdal, G, *Asian Drama: An Inquiry into the Poverty of Nations* (New York: Twentieth Century Fund, 1968).

Narokobi, CS, 'Citizenship Matters in PNG' (Port Moresby: unpublished, 1981).

New Zealand, Ministry for Environment, *Living for the Future: A Guide to Agenda 21* (Wellington: Ministry for the Environment, 1993).

Nonggorr, J, 'Development of Customary Law: Replacing the *Customs Recognition Act*', (1993) *Melanesian Law Journal* 21:49.

Nonggorr, J, 'The Development of an 'Indigenous Jurisprudence' in Papua New Guinea: The Past Record and Future Prospects', in J Aleck and J Rannells (eds), *Custom at the Crossroads* (Port Moresby: UPNG, 1995) 68.

O'Regan, R, 'The Common Law and English Statutes in the Territory of Papua and New Guinea', (1971) 45 *Australian Law Journal* 297.

O'Regan, R, *The Common Law in Papua and New Guinea* (Sydney: Law Book Co, 1971).

Oliver, N, 'Review of Land Dispute Settlement Organisations and Mechanisms' (Port Moresby: Department of Lands and Physical Planning, 1996).

Omar, I, 'Parliament, the Executive and the Court in Papua New Guinea', (1996) *Australian Law Journal* 70:313.

Ombudsman Commission of Papua New Guinea, *Report of an Investigation into the Spring Garden Road/Poreporena Freeway Project* (Port Moresby: Ombudsman Commission, 1992).

Papua New Guinea Department of Foreign Affairs and Trade, *Treaty List (No 2)* (Port Moresby, Department of Foreign Affairs, 1991).

Papua New Guinea Government Liaison Branch, 'Citizenship'. Information Paper Prepared for the Constitutional Planning Committee (Port Moresby: unpublished, no date).

Papua New Guinea Law Reform Commission, *The Role of Customary Law in the Legal System* (Port Moresby: Government Printer, 1977).

Papua New Guinea Law Reform Commission, *Final Report on Domestic Violence* (Report No 14) (PNGLRC: Port Moresby, 1992).

Papua New Guinea National Judicial System, 'The Judiciary and the Development of the Underlying Law', *Annual Report by the Judges: 1987* (Port Moresby: mimeo, 1987).

Papua New Guinea National Parliament, Final Report of the Select Committee on Expatriate Involvement in Business (Port Moresby: 1981).

Papua New Guinea, Government Paper, 'Proposals on Constitutional Principles and Explanatory Notes' (Port Moresby: unpublished, August 1974).

Rajan, M, *The Expanding Jurisdiction of the United Nations* (Bombay: Tripathi Private Ltd, 1982).

Rannells, J, 'Papua New Guinea Constitution and Organic Laws Citator, 20 Years On: 1975–1995', *Michael Somare Library Occasional Publications 23* (1995).

Redding, G, The *Spirit of Chinese Capitalism* (Berlin: Walter de Gruyter, 1990).

Regan, AJ, 'Limiting State Action: Some Comparative Perspectives on Constitutionalism, Participation and Civil Society in Papua New Guinea', paper for the 21st Waigani Seminar, Port Moresby (28 August 1995).

Regan, AJ, 'Competence and Compellability of the Spouse of the Accused as a Witness in Criminal Proceedings in Papua New Guinea', (1997) *Melanesian Law Journal* 25:87.

Regan, AJ, 'The Politics of Provincial Government', in RJ May and AJ Regan (eds), *Political Decentralisation in a New State: The Experience of Provincial Government in Papua New Guinea* (Bathurst: Crawford House Press, 1997).

Regan, AJ and EP Wolfers, 'Aids to interpretation of the Constitution: some preliminary thoughts', (1986) *Melanesian Law Journal* 14:153.

Roebuck, D, 'Custom, Common Law and Constructive Judicial Lawmaking', in R De Vere, D Colquhoun-Kerr and J Kaburise (eds), *Essays on the Constitution of Papua New* Guinea (Port Moresby, 1985).

Saffu, Y, 'January - December 1990', in C Moore with M Kooyman (eds), *A Papua New Guinea Political Chronicle 1967-1991* (Bathurst NSW: Crawford House, 1998) 482.

Sahlins, MD, 'Poor man, rich man, big-man, chief: political types in Melanesia and Polynesia', (1963) *Comparative Studies in Society and History* 5:285.

Sakora, B, 'Judicial Law-making under the Papua New Guinea Constitution', in P Sack (ed), *Pacific Constitutions* (Canberra: ANU, 1982) 257.

Schwartz, B, *The World of Thought in Ancient China* (Cambridge, Mass: Harvard University Press, 1985).

Seidman, R, 'Law and Development: A General Model', (1972) *Law and Society Review* 6:311.

Seidman, R, *The State, Law and Development* (New York: St Martins Press, 1978).

Sexton, M, War for the Asking: Australia's Vietnam Secrets (Ringwood Vic: Penguin, 1981).

Snyder, F, 'Law and Development in the Light of Dependency Theory', (1980) *Law and Society Review* 14:723.

Somare, M, 'Law and the Needs of Papua New Guinea's People', in J Zorn and P Bayne (eds), *Law Bilong Ol Manmeri* (Port Moresby: UPNG Press, 1975) 14.

Somare, M, 'The Challenges of Independence - My Yesteryears Vision of Papua New Guinea', Keynote Address for the 21st Waigani Seminar, Port Moresby (28 August 1995).

Srivastava, DK and D Roebuck, 'The Reception of the Common Law and Equity in Papua New Guinea: The Problem of the Cut-Off Date', (1985) *International and Comparative Law Quarterly* 34:850.

Srivastava, DK and MJ Le Brun, 'Development and underdevelopment of the underlying law in Papua New Guinea: A critique of State v Kamugaip', (1985) 1(3) *Pacific Law Digest* (Port Moresby: Faculty of Law, UPNG) 4.

Strathern, A, *A Line of Power* (London: Tavistock Publications, 1984).

Tay, A, 'Law in Communist China', (1969) *Sydney Law Review* 6:153-72 and 335.

Thomasetti, W, 'Australia and the United Nations: New Guinea Trusteeship Issues from 1946 to 1966', *New Guinea Research Bulletin 36* (1970).

Tordoff, W and R Watts, 'Report on Central-Provincial Government Relations' (Port Moresby: unpublished, 1974).

Trubek, D, 'Toward a Social Theory of Law: An Essay on the Study of Law and Development', (1972) *Yale Law Journal* 82:1.

Trubek, D and M Galanter, 'Scholars in Self-estrangement: Some Reflections on the Crisis in Law and Development Studies in the United States', (1974) *Wisconsin Law Review,* 1062.

Uganda Constitutional Commission, *The Report of the Ugandan Constitutional Commission: Analysis and Recommendations* (Kampala: Government of Uganda, 1993).

United Nations Centre for Human Rights, *Report of a Needs Assessment Mission to Papua New Guinea* (Geneva: UNCHR, 1995).

United Nations, *The World's Women 1995: Trends and Statistics* (United Nations: New York, 1995).

US Department of State, *Country Reports on Human Rights Practices for 1995* (Washington: US Government Printing Office, 1996).

van der Sprenkel, S, *Legal Institutions in Manchu China* (London: Athlone Press, 1962).

Vile, MJC, *Constitutionalism and the Separation of Powers* (Oxford: Oxford UP, 1967).

Wacks, R, *Legal Theory: China, Hong Kong and l997* (Hong Kong: University of Hong Kong Press, 1993).

Waiko, JD, *A Short History of Papua New Guinea* (Melbourne: Oxford University Press,1993).

Weisbrot, D, 'Integration of Laws in Papua New Guinea: Custom and the Criminal Law in Conflict', in D Weisbrot, A Paliwala, and A Sawyerr (eds), *Law and Social Change in Papua New Guinea* (Sydney: Butterworths, 1982).

Weisbrot, D, 'The Impact of the Papua New Guinea Constitution on the Recognition and Application of Customary Law', in P Sack (ed), *Pacific Constitutions* (Canberra: ANU, 1982) 271.

Wolfers, A, *Discord and Collaboration: Essays on International Relations* (Baltimore: Johns Hopkins Press, 1962).

Wolfers, EP, 'Defining a Nation: The Citizenship Debates in the Papua New Guinea Parliament', in FS Stevens and EP Wolfers (eds), *Racism, the Australian Experience, Vol 3: Colonialism and After: A Study of Race Prejudice in Australia* (Sydney: ANZ Book Company, 1977) 303.

Wolfers, EP, 'Discretion, Politics and Governors-General: Some Comparisons between Papua New Guinea and Australia', (1977) *Australian Quarterly* 49(2):75.

Wolfers, EP, 'Provincial Governments and Foreign Affairs', (1991) *Melanesian Law Journal* Special Issue:145.

Wolfers, EP, 'The Trusteeship Council, 1966', (1966-67) *New Guinea and Australia, the Pacific and South-East Asia*, 1(8):54.

Wolfers, EP, Race Relations and Colonial Rule in Papua New Guinea (Sydney: ANZ Book Company, 1975).

Wolfers EP, (ed), Beyond the Border - Indonesia and Papua New Guinea, South-East Asia and the South Pacific: Discussion and Documentation (Waigani: UPNG, 1988).

World Bank, *Governance: The World Bank's Experience* (Washington: World Bank, 29 November 1993).

World Bank, *Managing Development: The Governance Dimension* (Washington: World Bank, 29 August 1991).

Zorn, J 'Common Law Jurisprudence and Customary Law', in R James and I Fraser (eds), *Legal Issues in a Developing Society* (Port Moresby: UPNG, 1992) 103.

Index

[References are to page numbers]

www.ingramcontent.com/pod-product-compliance
Lightning Source LLC
Jackson TN
JSHW062338160926
108328JS00012B/21